# THE ULTIMATE PHOTOGRAPHY IDEAS BOOK

# THE ULTIMATE PHOTOGRAPHY IDEAS BOOK

**60 CREATIVE STEP-BY-STEP PROJECTS COVERING EVERY MAJOR GENRE OF PHOTOGRAPHY**

NIALL HAMPTON +

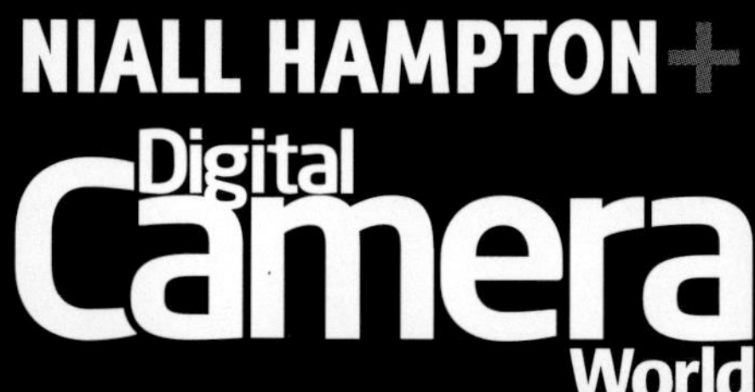


ilex

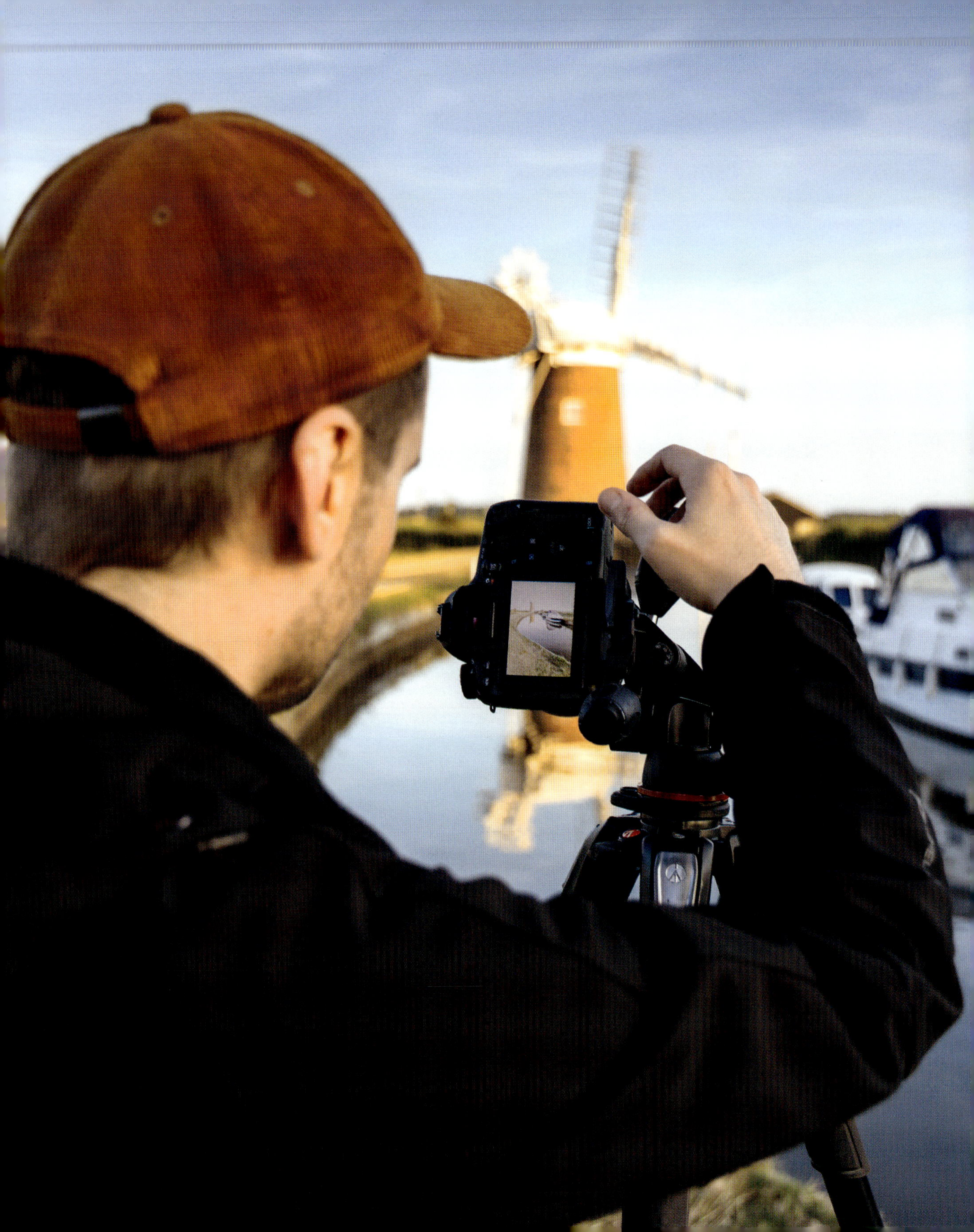

# CONTENTS

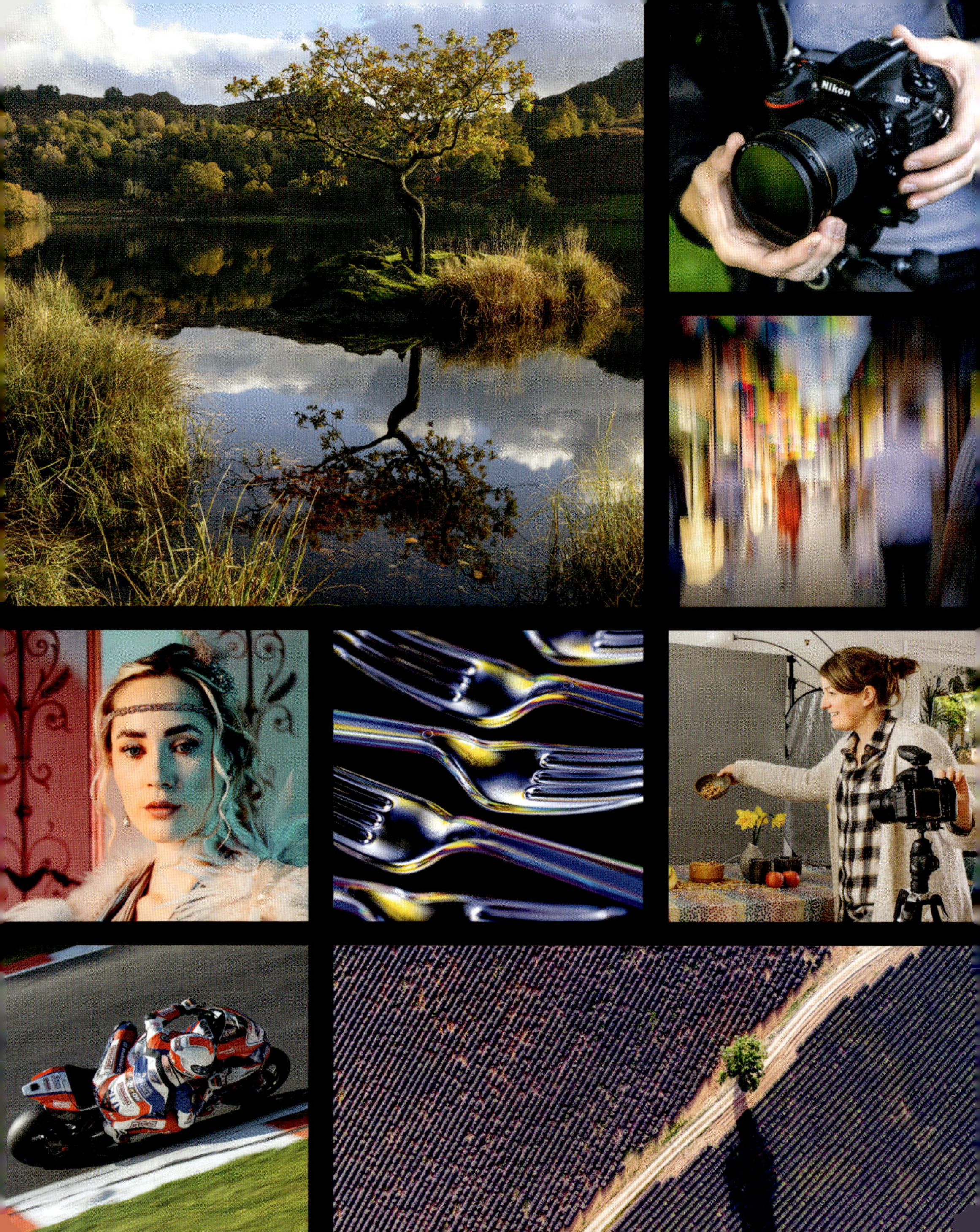
Nikon

# INTRODUCTION

**If you have bought this book, then you want to know how to take better photographs. And you're in the right place, as on the following pages you'll find 60 projects covering the most popular photographic genres today. We'll walk you through the practical steps involved and inspire you to apply these ideas to your own work.**

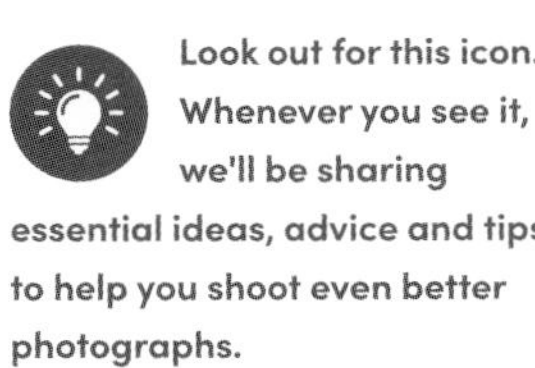

**Look out for this icon. Whenever you see it, we'll be sharing essential ideas, advice and tips to help you shoot even better photographs.**

Whether you're coming to photography from a smartphone, or already own a DSLR or mirrorless camera, the helpful technology at your fingertips means that compelling photographs can be taken by beginners. But to progress beyond the basics, you need to have a creative vision and be able to capture it, and that's where this book comes in.

With a chapter each dedicated to landscape, portrait, wildlife and macro, action, street and documentary and still life and creative photography, there really is something for everyone in this Ultimate Photography Ideas book. Expert contributors from *Digital Camera* magazine have produced a variety of projects with all the technique hints and tips you need, delivered in an accessible and easy-to-follow way, alongside camera and accessory recommendations.

But kit isn't everything. The best cameras and lenses that money can buy won't make you a better photographer; ask any professional and they'll tell you that it's all about what you can produce with the camera you have to hand. In fact, many of the projects in this book show you how to get great results using adapted or improvised equipment. Creativity isn't something you can buy, after all.

So read on and get inspired to take the next steps with your photography, whatever subjects you like to shoot. Thanks to the smartphones in our pockets, everyone is a photographer now, so moving beyond taking snaps and making your photos stand out from everyone else's has never been more necessary – or easier, thanks to this book.

– Editor, *Digital Camera* magazine

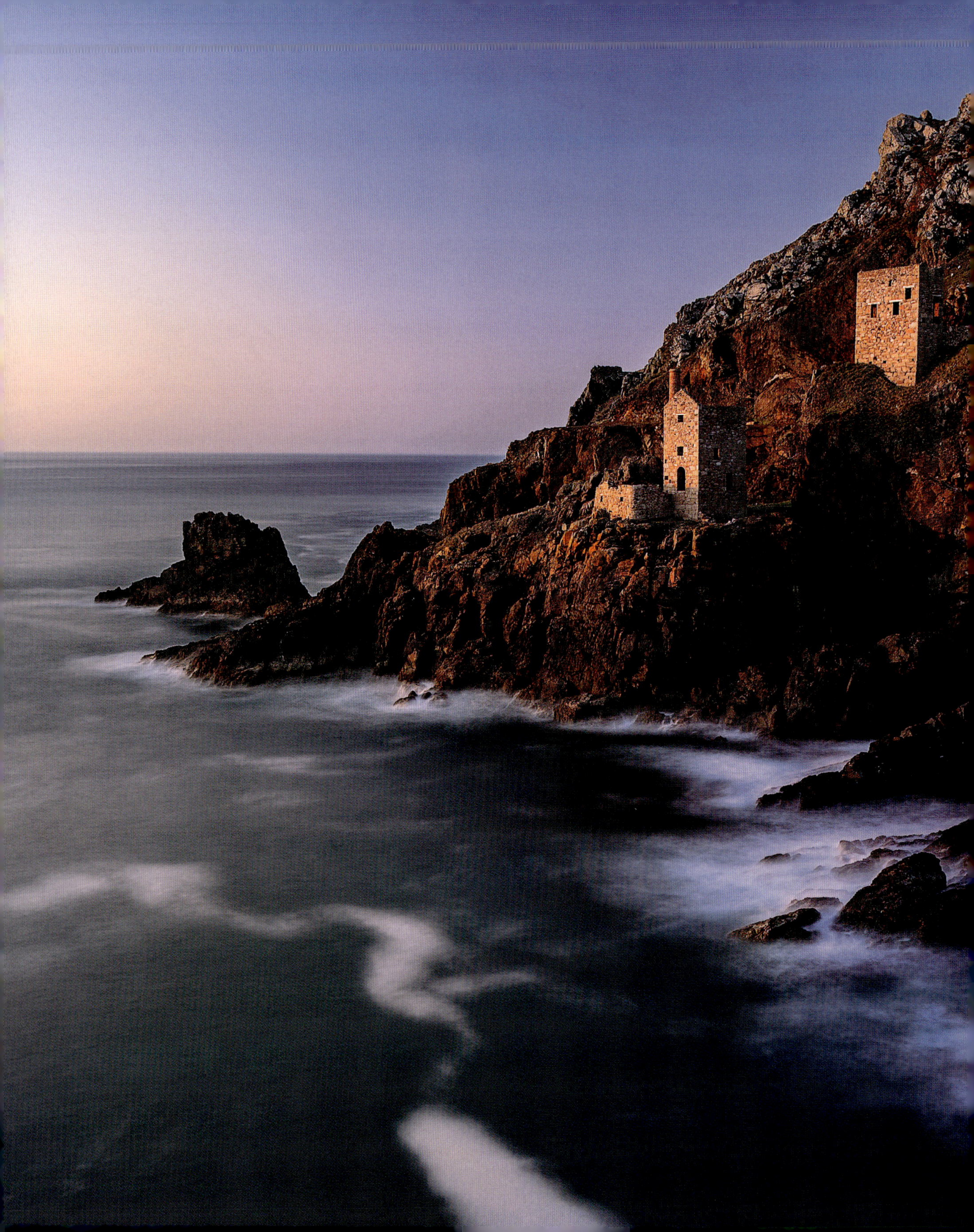

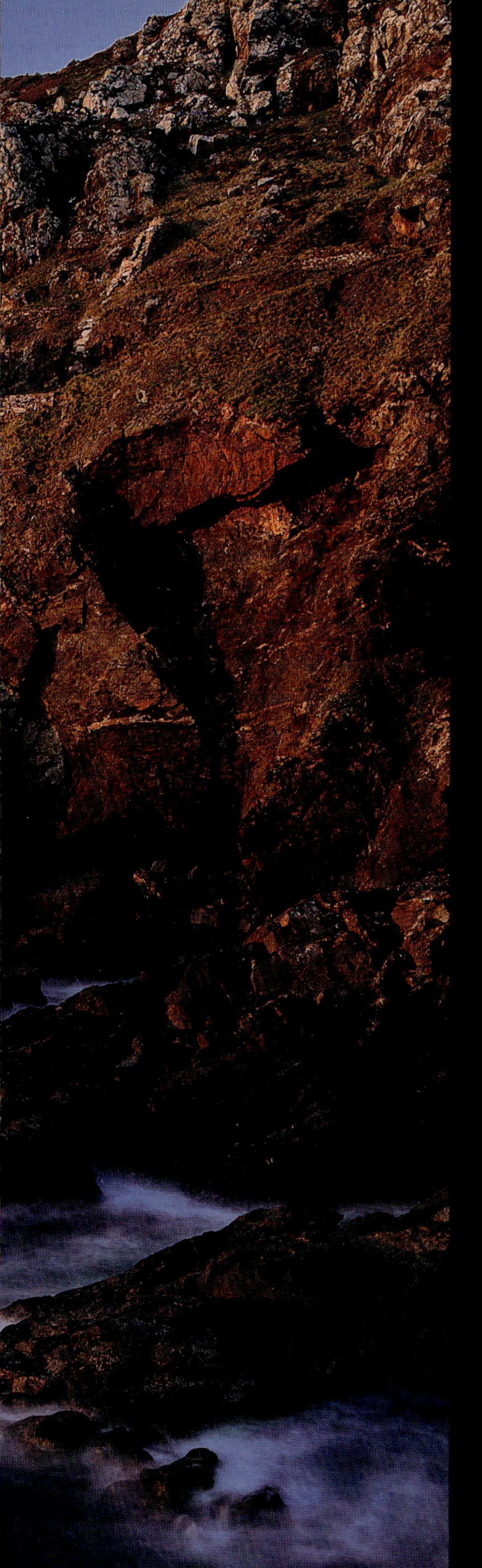

1

# LANDSCAPE IDEAS

**Master the most accessible photographic genre of all with a range of inspirational projects that will unleash your creativity**

# USE A TELEPHOTO LENS

**THE IDEA**
**Use a long lens to shoot landscapes that are more focused.**

**Time required:** 1 hour

**Kit needed:**
- DSLR or mirrorless camera
- Long lens
- Tripod
- Remote shutter release (optional)

**Camera settings:**
1/8 sec at f/8, ISO 100

**Skill level:**

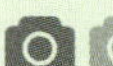   

**It's not surprising that wide-angle lenses are synonymous with outdoor photography. Wide fields of view can squeeze the vastness of a sprawling lake or the grandeur of a towering mountain into the frame, but they also have their limits.**

Wide fields of view cause subjects to diminish, so unless you're very close or your subject is very large, it can get lost in the frame. If you're not close enough to your subject, wide-angle lenses may cram in unwanted portions of a scene too, making the composition look unfocused, untidy and unbalanced.

This is particularly prevalent when you're shooting from a high vantage point like a hilltop. You may end up framing too much sky or unwanted foreground elements, such as the ground just in front of you.

One solution is to use a narrower field of view. This allows you to capture more focused compositions by cropping into the scene and allowing faraway subjects to dominate a larger portion of the frame. Lenses with a focal length of 70mm and above are considered telephoto and anything beyond 300mm enters super-telephoto territory. While you may encounter pincushion distortion (an easy fix in post-production) at longer focal lengths, you'll also find that barrel distortion is eliminated.

Long lenses are often thought of as the preserve of wildlife and sports photographers but introduce one to your kit bag and you'll find they can be an invaluable tool for landscapes.

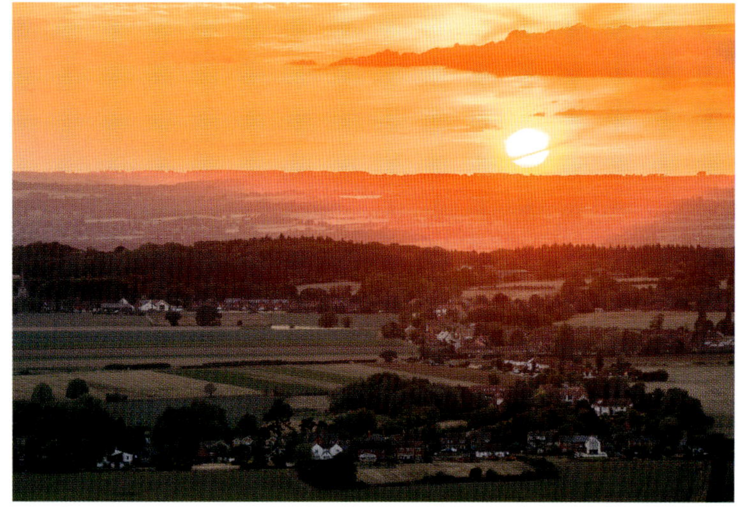

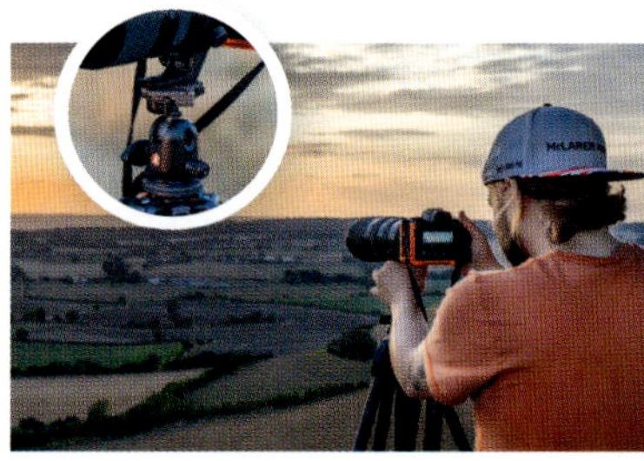

**1 Find your footing**
Camera shake is exaggerated at longer focal lengths, so a tripod is necessary. Top-heavy telephoto lenses can cause very gradual movement, especially if you're using a ball head, even when tightly secured. Some lenses come with a tripod collar and foot. This allows you to secure the camera to the tripod via the lens's foot, balancing the centre of gravity.

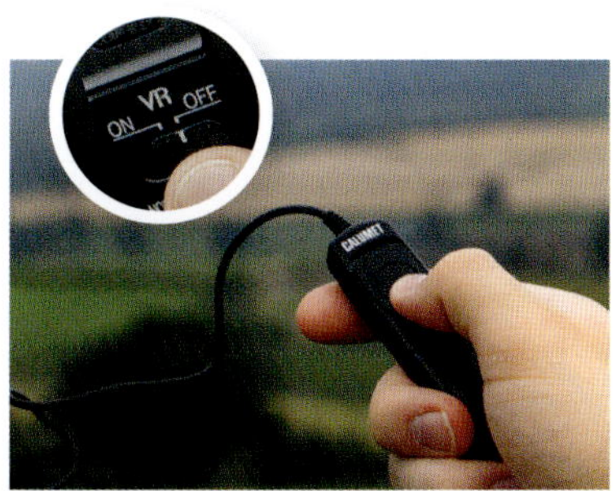


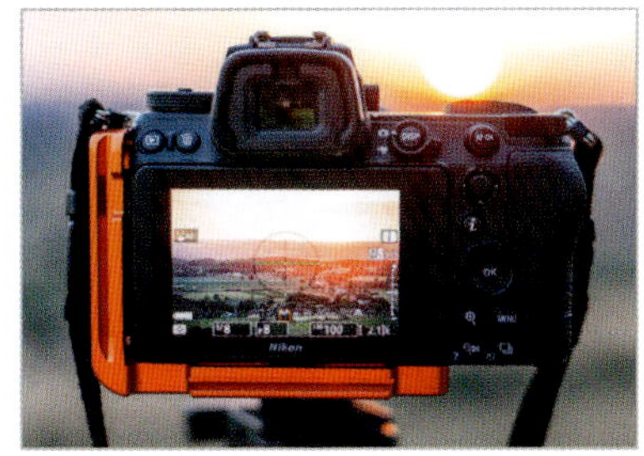

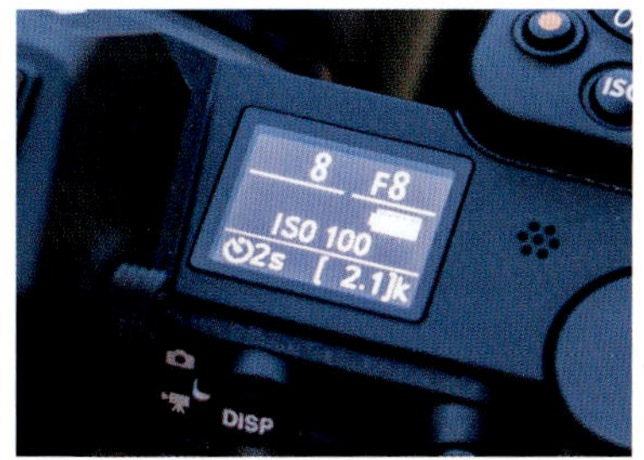


### 2 Keep it hands-free

The amplification of camera shake makes it imperative that you avoid inadvertently introducing movement when firing the shutter. Turn VR and/or IBIS off and use a remote shutter release. If you don't have the latter, use a self-timer or exposure-delay mode to shoot hands-free.

### 3 Composition

In this image, the layers of hills were used to split the frame via the rule of thirds. You could also use hedgerows or roads as leading lines and a particularly prominent building or tree as a subject. Use Live View to refine your composition and use the virtual horizon to ensure that it is perfectly level.

### 4 Camera settings

Switch to manual or aperture-priority mode. Since you're working on a tripod, the shutter speed doesn't matter. Set your aperture to around f/8 to f/11 to combat diffraction while still capturing a suitably large depth of field. Set ISO to 100 so image quality isn't compromised.

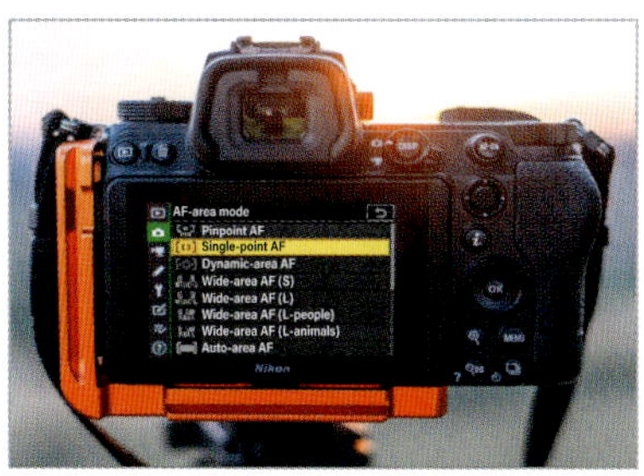


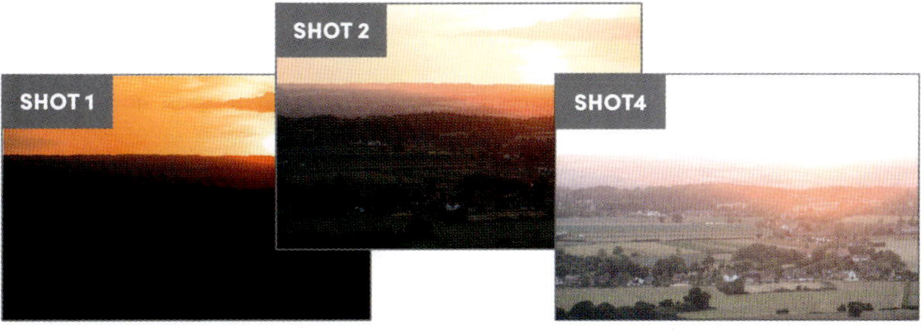


### 5 Find your focus

With no foreground interest, you should have no problem focusing a third of the way into the scene using single-point AF. Use back-button focusing to lock focus using the AF-ON button before firing the shutter without engaging AF again.

### 6 Shoot a bracket

If you're capturing a high-contrast scene, such as when shooting towards sunset, and you don't have an ND grad, shoot a bracket. This allows you to capture three or five shots of varying exposures, which you can then merge in post-production to create an HDR image. Merge images in Camera Raw by highlighting and right clicking the sequence before selecting Merge to HDR.

When a DSLR mirror flips up, just before the shutter is fired, it creates vibrations that can cause camera shake (mirror slap). Some cameras feature a mirror-up mode, which lets you press the shutter button to flip up the mirror and pause to quell vibrations before pressing it again to fire the shutter.

# MAKE THE MOST OF MIST

**THE IDEA**
**Embrace the opportunity of mist or fog on the horizon.**

**Time required:** 2 hours

**Kit needed:**
- DSLR or mirrorless camera
- 70–200mm lens
- Editing software

**Camera settings:**
1/640 sec at f/8, ISO 100

**Skill level:**

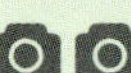  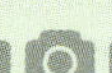

**Mist and fog occur when water droplets rise from the ground or a body of water, then condense and merge. Fog is denser, and is essentially a cloud on the ground, whereas mist is more transparent.**

You are likely to find mist or fog on a cool crisp morning after a clear night. Clear skies and low wind levels are both essential ingredients for getting mist or fog, which is why spring is a wonderful time of year to give this project a go.

The Dart Valley in Devon, UK, is a great fog and mist trap – the large body of water that makes up the River Dart and leads out to sea means you're far more likely to encounter this sort of weather due to the water evaporating from the surface; and the steep valley walls keep it contained for longer. On the day featured here, the townhouses were completely out of sight, and only the odd tree and other landmark stuck out from the dense fog carpet.

When it comes to composing your shot, you have two choices: either go wide and get the whole scene or use a telephoto lens to isolate just one part, for a more calming and abstract finish.

Converting to black and white helps emphasise the shape of the tree enabling it to act as the shot's focal point and also keeps the dense fog looking nice and clean.

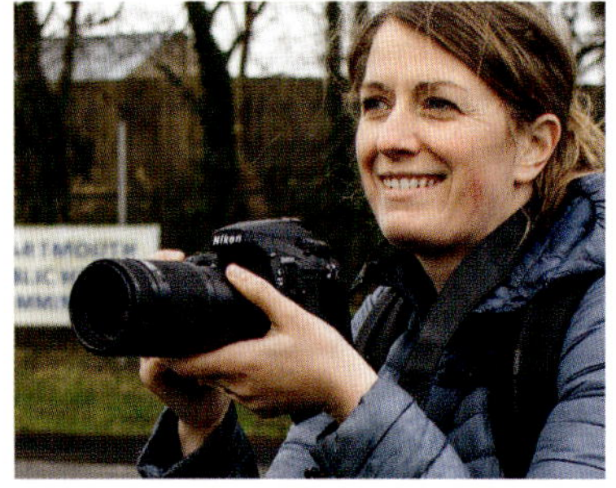

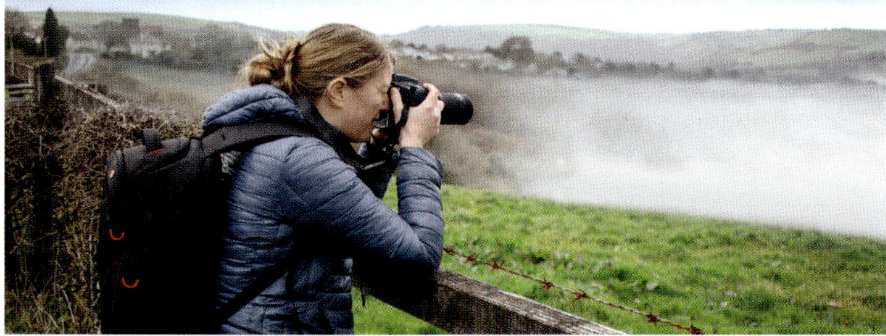

**1 Use a long lens**
A 70–200mm lens on a full-frame camera will do the job well enough. At the editing stage, you can always crop in a little to ensure your final composition includes only the vital ingredients – in this instance, the tree surrounded by the fog. Using just one landmark creates a striking result.

**2 Camera settings**
The general rule of thumb when using a long lens is to set the shutter speed to at least the length of the lens. For example, a 200mm lens needs at least a 1/200 sec shutter speed. Set the aperture to f/8 to keep everything in the frame sharp.

**3 Use a fence**
If you are using a long lens, it can help to rest your arms on a supportive surface while you are framing and shooting. In this instance, a fence provided some additional support. Some may prefer to use a tripod (which is fine to do), but you can be more flexible without one on a shoot like this.

## 4 Finishing touches

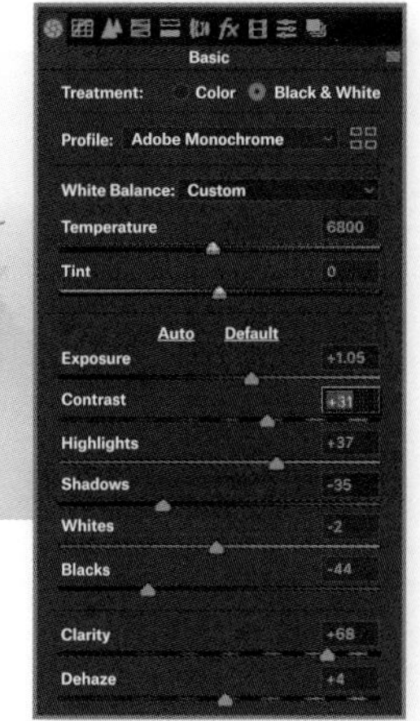


To convert your image to black and white, open Camera Raw and click on the Black and White Treatment option at the top of the Basics tab. After this, the main things you want to think about at this stage are checking if the exposure is correct, boosting the contrast and increasing the blacks and whites. Don't go too far with the whites, otherwise you'll lose detail.

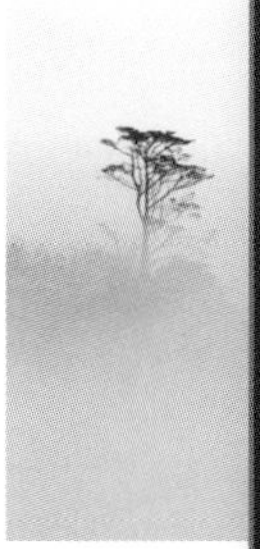

If your lens is old and produces an unwanted vignette around the outside of the image, click on the Lens Correction tab and increase Vignetting to lighten the edges.

Once happy with your ACR adjustments, use the Spot Healing Brush in Photoshop to clean any unwanted marks.

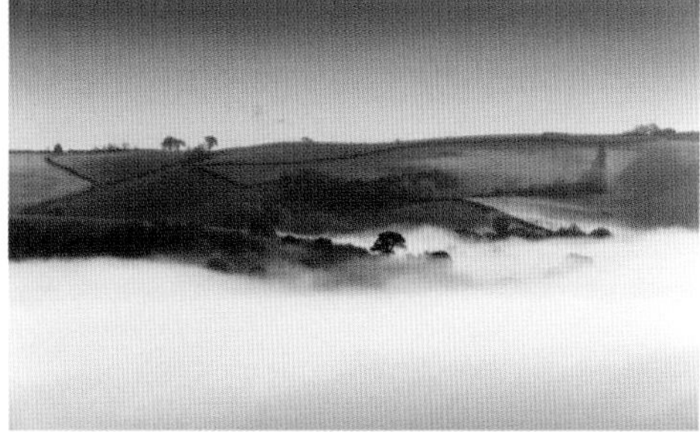

It's important at the editing stage to think about whether your image is better suited to a monochrome or colour finish. In this example, the final version lent itself better to colour: the soft pastel colours of the fields and the blue sky with the warmth of the sunshine are the main reasons for this. When it comes to editing white balance, be careful not to make the overall tones too warm, as this can make the fog look yellow and mucky.

# GET REFLECTIVE WITH A MIRROR

**THE IDEA**
**Take a mirror on location to bring a new dimension to the landscape.**

**Time required**: 1 hour

**Kit needed:**
- DSLR or mirrorless camera
- 16–35mm lens
- Mirror

**Camera settings:**
1/100 sec at f/11, ISO 100

**Skill level:**

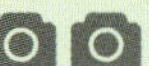  

**If you want to add a distinctive twist to your landscape shots, bring along a mirror the next time you're out in the wilderness. Reflections are a visually interesting topic to explore in photography – even more so when you are in control of what you want to be reflected.**

There are many shooting scenarios where using a mirror will add something to your shot: at the beach, in a woodland area, or when you have two visually contrasting scenes opposite each other that conflict, like a beautiful view and a power station.

For inspiration, look at artists Guillaume Amat and Murray Fredericks. Not only is their work visually engaging, it's also conceptually interesting. Their images explore space and composition in an enticing way, forcing you to consider authenticity and manipulation in a non-digital way.

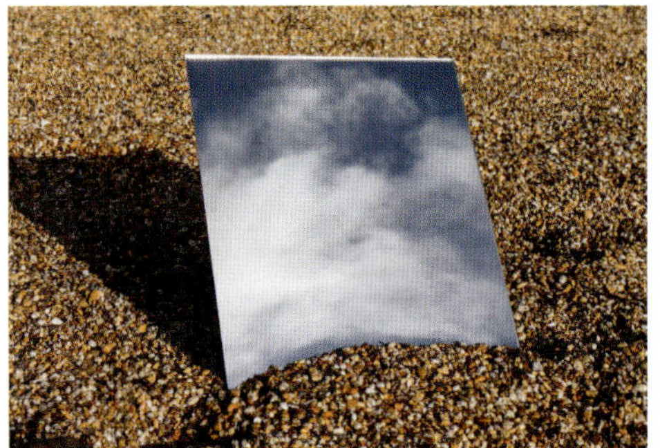

**1 The mirror**
Rather than lugging an expensive, heavy mirror out and about with you, pick up a piece of A3 acrylic mirror online very inexpensively. This lightweight material is easy to carry, and it doesn't matter if it gets damaged in the process. You can also bend the acrylic if necessary. Take a cloth and some glass cleaner out on location with you, to keep the reflective surface free from smudges.

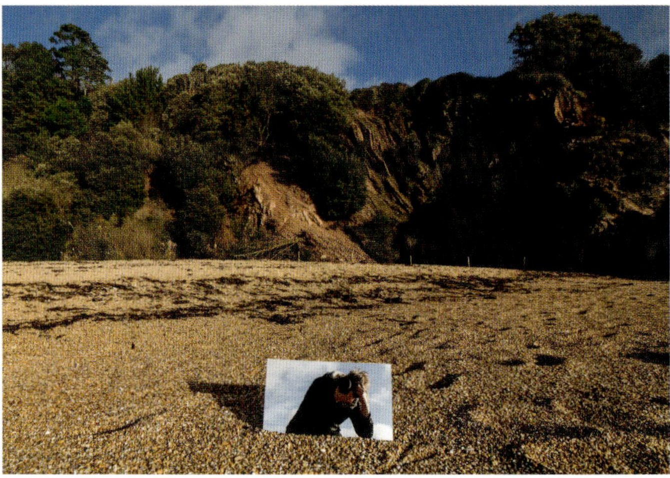

**2 Make a self-portrait**
For a fun spin on this technique, use the mirror to reflect yourself in the setting and create a self-portrait. When it comes to exposing your image, use a medium depth of field (try around f/11) to keep both the mirror and the background of your scene sharp.

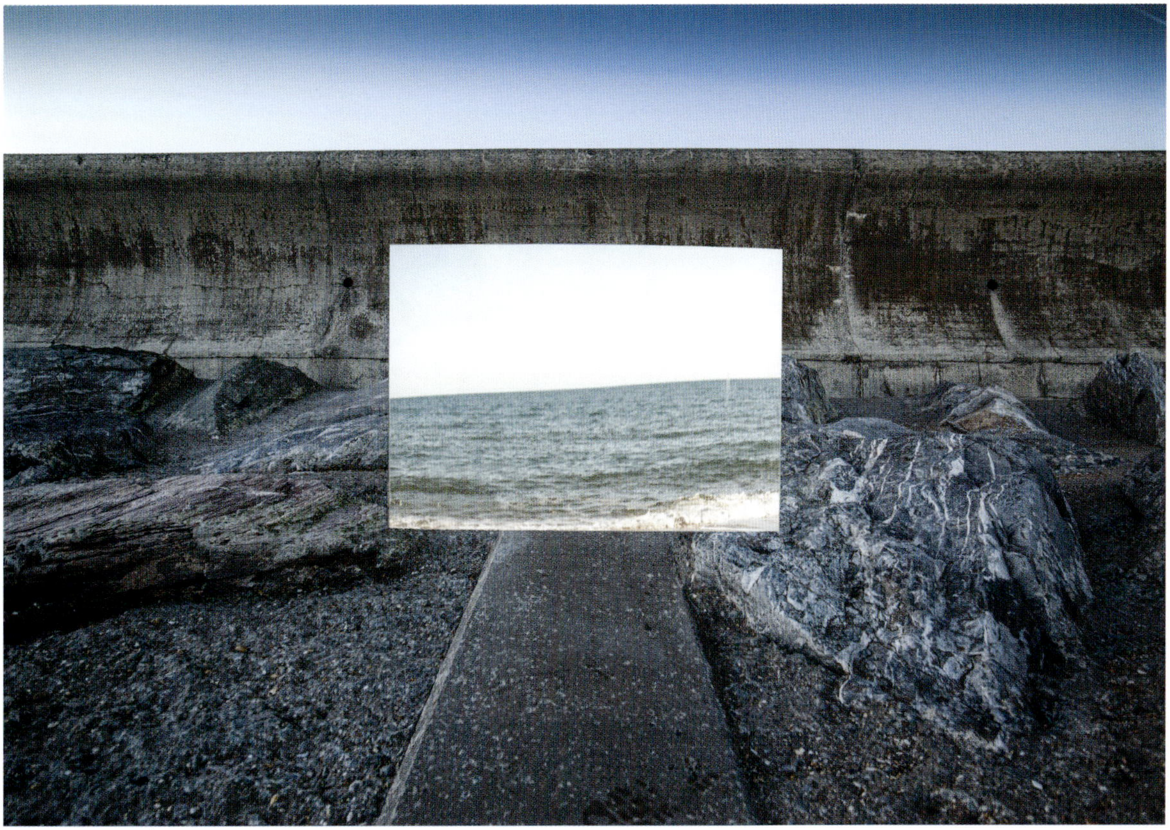

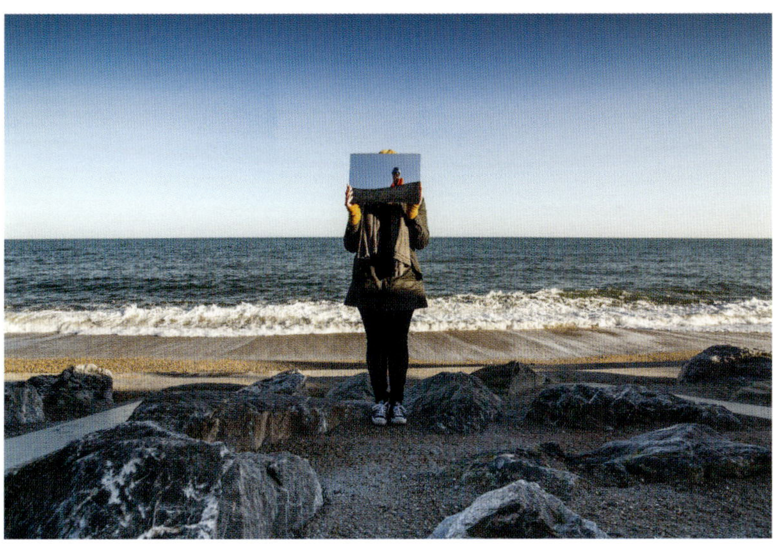

**3** **Get someone to hold the mirror** You can either hold the mirror yourself in the scene or get someone else to do it. You don't necessarily have to remove them from the image, as this set-up creates an interesting composition. Use a wide-angle lens to make the most of beach scenes.

# MAKE A SUNSET SPARKLE

**THE IDEA**
**Take low-light shots with a striking starburst effect.**

**Time required:** 2 hours

**Kit needed:**
- DSLR or mirrorless camera
- Wide-angle lens
- Lens hood
- Tripod
- Editing software

**Camera settings:**
1/40 sec at f/22, ISO 100

**Skill level:**

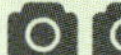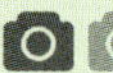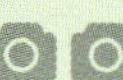

**It has long been established that shooting in the 'golden hour', the time around which the sun rises or sets over the horizon, bathes your landscape in a flattering, dreamy, warm light. But you can further this photogenic quality by giving the sun a dramatic starburst effect. The first step is to work out the direction in which the sun will set or rise, and where to shoot from. You also need to learn how to compose your scene with the sun in it safely, as looking at the sun through the viewfinder can damage your eyes.**

Camera settings play a large part in creating the starburst effect. You'll need to close your aperture down to a value such as f/22 to exaggerate the flare and restricts the light flow to a mere trickle, which is useful when you're shooting towards such a bright light source.

The flare effect is caused by light hitting the corners of your camera's aperture blades at the precise moment the sun hits the horizon. If you have a five-bladed aperture diaphragm, you'll end up with a five-point starburst; if it's made up of eight, you'll end up with eight points, and so on.

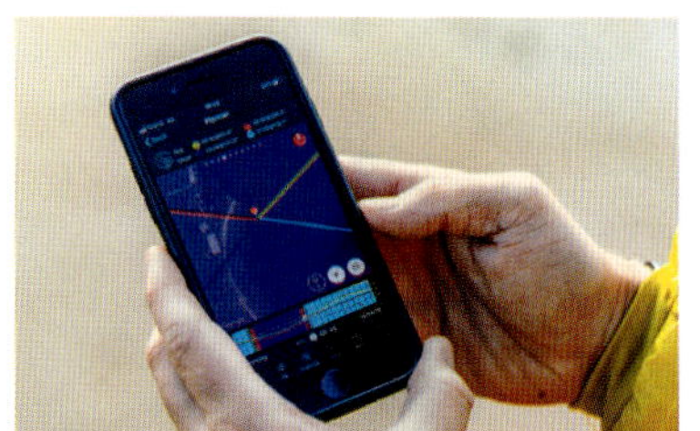

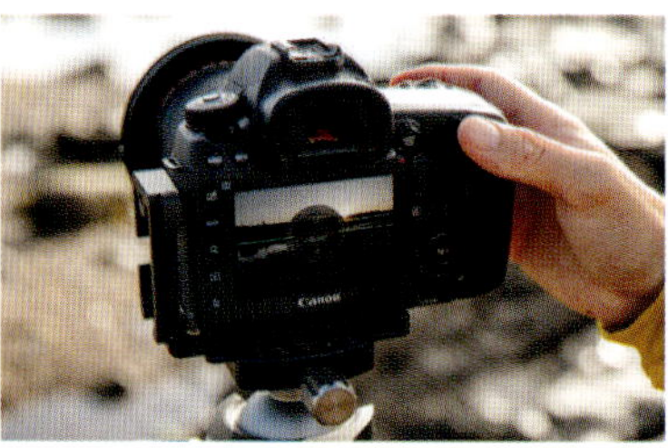

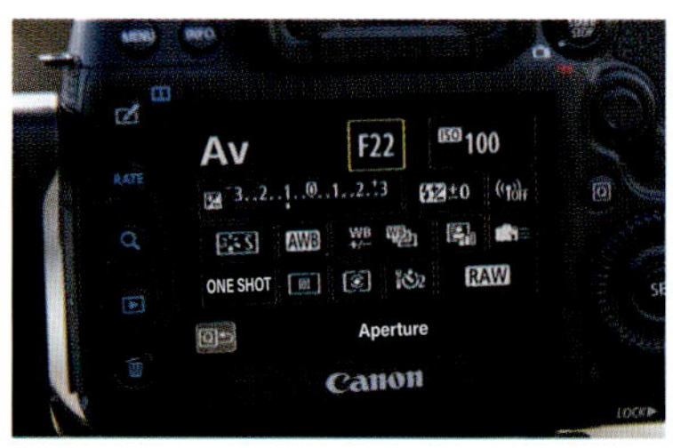


**1 Find the angle of the sun**
To shoot towards the sun, you first need to know where it's going to set. Apps such as PhotoPills or The Photographer's Ephemeris will reveal the angle at which the light from the setting sun will be coming towards you at any given time or location. This can make it much easier to plan and compose your landscape while you're waiting for the sun to set.

**2 Frame up the shot**
The bright sun can easily damage your eyes, so you should never look directly at it – or even view it through the optical viewfinder of a camera that's pointing towards it. Instead, use your camera's Live View mode to frame up the scene on your rear screen, and make sure your composition is finalised, focused and locked off on a tripod well before the sun is due to set.

**3 Close down your aperture**
Make sure you're shooting Raw files. Go into aperture-priority mode and set a narrow value such as f/22 (the narrower the aperture, the greater the starburst effect). Set the ISO to its lowest native setting (usually 100) and switch on the self-timer mode to avoid camera shake. As soon as you see the sun hit the horizon on your camera's rear screen, take the picture.

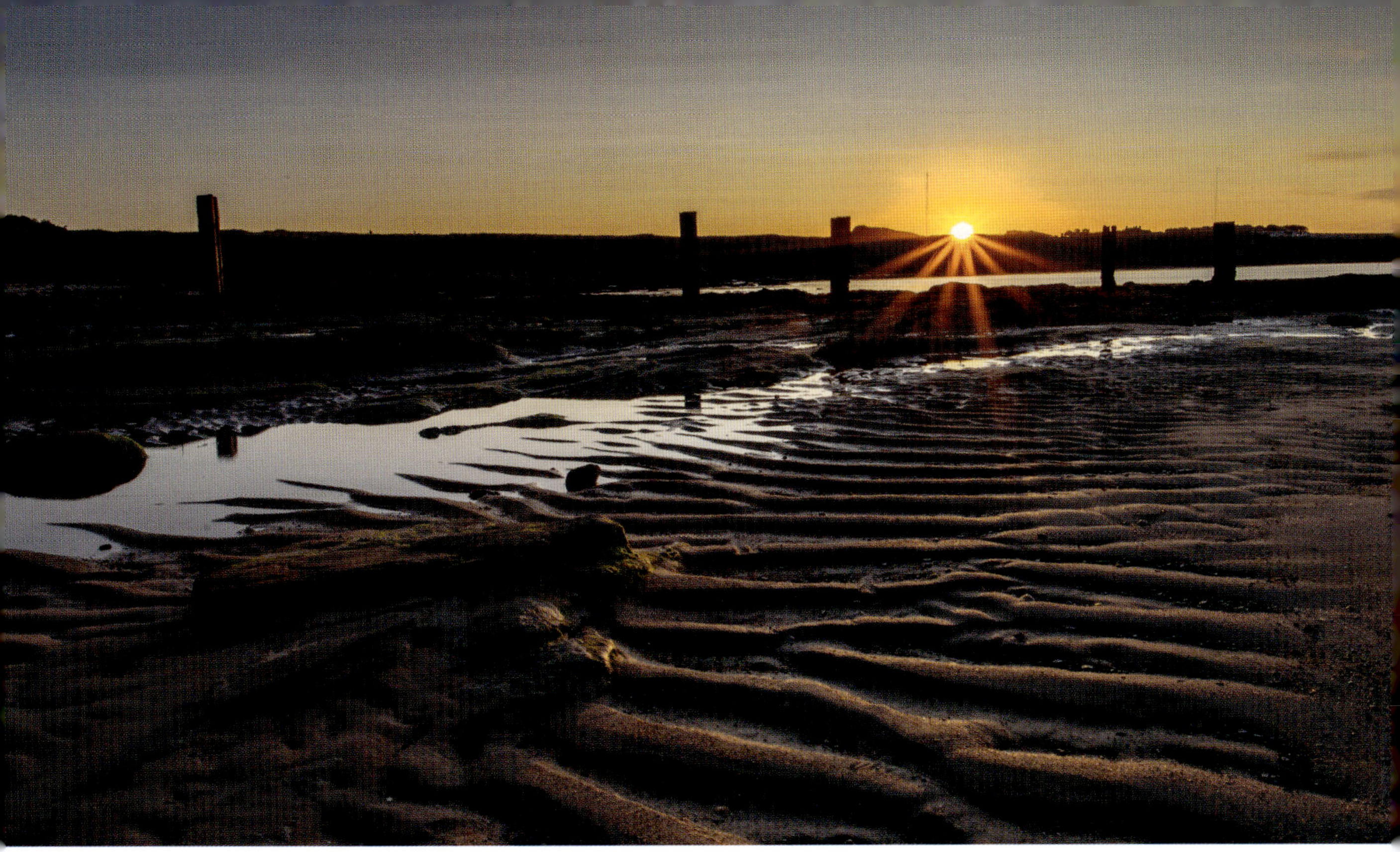

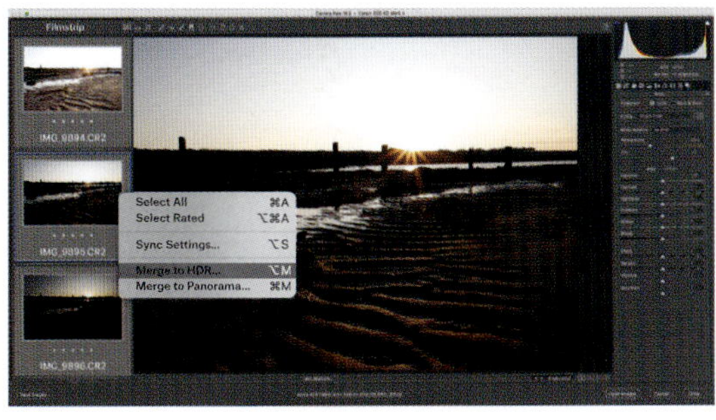

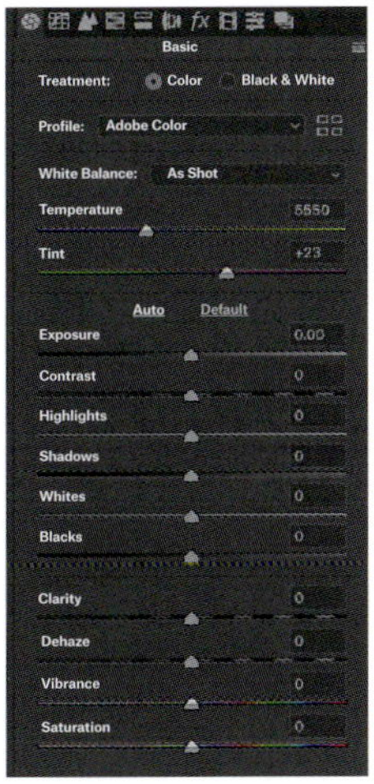

## 4 Expand your dynamic range

Because the contrast is so high, sunset images are perfect for a high dynamic range (HDR) treatment. Here, multiple exposures are merged so you get the full range of tones from deep shadows to bright highlights, making colours and tones look much richer. Activate your camera's auto-bracketing mode and set it to take three pictures, each 2 stops apart. Select all three shots in Camera Raw and choose Merge to HDR to create a single Raw file with more exposure information.

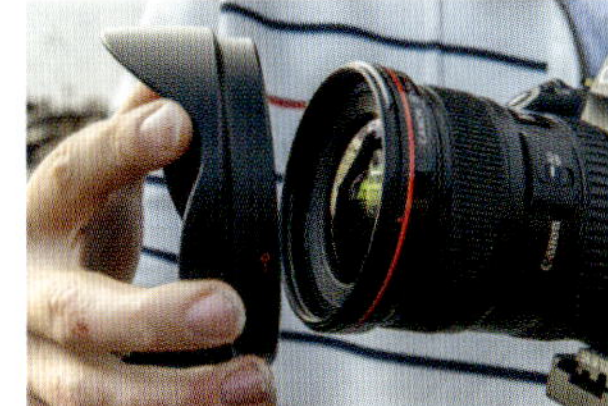

The idea of this technique is to capture the amazing flare effect that occurs when the sun hits the horizon. To add a little bit of clarity and stop the picture looking too washed out, attach your lens hood. Alternatively, increase the value of the Dehaze slider when you're editing the Raw file in Adobe Camera Raw or Lightroom.

# TAKE TO THE SKIES

**THE IDEA**
**Understand drone flying laws in your country to elevate your images.**

**Time required**: 1 hour

**Kit needed:**
- Camera drone
- Smartphone for controller

**Camera settings:**
1/50 sec at f/2.2, ISO 100

**Skill level:**

   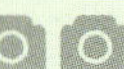

**Whether you use your drone to shoot video clips or still images, it's a fantastic tool to have – as long as you're following the rules.**

The UK requires anyone using a drone over 250g, or a drone that has a camera, to register with the Civil Aviation Authority (CAA) and get a Flyer ID. There is a simple online course that teaches the basic rules of flying a drone.

In the USA the FAA (Federal Aviation Administration) operates a similar system for recreational pilots with a 'TRUST' certificate, but if you want to fly a drone for profit you also need to seek a 'Part 107' licence. For more detailed information, check out the CAA website (www.caa.co.uk) or your local regulatory authority to ensure compliance with regulations.

Even if you just fly drones as a hobby, there are some basic rules to follow to stay out of trouble with the authorities. It's mostly common-sense stuff, such as not flying your drone within 1km of an airport and ensuring you always keep a direct line of sight with it. You also need to make sure your drone stays under 120m (some models feature a height limiter) and keep a distance of at least 50m from buildings and people.

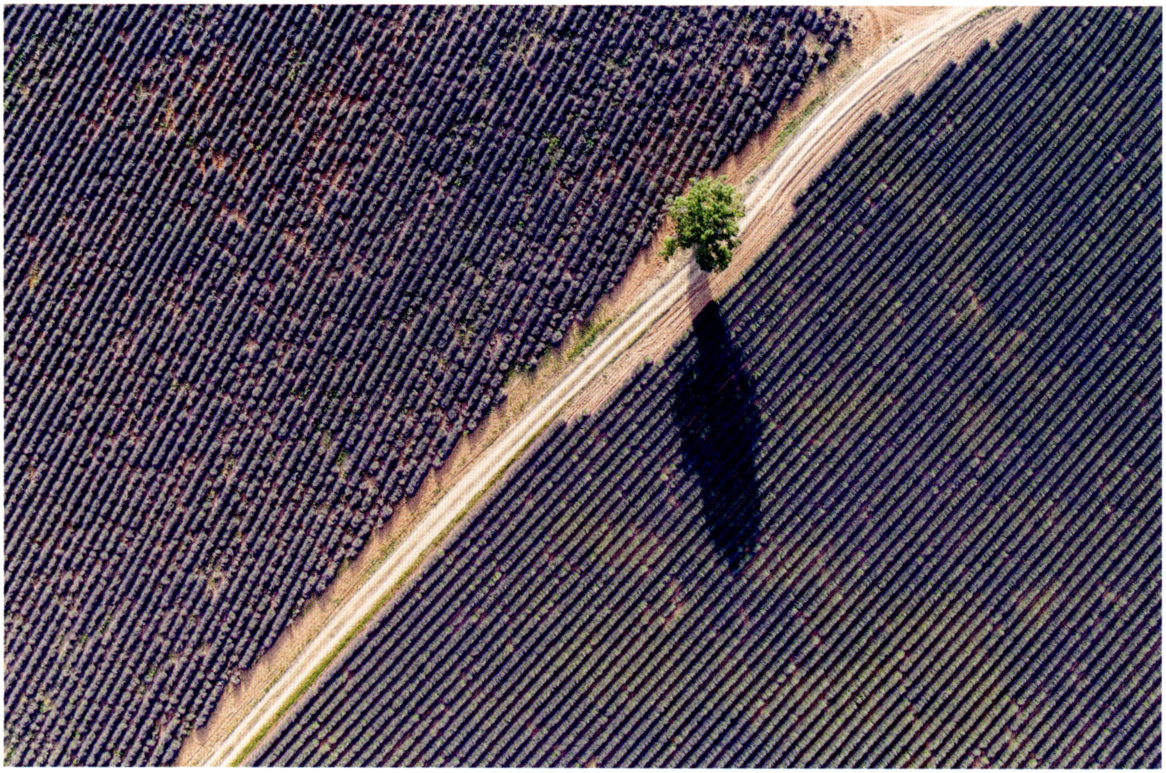

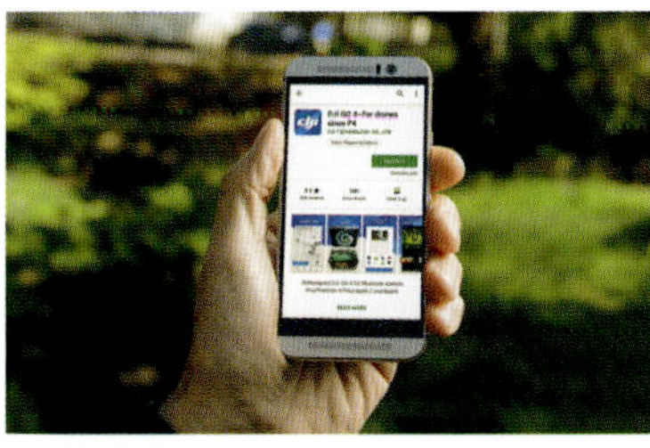

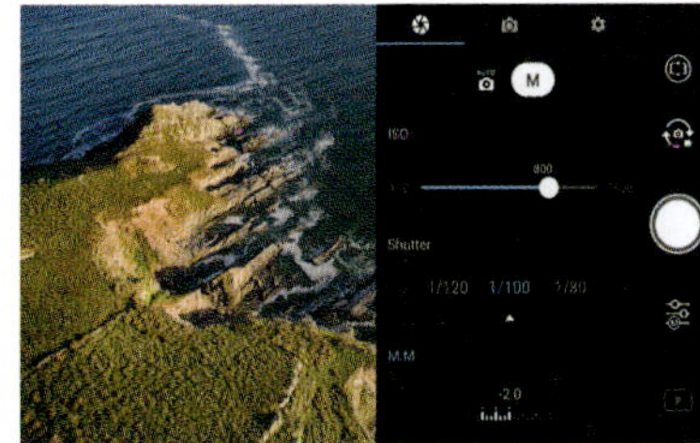

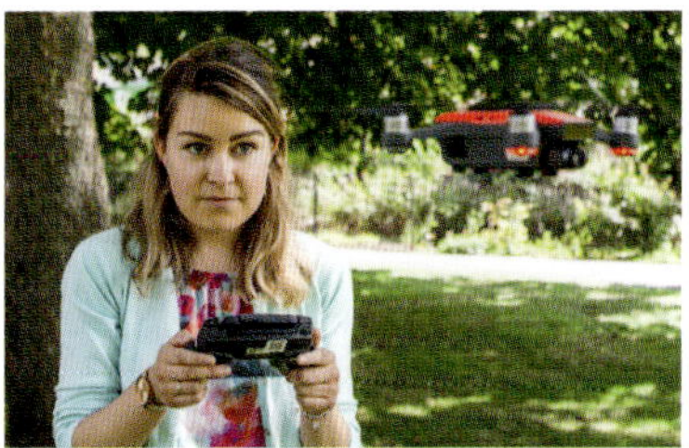

**1 Download the app**
Drones are directed either by their own advanced controller, or in the case of entry-level models, by linking to a smartphone to display a live video feed. A mobile device tends to provide flight controls, GPS and mapping, so it's a good idea to keep the drone controller firmware up to date. Before flying, make sure you have the latest version of the app.

**2 Settings and power**
Head to the relevant menu on the controller or app, choosing Raw for stills (if available) and a high-quality video output. 4K is preferable, allowing you to crop in on footage but still output in Full HD. Fly time is limited with consumer drones, as it takes a lot of power to keep them up in the air. Invest in spare batteries and you'll be able to shoot for longer.

**3 Learn special modes**
Drones such as DJI's Neo have modes such as gesture control, target tracking and panoramic shooting. It's worth reading the manual and getting to grips with the modes specific to your model. Before concentrating your efforts on photography, practise taking off and landing, hovering close to the ground as you get used to the controls.

**4 Pre-flight checks**
Inspect your drone, replace any damaged rotors, and clean the camera lens with a microfibre cloth. Make sure you're 50m away from buildings, people and vehicles and 1km from airports and airfields. Check the weather forecast to avoid flying in adverse conditions such as rain, fog, snow and strong winds. After you take off, let your drone hover for around 30 seconds to check its stability.

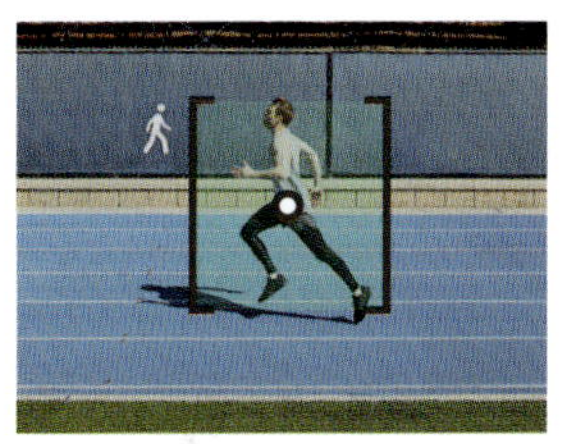

Most drones have a feature that enables you to lock on to a chosen subject as it moves. DJI, one of the most popular drone manufacturers, has the ActiveTrack function, designed to give an easier, safer way to achieve a cinematic shot while flying. When enabled, ActiveTrack follows a subject throughout the shot, whether they're walking along a trail, driving a car or even swimming. Bear in mind that the feature needs a strong GPS signal and use of the drone's vision systems. If you've got a compatible DJI drone, set it to P mode (position mode) so you can use ActiveTrack. Once you're in ActiveTrack mode, tap or draw a box around the subject on screen. Try to include the whole subject within the box, keeping out as much of the background as possible.

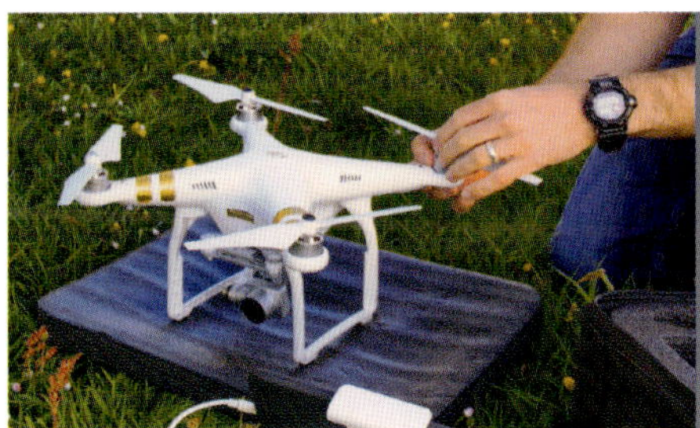

## Check ahead

**Even if you satisfy the conditions for drone use set out by the CAA and follow its safety guidelines, you are not free to release your drone wherever you like. Landowners including the Forestry Commission and the National Trust have strict policies about the use of drones on their properties, so you should always get permission first.**

# FLATTEN PERSPECTIVE

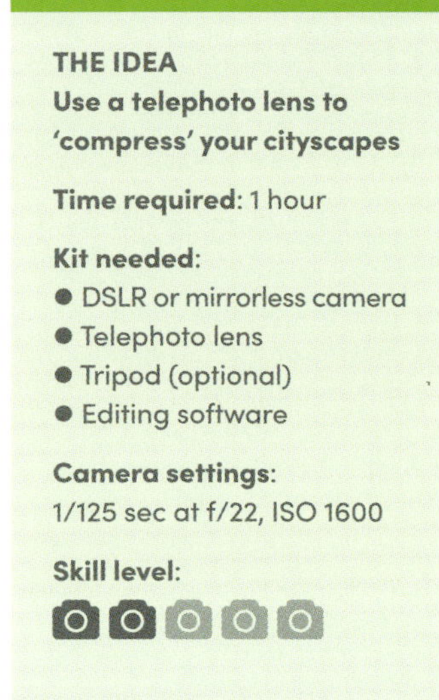

**THE IDEA**
**Use a telephoto lens to 'compress' your cityscapes**

**Time required:** 1 hour

**Kit needed:**

- DSLR or mirrorless camera
- Telephoto lens
- Tripod (optional)
- Editing software

**Camera settings:**
1/125 sec at f/22, ISO 1600

**Skill level:**

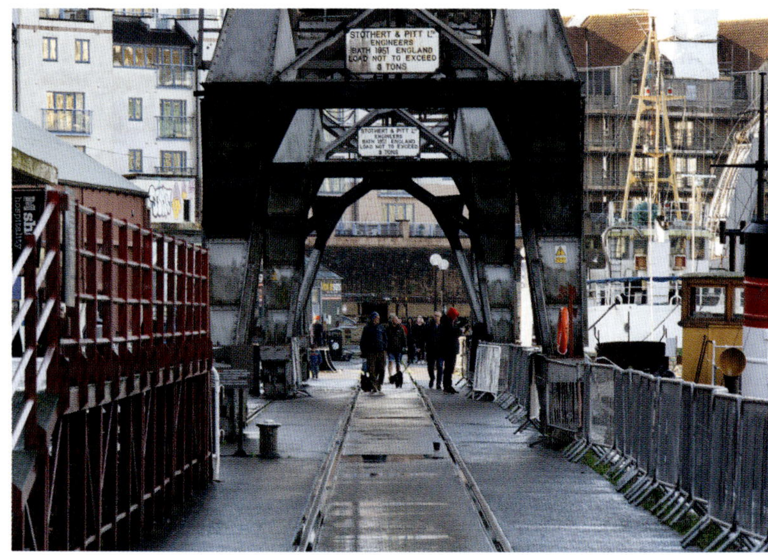


**We all have our own perspective on the world, and camera lenses aim to replicate these optical viewpoints as faithfully as possible. To record in a photograph what we see with our eyes, we choose the appropriate lens for the job, whether it has a fixed or adjustable focal range. But you can also use specific lenses to move away from simply reproducing a scene, instead flattening, or 'compressing' it. One of the best ways to achieve a flattened perspective for effective creative results is to use a telephoto lens.**

Flattened perspective is achieved when the visual depth between subjects is reduced; the relative subjects in the image will therefore appear closer to one another than they are in reality.

Distances now become more important when you are shooting – the further away you are from the subject, the more enhanced the flattening effect will be. You will need to adapt to a new way of aligning your composition, as there is a greater distance for all the subjects you want to portray to be included.

When you use a telephoto lens, make the most of high vantage points within the environment to experiment with the technique. This shot was taken from a point high over the streets at Cabot Tower in Bristol, UK.

Taking out a tripod is not essential, but if lighting conditions are poor, mounting the camera on a tripod will allow you to shoot at slower shutter speeds, which will be useful, as you'll be using narrower apertures to get everything in focus. Plus, a telephoto lens will be bigger and heavier than a standard zoom lens, so a tripod will make your life easier.

It also helps to have an open mind when you're hunting for locations. Successful images will come from exploring different areas and finding viewpoints that haven't been considered beforehand.

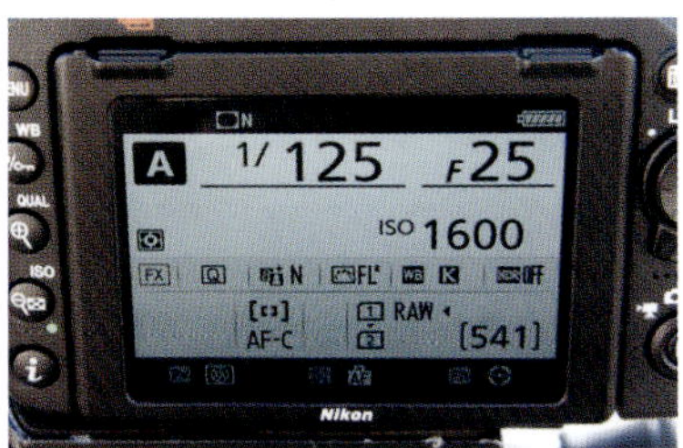


**1 Aperture priority**

As you need to control the depth of field in your image, set the camera to aperture-priority mode. To obtain a flattened perspective, you need to capture a large depth of field, and the foreground and background must be in full focus. Set a narrow aperture of f/16 or f/22 to achieve this.

If required, adjust your ISO to a higher setting – you can still get great results at ISO 6,400. This will combat motion blur from the shutter speed being too slow. Try to keep your shutter speed faster than 1/60 sec.

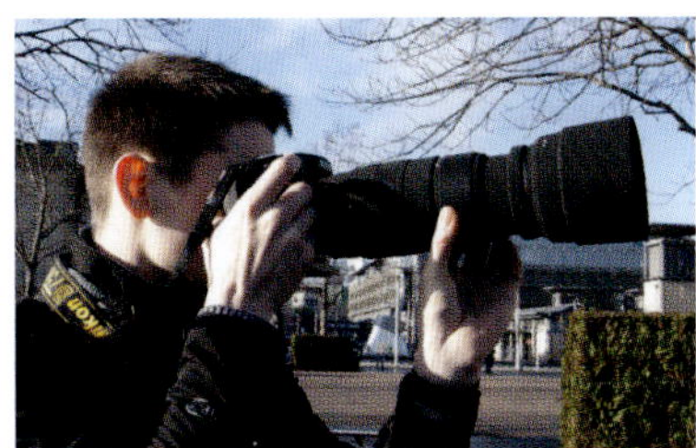

**2 Telephoto lens**

As they possess higher focal ranges then standard lenses, it's essential to use a telephoto lens. A large telephoto with a focal range of 120–400mm is ideal for covering both short and long distances. However, you can also get good results using a telephoto offering between 85 and 135mm.

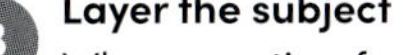

**3 Layer the subject**

When scouting for a location, check which subjects will be in your line of sight. Try to find subjects located within the foreground of the image and ones further in the background, too. Buildings work well when you 'layer up' your composition, as they effectively merge and intersect with each other in the frame. As buildings are usually flat to the focal plane, it is easy to get the compressed effect, enabling photographs to be taken at a larger scale. You could use passers-by as elements in the image to give a sense of scale that will enhance the compressed effect but be discreet and mindful of people's right to privacy.

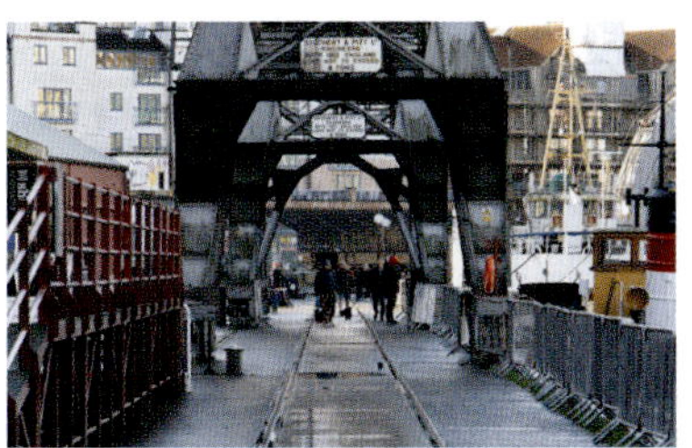

**4 Know your angles**

Always consider your angles in urban and rural landscape photography. As this technique is all about altering and flattening perspective, keep an eye on getting straight horizontal and vertical lines throughout, for a tidier final image. To practise this, open one of your images in Photoshop. Go to View > New Guide, then select Horizontal or Vertical. Using the Move Tool, reposition the guides in line with the edges of your subjects to see if you are capturing everything straight.

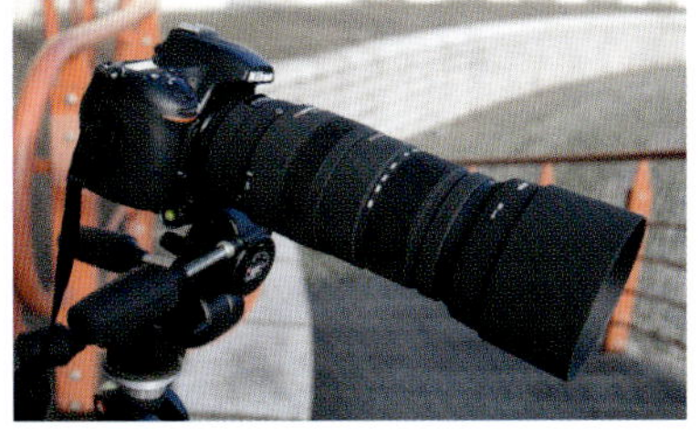

**5 Ditch the rule of thirds**

In conventional landscape photography, around one-third of the sky is included to balance the image. With the style and effect we are aiming for, though, it is better to move the lens further down to get more subject matter into the frame. To achieve this, shoot from higher vantage points so your composition includes more elements over a greater distance.

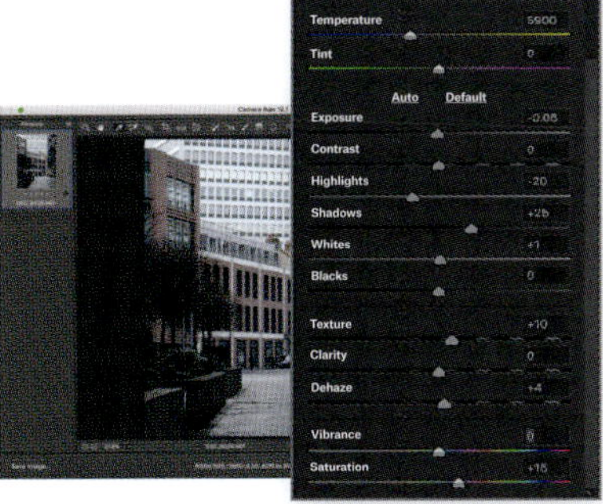


**6 Camera Raw**

When viewing the resulting images in post-production, some key tools can be of benefit. It's important to keep control of Shadows and Highlights adjustments, and to reduce the effect of shadows in the photograph. Be mindful of boosting Contrast – you want the subjects to merge with each other as much as possible for the flattened perspective to be more effective.

# PAINT WITH LIGHT

**THE IDEA**
**Reveal detail in low-light scenes using a flashgun.**

**Time required**: 1–2 hours

**Kit needed**:
- DSLR or mirrorless camera
- Wide-angle lens
- Off-camera flash
- Tripod
- Editing software

**Camera settings**:
8 secs at f/4, ISO 12,800 and 15 secs at f/10, ISO 400

**Skill level**:

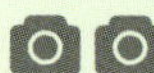   

**Using a flash or a torch is a great way to reveal detail in low-light scenes, but the light from the bulb alone can look a bit plain. You can add flash gels – little strips of coloured plastic – in front of the flashgun so the flashlight takes on the colour of the gel, meaning you can paint areas of your scene with vibrant reds, greens, blues and so on. You can do the same with your torch, and if you're on a tight budget, semi-translucent sweet wrappers work a treat.**

Shine a bright torch on your landscape so that you can see the scene and get the framing you want on a tripod, then lock off the framing and focus.

Set your flashgun to manual mode and 1/16 power. Start your camera's long exposure and use the test button on your flash to manually fire it off-camera and flash every part of the frame to get good coverage. Once the exposure has finished, play it back. If it's still too dark, you'll need to either increase the flash power or fire the flash more times throughout the exposure.

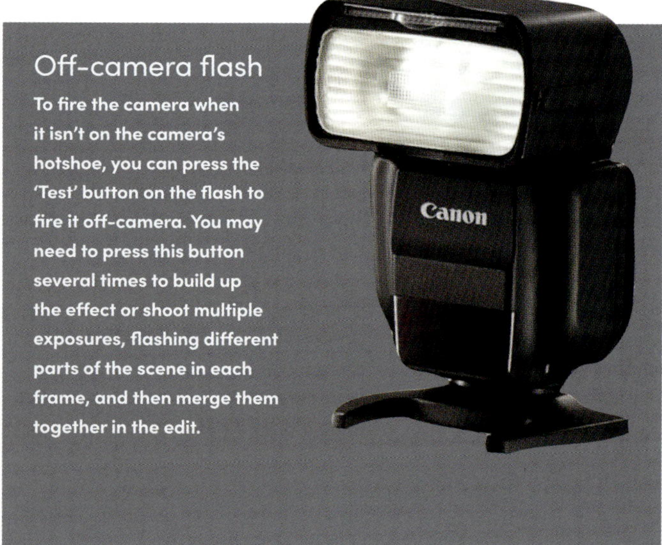


## Off-camera flash

**To fire the camera when it isn't on the camera's hotshoe, you can press the 'Test' button on the flash to fire it off-camera. You may need to press this button several times to build up the effect or shoot multiple exposures, flashing different parts of the scene in each frame, and then merge them together in the edit.**

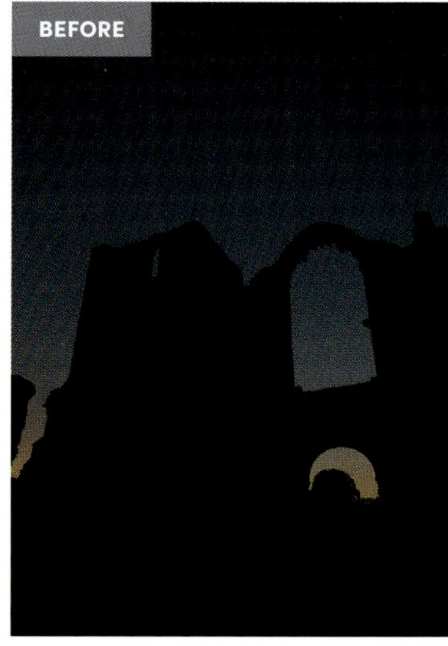


**Above and right: In the original scene, the building was a stark silhouette against the starry backdrop. Adding a little 'fill' light from a hand torch or flashgun reveals the shadow detail.**

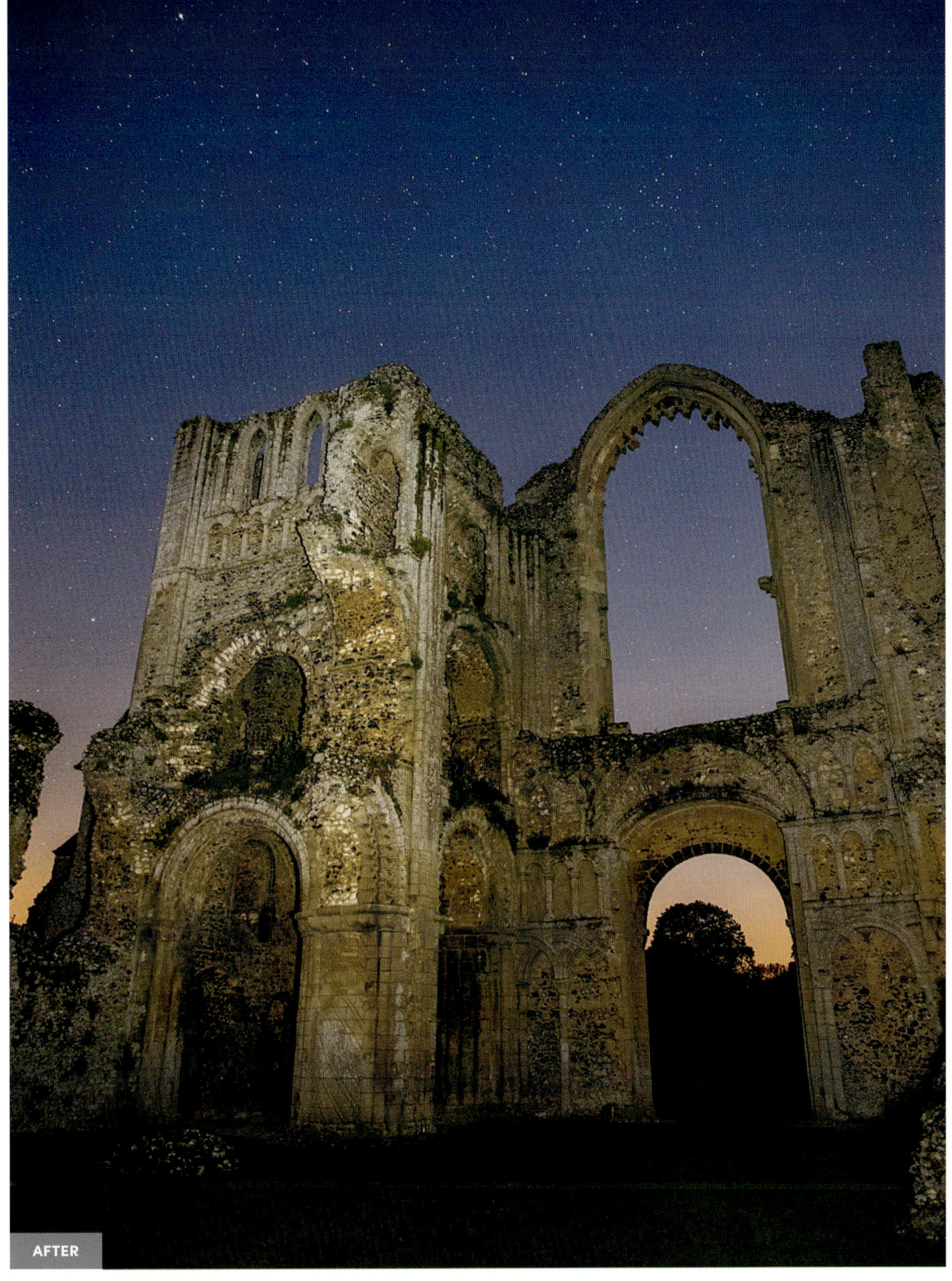
AFTER

# ADD A SPOOKY MIST EFFECT

**Adding spooky mist to your shots is simple and cost-effective with L-wire (also called EL-wire). You can buy them from online retailers very inexpensively.**

They come in different colour variations, and as they're very affordable, it's worth picking up a few colours to experiment with. They consist of a long, thin strip of plastic that lights up and is powered by a battery pack.

The wire is spread out and thrown across the floor of the scene during a long exposure to build up the ghostly 'mist' effect.

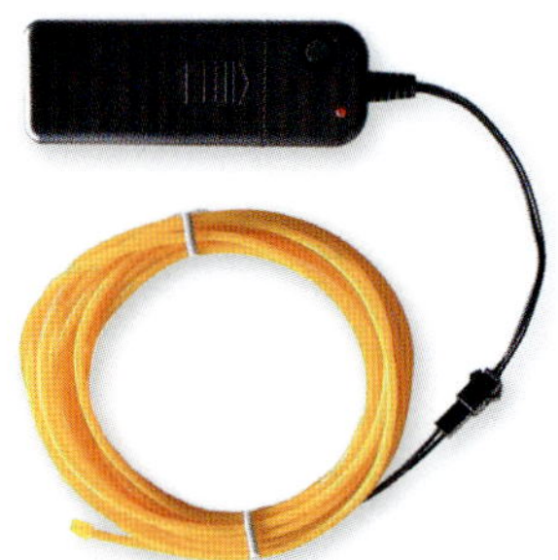

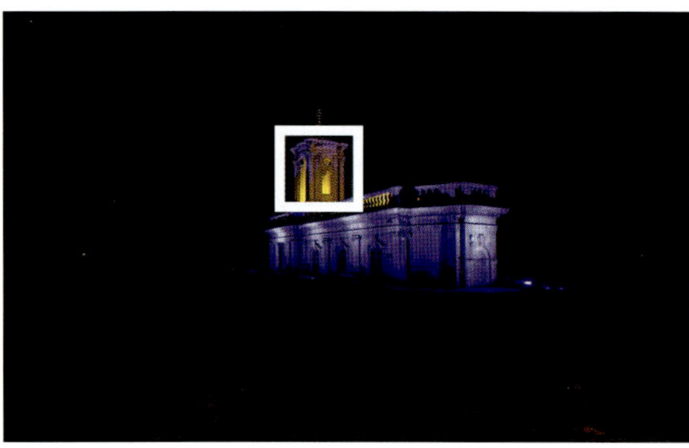

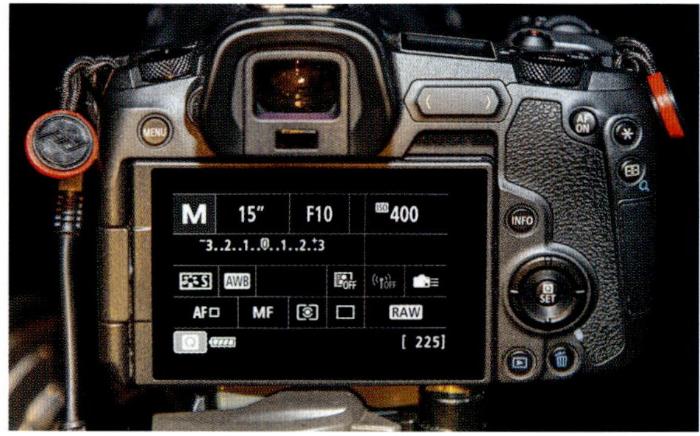


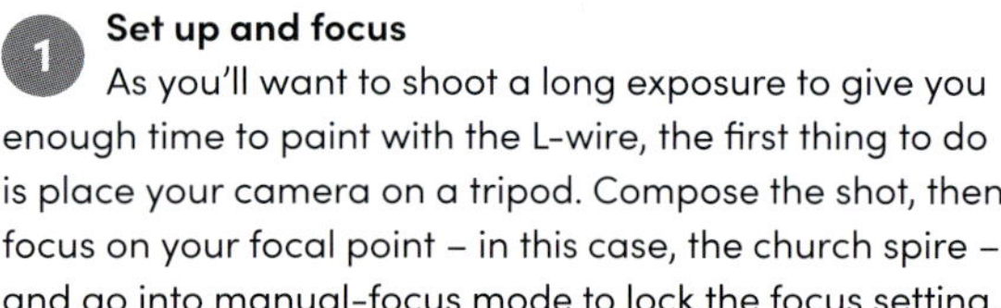

**1 Set up and focus**
As you'll want to shoot a long exposure to give you enough time to paint with the L-wire, the first thing to do is place your camera on a tripod. Compose the shot, then focus on your focal point – in this case, the church spire – and go into manual-focus mode to lock the focus setting.

**2 Dial in the exposure**
In manual mode, dial in an aperture of f/10, a shutter speed of 15 sec and an ISO of 400. Then set continuous drive mode and attach a shutter-release cable. Lock the shutter on the cable release down in the firing position so that it will continually take 15 sec exposures.

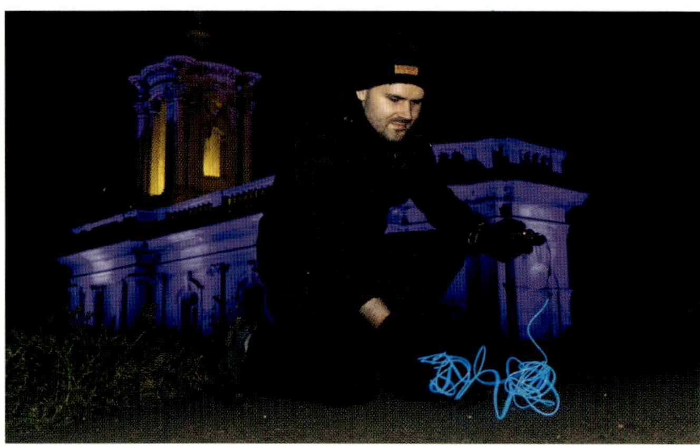

**3 Paint with your L-wire**
Wear dark clothing to minimise how much you will show up in the exposures, then switch on your L-wire and throw the wire across the foreground until you've covered it all. Now, stack your exposures with Layers in Photoshop and blend them together with the Lighten blend mode.

It took many exposures to cover the entire pathway with the blue L-wire that creates an ethereal mist in the shot opposite.

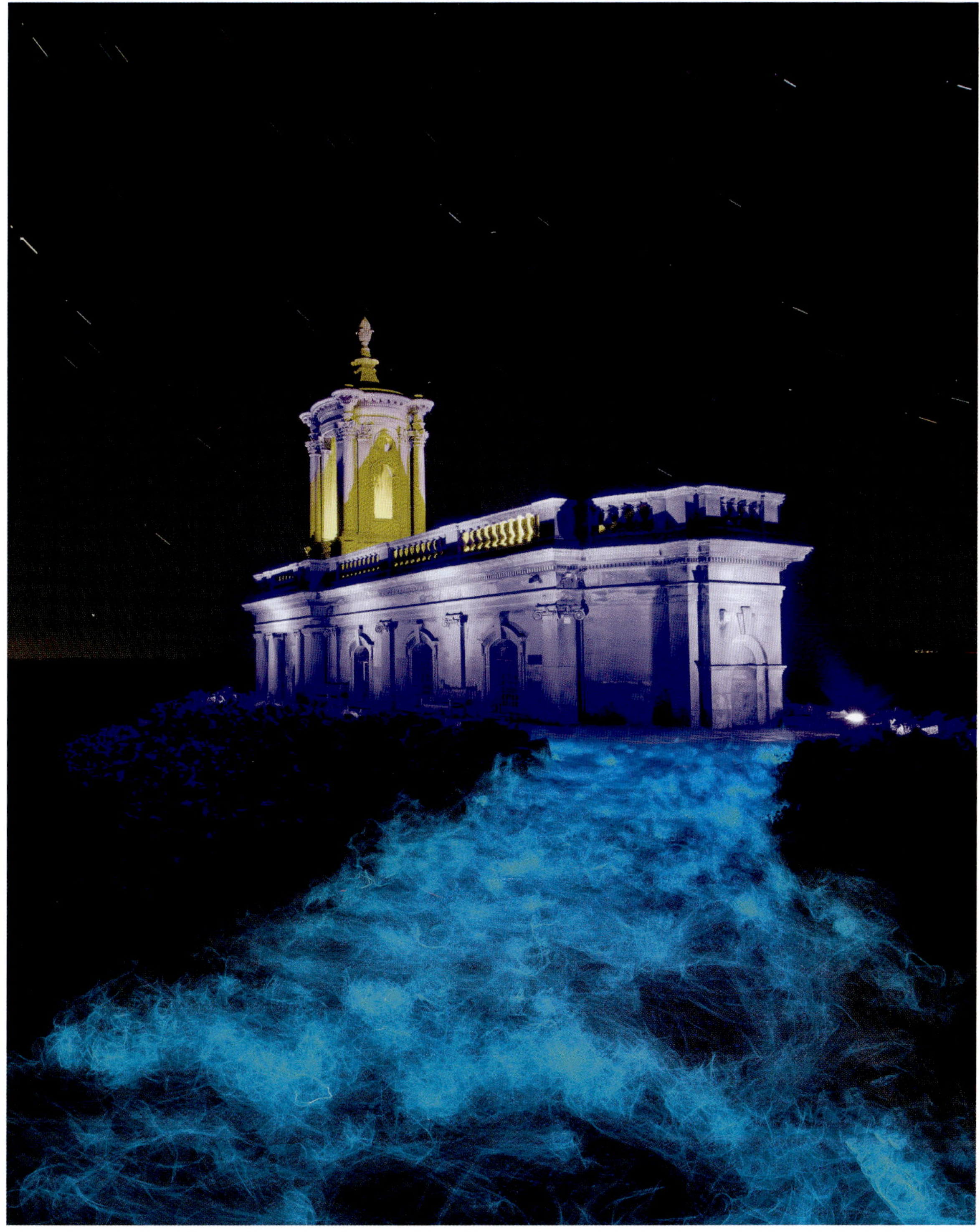

# LEARN TO POLARISE

**THE IDEA**
**Understand what a polarising filter is, and how best to use it.**

**Time required:** 1 hour

**Kit needed:**
- DSLR or mirrorless camera
- 28mm lens or longer
- Circular polarising filter

**Camera settings:**
4 secs at f/8, ISO 100

**Skill level:**

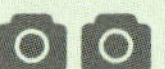   

**The polariser isn't just a landscape photography essential, it's the multitool of filters. Its ability to block polarised light from a specific direction reduces glare from sunlight, and boosts both contrast and colour saturation. This results in the punchier skies most people associate with polarisers, but also the ability to cut through reflections in water. If that wasn't enough, a polarising filter's light-blocking properties allow it to double as a handy one- or two-stop neutral-density filter.**

CPL stands for circular polariser, and the name derives from the way CPLs filter light, not their shape. As such, they're available as either screw-in filters or fit-square slot-in systems, which usually have a special recess built into the holder. Not all polarisers are circular polarisers, though. Linear polarisers also exist, but the way they filter light has been known to affect metering and autofocus systems, which is why CPLs are more commonly used. For more information on how polarisers work, turn to page 141.

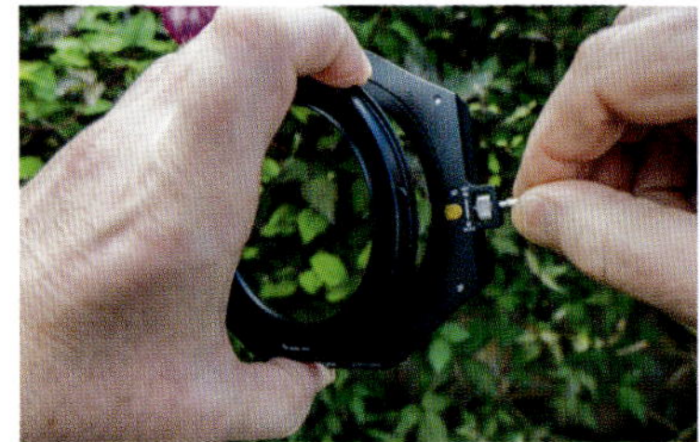

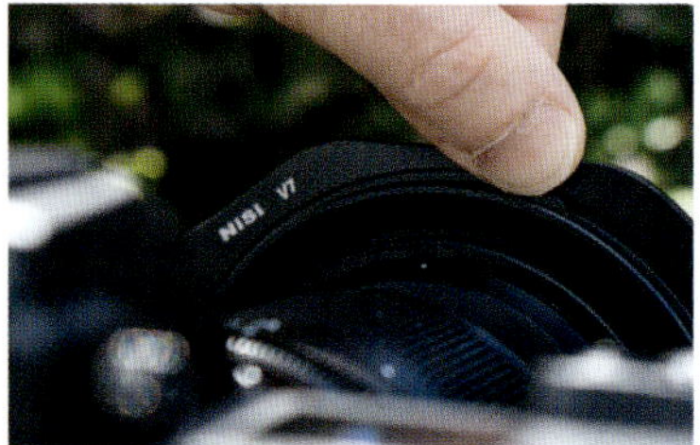

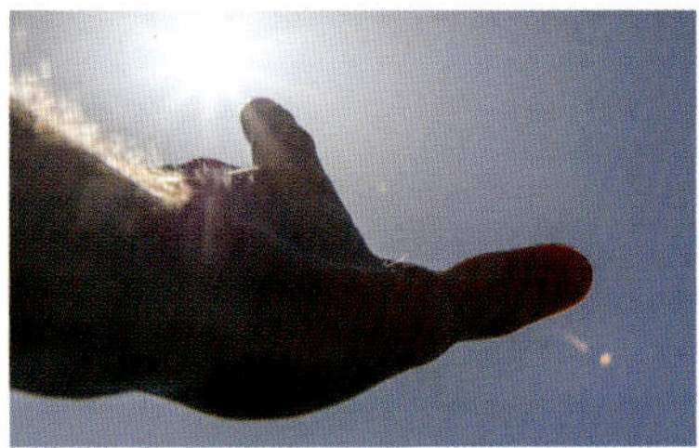

**1 Fit the filter**
Some filter systems feature a special recess at the rear of the filter holder, and so the polariser needs to be fitted before the holder is attached to the camera. Screw-in polarisers mount directly onto the filter thread at the front of the lens.

**2 Adjust the strength**
With the filter mounted, slowly turn the rotating polarising element. On a screw-in filter, there may be a mark on the rotating ring. As you turn it, you will see the filter's effect through the viewfinder or Live View.

**3 Fingers and thumbs**
The polarising effect is at its strongest at a 90-degree angle to the sun. A quick 'ready reckoner' for the best direction to shoot is to create a finger gun with your thumb and forefinger. Point your finger at the sun (without looking at it), and your thumb will indicate where the effect will be strongest.

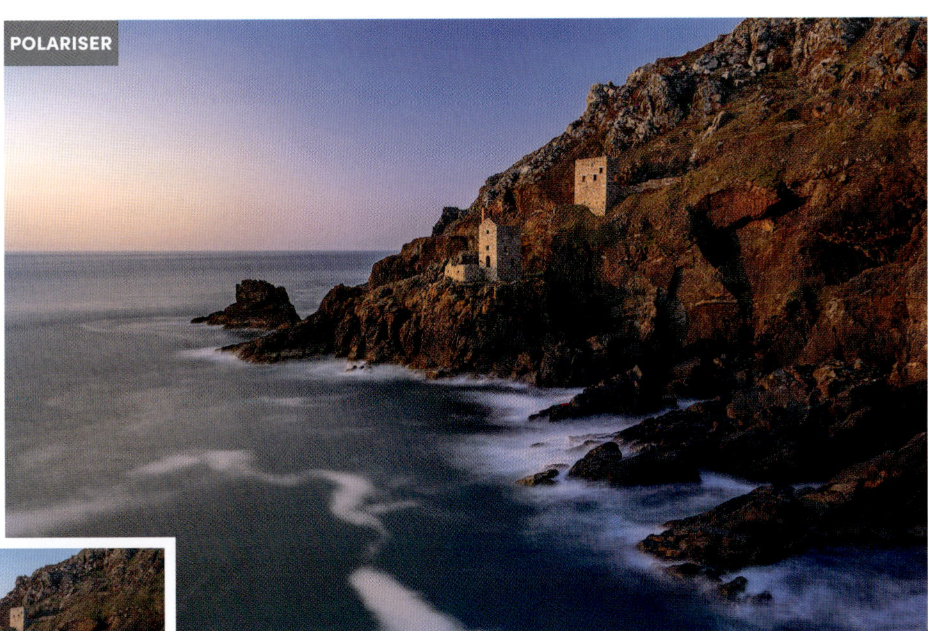


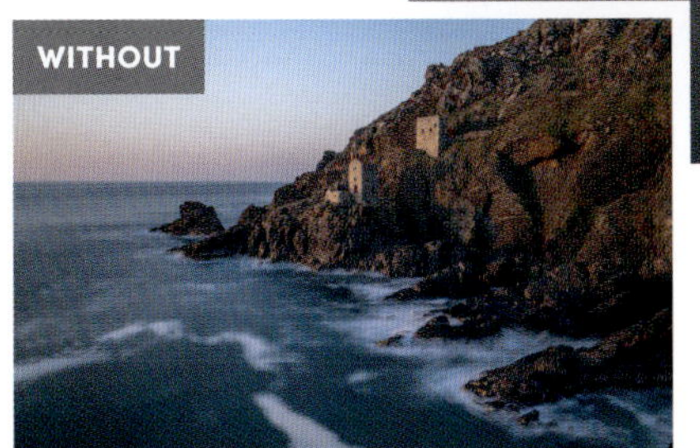


Because polarisers work best at a 90-degree angle to the sun, very wide fields of view will frame areas beyond this parameter, where the filter will prove less effective. This can create patchy skies, so we'd recommend going no wider than 28mm on a full-frame camera.

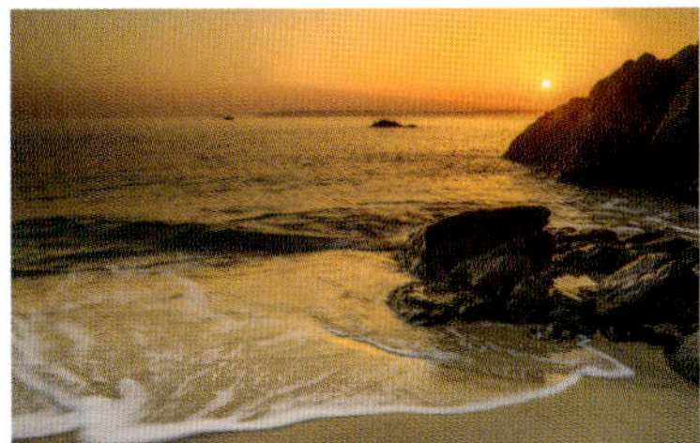

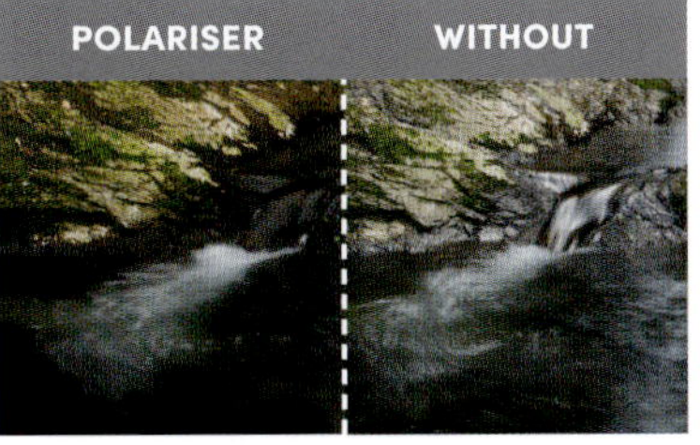


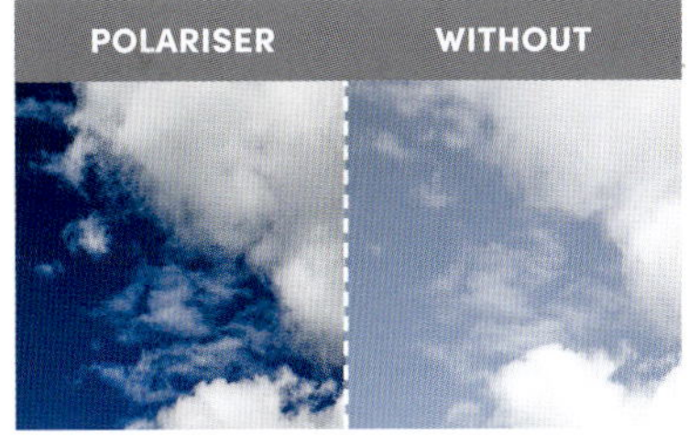


### 4 The ND effect

It's worth noting that the greater the polarisation effect, the less light will be transmitted, typically by up to a couple of stops. In effect, a polariser also acts like a weak ND filter and can gently blur moving elements. Try using it to add a dash of movement to running water.

### 5 Remove glare

Here, you're not targeting the polarisation effect towards the sun itself, but the reflected light. This enables you to shoot 'through' a river to the riverbed below, boost the vibrancy of foliage by removing reflections from leaves, or reduce the glistening effect of damp rocks.

### 6 Add some punch

The most characteristic use of a polariser filter is to transform a wispy, hazy and indistinct sky into one with deep blue shades and well-defined, punchy white clouds. While the effect will be at its strongest when the filter is rotated at 90 degrees to the sun, on bright days too strong an effect can result in near-black skies, so you may need to dial it back a little.

# USE SOME MOTION BLUR

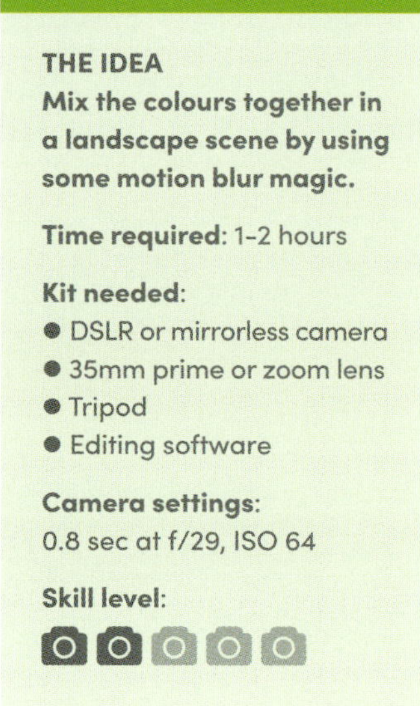

**THE IDEA**
**Mix the colours together in a landscape scene by using some motion blur magic.**

**Time required:** 1–2 hours

**Kit needed:**
- DSLR or mirrorless camera
- 35mm prime or zoom lens
- Tripod
- Editing software

**Camera settings:**
0.8 sec at f/29, ISO 64

**Skill level:**

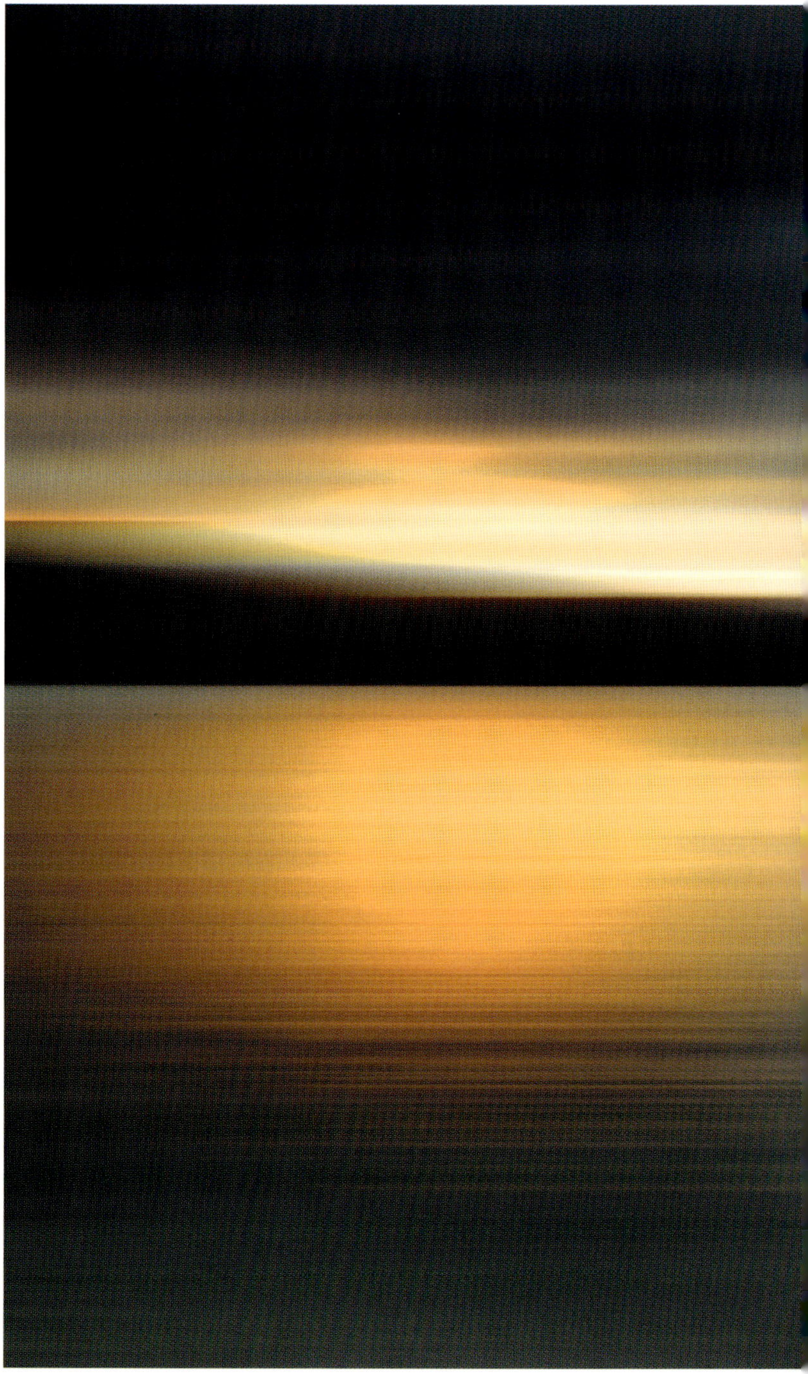

**There are two ways you can mix the colours in a scene. The first is to shoot it in-camera with a technique called camera dragging. Reduce your shutter speed (start at 1 sec and adjust if needed) and pan the camera across the scene as you release the shutter. You can either do this by hand or by using a tripod.**

The latter will produce a cleaner and straighter blur, but experiment with both to see which you prefer. If you can't achieve a slow enough shutter speed by reducing the aperture and keeping ISO low, attach an ND filter.

The second technique is to cheat a little and edit the blurred effect in Photoshop using the Motion Blur tool.

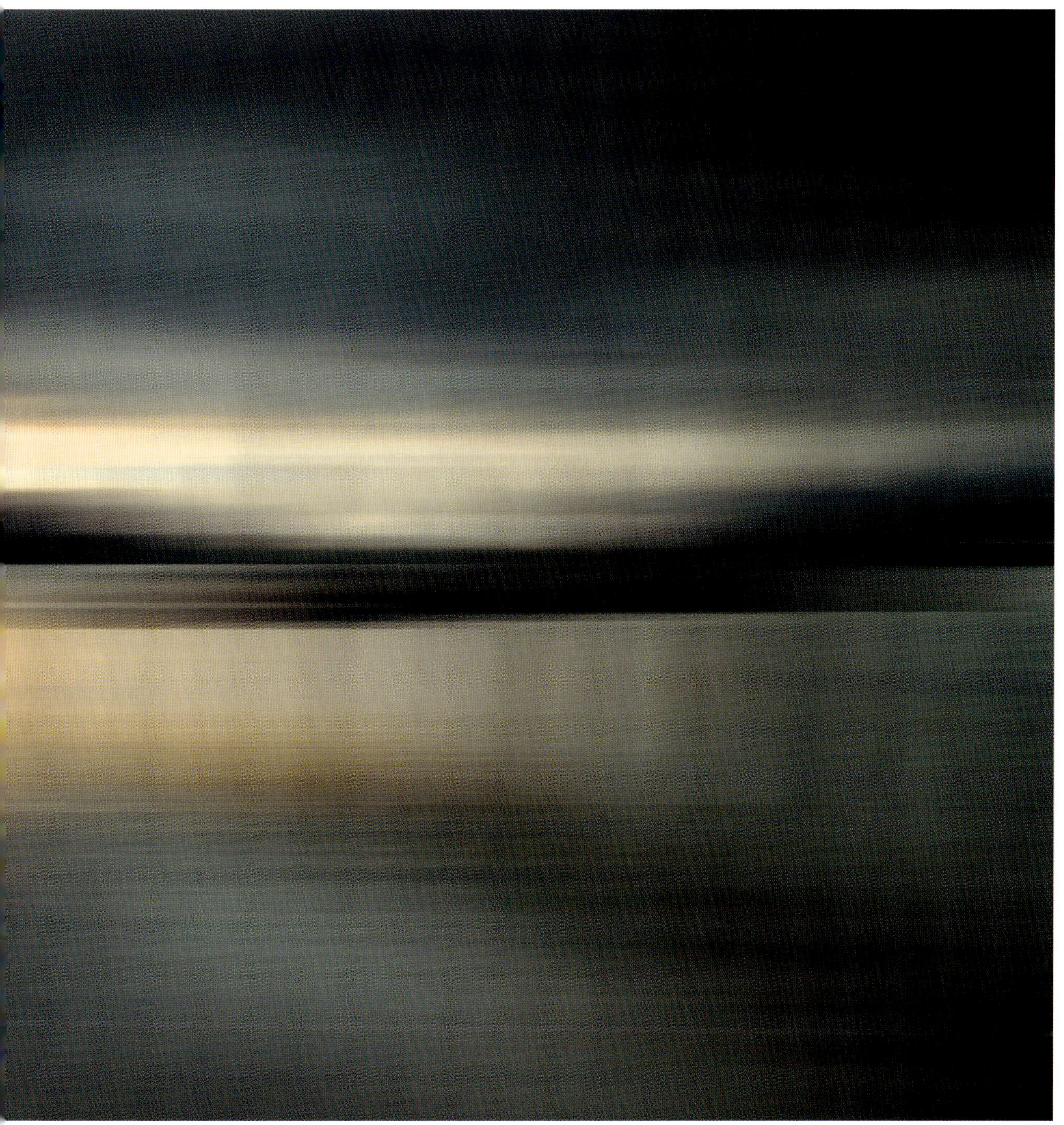

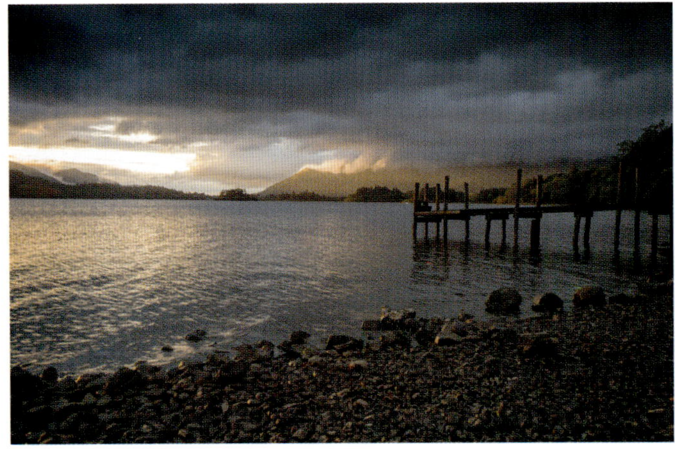

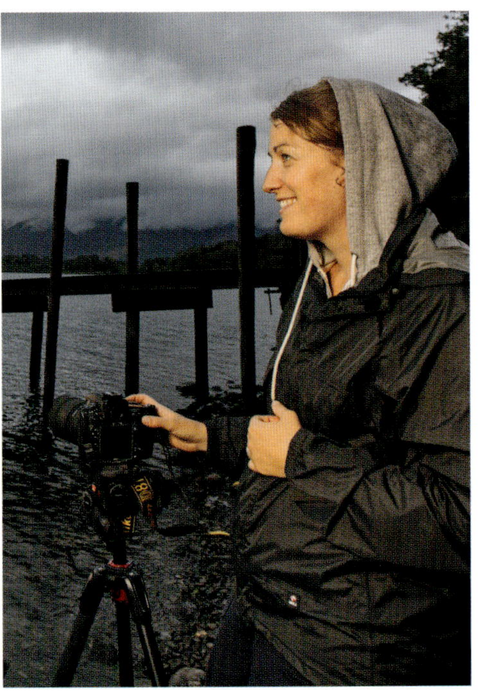

**1 Low light**

This image was taken at the end of a very wet day. Around sunset, the clouds lifted, and the warm tones of the sun setting behind the hills contrasted nicely against the stormy, gloomy colours of the clouds and water. It just goes to show that you should head out whatever the weather – you never know what you're going to get.

**NO MOTION**

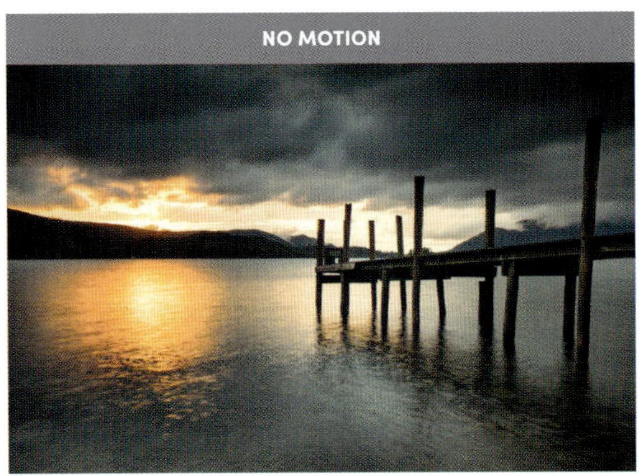

**WITH MOTION ADDED**

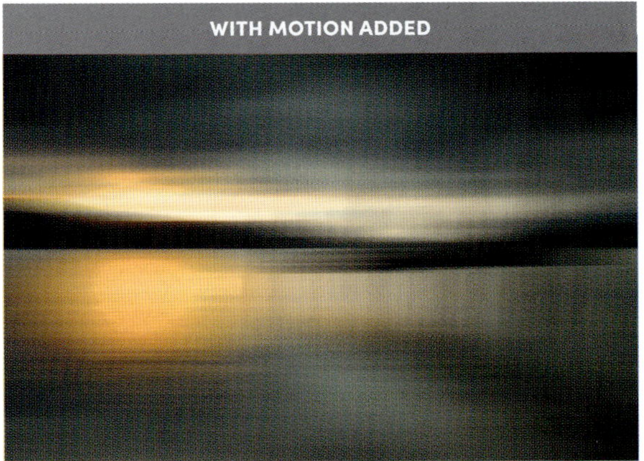

**2 No movement**

Despite the colours looking great, the water lacks interest. If you don't have a filter to hand, to reduce the shutter speed to a slow enough time to get that blurred and silky effect, create movement at the post-production stage.

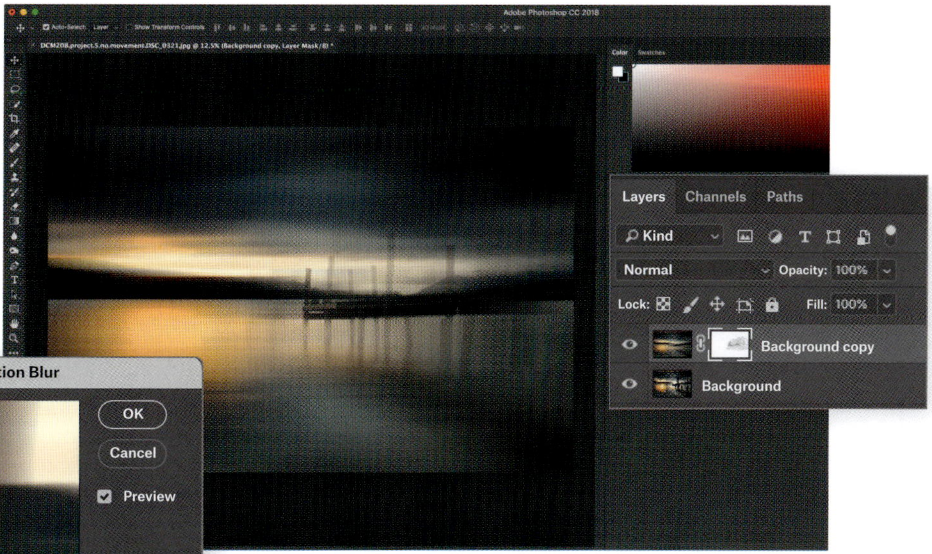

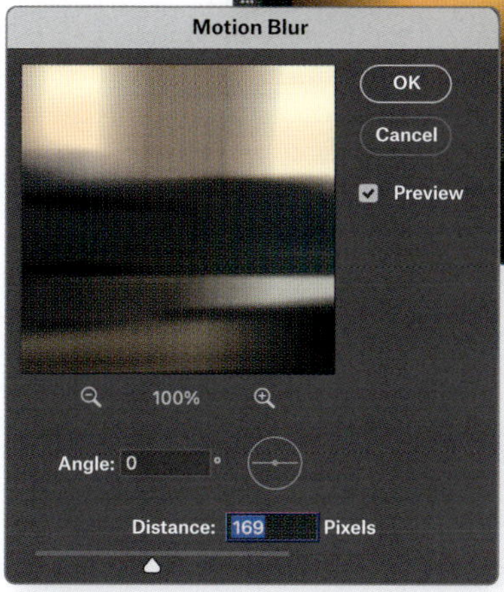

### 3 Add motion using Photoshop

To achieve the final effect in Photoshop, first duplicate the Background layer. To add the motion, go to Filter > Blur > Motion Blur and use the slider to adjust the intensity of the blur. Then add a Layer Mask and use a Black brush at 15% Opacity to paint any features you want to keep.

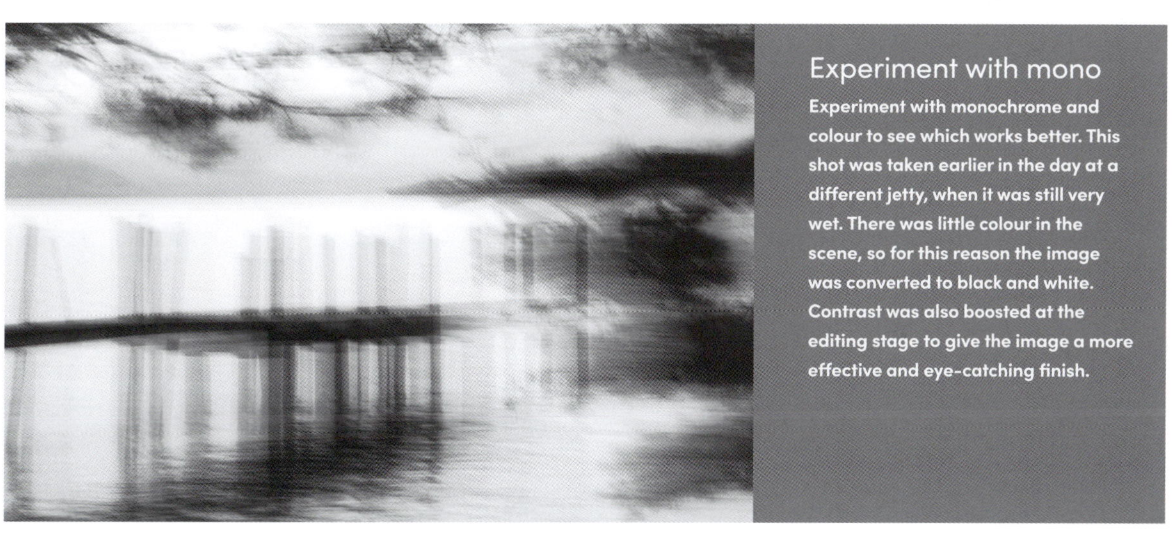

## Experiment with mono

**Experiment with monochrome and colour to see which works better. This shot was taken earlier in the day at a different jetty, when it was still very wet. There was little colour in the scene, so for this reason the image was converted to black and white. Contrast was also boosted at the editing stage to give the image a more effective and eye-catching finish.**

# ADD A TWIST TO COASTAL SHOTS

**THE IDEA**
**Shoot cloudy skies at sunset to add atmosphere to your landscapes.**

**Time required:** 2 hours

**Kit needed:**
- DSLR or mirrorless camera
- ND filter
- Tripod
- Editing software

**Camera settings:**
25 secs at f/8-f/11, ISO 100

**Skill level:**

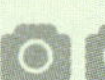

**Heading out to shoot a sunset on a cloudy evening is always a bit of a gamble because if the clouds completely obscure the sun, you might miss the big event altogether. But if the light is right, a cloudy sky can present a dramatic backdrop as the sunset illuminates the cloud cover in interesting ways.**

An effective way to add even more drama to the sky is to shoot through a neutral-density filter, so you can dial in a long exposure and capture a sense of movement in the clouds. Another element to consider when photographing a moody landscape is your subject. Gnarled trees, craggy rocks and crashing waves look particularly intense against a dark and brooding backdrop.

Flamborough Head Lighthouse in East Yorkshire, UK (pictured), is an ideal location. Not only are lighthouses synonymous with stormy weather, but the bright white structure will stand out effortlessly against a darker sky.

Use The Photographer's Ephemeris app to quickly work out where the sun will be in relation to your subject. This allows you to work out the angle you need to capture the best light.

Underexpose to ensure you have plenty of detail to work with in post-production.

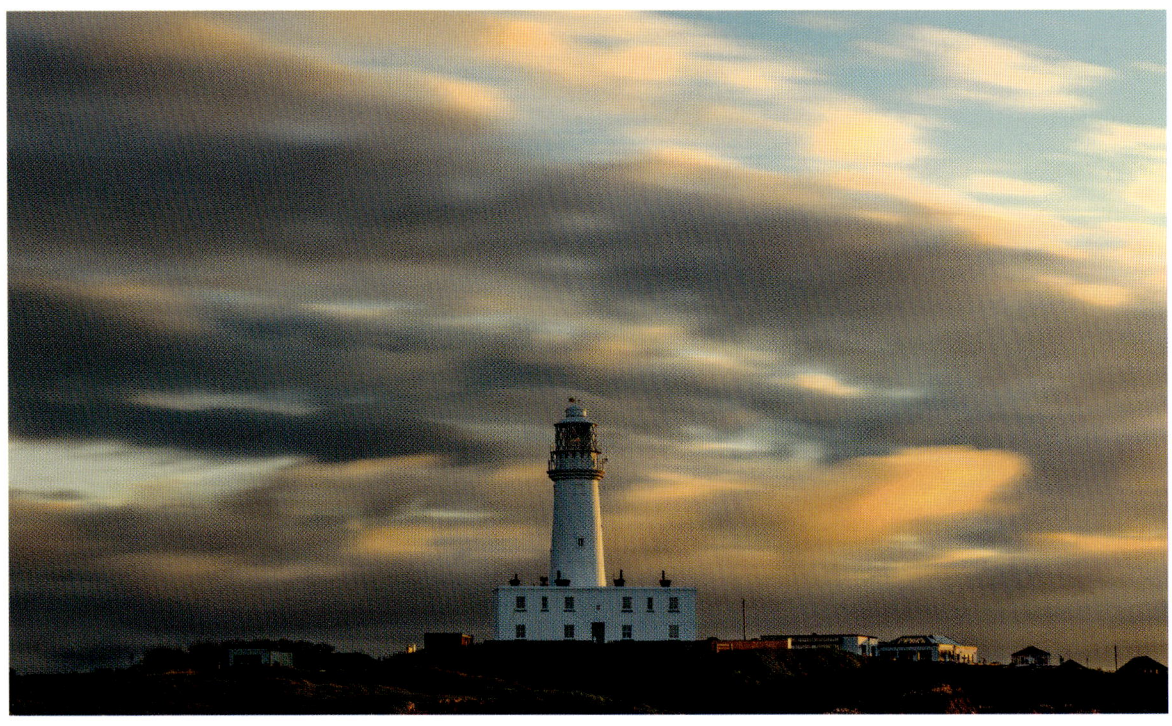

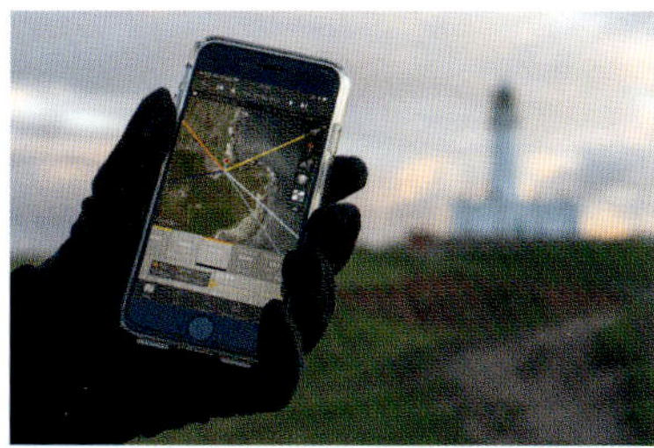

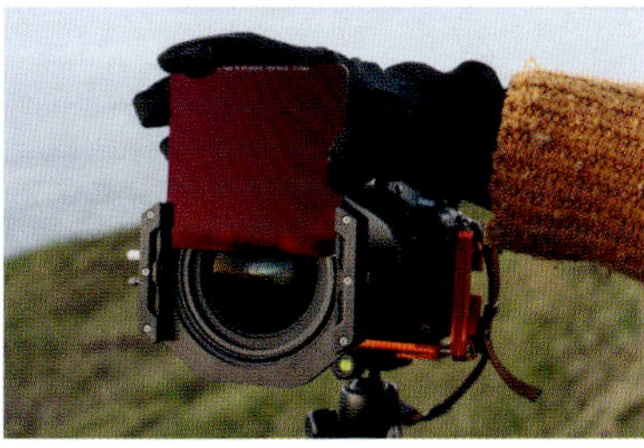

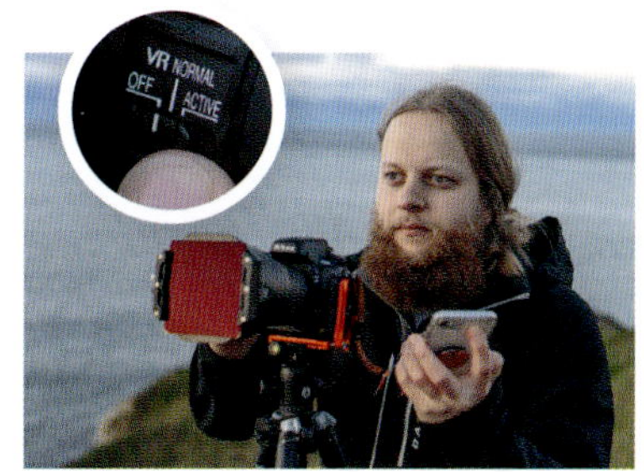


**1 Subjects matter**
Choose a subject that complements your dramatic sky. Once you've selected a location, a companion app such as The Photographer's Ephemeris will allow you to pinpoint where the sun will set in relation to the subject. This allows you to work out the optimum angle from which to shoot.

**2 Test shot**
Fix the camera on a tripod and compose. If using a filter holder, make sure it's attached to the lens, but refrain from attaching a filter. Set the camera up for a slightly underexposed image and take a test shot. Once happy, attach the filter.

**3 Set for success**
Switch to MF if using AF to prevent the camera from refocusing when the shutter button is pressed. If you don't have a remote shutter release, set a two-second self-timer to help prevent camera shake and use an exposure calculator app to work out the required exposure settings.

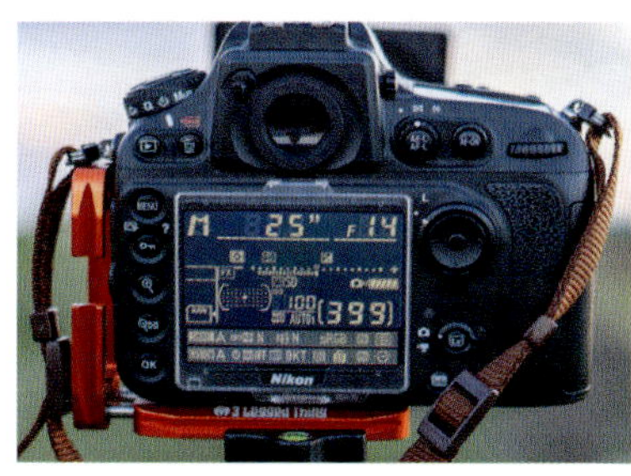


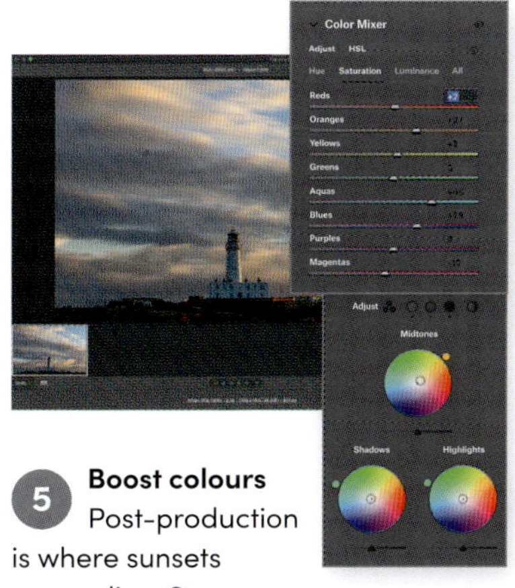


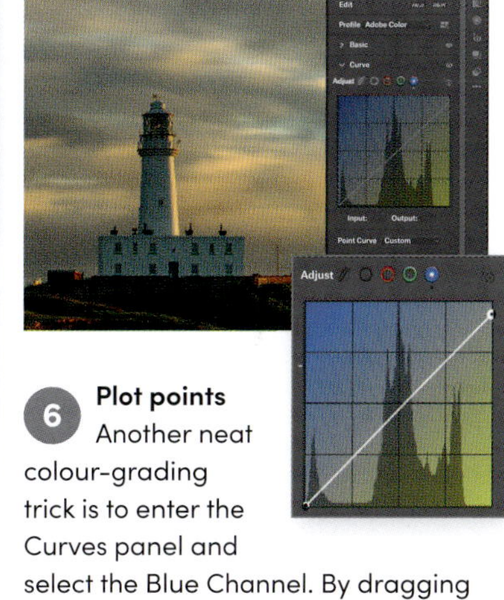


**4 Just keep shooting**
Select an aperture between f/8 and f/11 to ensure the best image quality. Don't stop shooting – the light and clouds will continue to change, so shoot the whole sunset so you have lots of images to choose from.

**5 Boost colours**
Post-production is where sunsets come alive. Camera Raw's Color Mixer panel allows you to control the saturation and luminance of colours, while the Color Grading panel controls the hue, saturation and luminance of midtones, shadows and highlights. Focus on warm colours to add plenty of punch.

**6 Plot points**
Another neat colour-grading trick is to enter the Curves panel and select the Blue Channel. By dragging the top anchor point down slightly, you can add a touch of yellow to the highlights, to really enhance the golden light.

Colour grading is a difficult editing skill to master, and if you've been working on an image for a while, it's easy to become overwhelmed. Once you've graded an image, save it, and return to it the following day. You'll find it easier to recognise whether you've pushed the colours too far with a clear mind and fresh eyes.

# PLAN FOR THE BEST LIGHT

**THE IDEA**
**Increase your chances of capturing glorious lighting with a mixture of planning and patience.**

**Time required**: 30 minutes

**Kit needed:**
- DSLR or mirrorless camera
- Filters
- Remote shutter release
- Tripod
- Weather/photo apps
- Waterproofs

**Camera settings:**
1/3 sec at f/16, ISO 64

**Skill level:**

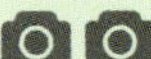  

**There are plenty of techniques out there to help improve your landscape photography, but a good landscape hinges on three things: subject, composition and light. We have complete control over the first two, but the latter is what can send even the most promising photo shoot into disarray.**

Planning is a key factor when it comes to getting perfect lighting. Keeping an eye on weather forcast websites or using a weather app is a good place to start, but what can you do to improve your chances of capturing stunning light when you're out in the field? You wait and wait... and wait some more.

People who don't take photographs might assume a good landscape is down to being in the right place at the right time, and while that's partially true, you also make your own luck.

Professionals will tell you that you should wait around even if light conditions are ideal, because they could always get better. This image of a lone tree surrounded by a body of water is a prime example.

The key to this photo is how the light frames and separates the tree from the busy background. Without it, the subject would get lost in the busy melee of colours on the far side of the lake. Weather reports promised intermittent bursts of sunshine, and with the sun behind and slightly to the photographer's right, there was a good chance of experiencing ideal lighting conditions. It was just a case of waiting for them to occur.

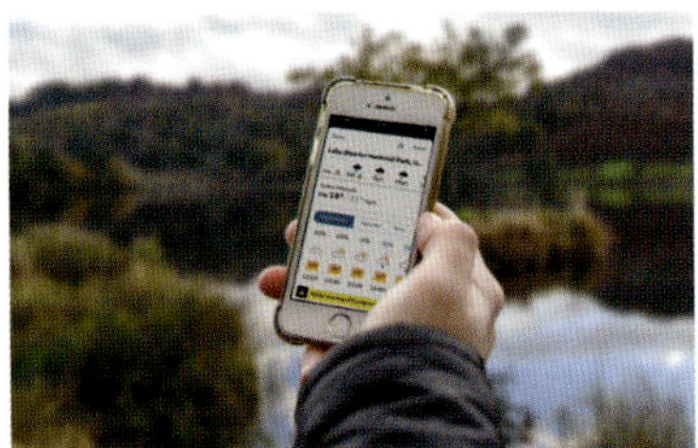

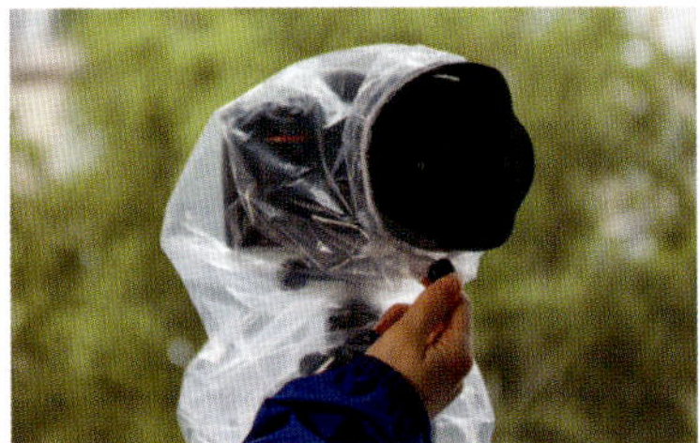

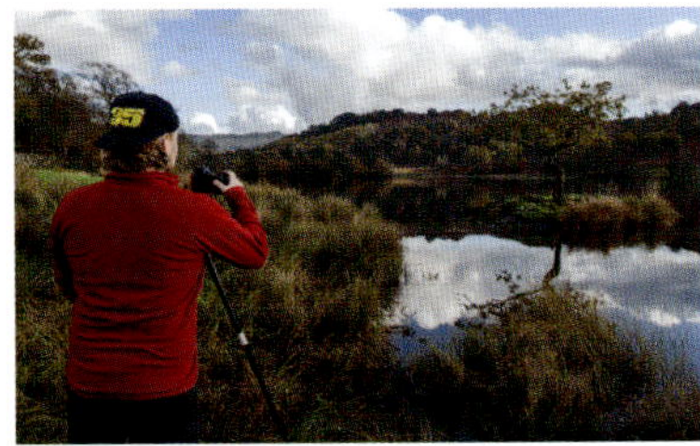

**1 Read the weather**
Apps like Met Office Weather Forecast are invaluable when it comes to predicting the weather. Combine this with a photography planning app, such as PhotoPills, and you can work out precisely what direction light comes from at specific times and dates.

**2 Come prepared**
The weather can quickly turn bad, but it can clear up just as fast. Carry waterproofs and a camera rain cover on every shoot. There's nothing worse than heading off in defeat, only to witness the glorious conditions you wanted all along.

**3 Ahead of time**
If you've planned where you're going to stand to capture the best light, the last thing you want is to arrive late and find out another photographer has taken your spot. If you're shooting popular hotspots that are known to get busy, ensure you get there first.

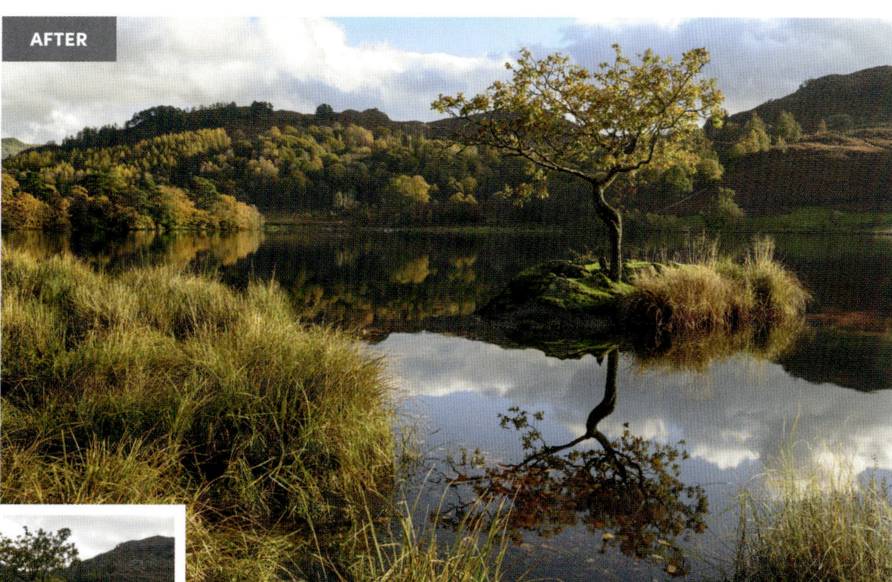


BEFORE

Many landscape photographers are creatures of habit. If you live near or regularly visit a beauty spot, keep photographing it. Everything mentioned here will boost your chances of capturing the right light, but the more you visit a location, the better your chances of capturing that once-in-a-lifetime photo where the stars align.

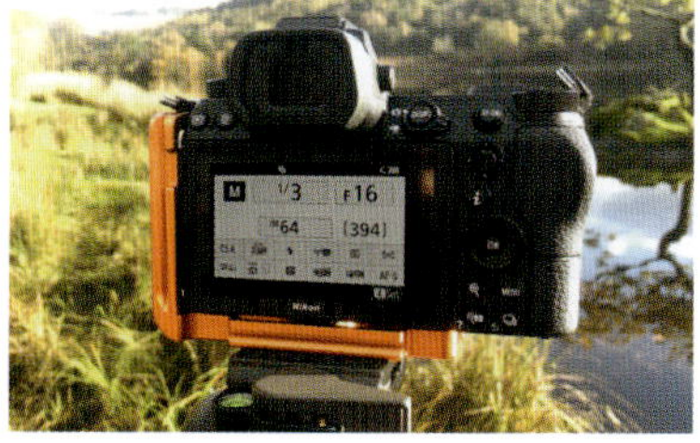

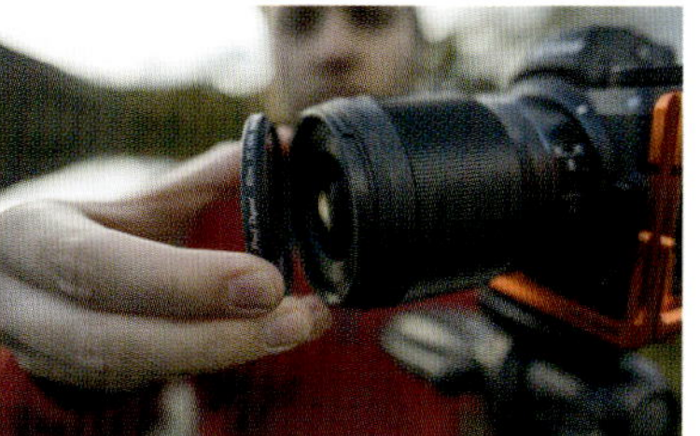

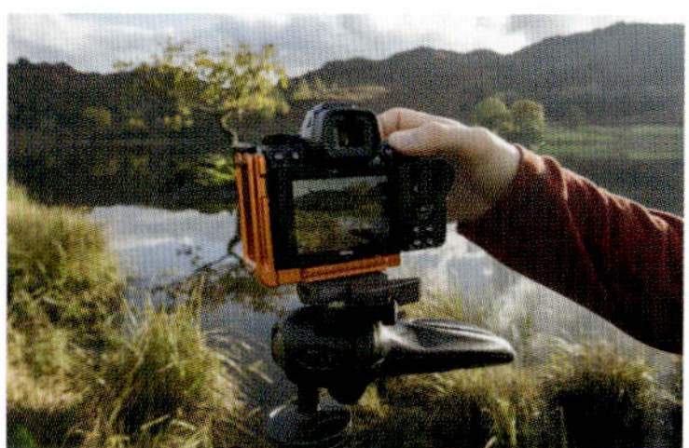

**4 Set for success**
Even with the light changing, it's still good to get your settings right and lock the focus. Select the lowest ISO setting and set aperture to be about f/8 to f/16. From there, alter the shutter speed to suit the lighting.

**5 Fast filters**
The best light is often fleeting, so set up any filters as quickly as possible. Calculating exposure with the Lee Filters app will also save time, although your camera's electronic viewfinder will clearly show any changes to exposure in real time.

**6 Wait for it...**
Patience won't guarantee results, but it'll shift the odds in your favour. A remote shutter release is invaluable at moments like these because the light might only last a few seconds.

# SHOOT LANDSCAPES AT NIGHT

**THE IDEA**
**Take a photograph of the moonlit sea.**

**Time required**: 1 hour

**Kit needed**:
- DSLR or mirrorless camera
- Long lens
- Tripod
- Weather/photo apps

**Camera settings**:
30 secs at f/5.6, ISO 800

**Skill level**:

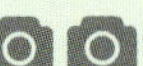  

**As winter kicks in and the light begins to drop earlier in the day, now is the perfect time to try your night shooting skills. The beach is a wonderful location once the sun has set – the moving body of water, the curves of the bay and the natural surroundings create a match made in heaven.**

This image was taken at Blackpool Sands near Dartmouth, Devon, UK, using the moon's light to illuminate the seascape. The result is wonderful, as the light is much softer and has a different tone to sunlight.

Shooting in the dark is no easy task and requires a bit of forward planning and thinking. Knowing your location well will help, so do a recce in the daylight so you have a composition in mind before you start.

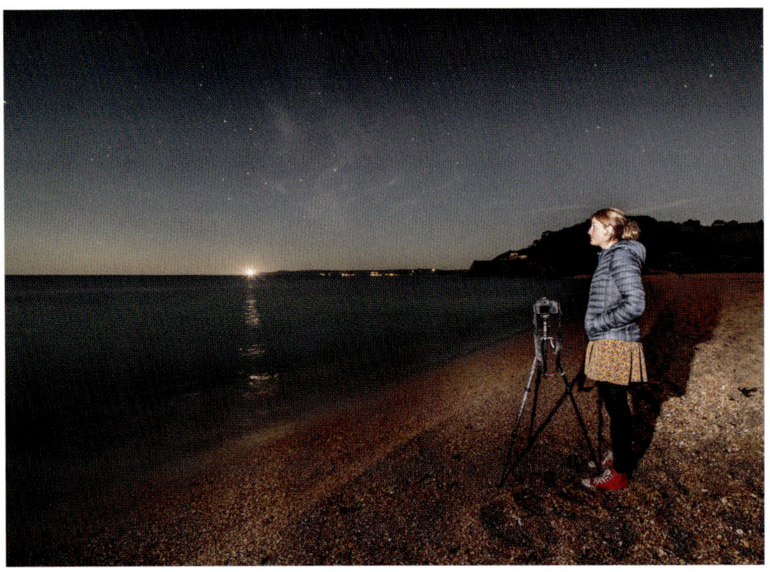

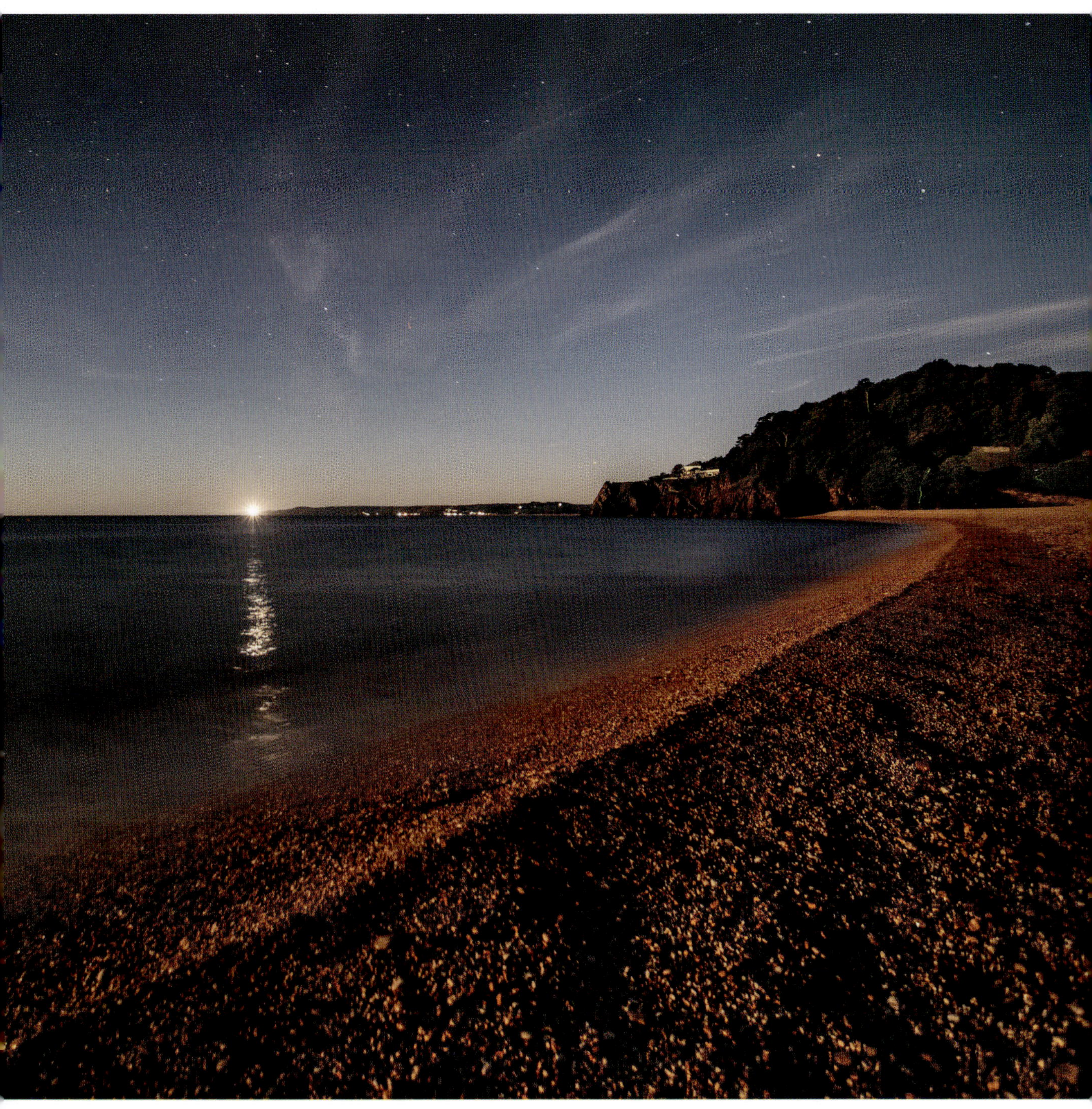

## 1 Plan your shoot

To ensure you have the perfect conditions, plan your shoot well. First, check the weather forecast and moon phase. It is possible to shoot a few days either side of a full moon, but you'll get best results with it being a complete circle. To find out the moon's position and when it will be rising, check out The Photographer's Ephemeris. There is an app or web version where you can pinpoint your exact location.

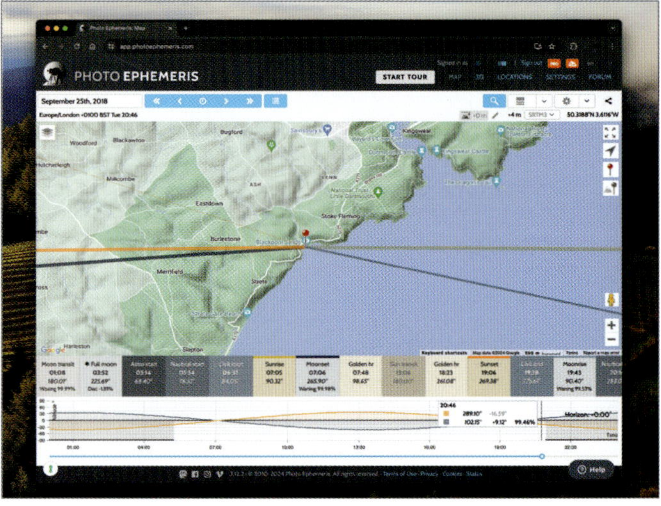


## 2 Camera set-up

Mount your camera onto a tripod and secure it in place. For shots like this, the wide end of a 15–30mm zoom lens will help you achieve the most dramatic compositions. To ensure your tripod doesn't move, push it down firmly into the sand and avoid walking nearby after you've released the shutter to take an exposure.

**A head torch will come in handy when shooting at night. Alternatively, you could use the torch on your mobile phone.**

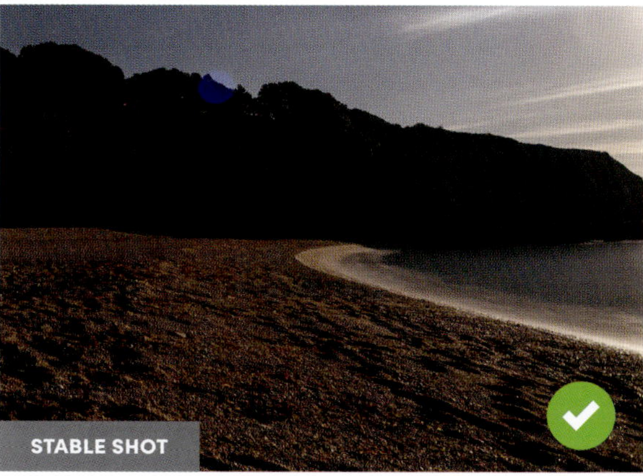


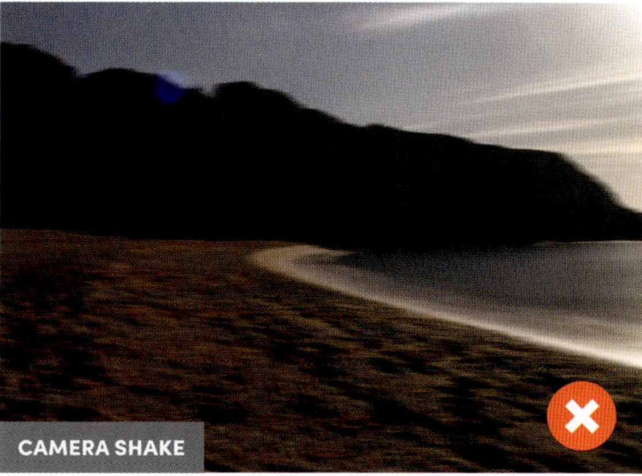


### 3 Avoid camera shake

Camera shake occurs when your camera gets touched or moved during an exposure and creates a blurred effect. As you're opening your shutter for such a long period of time, you really want to avoid this technical issue. A remote shutter release will come in handy, as it means you can avoid touching your camera altogether. If you don't have one, set your camera to its self-timer mode and engage the mirror lock-up feature.

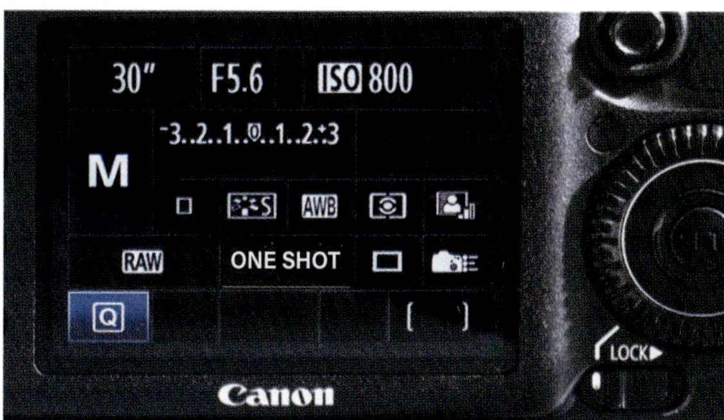

### 4 Open the aperture and push the ISO

When it comes to capturing the night sky and stars, avoid shooting for long periods of time unless you're after a star trail effect. So, to keep the stars twinkling in the sky as small dots, don't go past 30 seconds. To ensure you do this, use a wide aperture and push ISO up. Modern cameras are much better at handling noise but take some test shots, so you know the limitations of your camera. Select manual mode and try variations on the exposure until you're pleased with the results.

### 5 Shooting the moon

A full moon emits a lot of light and will overexpose. If you want detail in the moon, your landscape will be dark; if you want detail in the landscape, the moon will be overexposed and appear like the sun. By way of compromise, shoot two separate exposures and blend them in Photoshop.

# CREATE A SENSE OF ZEN

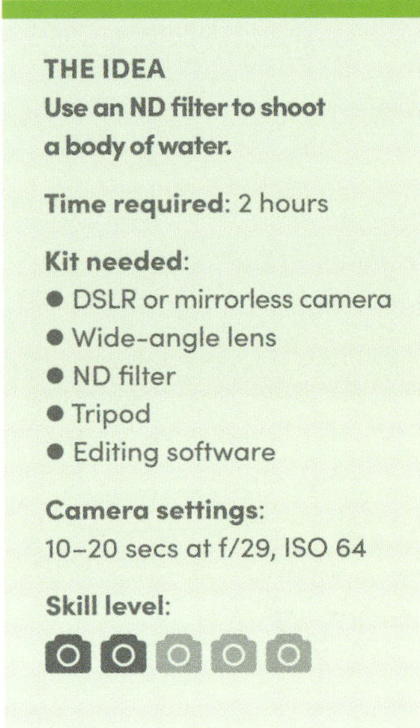

**THE IDEA**
**Use an ND filter to shoot a body of water.**

**Time required**: 2 hours

**Kit needed**:
- DSLR or mirrorless camera
- Wide-angle lens
- ND filter
- Tripod
- Editing software

**Camera settings**:
10–20 secs at f/29, ISO 64

**Skill level**:

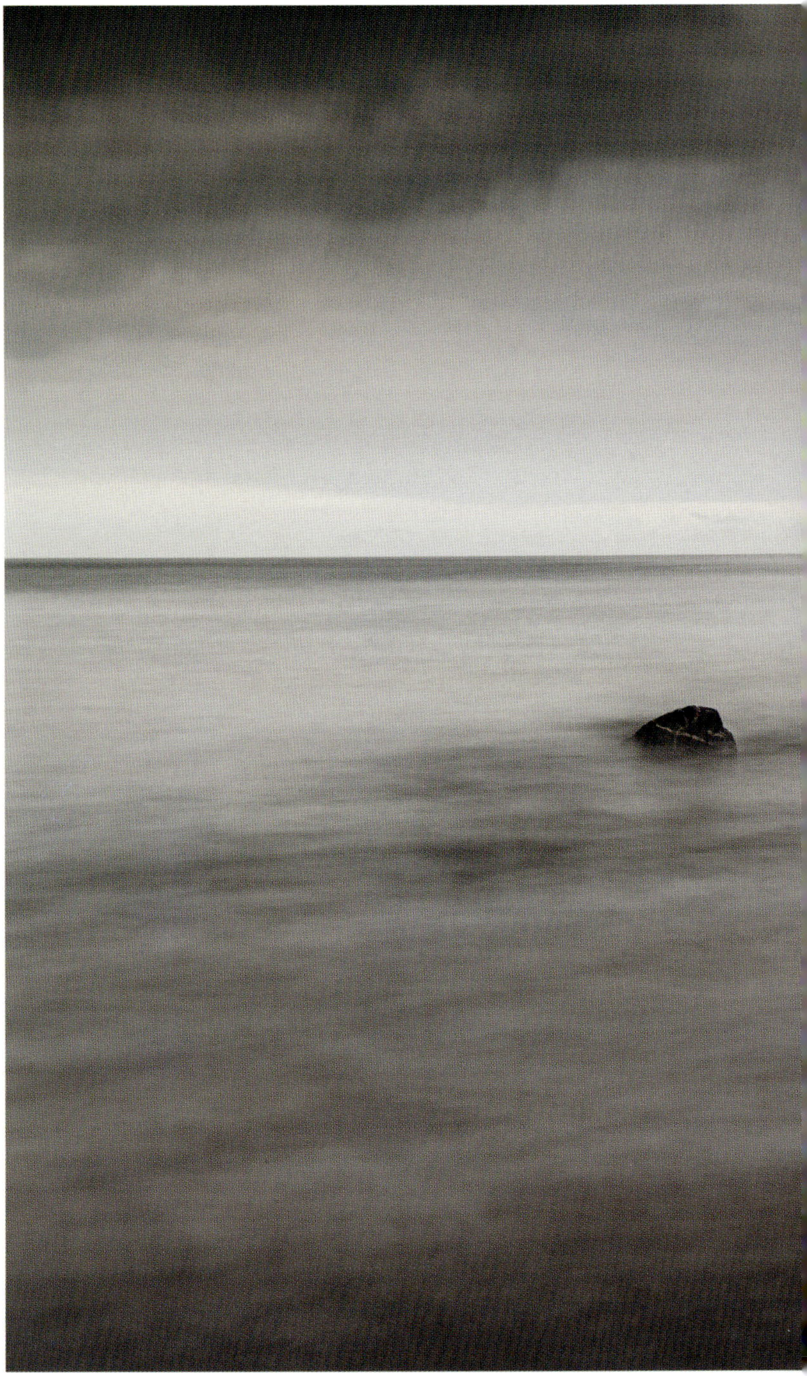

**We often don't take the time to slow down and just absorb our surroundings. So, in this project, you'll discover the necessary steps to capture a slow seascape that encompasses that Zen feeling. To give this a go, you will need to find a seaside view, but it doesn't matter if there isn't a convenient shoreline within easy reach – you could go to a lake, a waterfall or a river. You just need to make sure there is moving water to capture the effect.**

To make sure you're fully equipped, you will need a tripod and preferably a variable ND filter (this gives you flexibility when it comes to the amount of light reaching your sensor). Now, take some deep breaths and prepare to become a Zen master...

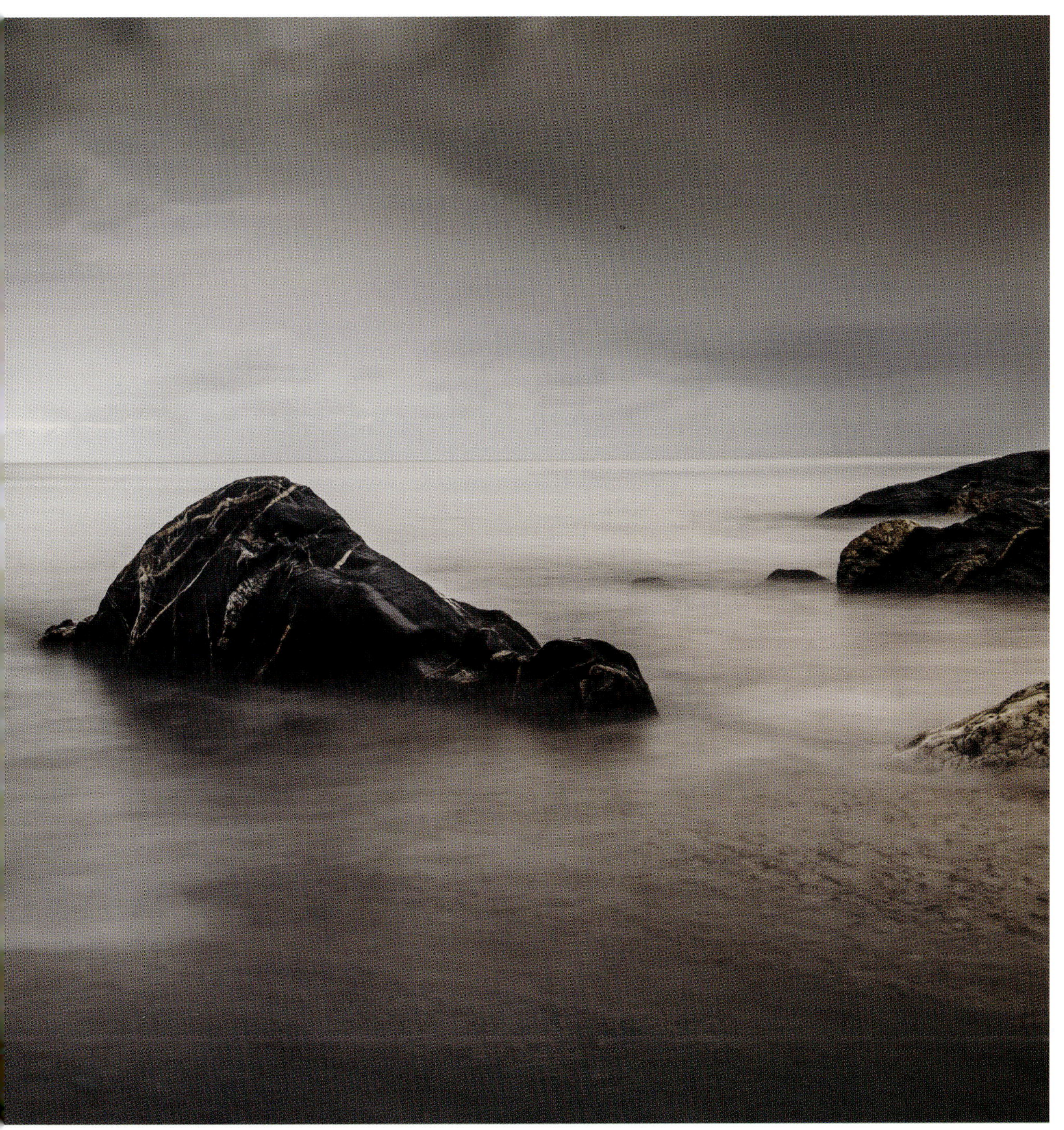

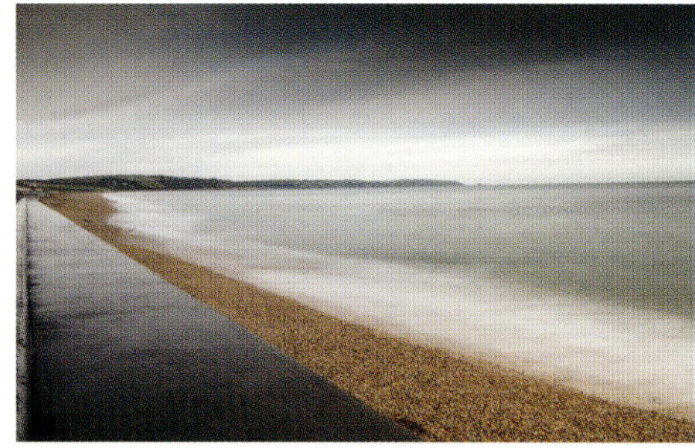

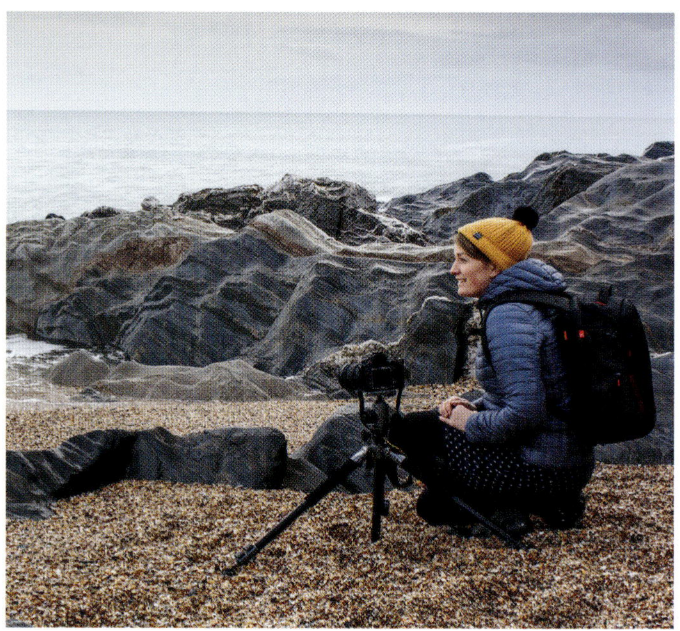

### 1 The right place at the right time

You'll first need to scout for the ideal location. If you're heading to the sea, find some rocks or wooden posts in the water, so you have something that's both still and of interest. The weather is another important consideration. Although the ND filter helps, you still don't want the conditions too bright, as you won't get a slow enough shutter speed setting. If you can, head out earlier in the morning or later in the day.

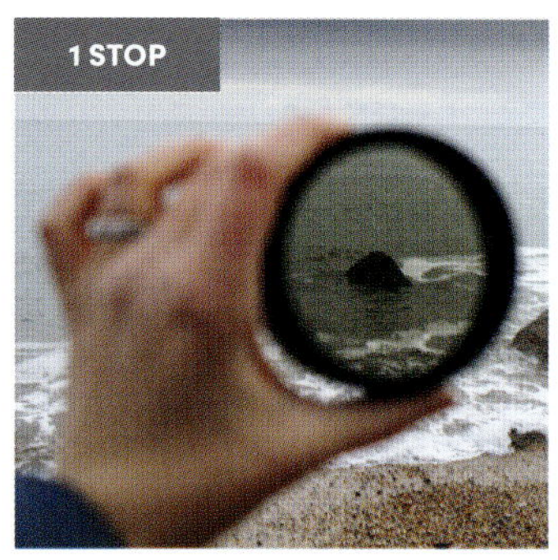

1 STOP

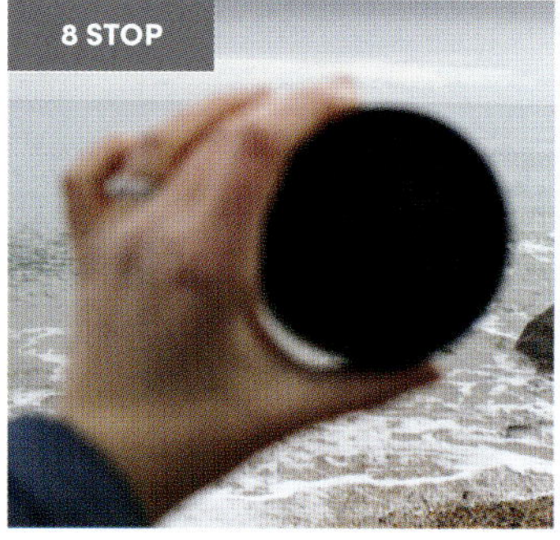

8 STOP

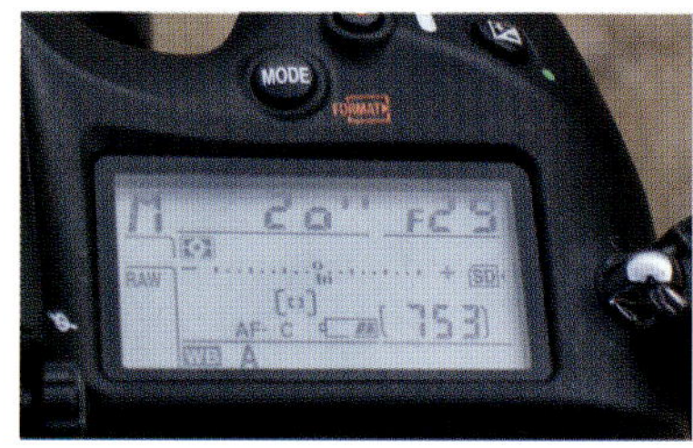


### 2 Get the kit

You will need an ND filter (either variable or fixed) to slow down your shutter speed setting, as well as a tripod to mount your camera on. Ideally, you want a wide-angle lens, but this is not essential, and you can play around with your composition on location.

**If using a variable ND, you can adjust the filter between 1 and 8 stops of light. To get a slow enough shutter speed to blur the water, set the strength to maximum, then increased the shutter speed setting by 8 stops.**

### 3 Camera settings

To ensure a shutter speed between 10–20 sec, reduce the ISO to 100 and close the aperture down to the maximum it can go on your lens. Set the camera to manual mode and keep an eye on the exposure meter. It's best to check the histogram after each shot to ensure you've got the exposure correct rather than relying on the LCD screen.

Switch on Live View to lock up the mirror and set the camera to its self-timer mode.

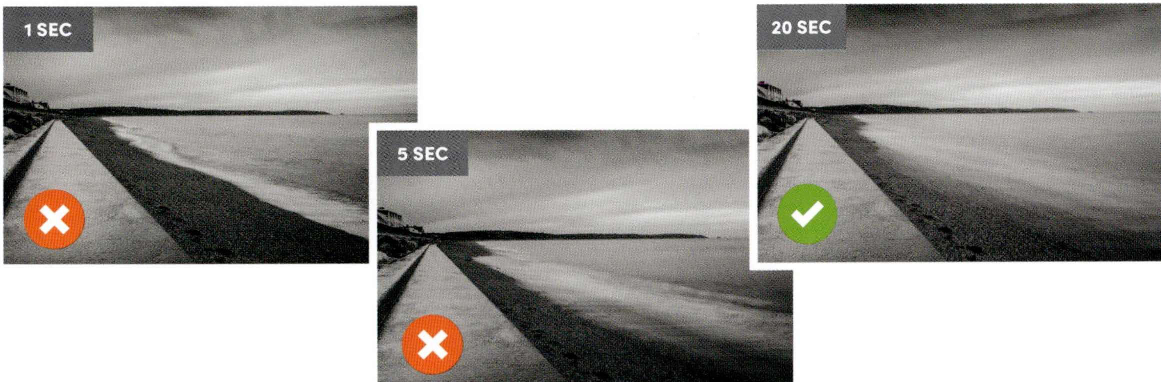


**4** **Different shutter speeds**
Although 1 sec can feel like a long time when you're holding a camera in your hand (and yes, it would be blurred), when it comes to capturing water movement, it doesn't really do the job. The examples pictured here show the results of shutter speeds set to 1 sec, 5 secs and 20 secs. To ensure you have that milky effect, use at least a 10 sec shutter speed. As long as you keep checking the histogram, you can overexpose your image a little. Shoot in Raw and ensure no highlights are clipped – you can reduce the exposure setting at the editing stage to bring out the tones in the sky.

**5** **Editing tricks**
This type of image requires a basic edit. Open your image into the Camera Raw editor in Photoshop and tweak the Contrast and Clarity settings to boost the tones. Play around with the White, Highlights, Blacks and Shadows sliders to make further small adjustments. If you want to convert your image to black and white, you can also do this at this stage. To darken the sky, use the Graduated Filter (fifth from the right in the top bar). Hold down Shift as you drag the cursor down to keep a straight line.

Finally, make any isolated adjustments with the Adjustment Brush (sixth from the right in the top bar). This tool is very handy if you just want to increase the exposure in one part of the image. Simply paint over the area, then tweak the sliders to your desired effect. Once these changes are made, use the Spot Healing Brush in the main Photoshop editor to remove any spot marks from the sky and sea.

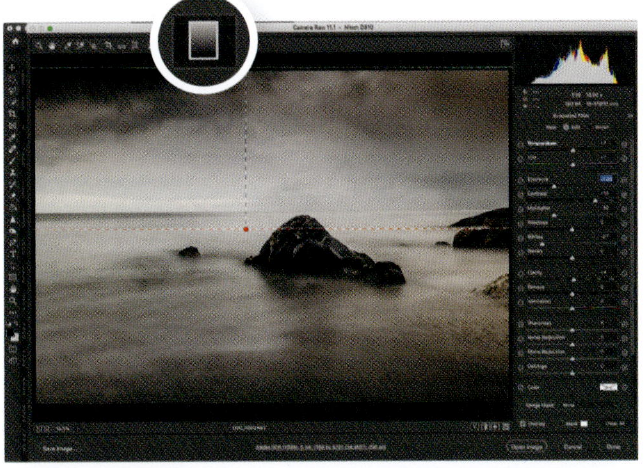

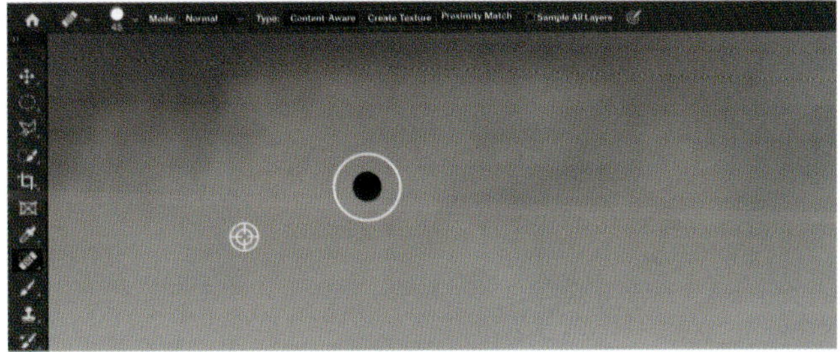

# BLUR A WATERFALL

**THE IDEA**
**Use an ND filter to capture slow-motion watery scenes.**

**Time required**: 1–2 hours

**Kit needed**:
- DSLR or mirrorless camera
- 16–85mm lens
- ND filter
- Tripod

**Camera settings**:
2.5 secs at f/20, ISO 100

**Skill level**:

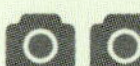  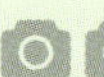

**Slowing down water motion with a neutral-density filter is nothing new, but it's one of those quintessential landscape techniques that's always good to have a grip on.**

The skills you need – learning to balance and calculate exposures and focus before adding a filter – can come in handy for a whole host of other projects and scenarios.

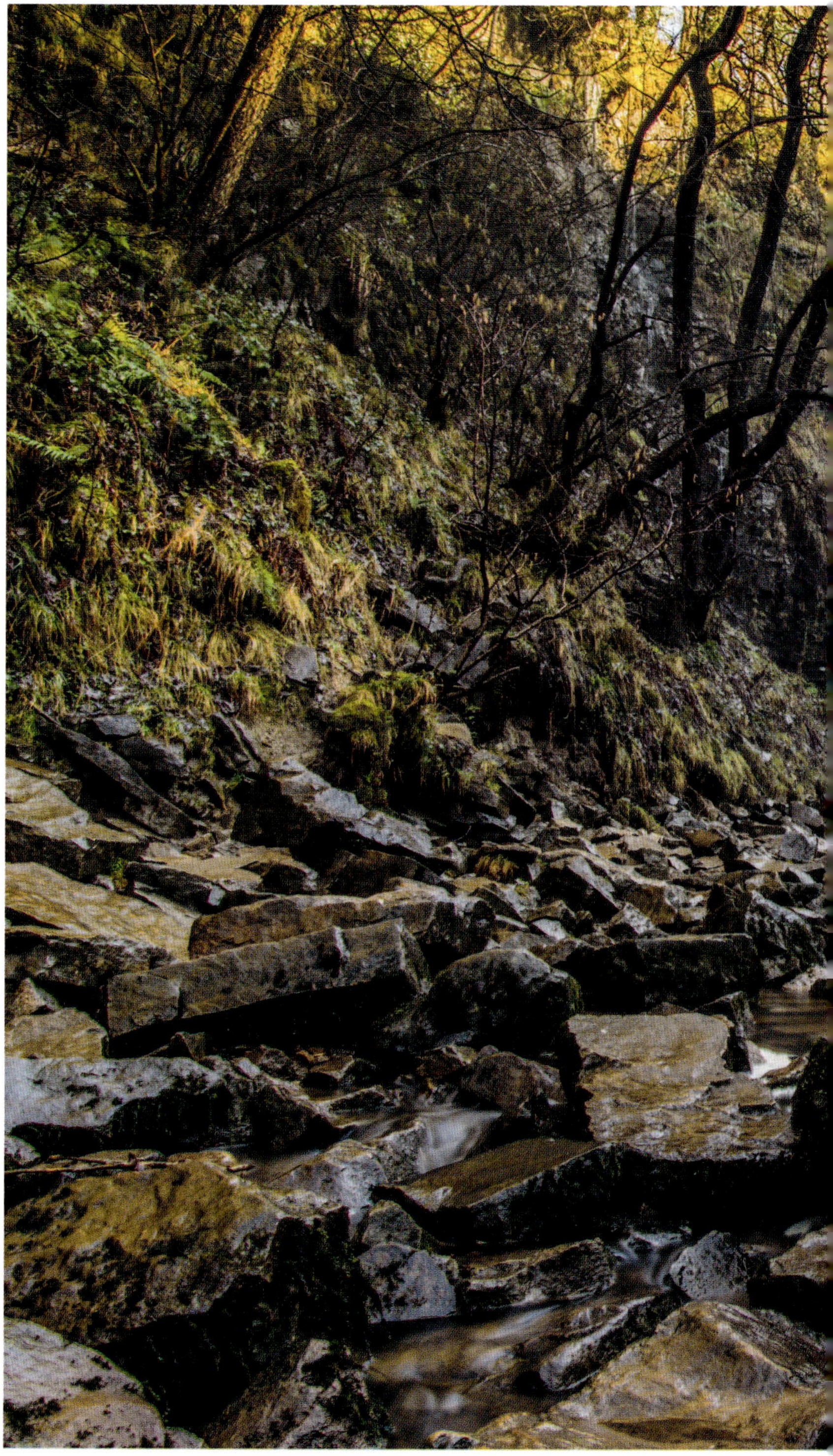

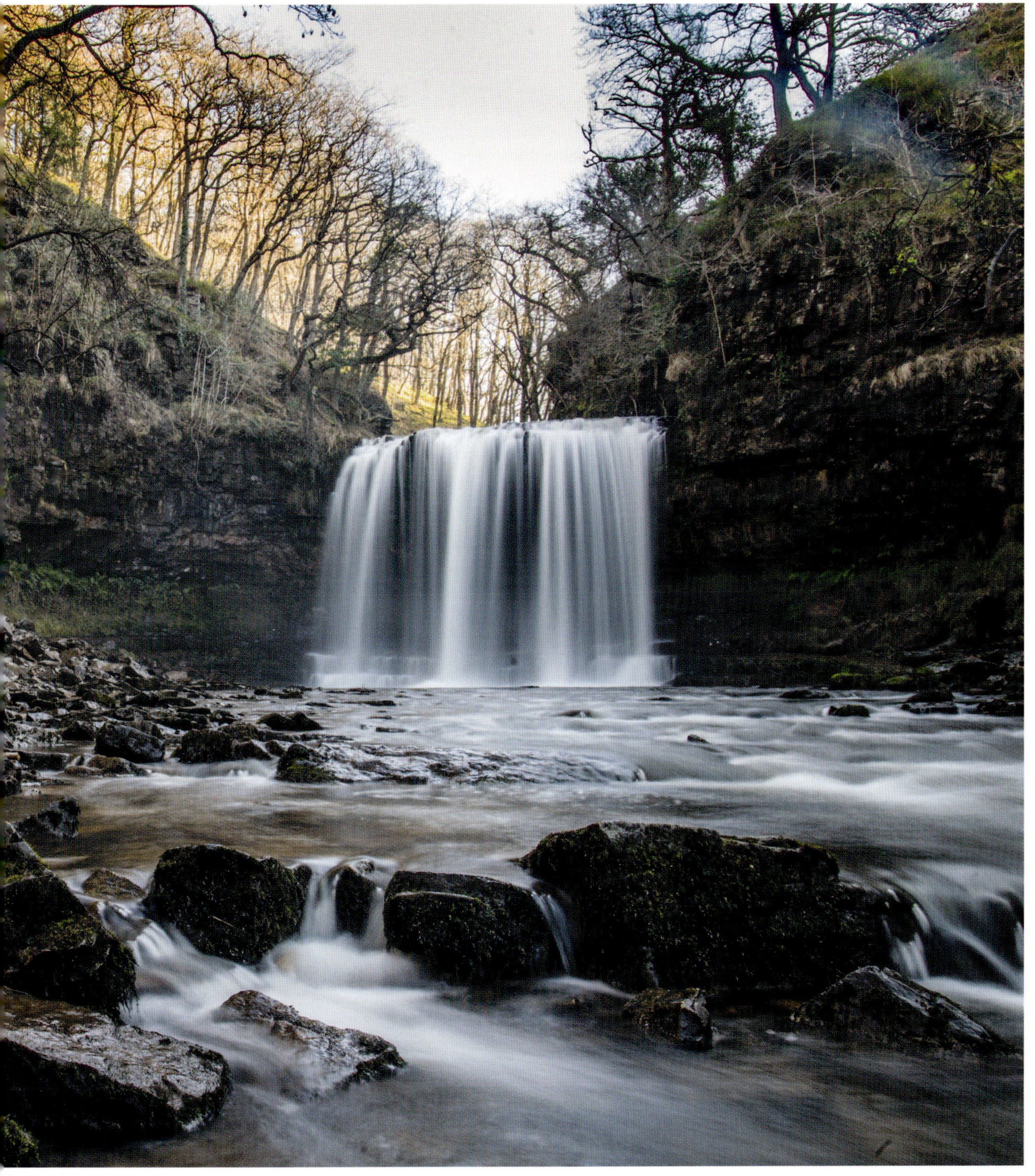

Getting silky smooth water shots is challenging, but having the right equipment helps. You'll need an ND filter to limit the light entering the lens and allow for long exposures to be set. At extended shutter speeds, a sturdy tripod and remote cable release are also necessary to keep everything sharp.

Lens choice is likely to be dictated by your location. At the beautiful Sgwd yr Eira waterfall in Wales, UK, a 16–85mm zoom gave a good focal range to compose scenes with. While a telephoto lens enables you to fill the frame with water features from a distance, a wide-angle lens is your best bet if the falls are smaller or you're closer to them.

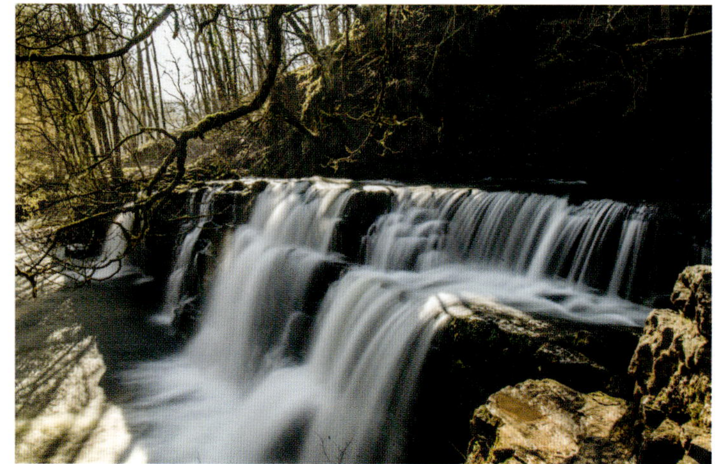

**1 Create a composition**

When it comes to positioning waterfalls in the frame, the idea is to add interest and lead the viewer through the scene. If you want to capture more interesting viewpoints and perspectives, wade into the river (waterproof boots needed) with your camera and tripod. Consider whether you want the waterfall to fill the whole frame, or for it to be part of a wider scene.

**2 Focus the frame**

Once you've got your positioning sorted, focus on the waterfall. It's impossible to focus through a dark ND filter, so this step needs to be done before you screw it on. You can either use autofocus first and then switch to manual focus or use manual focus with Live View to help you check sharpness. If you're using a sliding ND filter, simply slot this into the holder once you've focused.

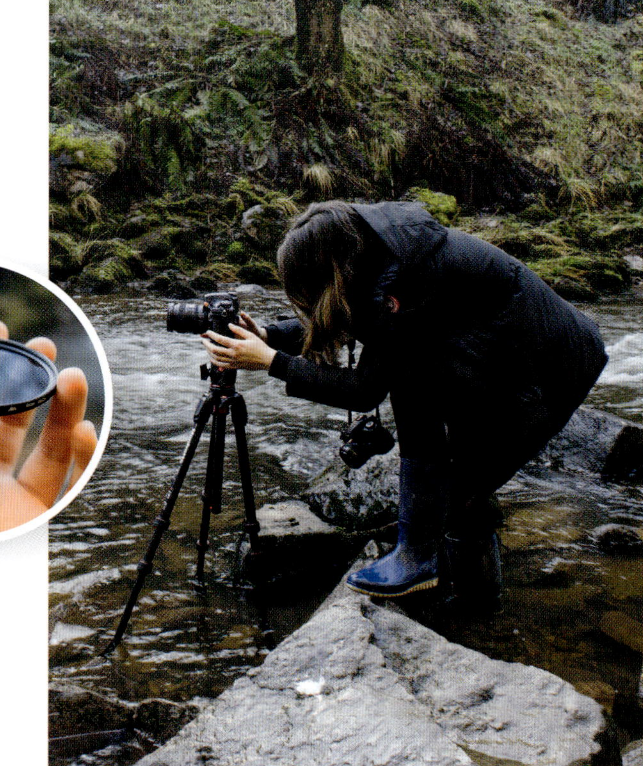

### 3 Calculate exposure

Use manual mode to shoot. Set your desired aperture and ISO values, then note the initial shutter reading. You'll need to tweak this shutter speed for the ND filter you're using. To work out (roughly) how long you need your exposure to be, use an app such as Long Exposure Calculator. As an example, with an 8-stop filter, 1/100 sec becomes 2.5 sec.

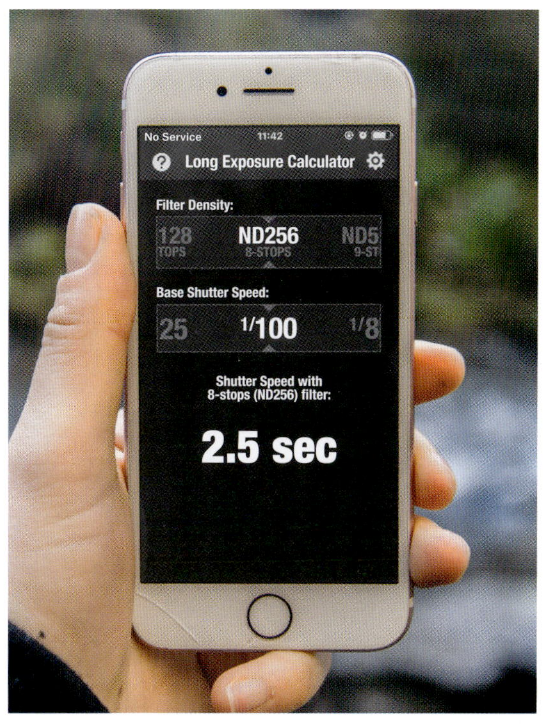


Every body of water flows at a different speed, and this means that there is no one 'right' exposure to aim for. Higher waterfalls – which allow gravity to accelerate the plunging water – are faster, so you'll need shorter exposures than you would for slower water to get the same effect. The best approach is to take several shots at varying speeds, then review these in the field by checking your LCD. See how the different shutter speeds are rendering the waterfall, then decide whether you want the spray and trails to be discernible in the images, or whether you want to completely blur the movement.

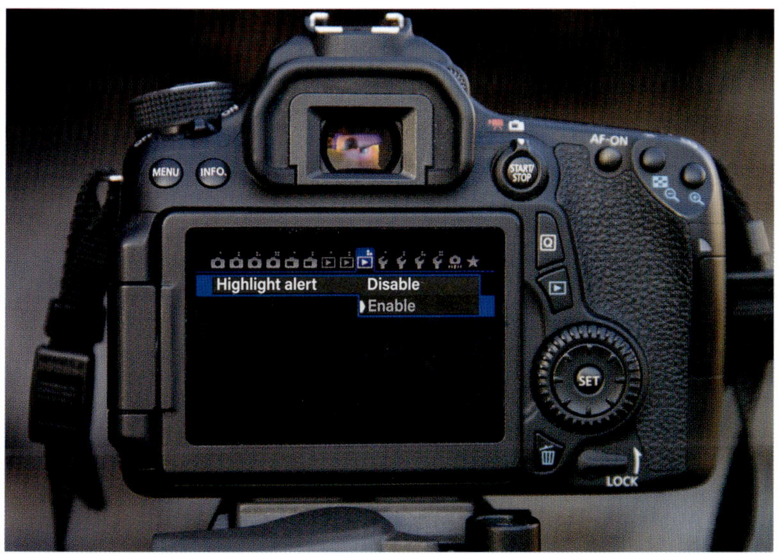


### 4 Check your highlights

When water moves and drops at high speeds, it generates so much turbulence that the water appears white. When photographing white water and using long exposures, it's easy to overexpose scenes and blow out detail in the highlights of the river. For the best results, underexpose by lowering the ISO or increasing the f/stop number and enable your camera's Highlight Alert feature.

# CAPTURE A WINTER DAWN

**THE IDEA**

**When the daylight hours are short, head out for first light to capture those amazing skies and warm natural light.**

**Time required**: 1–2 hours

**Kit needed**:

- DSLR or mirrorless camera
- Wide-angle lens
- ND filter
- Tripod
- Editing software

**Camera settings**:
1/320 sec at f/11, ISO 100

**Skill level**:

 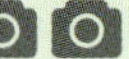 

**There is nothing better on a crisp winter morning than watching the sun rising over the horizon and breaking through the clouds. Winter is the perfect time of year to shoot sunrise. For starters, you don't need to wake up in the middle of the night to be there. This sunrise was photographed at 7.40 a.m., which meant leaving the house at a reasonable 6.30 a.m. to be there at the right time.**

This image was taken from a viewpoint at Gallants Bower, near Dartmouth Castle in Devon, UK, and looks out over the sea at the mouth of the River Dart. In the distance, the iconic Kingswear Daymark beacon sits within the rule of thirds, with the foliage in the foreground adding interest.

A wide-angle zoom lens will allow you to include lots of wonderful sky, which will really come alive once the sun breaks through. If you're lucky, a flock of birds might soar through the sky at the optimum moment, adding an extra sparkle to your sunrise image.

There are many elements to consider when trying to predict if you're going to have a good sunrise or not. First, look on the weather forecast for clouds. The shot will work best if the cloud coverage is somewhere between 30–70%. Other things to take into consideration are humidity (low, but not too low), visibility (the more the better) and wind speed (low).

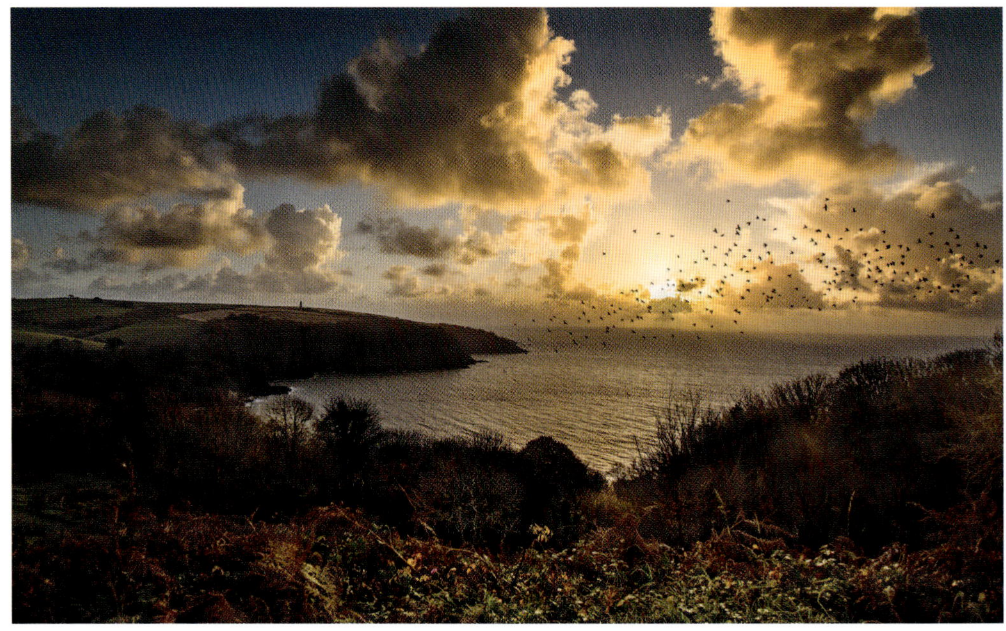

## 1 Be prepared

Arrive at your location at least 30 minutes before sunrise, and be prepared to wait – the light may not sparkle until 20-30 minutes after the sun creeps above the horizon. It helps to shoot a location you are familiar with, as you can frame your shot a few days in advance.

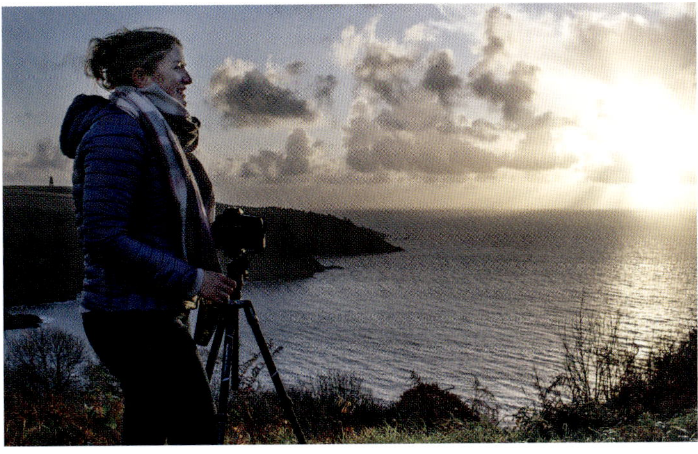

## 2 Get multiple exposures

When you shoot a scene like this, it can be tricky to keep the detail in the sky around the sun and expose for the foreground. For this reason, bracket your exposures, then blend them together. The other way to get around this problem is to use a graduated ND filter if you have one. When bracketing exposures, set your camera up on a tripod so you can produce a flawless blend.

## 3 Aperture setting

Set your aperture at f/11 to ensure both the foreground and the background are sharp, and set ISO to 100. When there is lots of light in the sky, your shutter speed should be fast enough to handhold your camera, but if you want to bracket your exposures, keep the camera on a tripod.

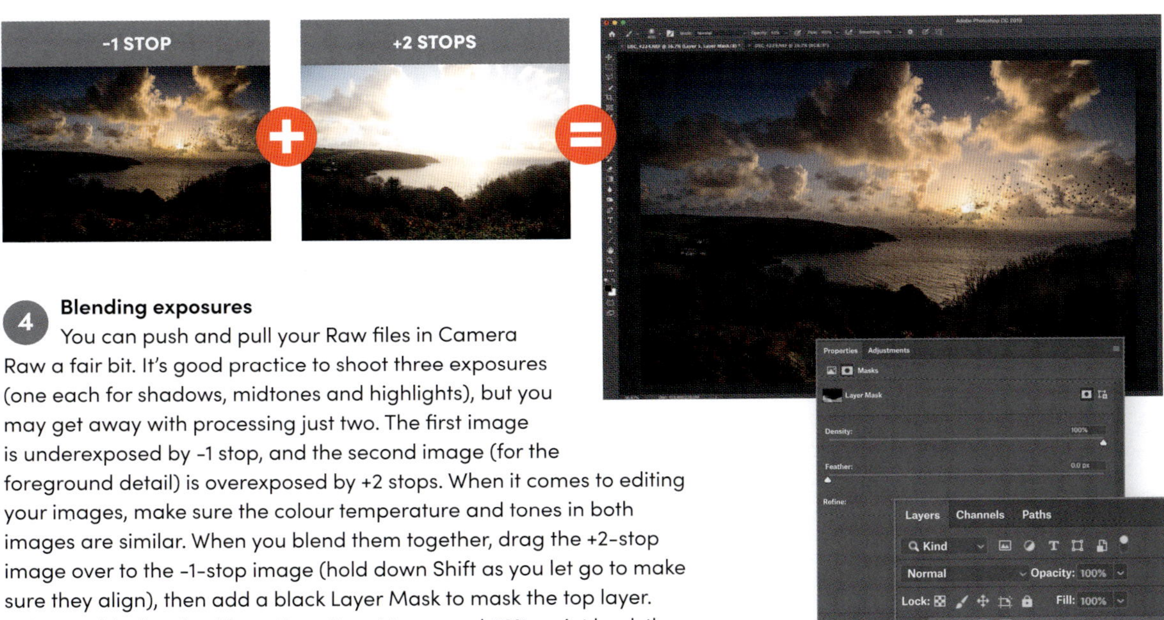


## 4 Blending exposures

You can push and pull your Raw files in Camera Raw a fair bit. It's good practice to shoot three exposures (one each for shadows, midtones and highlights), but you may get away with processing just two. The first image is underexposed by -1 stop, and the second image (for the foreground detail) is overexposed by +2 stops. When it comes to editing your images, make sure the colour temperature and tones in both images are similar. When you blend them together, drag the +2-stop image over to the -1-stop image (hold down Shift as you let go to make sure they align), then add a black Layer Mask to mask the top layer. Using a white brush with an Opacity set to around 50%, paint back the parts of the image you want lighter in the foreground.

# TILT AT WINDMILLS

**THE IDEA**
**Capture some amazing windmill landscape photos.**

**Time required:** 1 hour

**Kit needed:**
- DSLR or mirrorless camera
- Wide-angle lens
- Tripod
- Editing software

**Camera settings:**
117 secs at f/11, ISO 100

**Skill level:**

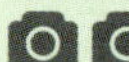   

**Landscape is a fantastic genre of photography that really allows you to take your time, grow your craft, experiment with camera settings and get out into the great outdoors.**

It can be difficult to find that perfect focal point to anchor your landscape shot. Luckily, windmills can be found in many regions across the world, each with its unique style and history. One example is the stunning Horsey Windpump in the UK (pictured). Horsey is one of the biggest windpumps in Norfolk. Type 'windmill' into Google Maps to find some windmills close to you.

A good rule for shooting landscapes is to set up on a tripod, so you can take your time to compose and eliminate camera shake. Switch off image stabilisation and select aperture-priority mode, then dial in a medium aperture value such as f/11 for strong sharpness, and ISO 100 for good image quality.

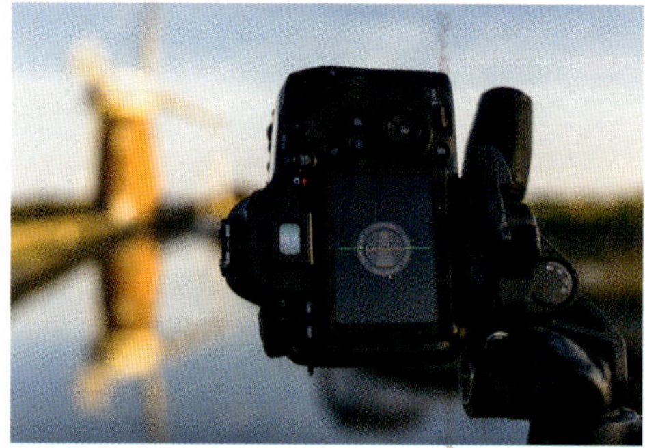

Set up on a tripod and use the in-camera spirit level to ensure the horizon is perfectly straight. Don't worry if you aren't faced with glorious sunshine – landscapes can look dramatic in rainy and stormy weather too.

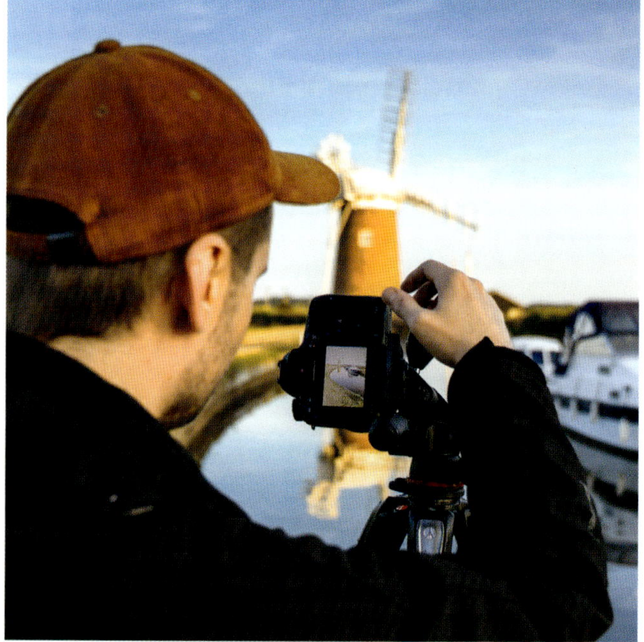

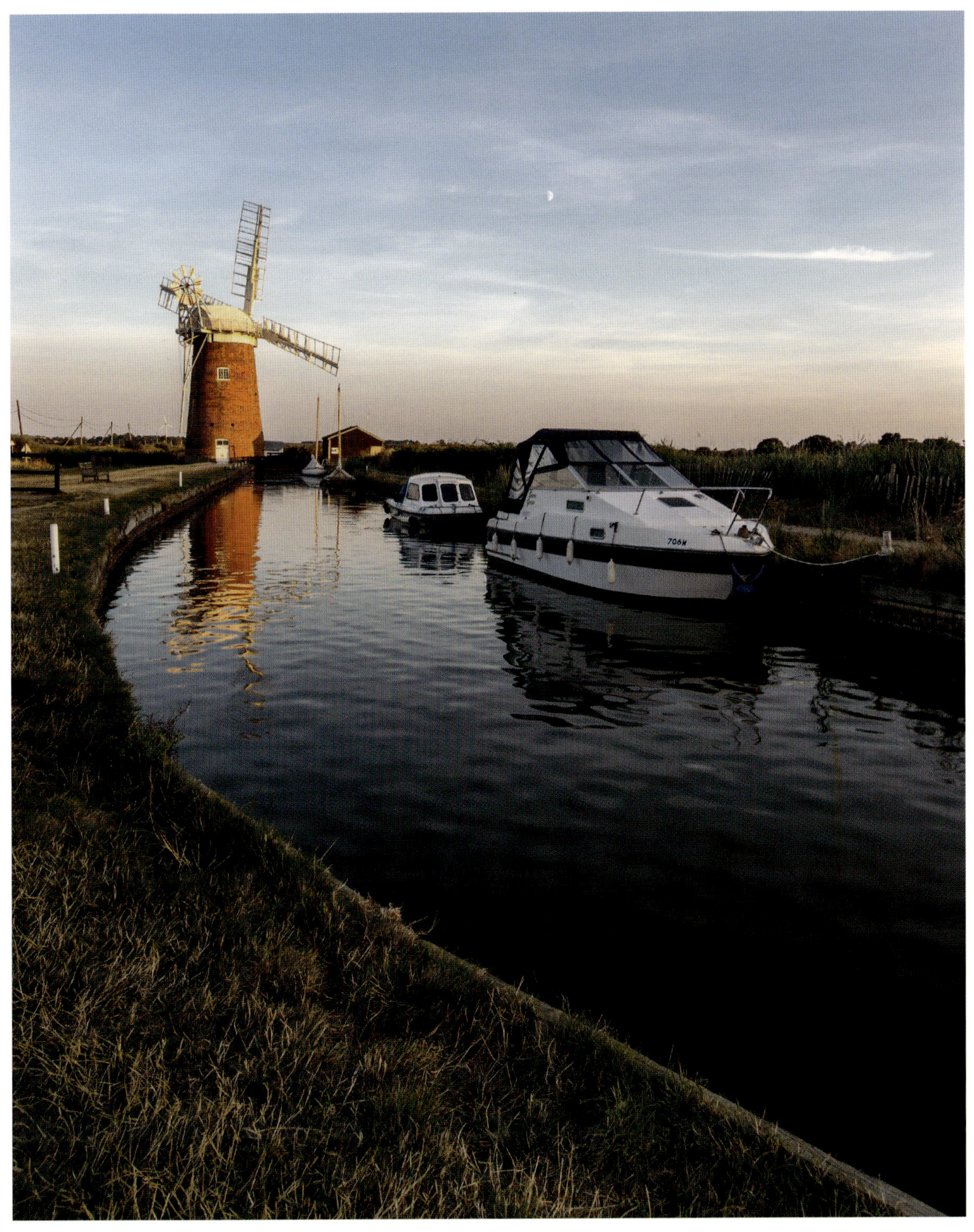

**1 Shutter speed**

Shutter speed determines how long the camera's shutter stays open to expose the digital sensor to light. With fast shutter speeds, the scene will be frozen still, but slowing the shutter speed down will help to smooth out the ripples in the water and blur moving clouds for a dream-like, painterly quality.

Shooting at dusk or dawn, when the light levels are gentler, will enable you to shoot longer exposures, although you can shoot for even longer with a filter such as a 3-, 6-, 10- or even 15-stop ND.

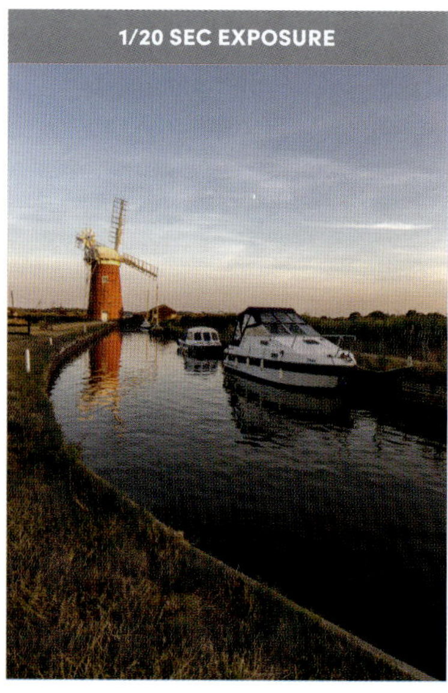

1/20 SEC EXPOSURE

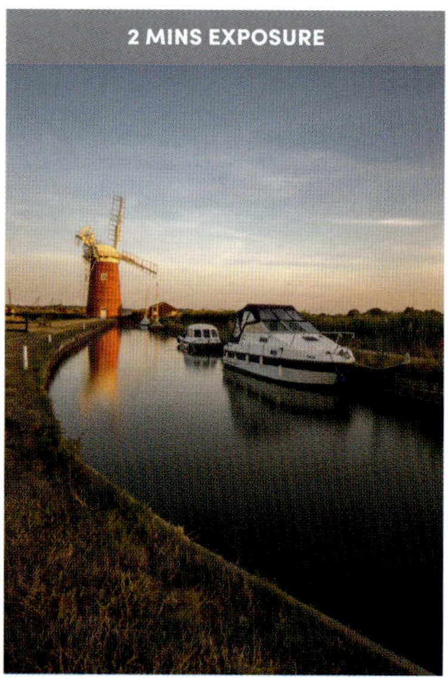

2 MINS EXPOSURE

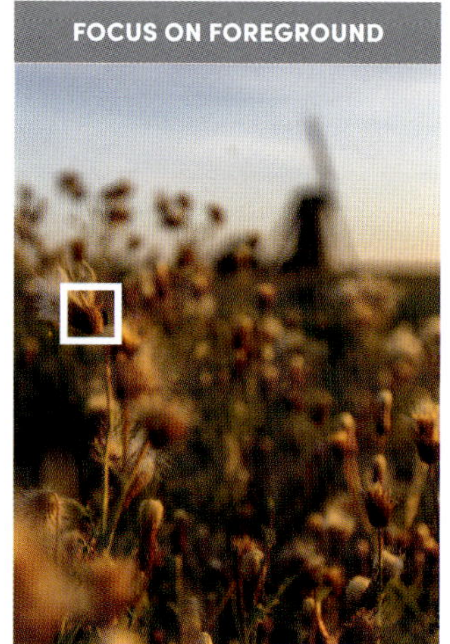

FOCUS ON FOREGROUND

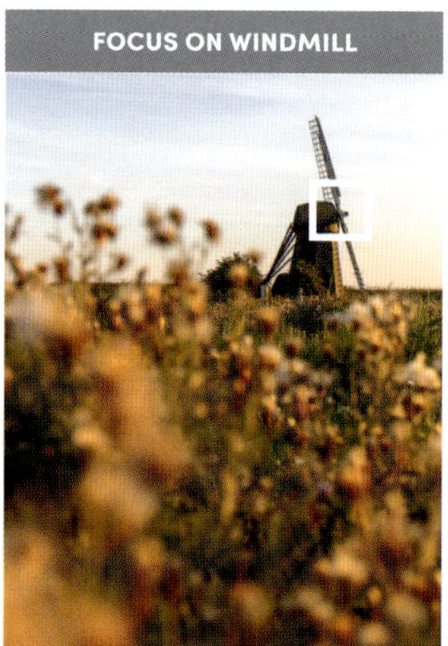

FOCUS ON WINDMILL

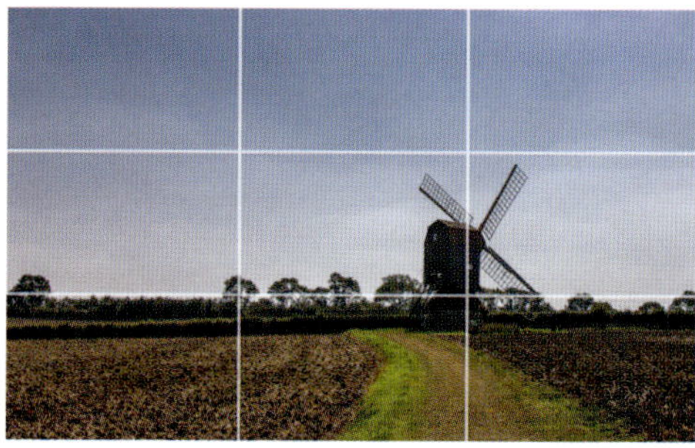

**2 Compose and focus**

Composition can be improved by using the rule of thirds. Place your horizon on one of the lines, then place your subject on two of the intersecting points.

It's also worth looking for foreground interest that you can include in your shots to add depth. Make sure you focus on the windmill, so it's pin sharp. Use a middle aperture value between f/11 or f/16 so that the scene has a deep zone of focus or shoot wide open to blur the foreground.

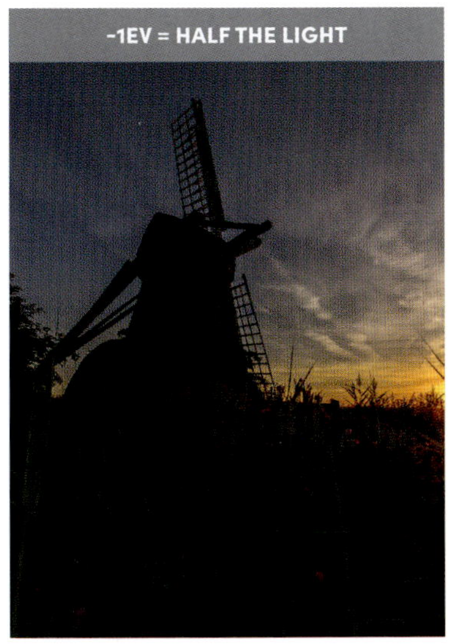


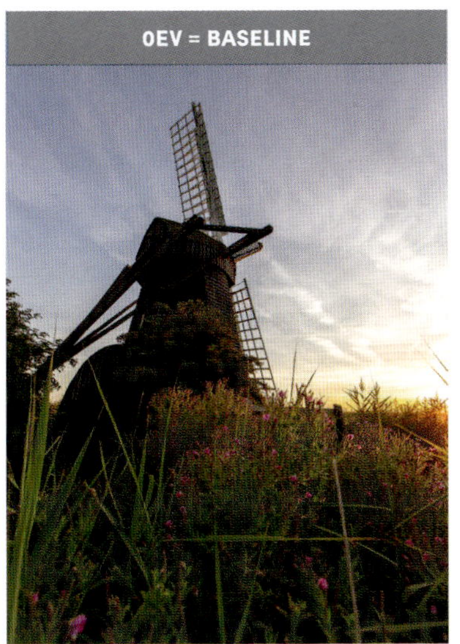


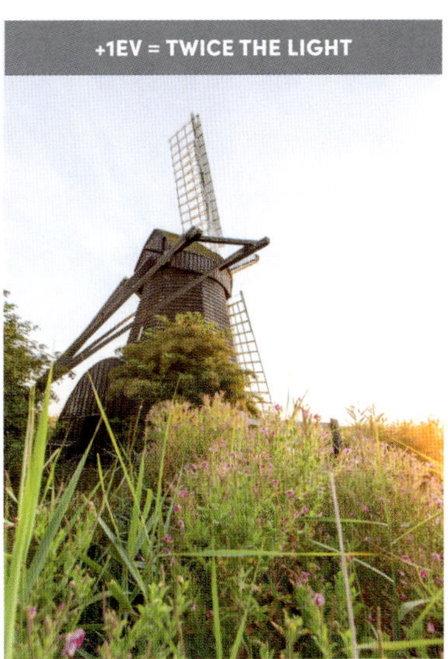


### 3 Expand your dynamic range

It can be tricky to expose for landscape scenes, especially in high-contrast situations such sunrises or sunsets. One option is to try a high dynamic range (HDR) image. Frame up on a tripod and lock off focus, then shoot a series of pictures in quick succession at different exposure values. You'll then have a batch of shots, both over- and underexposed, which you can merge in Photoshop to broaden the highlight and shadow detail within a single image. Use your camera's auto bracketing feature to simplify taking your group of images, then open the Raw files into Camera Raw, select them, right-click and choose Merge to HDR.

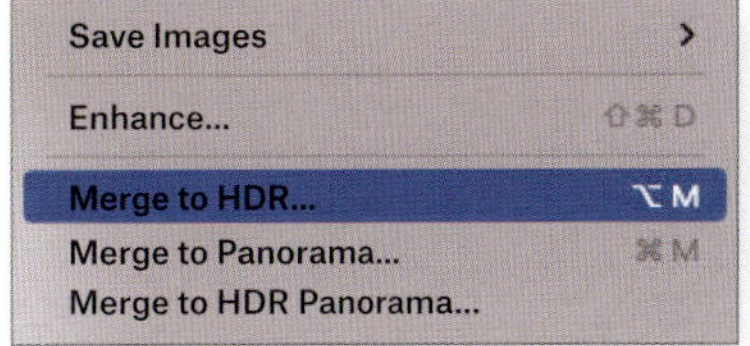


### 4 Targeted edits

Windmills often have a white top that may easily burn out and clip, resulting in a loss of detail. To avoid this, shoot in the Raw format, so that you have more exposure information to play with, then open that Raw file in Camera Raw or Lightroom. Paint over the windmill with the Adjustment Brush to select it, then edit this specific part of your photo. Tick the Overlay box so that you can clearly see where you've painted while working with the Adjustment Brush. If the highlight detail is starting to burn out, reduce Exposure, Highlights and Whites. You may also want to increase Clarity, Sharpness and Contrast to really help your windmill pop out from the landscape.

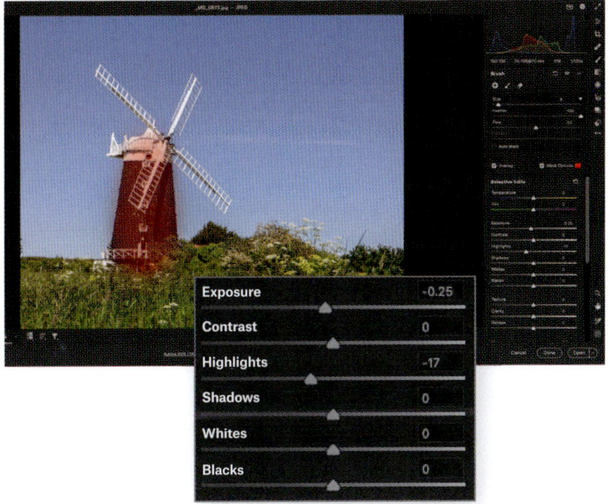

# PUT A FIGURE IN A LANDSCAPE

**THE IDEA**
**Photograph and edit a figure in a landscape.**

**Time required**: 1 hour

**Kit needed**:
- DSLR or mirrorless camera
- 35mm lens or similar

**Camera settings**:
1/160 sec at f/2, ISO 100

**Skill level**:

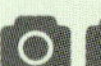   

**Adding human interest to a landscape is a fantastic way to introduce a subject to a flat scene. It also affords you a little bit more control over your composition. Social media is teeming with figure-in-a-landscape photos and we're going to show you just how effective this technique can be.**

This sunrise image was taken at Windermere in the UK's Lake District. With no interesting subject, and the lake and sky dominating the frame, a traditional landscape would have been uninspiring. But with a figure positioned on a partially submerged rock, a clear subject was added. You could even include yourself by setting the camera's self-timer.

As with any landscape shoot, planning is crucial. The Photographer's Ephemeris app will tell you when and where the sun will rise. A focal length of around 35mm will allow the figure to feature prominently while also allowing you to fit in plenty of the surrounding scenery.

Tell your 'model' what you are trying to achieve before they get into position, and discuss the poses you would like them to cycle through. Be sure to take plenty of shots to increase your chances of capturing something that is unexpected.

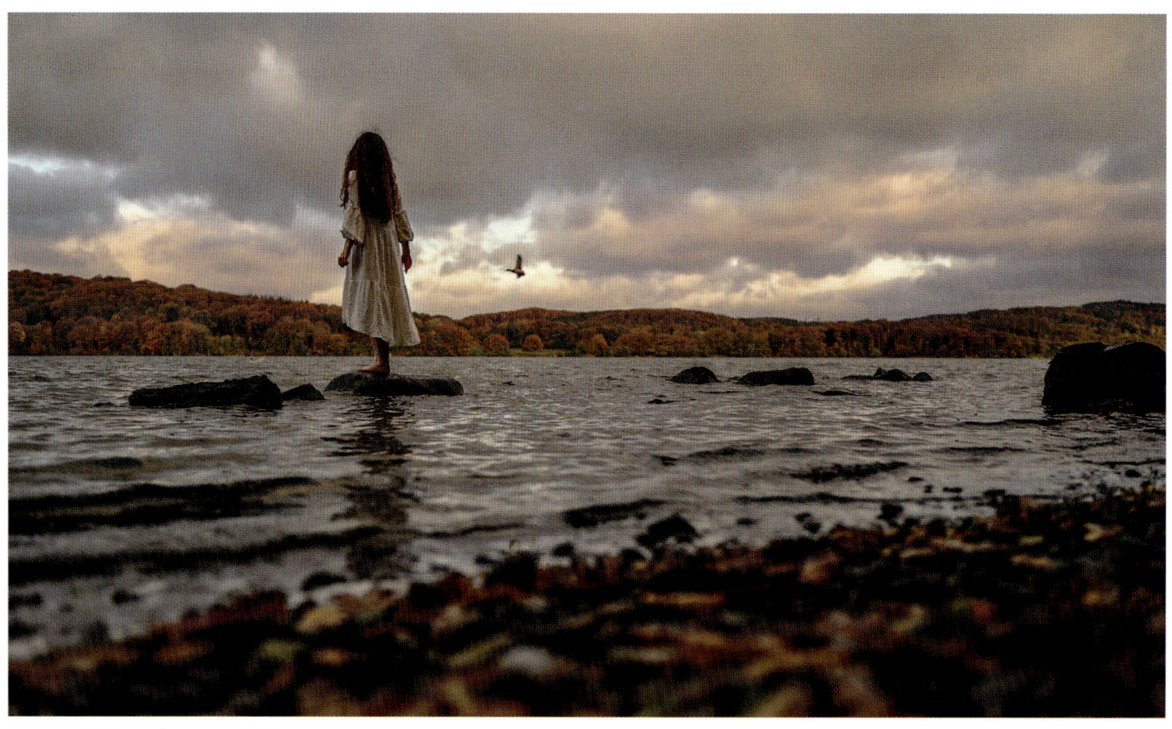

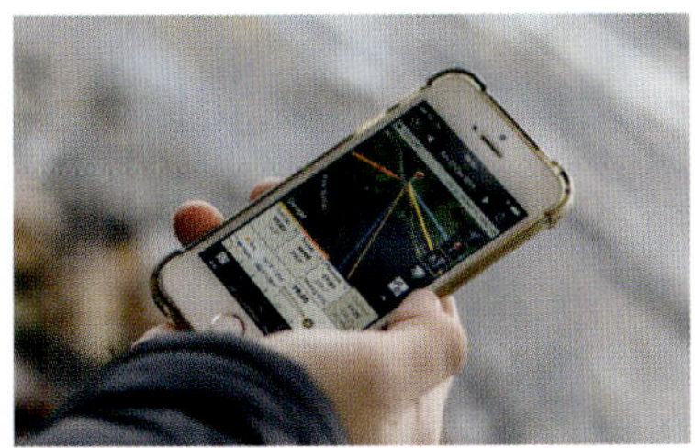

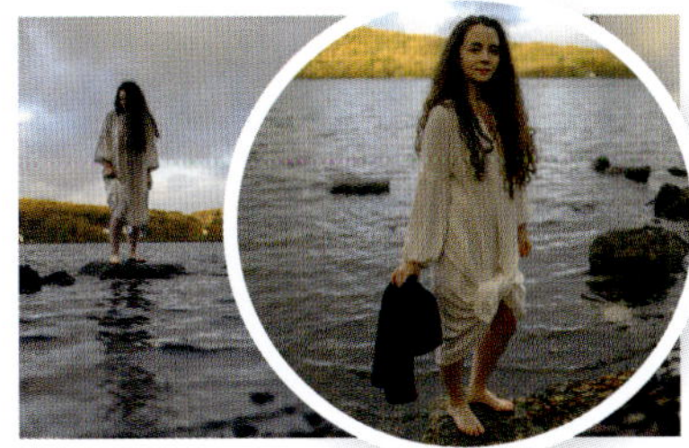

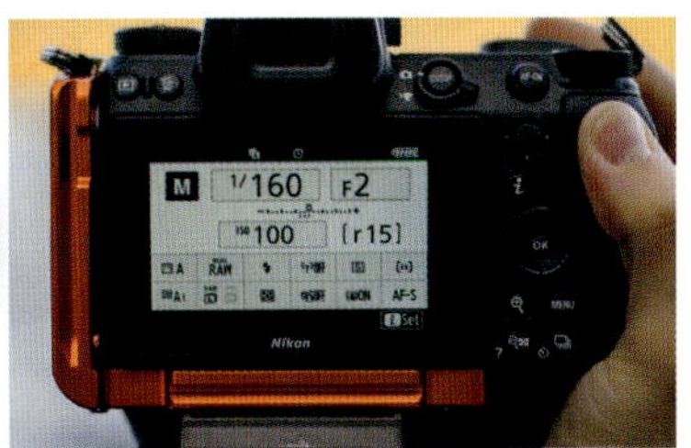


**1 Location, location, location**
Decide where you want to position your figure. Use The Photographer's Ephemeris app to work out where the light will be coming from and shoot with the light behind you. In this instance, the light was hitting the trees and clouds in the background.

**2 Dress to impress**
Think about what your figure is wearing. It can be difficult to see the details on dark clothing, and your figure can get lost in the expansive background. The white dress in this example contrasts against the dark clouds, and plenty of detail is visible despite the moody conditions.

**3 Camera settings**
Freeze any movement from the wind by using a shutter speed of around 1/160 sec. Bright weather will allow you to shoot at ISO 100, and an aperture of around f/2 will help to blur extreme foreground details and produce a shallow enough depth of field to make the figure pop against a busy background.

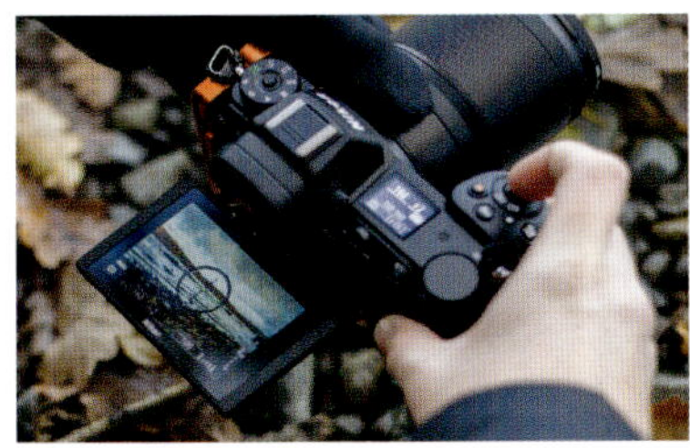

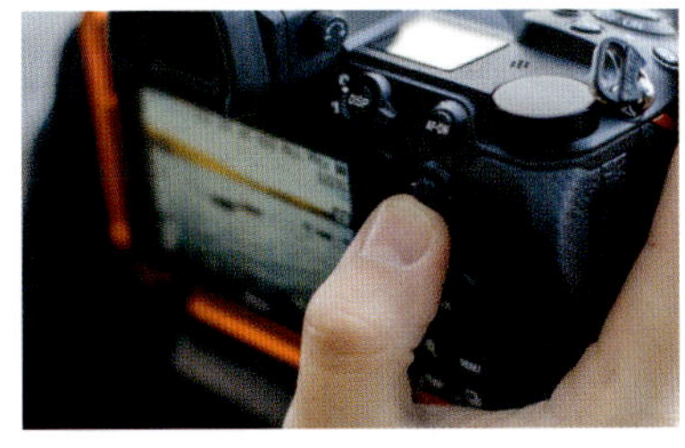

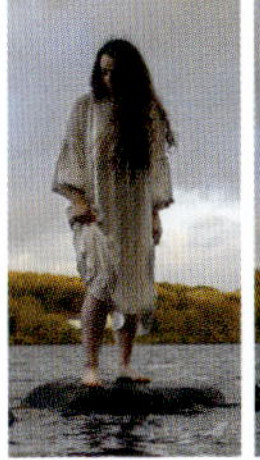

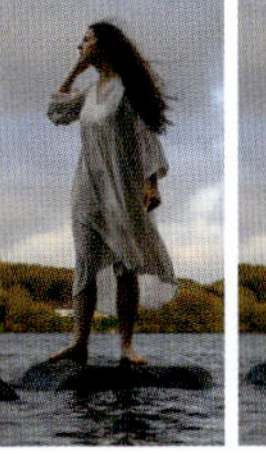

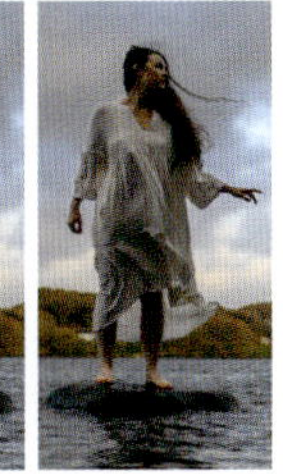

**4 Get low with your lens**
Shooting from a low angle will make your figure look more powerful. This is where your camera's tilting screen comes in very handy. Also, ensure your camera's virtual horizon is activated, as this will help you avoid wonky horizons.

**5 Focus point**
Set your camera's focus mode to single-shot and your AF-Area mode to single-point. Use the joystick or touchscreen to move the focus point over your figure, or half-press the shutter button and recompose. The latter can also be done in continuous-shooting mode if you're using back-button focusing. Back-button focus will also enable you to shoot burst sequences without any fear of the camera refocusing or hunting.

**6 Direct your model**
Windy weather can make it difficult to communicate with your model once they're in place. Talk them through your vision and discuss a variety of poses that you'd like them to cycle through beforehand. This enables you to take plenty of shots in quick succession, and experiment while doing so.

**Photographers often talk about taking one good shot, but light moves quickly, especially at sunrise or sunset. Take plenty of shots so you can select the best lighting in post-production. Each moment presents subtle changes in colour, intensity, and shadows that can dramatically alter the mood of a photograph.**

# ADD MOOD WITH AN ND FILTER

**THE IDEA**
**Use a neutral-density filter to photograph a minimalist seascape.**

**Time required**: 30 minutes

**Kit needed**:
- DSLR or mirrorless camera
- 24–70mm zoom lens
- ND filter
- Tripod

**Camera settings**:
10–20 secs at f/11, ISO 100

**Skill level**:

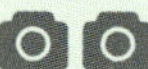  

**If you regularly forego heading out with your camera on days with grey skies and muted lighting, you may be missing out. Drab weather is ideal for shooting minimalist seascapes and is the perfect chance to brush up on taking long exposures.**

At the Philip Lucette Beacon in Devon, UK, the lone subject, surrounded by sea and sky, provided a fine minimalist composition. A 10-stop ND filter produced a 6 sec exposure, which smoothed out the sea and softened the clouds.

The hardest thing to grasp when using an ND filter is the formula for calculating the shutter speed, but with the help of a simple app, you can calculate this in no time. Exactly what ND filter you use will depend on the lighting. A bright setting might warrant a 16-stop filter, while a darker day might warrant a 6-stop filter.

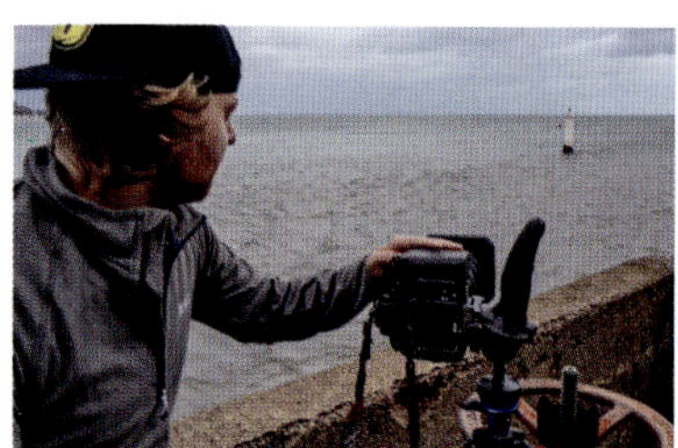

**1 Subjects matter**
Minimalist photos tend to feature negative space, clean compositions and very little to detract from the subject, so choose your subject carefully. At high tide, the sea surrounds the Philip Lucette Beacon in Shaldon, Devon, making it an ideal subject.

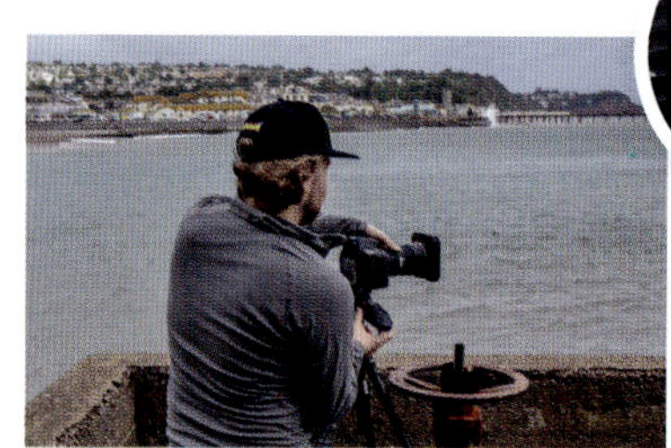

**2 Frame by frame**
Set up your camera and lens (with filter holder) on a tripod. Activate Live View and use the virtual horizon overlay to ensure a straight horizon. Try both portrait and landscape orientations.

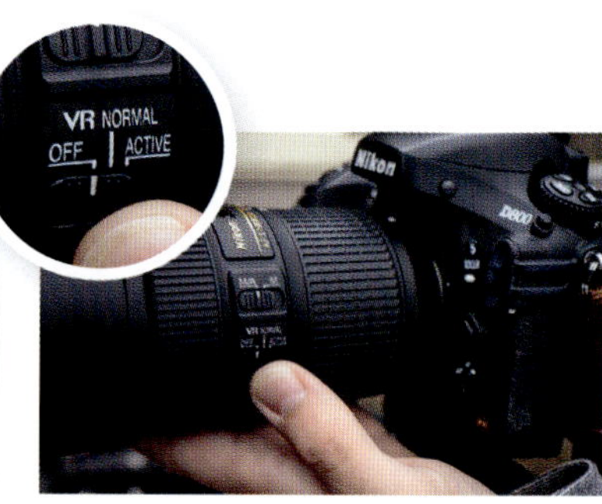


**3 Lens and VR**
Minimalist photos can be taken with almost any lens – the image of the Philip Lucette Beacon shown here was taken with a 24–70mm zoom at 70mm. Switch off any form of image stabilisation – when using a tripod, some systems can add blur by correcting for movement that doesn't exist.

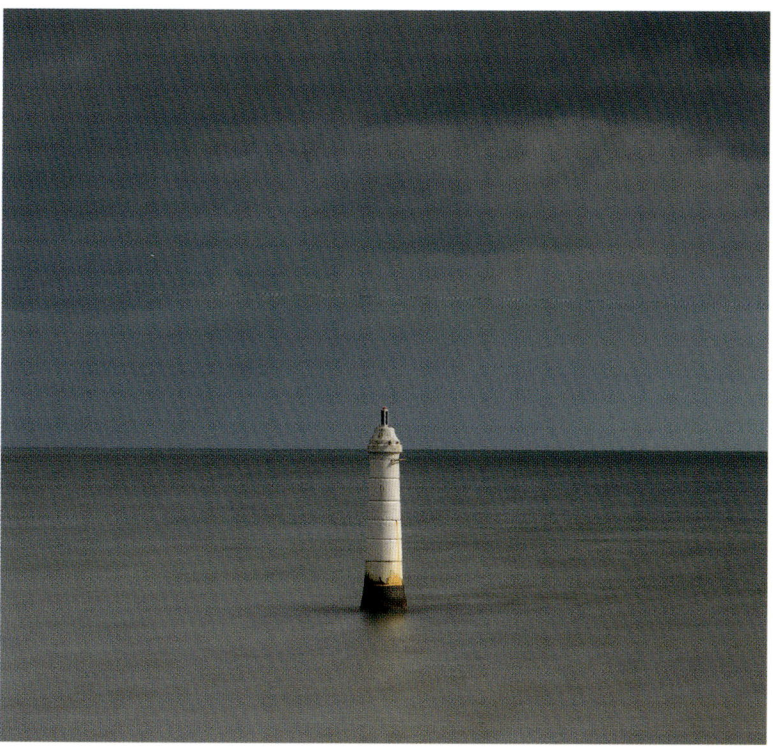

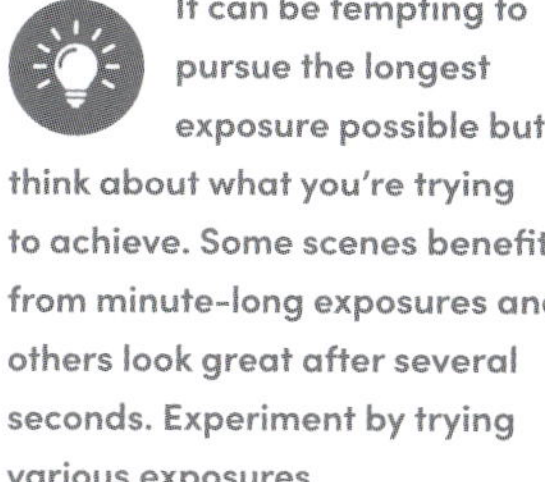

It can be tempting to pursue the longest exposure possible but think about what you're trying to achieve. Some scenes benefit from minute-long exposures and others look great after several seconds. Experiment by trying various exposures.

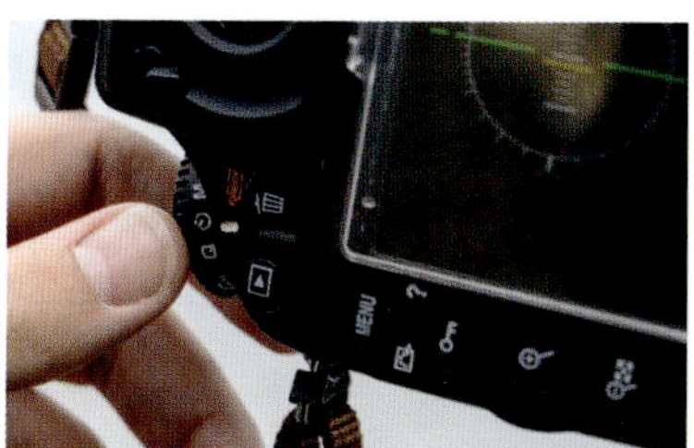


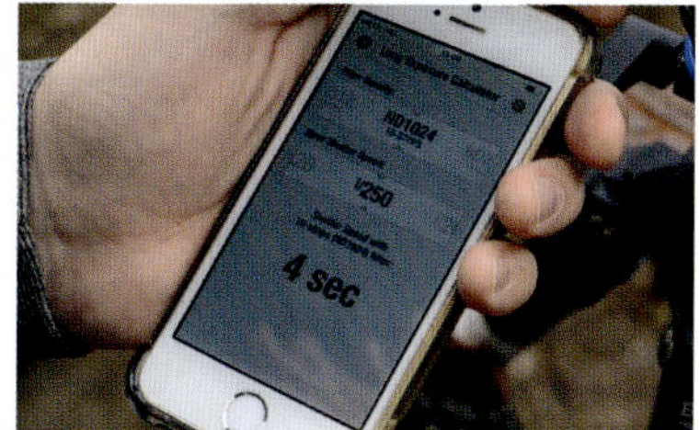


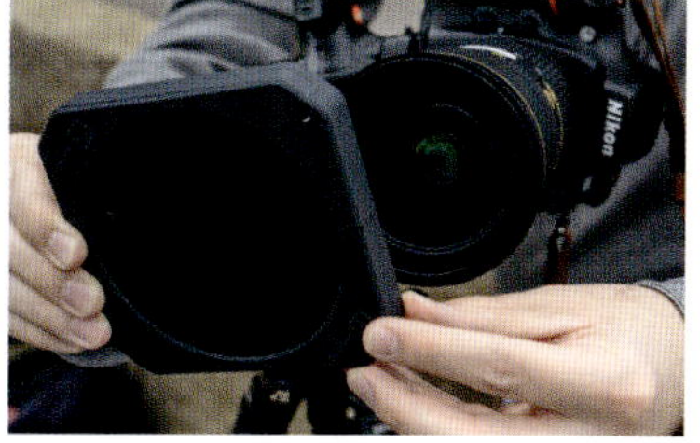


**4 Hands free**
Pressing the shutter button can cause unwanted movement when taking a long exposure. Mitigate this by activating your camera's self-timer function. Set the AF-Area mode to single point and use AF-S to focus.

**5 Skip the maths**
Select your camera's base ISO and choose a suitable aperture while in aperture-priority mode to find your base shutter speed. Switch to manual mode and input the same settings. Use an app such as Long Exposure Calculator to calculate exposure.

**6 Fix filter and shoot**
Back-button focusing allows you to press the shutter button without engaging focus lock. However, if you're not using back-button focusing, you'll need to turn autofocus off to prevent hunting or refocusing when you press the shutter button. Finally, carefully attach your filter and activate the shutter when you're ready to capture your minimalist seascape.

# KING OF THE CASTLE

THE IDEA
**How to include buildings in your landscape photos.**

**Time required:** 1 hour

**Kit needed:**
- DSLR or mirrorless camera
- Wide-angle lens
- ND filter
- Tripod
- Editing software

**Camera settings:**
1/100 sec at f/16, ISO 100 or try 30 secs at f/22 with a 10-stop ND filter

**Skill level:**

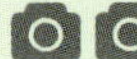 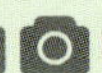 

**The countryside offers a wealth of landmarks, from lighthouses to trees and historic listed buildings to castles. When traveling, always be on the lookout for suitable subjects like this.**

If your landscapes are failing to have the impact you'd like, an iconic landmark, such as a castle, can really help to anchor your scene and demand the viewer's attention.

When framing your shot, pay attention to the light's angle and its impact on the building's textures. Use the rule of thirds to balance the composition and leading lines to guide the viewer's eye. For different effects, experiment with camera settings: 1/100 sec at f/16 will produce a sharp, well-exposed image suitable for daylight conditions. Conversely, try out long-exposure shots with smooth motion blur and a deep depth of field.

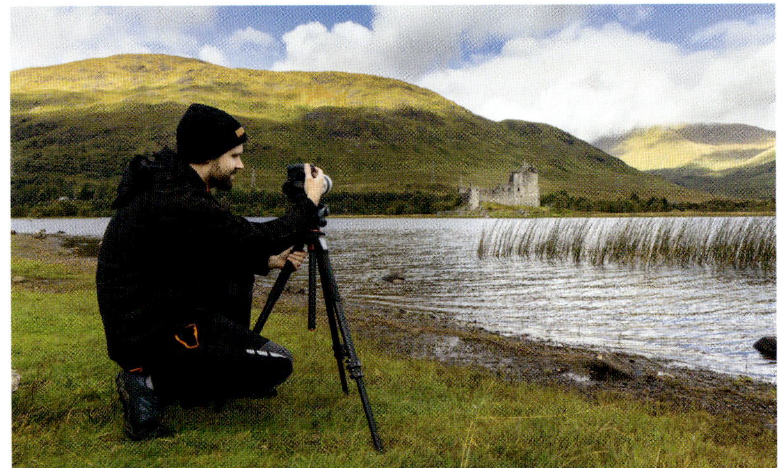

## Experiment with mono

**Experiment with monochrome and colour to see which works better. This shot was taken earlier in the day at a different jetty, when it was still very wet. There was little colour in the scene, so for this reason the image was converted to black and white. Contrast was also boosted at the editing stage to give the image a more effective and eye-catching finish.**

BEFORE

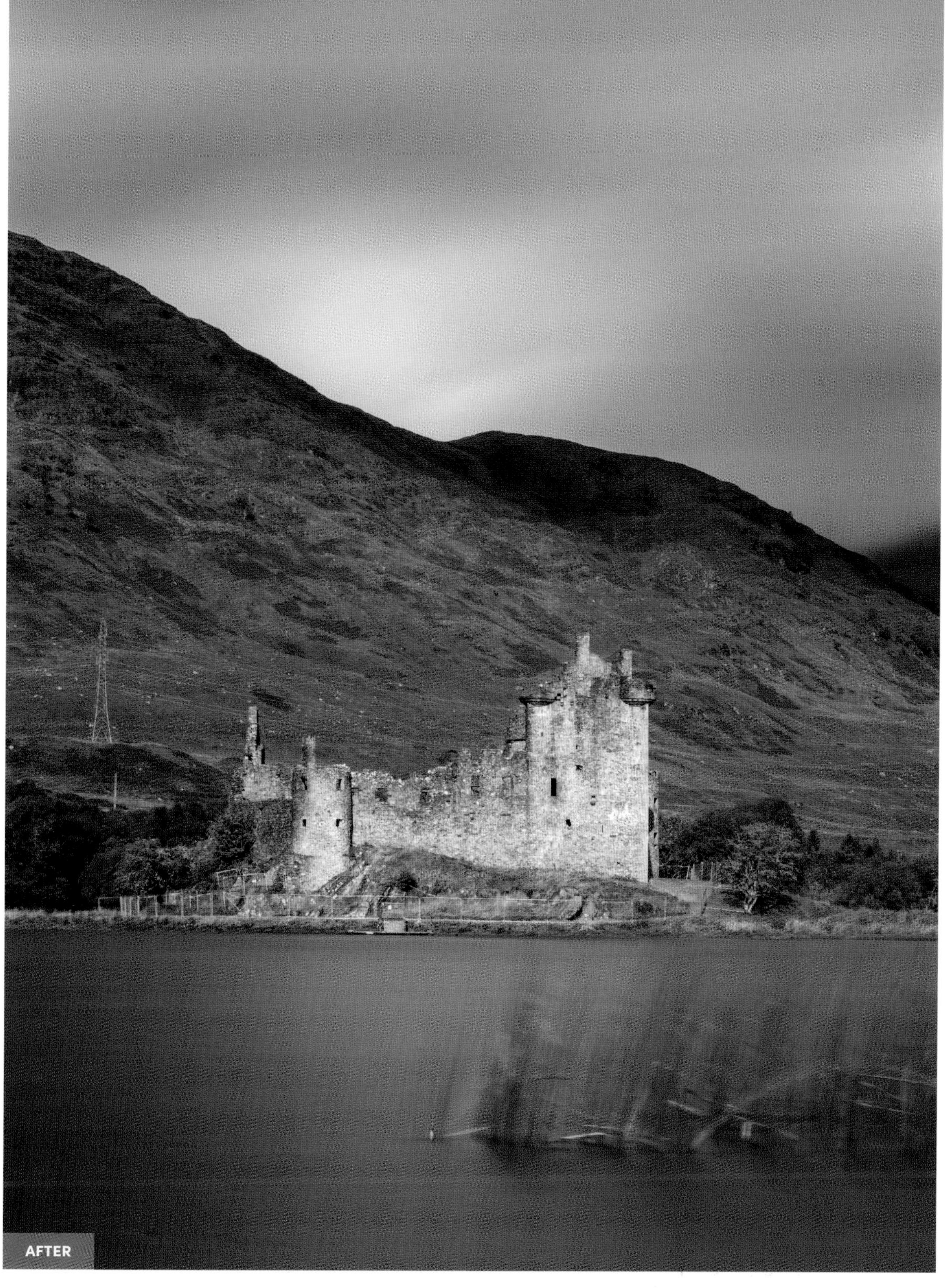
AFTER

## 1 Get set up

When shooting a landscape you often have plenty of time to spare as you sit and wait for the perfect light to materialise, which means you can take your time to set up on a tripod and perfect your composition. Go into Live View and compose your shot, making sure the horizon is perfectly level. The rule of thirds is a classic trick you can use when composing to enhance your landscape scenes as it helps offset your focal point so it isn't in the middle of the frame. You can use the camera's grid to help with this.

While wide-angle lenses are associated with landscape photography, you can get great results by zooming in with a long telephoto to compress the perspective. It's down to personal preference on how much of the scene you want to include in shot.

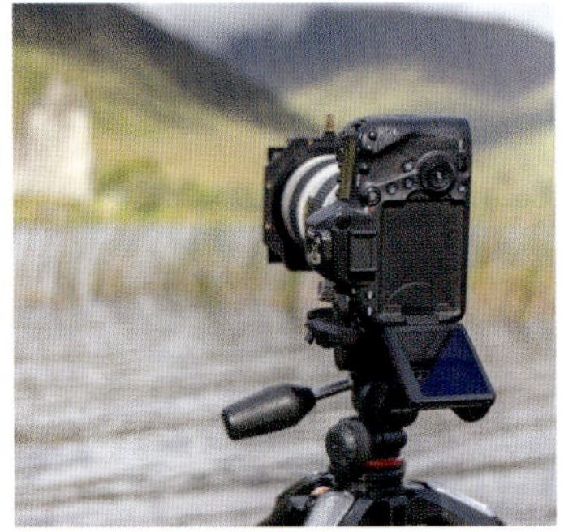

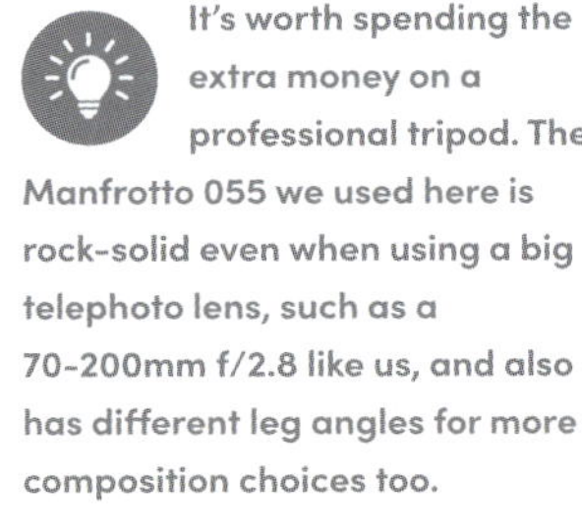

It's worth spending the extra money on a professional tripod. The Manfrotto 055 we used here is rock-solid even when using a big telephoto lens, such as a 70-200mm f/2.8 like us, and also has different leg angles for more composition choices too.

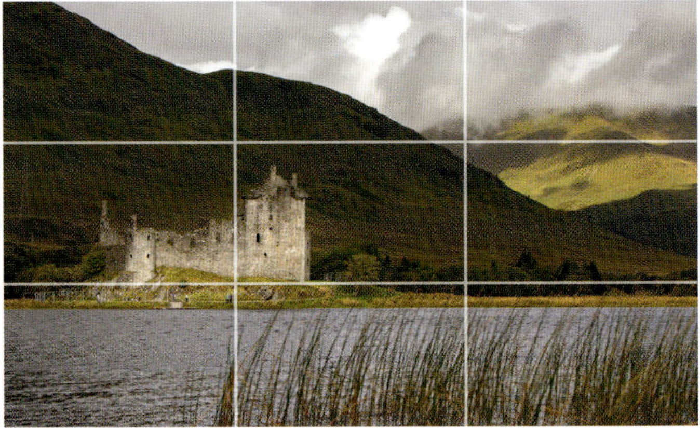

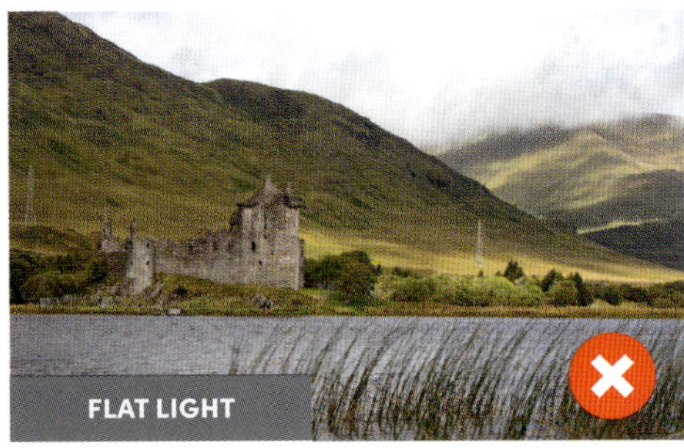
FLAT LIGHT

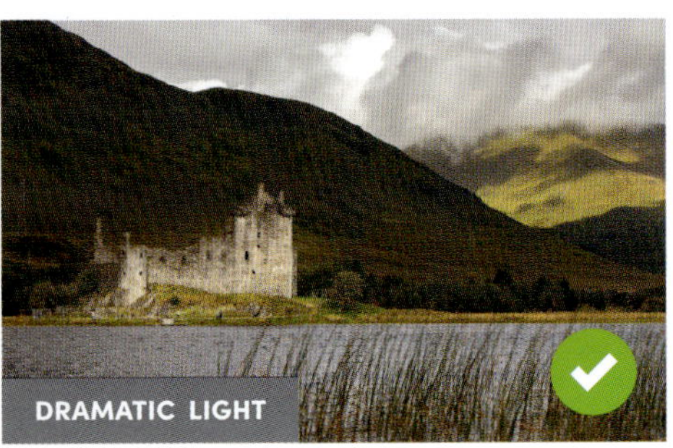
DRAMATIC LIGHT

## 2 Be patient

Light can change quickly when shooting landscapes, especially on overcast days when the sun can suddenly break through cloud cover and bring your scene to life. It pays to be attentive and ready to take the shot. The quality of light will also change throughout the day, when the sun is overhead in the middle it can look harsh and unflattering, while at sunrise or sunset you have the blue and golden hours, producing softer light which is much more photogenic.

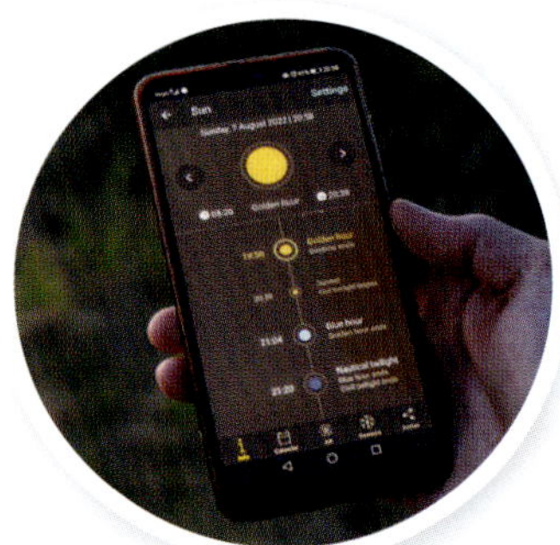

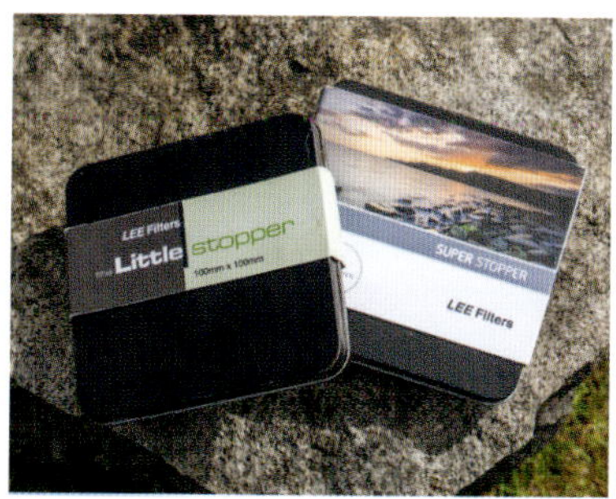


## 3 Long exposures

A great way to make your landscape shots look more professional is to experiment with your shutter speed. In bright daylight, the light levels are often too high for long exposures. To address this, you can use a Neutral Density (ND) filter, which attaches to your lens and reduces the amount of light entering it, similar to sunglasses. This allows you to use a longer shutter speed. For example, a regular shutter speed of 1/30 sec might freeze the clouds and water ripples, while using a 10-stop ND filter to extend the exposure to 30 seconds can create a smooth, ethereal blur in the scene.

**Bright skies in landscapes are prone to dust spots. Quickly remove them in Photoshop with the Spot Healing Brush.**

**1/30 SEC SHUTTER SPEED**

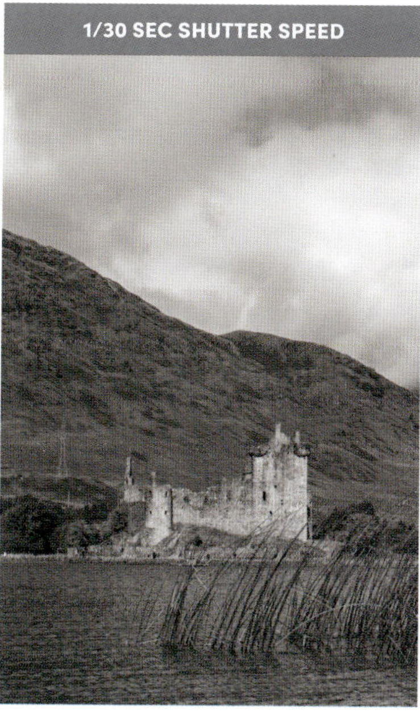

**30 SECS SHUTTER SPEED**

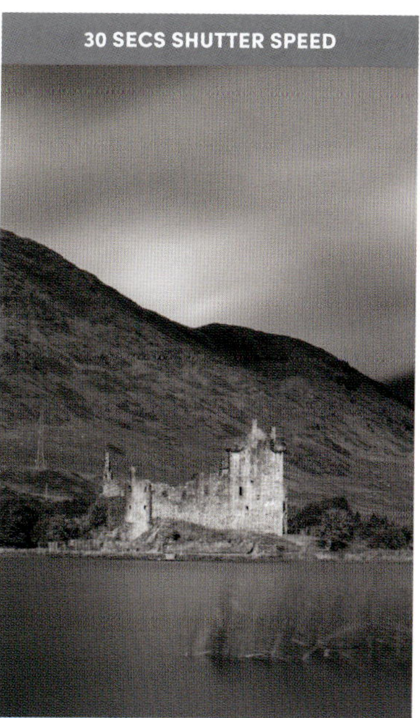

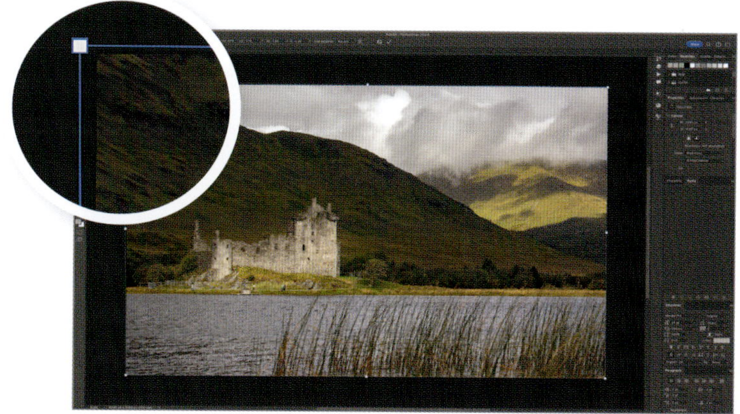

## 4 Watch horizontal and vertical lines

Converging verticals are when straight lines of buildings appear to lean inwards. This is most apparent when shooting with a wide-angle lens and positioning a building off-centre, or shooting from a low perspective. To fix this, start by opening your image in Photoshop and duplicate it with Ctrl/Cmd+J. Enter Free Transform mode using Ctrl/Cmd+T. While holding Ctrl/Cmd+Shift+Alt, drag one of the top corner handles outward until the vertical lines are aligned. If the image looks a bit squished, hold Shift and drag the top middle handle upwards to stretch it back to the right proportions.

# SHOOT THROUGH A LENS BALL

**THE IDEA**
**Shoot landscape scenes through a crystal ball.**

**Time required:** 1 hour

**Kit needed:**
- DSLR or mirrorless camera
- 50mm or above prime or telephoto lens
- Lens ball

**Camera settings:**
1/1000 sec at f/2.8, ISO 100

**Skill level:**

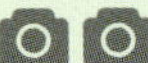  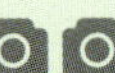

**There's something very satisfying about holding a glass ball. The subject is projected upside-down, and inside the ball there is an encapsulated scene.**

When selecting a suitable location, watch out for unwanted reflections. If you shoot during the day, you'll want to pick a shady spot. It can look effective to play around with a lens flare technique, which is a technical flaw, but if you want to avoid this, stay out of the sun. It's also vital to take a cloth and wipe away any fingerprints on the ball which could ruin the result.

Play around with how and where you place your ball. Try balancing it on rocks, sand, earth, in your hands: there are many different possibilities.

During editing, flip the scene round 180 degrees so the scene in the ball is the correct way up.

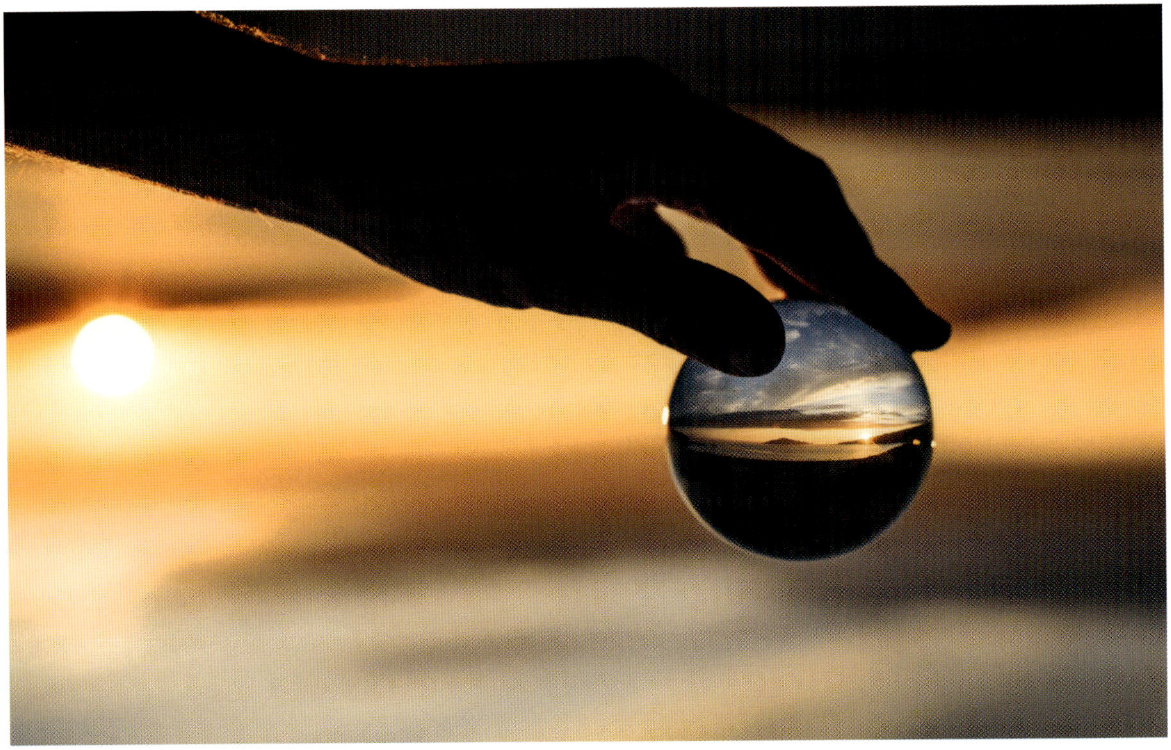

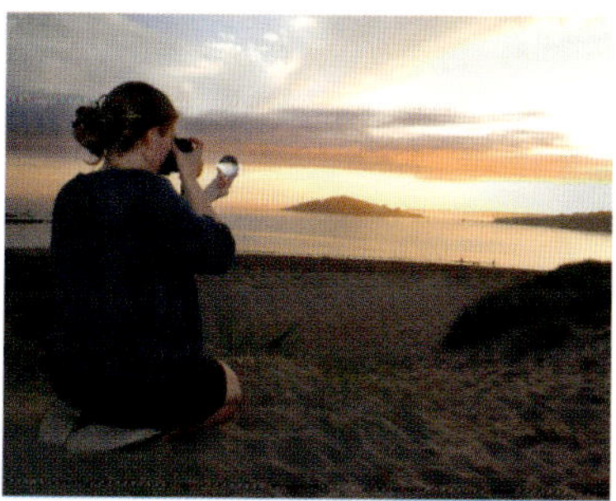

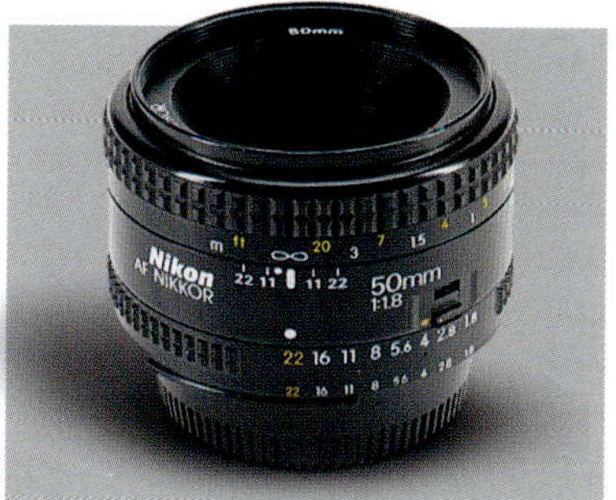



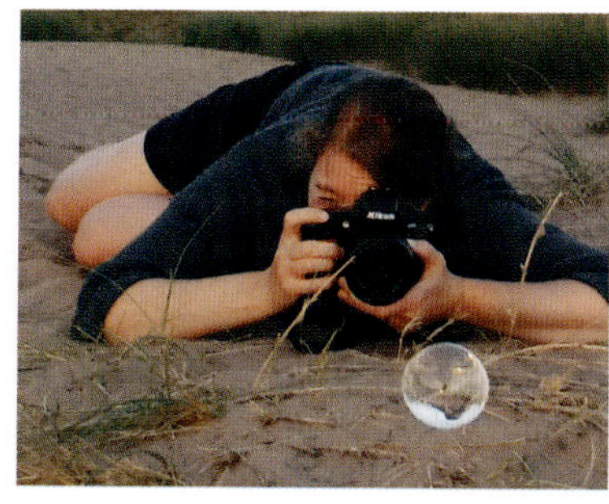

**1 The setting**

Pick a stunning setting with a strong focal point to achieve the best results. Head down just before sunset and shoot during the golden hour to ensure that the colours in the sky are warm and appealing in the final shot.

**2 Lens choice**

Prime or telephoto lenses with a longer focal length (50mm or above) are best for this subject, as they compress the elements in the scene. Prime lenses are also much faster and can be opened to wider apertures to give you control over depth of field.

**3 Camera settings**

Select aperture-priority mode and open the aperture to f/2.8. This will blur the background nicely while keeping the scene in the ball sharp. Due to the wide aperture setting, you will still be able to handhold the camera at ISO 100, eliminating the need for a tripod.

## Why is the scene upside-down?

**A glass ball is a convex structure. In simple terms, the ball's shape makes the light change direction when it travels through the ball – a process known as refraction – and is then projected out the other side upside-down. The glass in camera lenses is also convex, so the same thing happens, and the glass turns the image upside-down. Cameras either have an optical viewfinder, which uses mirrors to project your image the right way up, or an electronic viewfinder which does it electronically.**

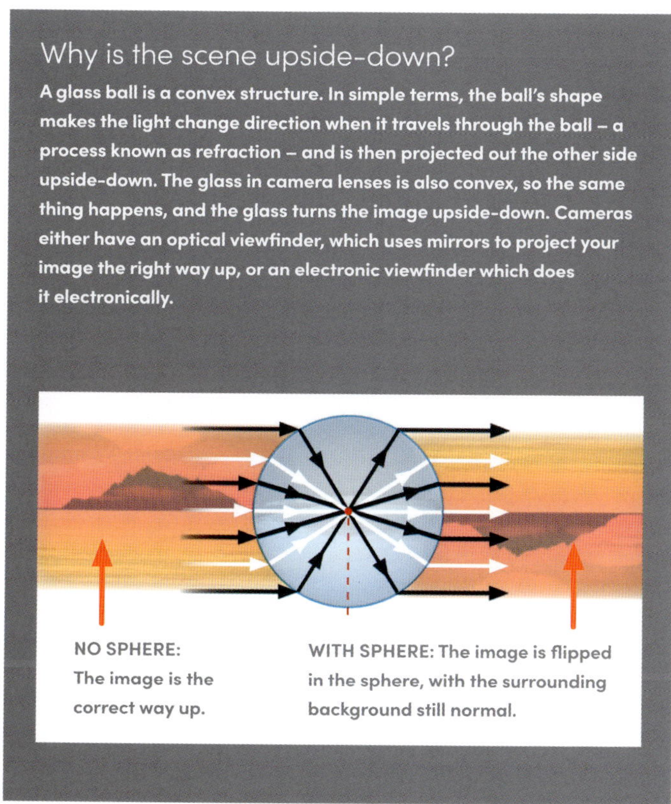



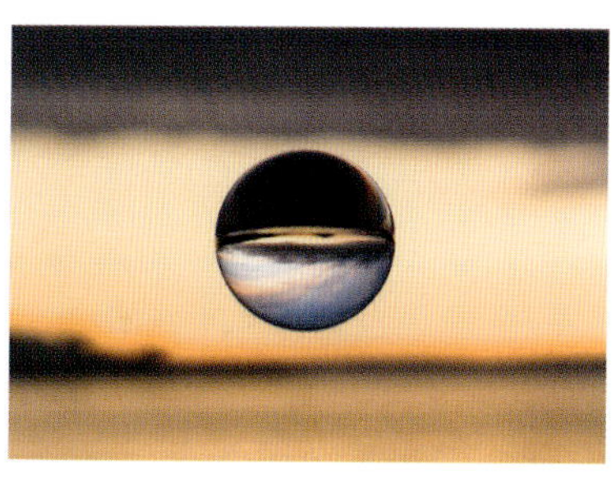

**THROW IT IN THE AIR**

You'll need some assistance with this, and it's good to make sure your on-hand help can throw accurately. Get your assistant to hold the ball still in the air and pre-focus where you want it to end up. Set your camera to shoot in burst mode and fire a succession of shots as the ball is released. It's a trial- and-error approach, but when you succeed in getting the shot, it's worth it.

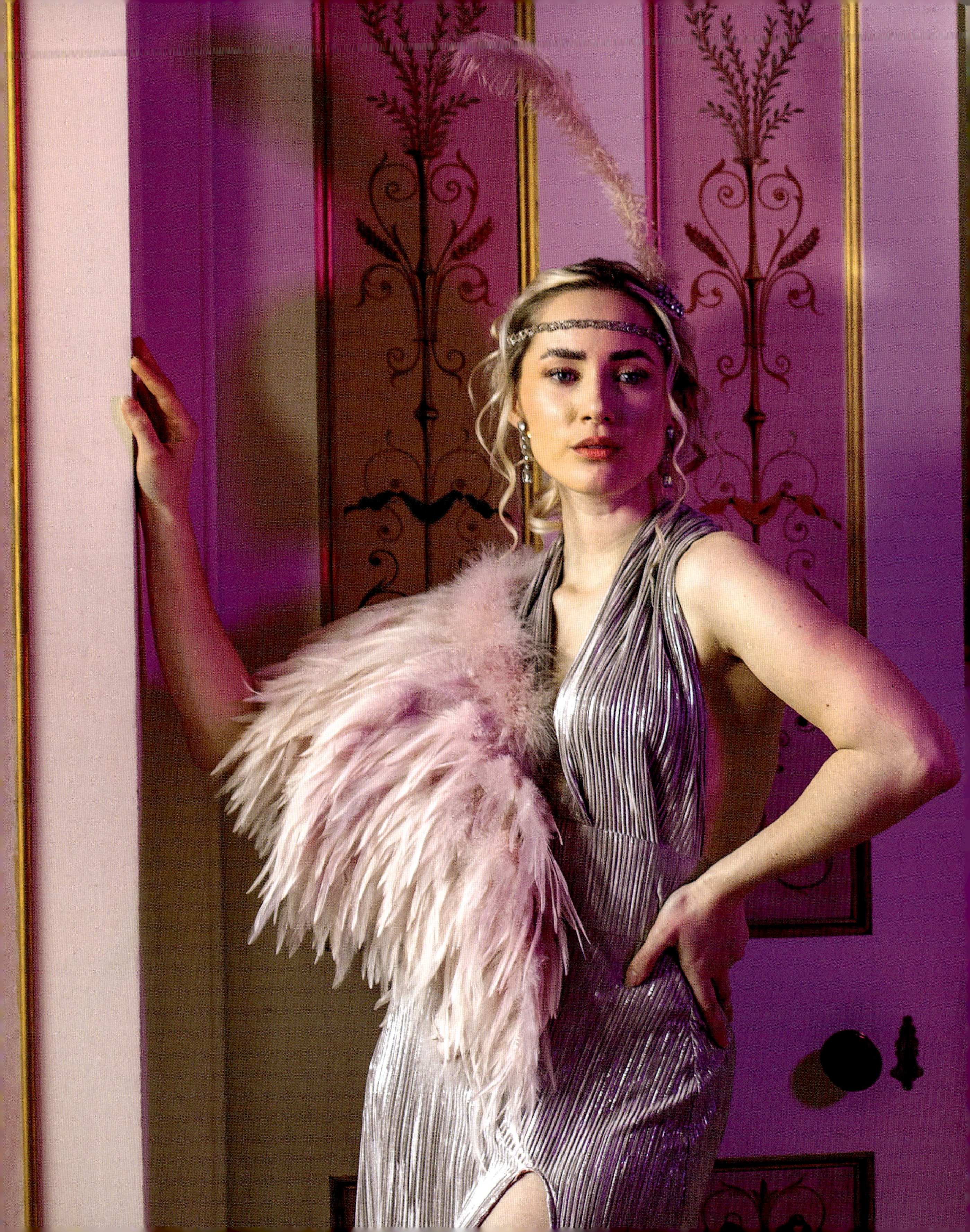

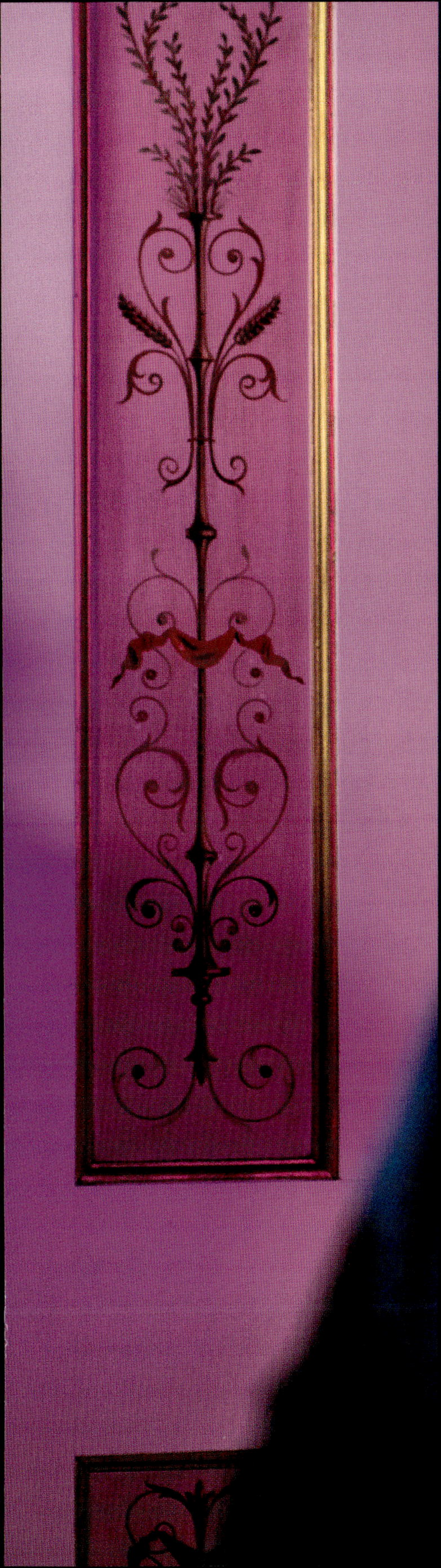

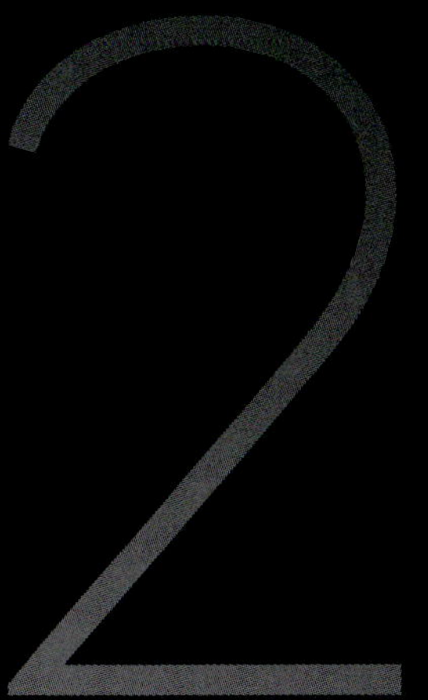

# PORTRAIT IDEAS

**Expert advice for capturing the essence of a person using a variety of approaches, many using straightforward lighting setups**

# CREATE SILHOUETTES

**THE IDEA**
**Use a long lens to capture a distinctive photo.**

**Time required**: 1 hour

**Kit needed**:
- DSLR or mirrorless camera
- 300mm lens
- Lens hood
- Editing software

**Camera settings**:
1/2000 sec at f/4, ISO 100

**Skill level**:

**When travel plans go awry, remember that there are still photo opportunities to be had, wherever you are. In this instance, stormy weather delayed the photographer's journey to Skomer Island off the Welsh coast, leaving an extra day for practising with a new telephoto lens.**

Most people reach for a wide-angle lens when confronted with long, sweeping beaches, but a long focal length allows you to experiment with compressing the perspective of a scene instead.

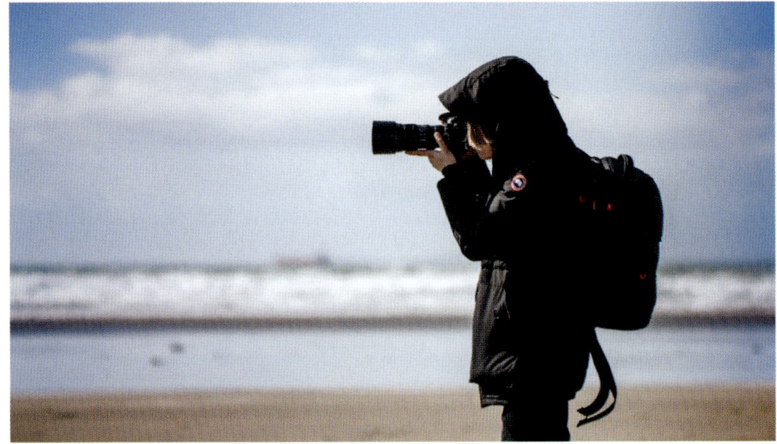

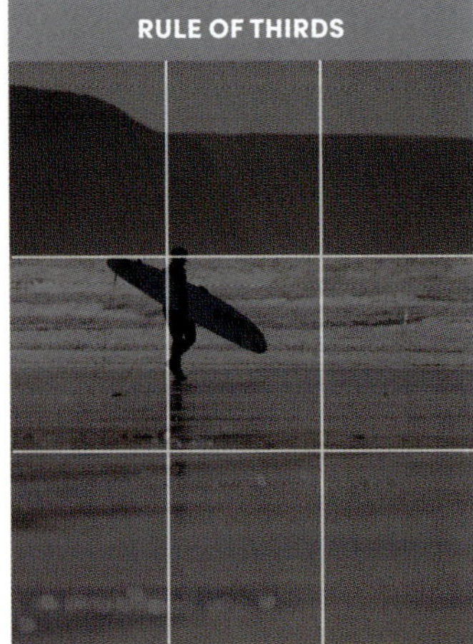


**1 Adapt your approach**
Explore different angles with your telephoto lens and look for elements that draw you in. In this example, this was the reflective sand at low tide and the sparkling bokeh from the sun. Select your lens's maximum aperture and focus on the person in the distance. Here, the wide aperture and 300mm focal length threw the sand into soft focus, while keeping the point of interest clear.

The surfer was positioned a third of the way into the frame to create a pleasing composition.

**2 Edit for impact**
Everyone processes their photos to different extents, but it's often useful to imagine how you're going to edit a shot when you take it. For example, this image was underexposed to ensure there was no clipping in the sparkly sand.

**3 Be aware of the weather**
Although this scene looks picturesque, there were strong gales whipping across the beach. A lens hood protected the front element from swirling sand particles.

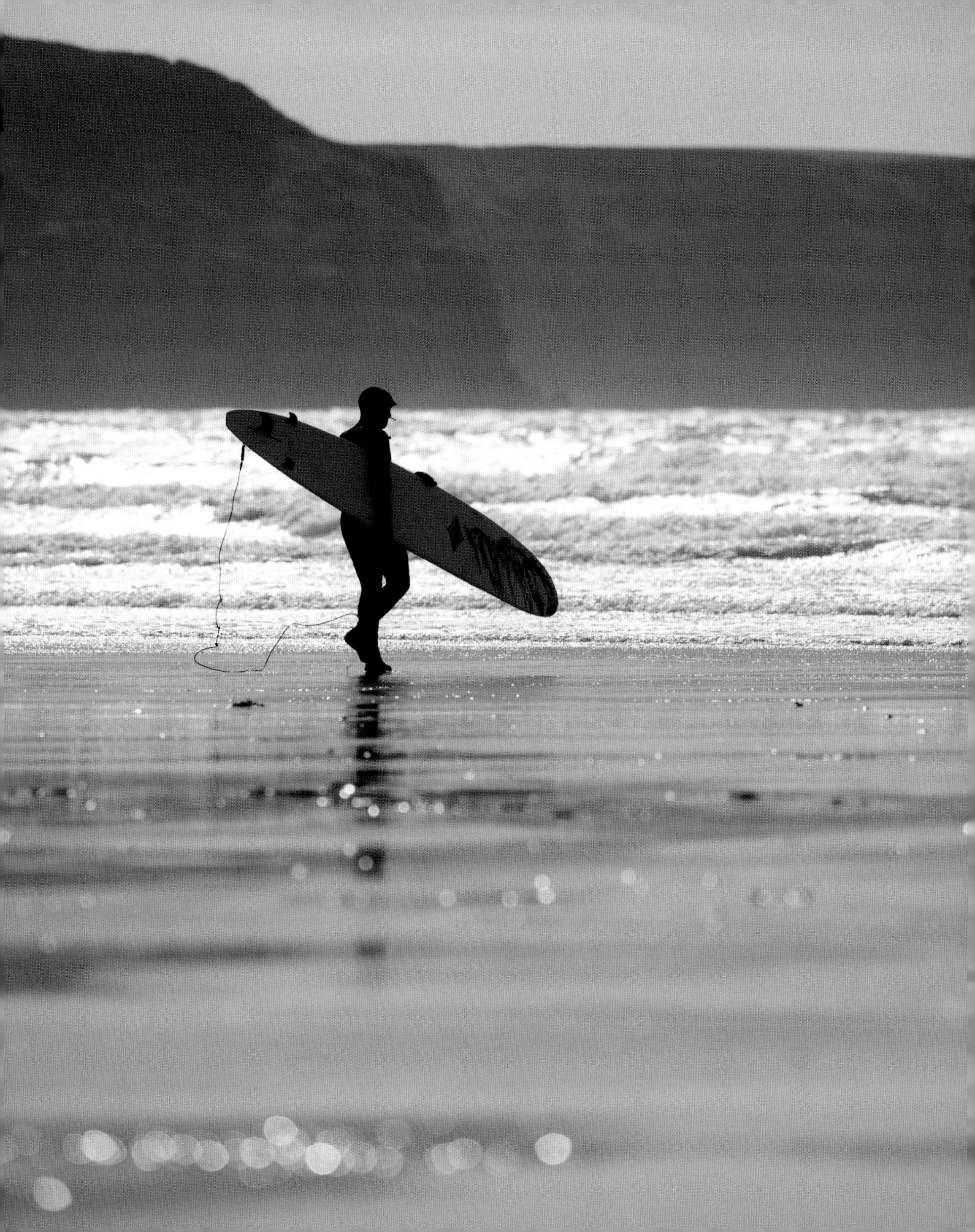

# GO MONOCHROME

**THE IDEA**
**Sculpt and shape the male figure with light and shade.**

**Time required**: 2 hours

**Kit needed**:
- DSLR or mirrorless camera
- 50mm lens
- Flashgun and blue cellophane (optional)
- Editing software

**Camera settings**:
1/125 sec at f/14, ISO 400

**Skill level**:

**When we think of a fine-art nude image, we often picture a female figure. However, the male figure is also an interesting shape to capture, especially when lit with a torch against a black background to highlight muscle form and shape using shadows and intense lighting.**

Setting up the shot is relatively easy. For this image, a blackout blind was pulled down in an office space, with a torch placed on a desk to one side, in line with the model. If space is limited, shoot just the top half of the body; if you have more space and a longer backdrop, shoot the whole figure. To keep your model in the correct position, put a reflector case on the floor to mark the spot and ensure his body stays within the boundaries of the backdrop.

Look at other photographers' work to see how they light and pose their models. You could also refer to paintings, statues and sculpture to get some great ideas.

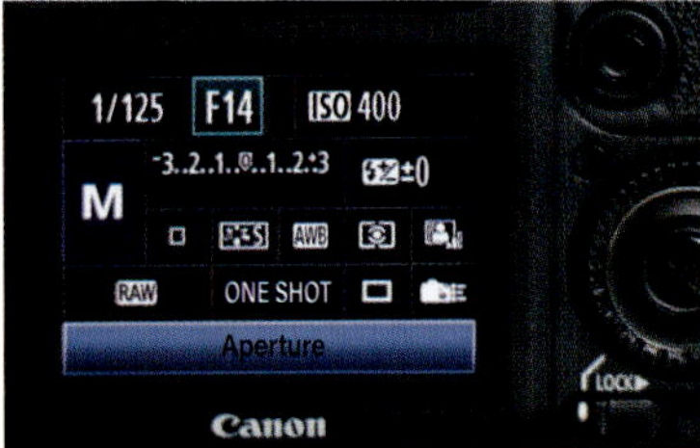


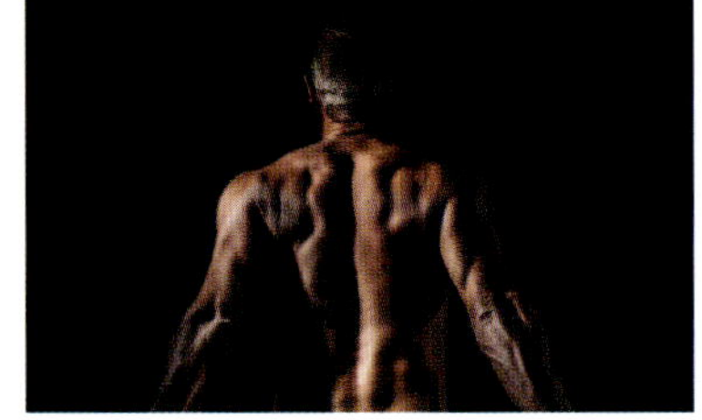

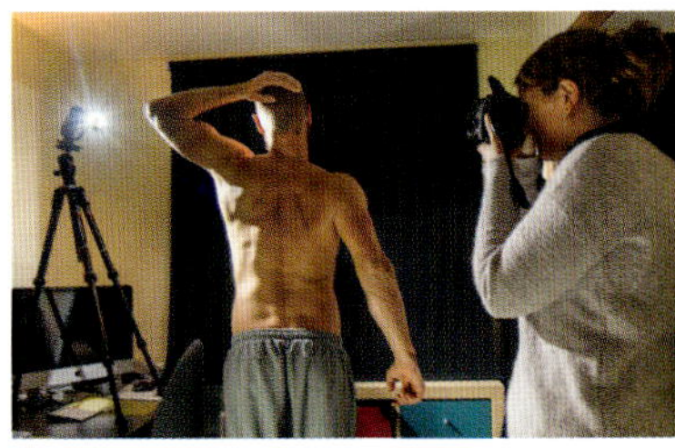

**1 Camera settings**
When you want to use flash, it's easiest to set your camera to manual mode. You then need to sync your shutter speed setting to the flashlight. Start with your flash firing at 1/8 power and balance the flash power and aperture setting when you set up your shot.

**2 Poses**
Ask your model to tense their muscles and create shapes. Although the male figure isn't as curvaceous as a female one, you can still capture curves and lines by getting them to exaggerate their pose. Get them to arch their back and create angles with their arms, like a Greek statue. Before you start, look around for inspiration and possible poses, so you know what you're after.

**3 Background and light**
A quick and easy solution for a black background is to use a blind. If you don't have one of these, hang a sheet, a paper roll or a blanket behind your model. You won't be lighting your background, so if it is dark, it will appear black in your shot. You don't want your flash to hit the background at all – only your model – so angle the flash head to the side and slightly behind your model, facing forwards.

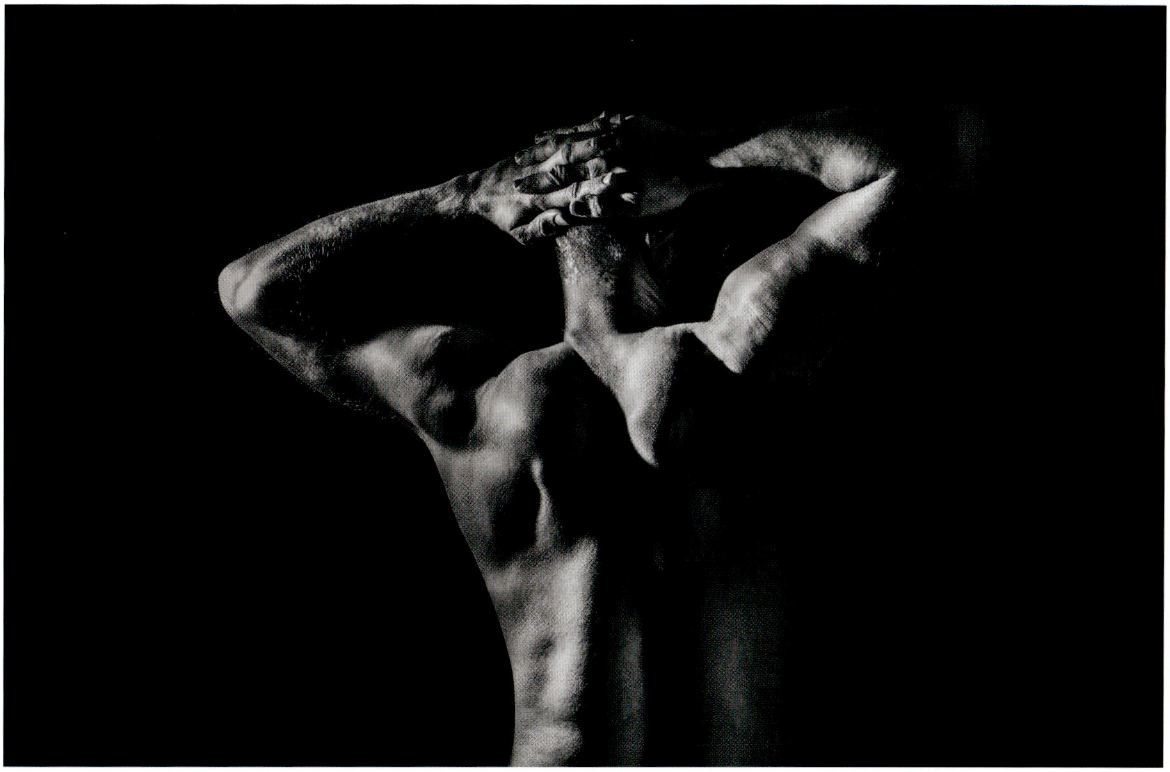

**4** **Editing tips** At the editing stage, there are a few things that you can do to boost tone and contrast. In Camera Raw, push the Clarity setting all the way up to increase the midtone contrast. Boost contrast and reduce highlights if necessary. In Photoshop, use the Dodge (set to Highlights) and Burn (set to Shadows) tools to fine-tune the overall effect, then smooth any wrinkles using the Spot Healing Brush. Finally, use a Curves Adjustment Layer to tweak the overall contrast and look.

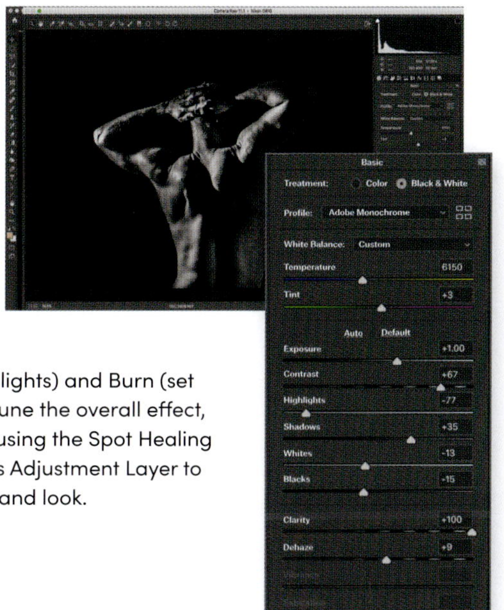


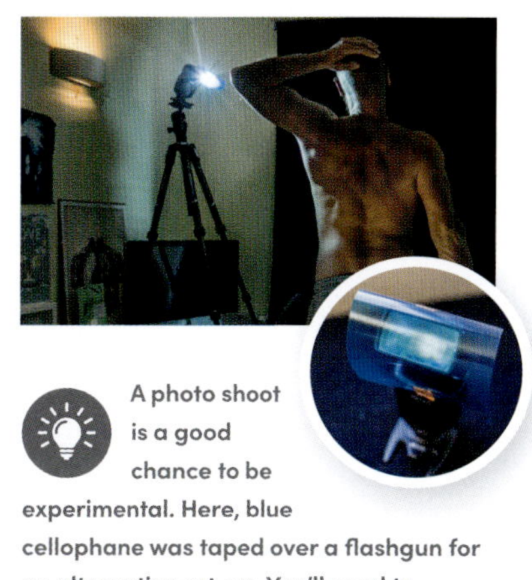

A photo shoot is a good chance to be experimental. Here, blue cellophane was taped over a flashgun for an alternative set-up. You'll need to increase the flash power from your original setting if you want to try this.

# ADD SMOKE TO A FASHION SHOOT

**THE IDEA**
**Use smoke grenades to create a vibrant scene.**

**Time required**: 1-2 hours

**Kit needed**:

- DSLR or mirrorless camera
- 24-70mm lens
- Off-camera flash
- Smoke grenades

**Camera settings**:
1/200 sec at f/11, ISO 100

**Skill level**:

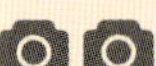   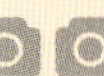

**Smoke can elevate the look of the image to an incredible extent, but white smoke is reflective and bounces the light around, sometimes leading to an overexposed image. Coloured smoke, however, presents no such problems.**

Smoke grenades are powerful tools and must be handled with extreme caution. Always read and follow the manufacturer's instructions, and ensure you are in compliance with local laws and regulations when using smoke grenades. Maintain a safe distance from flammable materials and ensure proper dispoal.
Smoke is a bit of a wild beast and, depending on the weather on the day, can be almost uncontrollable. If you use white smoke and are working fast before the smoke evaporates, you can be in such a rush to capture the moment that when you finally look down at your camera, all your images are extremely bright. Coloured smoke is darker, so your overall image exposure is more consistent.

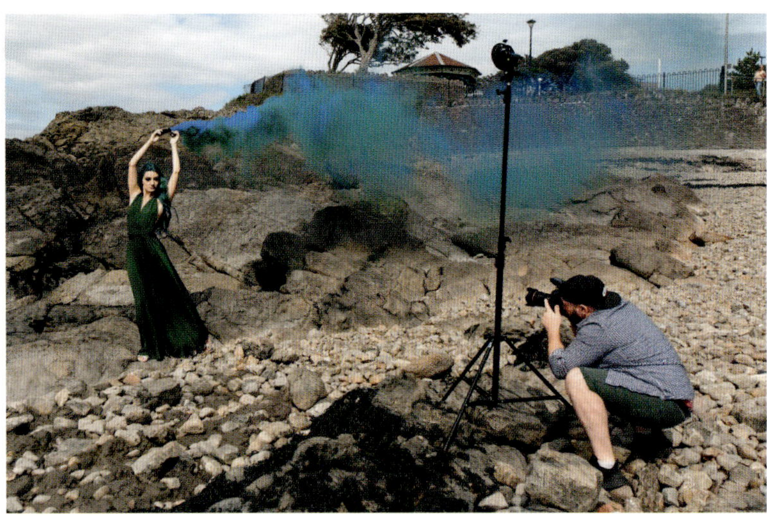

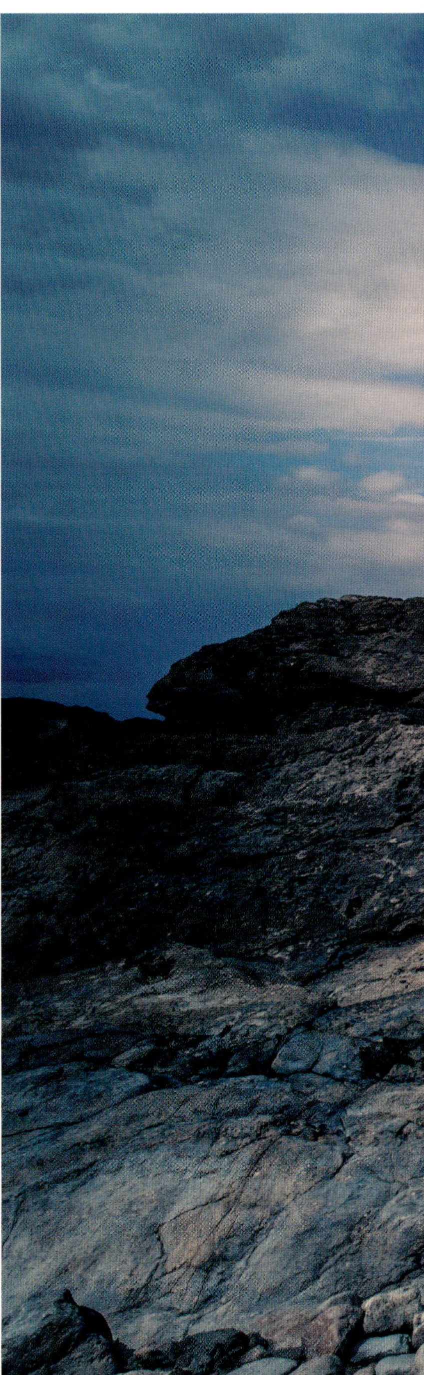

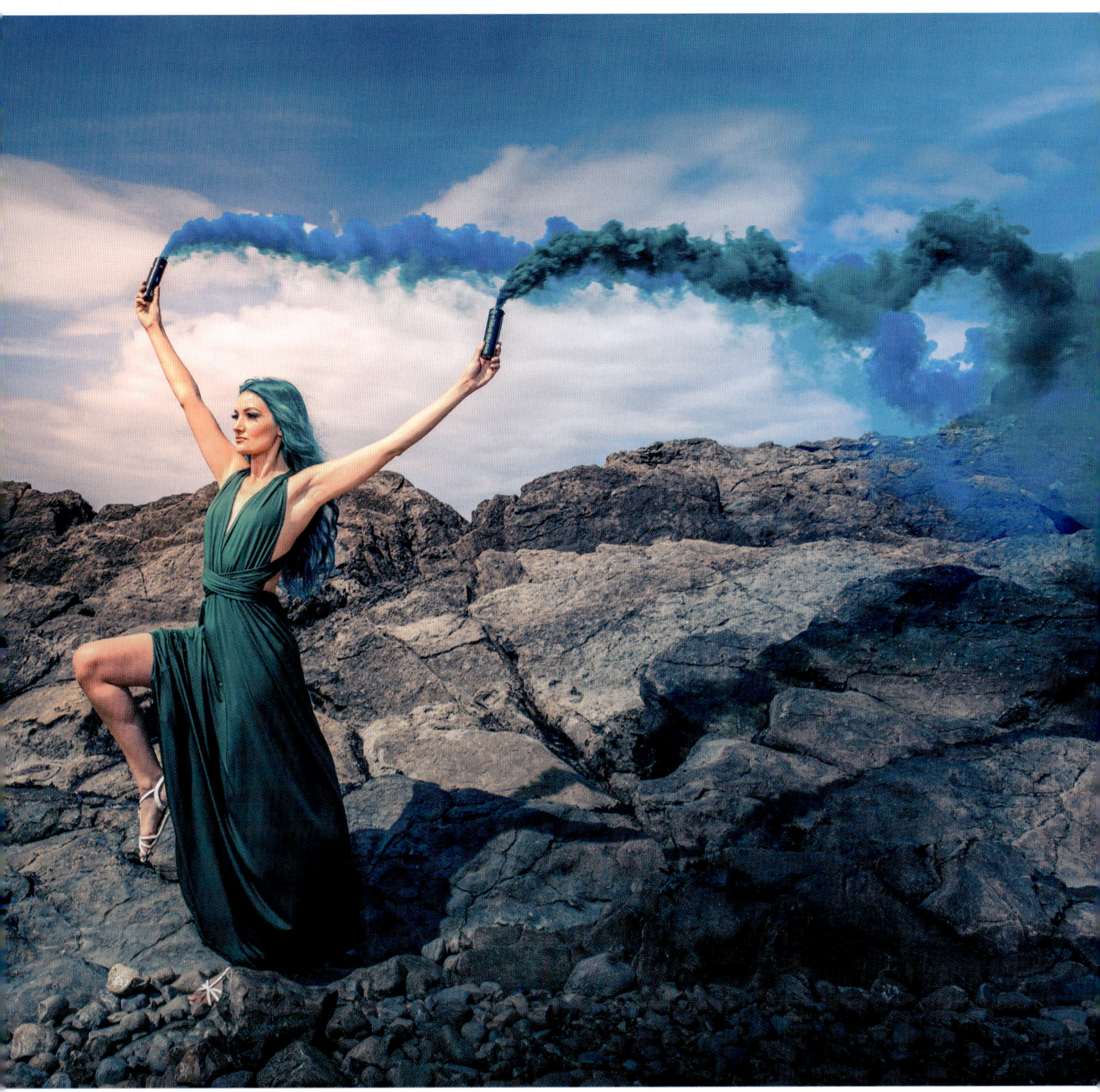

**1** **Find your background**

Give yourself different options. For this shot, the photographer could have shot directly out towards the sea for a clean sky backdrop. Alternatively, they could have used the more textured background of the rocks to add another layer. Take a quick test shot with your model to see how things are looking.

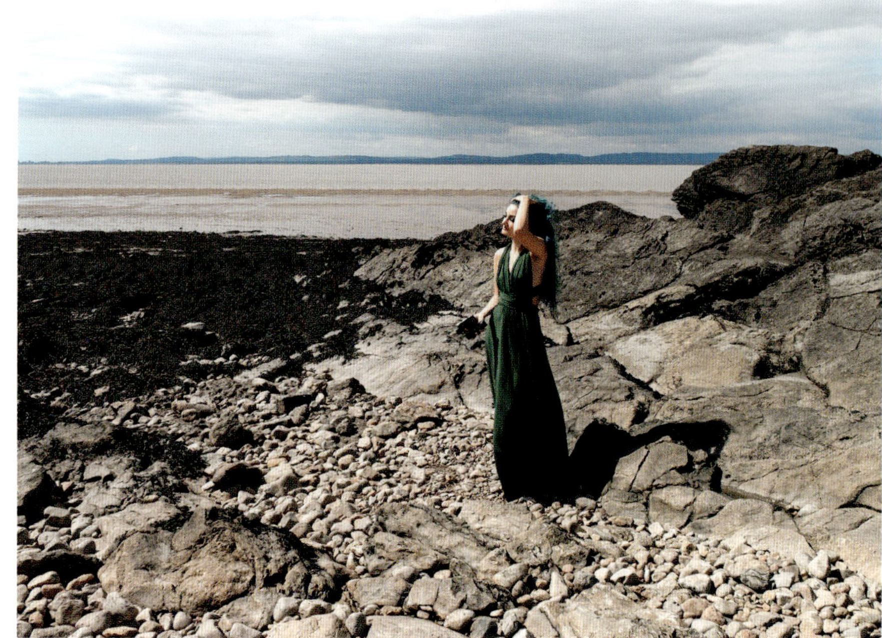

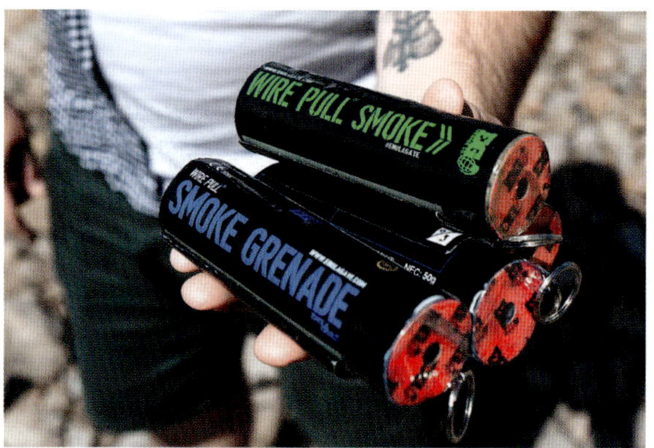


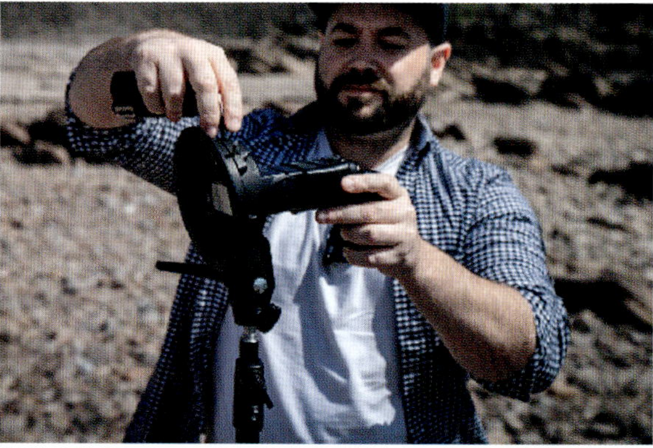

**2** **No smoking please**

If you're at all concerned about using smoke grenades in a certain area, you should pause and re-evaluate. They can get hot, so make sure you have some water nearby to extinguish any accidental flames. A standard smoke grenade will give you around 90 seconds of smoke.

**3** **Add off-camera flash**

If you're shooting in harsh sun, with cloud cover moving in and out, you could probably use 100% natural light, but using an off-camera flash will help you to lift the exposure on your model. You can easily switch it off during the shoot if you need to.

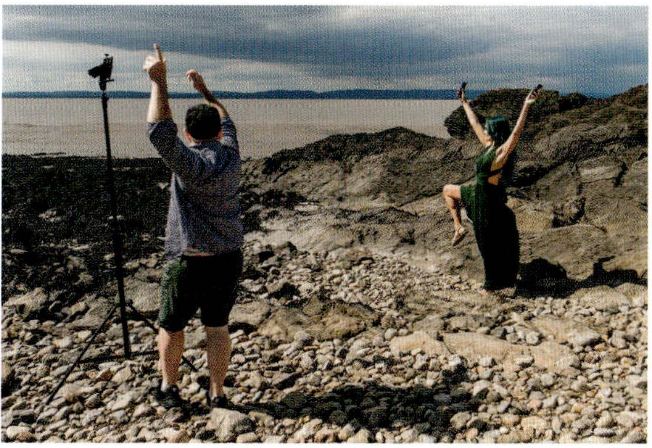

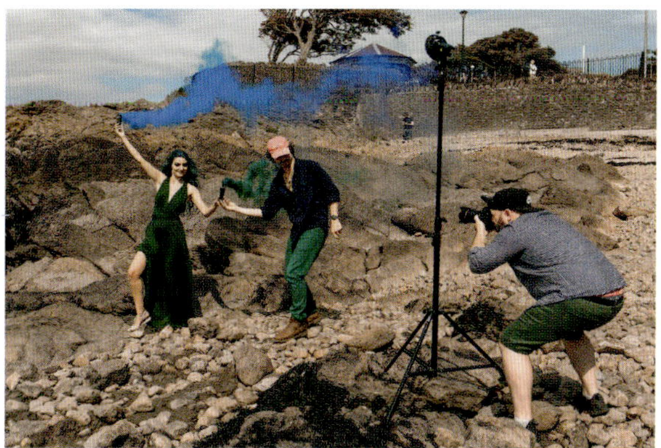

**4 Rehearse before you shoot**
This is possibly the most important part of a shoot using smoke grenades. Establish the frame's edge with your model, so they don't walk out of shot, and practise the movement together. Ninety seconds may seem like a long time, but once you start, it's over all too quickly.

**5 Have a helping hand**
It's not always possible but whenever you can, try to have an extra pair of hands available, as this will enable you to get the smoke grenades open much faster, before they quickly jump out of shot.

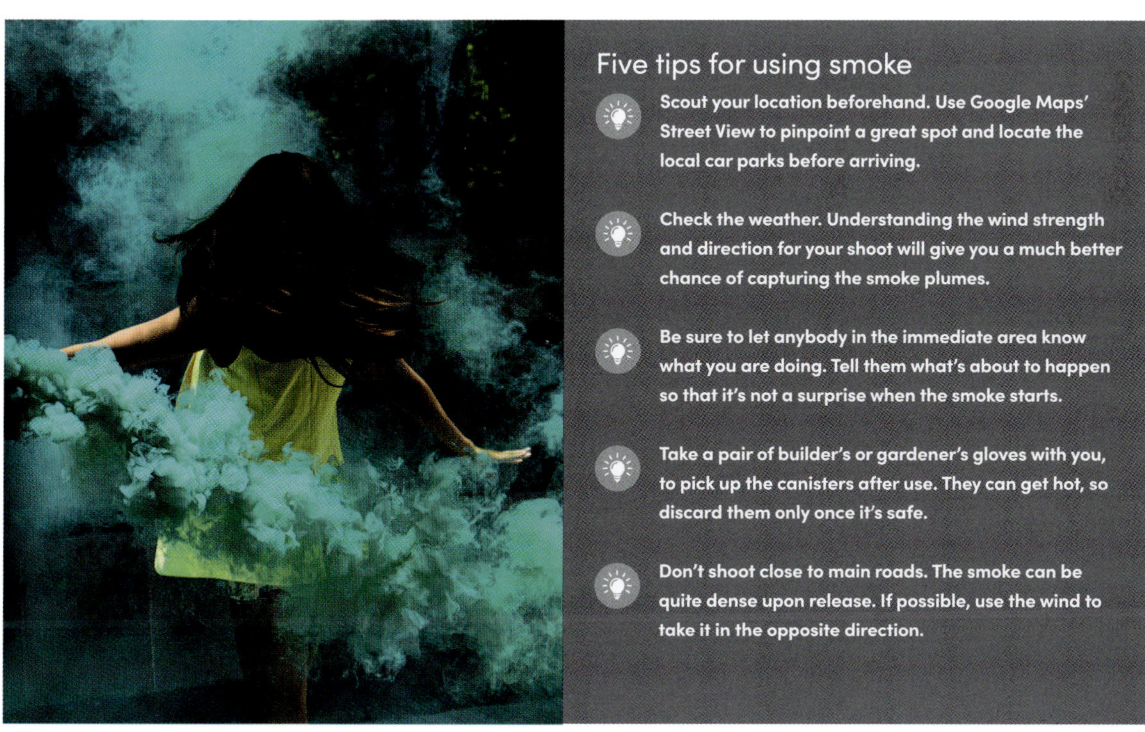

## Five tips for using smoke

- **Scout your location beforehand. Use Google Maps' Street View to pinpoint a great spot and locate the local car parks before arriving.**
- **Check the weather. Understanding the wind strength and direction for your shoot will give you a much better chance of capturing the smoke plumes.**
- **Be sure to let anybody in the immediate area know what you are doing. Tell them what's about to happen so that it's not a surprise when the smoke starts.**
- **Take a pair of builder's or gardener's gloves with you, to pick up the canisters after use. They can get hot, so discard them only once it's safe.**
- **Don't shoot close to main roads. The smoke can be quite dense upon release. If possible, use the wind to take it in the opposite direction.**

# TRY ANIMAL PORTRAITURE

**THE IDEA**
**Take a horse portrait with bags of character.**

**Time required**: 1-2 hours

**Kit needed**:
- DSLR or mirrorless camera
- 50mm lens
- Off-camera flash

**Camera settings**:
1/200 sec at f/2.8, ISO 400

**Skill level**:

**Like photographing any animal, taking pictures of horses certainly comes with its challenges. If you want to try this for yourself, you will need a pair of helping hands – and a bit of patience too, as the horse might not always look or perform as you want it.**

The horse in this photo shoot was called Rocky, and his owner was on hand to help position him, and to generally keep him happy with strokes and treats.

When it comes to finding the ideal location, look no further than the stables. By bringing the horse out into the doorway and using natural light, you can get a great result. Set your exposure to read from the horse – as there is less light in the background, it will darken down anyway.

A mixture of natural light and flash was used for this shoot. Before using flash, though, it's a really good idea to check with the owner that the horse won't be scared by the light. Their safety and well-being should come before anything else. It helps to spend a bit of time at the beginning bonding with the horse, showing it your camera and making it comfortable in your presence before you start shooting.

**1 Camera settings**
If you're using flash, you'll need to sync your shutter speed with the flashlight. This means you'll need to select a shutter speed of 1/200 sec or slower. You can then balance your ISO, aperture and flash setting with the ambient light. Here, the flashgun was placed slightly to the side and behind Rocky for a dramatic result.

**2 Flash assist**
If you are going to shoot using flash, it can help to get an assistant to hold the flashgun rather than placing it on a stand. That way you don't need to worry about the horse knocking it over as it moves around. Being flexible and telling your assistant where to fire the flash from is crucial. Make sure the sensor from your flashgun is in line with your camera so it will fire.

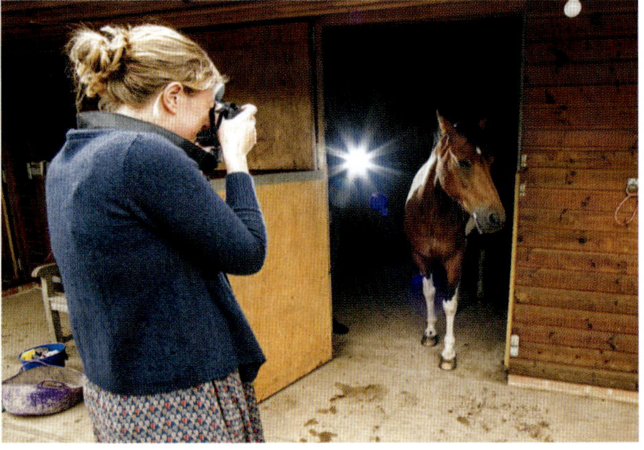

**3 Right pose**
Timing is everything. Be prepared to keep shooting, as you're unlikely to get it right first time. A horse indicates happiness by pointing its ears forward, so aim to capture this. You'll also need to direct the owner to keep repositioning the horse into the light, as it won't stay still for long.

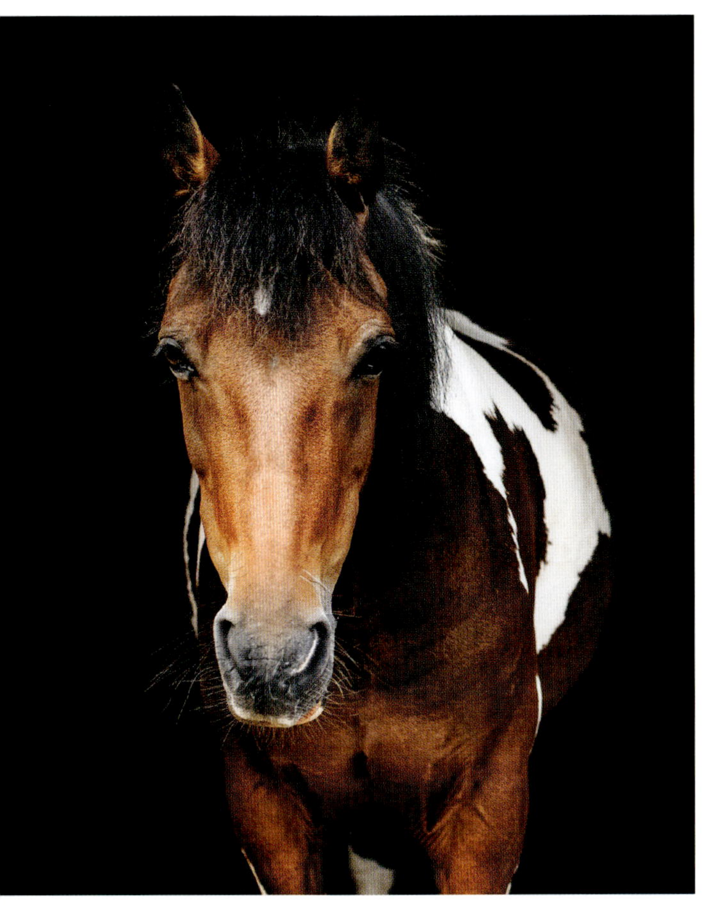

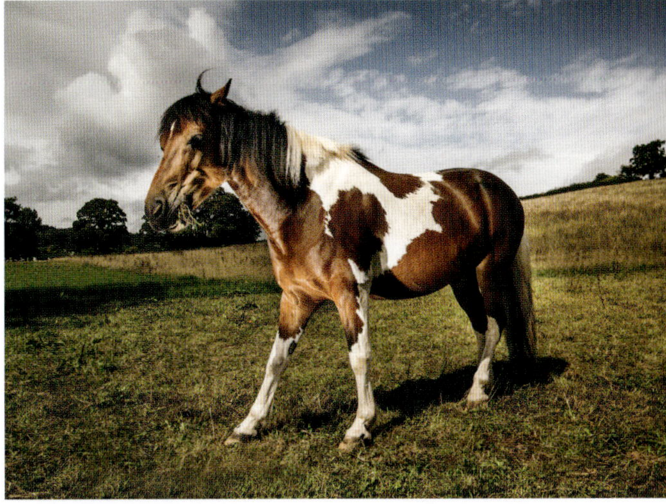

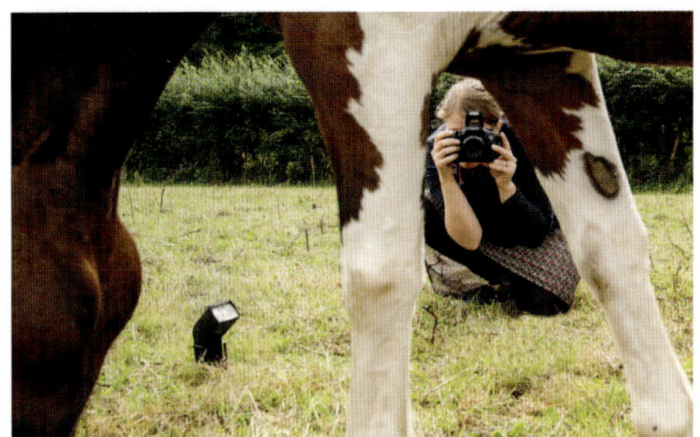

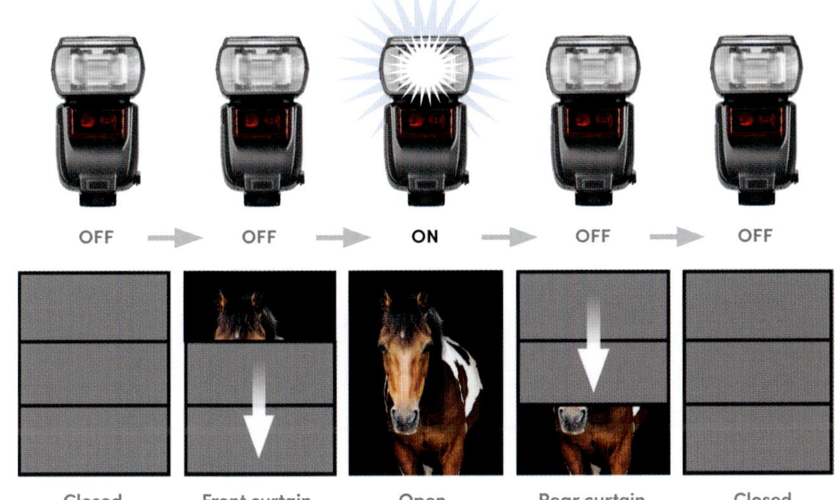


When using flash on a shoot, you should always aim to use a shutter speed of 1/200 sec or slower, so that the light from the flash has time to reach the sensor on the camera before it closes. DSLRs use a focal-plane shutter system, with a front and rear curtain. When you press the shutter button, the front opens first, followed by the rear. If the shutter speed is too fast, the flash will only reach some of the sensor, and you will have a black bar across your image.

# USE COLOURED LIGHTING

**THE IDEA**

**Mix opposing coloured lighting effects for portrait and fashion shoots with punch.**

**Time required**: 2 hours

**Kit needed**:

- DSLR or mirrorless camera
- 50mm or 85mm lens
- Off-camera flash
- Gel diffusers or coloured LED light panels

**Camera settings**:
1/1000 sec at f/1.2, ISO 400

**Skill level**:

  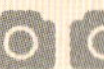

**Colour is one of the main creative tools in photography, and coloured lighting allows you to experiment with colours in a variety of different ways. Whether you use tried-and-trusted techniques like placing coloured gel diffusers over flashguns, or LED light panels that offer millions of built-in colours at your fingertips, the corrective colour techniques covered here will help you produce highly creative environmental scenes or editorial-style fashion and portrait shots that pack a punch.**

A great way to get started is to use a pair of complementary colours. Blue and orange is a popular combination, and can be seen in the teal-and-orange film look that's popular in so many Hollywood movies.

You don't have to stick to only complementary colours, though – let your imagination run wild and trust your intuition. As colour harmonies look pleasing to our eyes, you can rely on your intuition to instinctively pick colours that go well together.

If you want to know more about how colours work together, then research analogous, complementary, split complementary, triadic and tetradic harmonies.

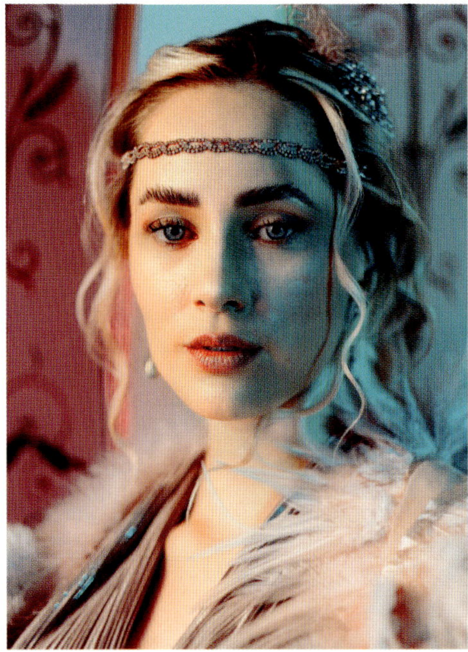

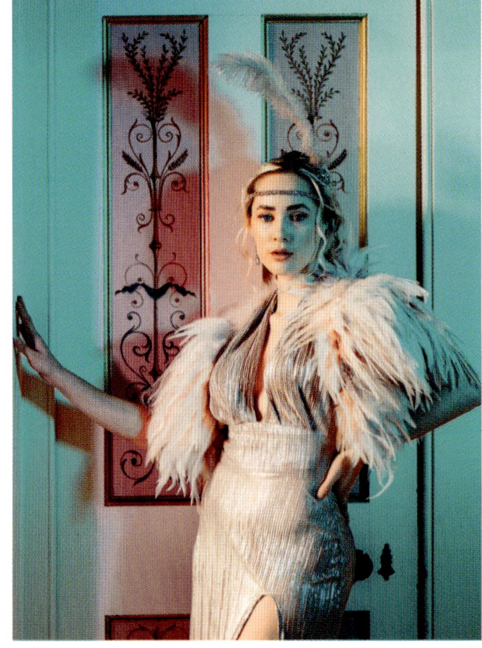

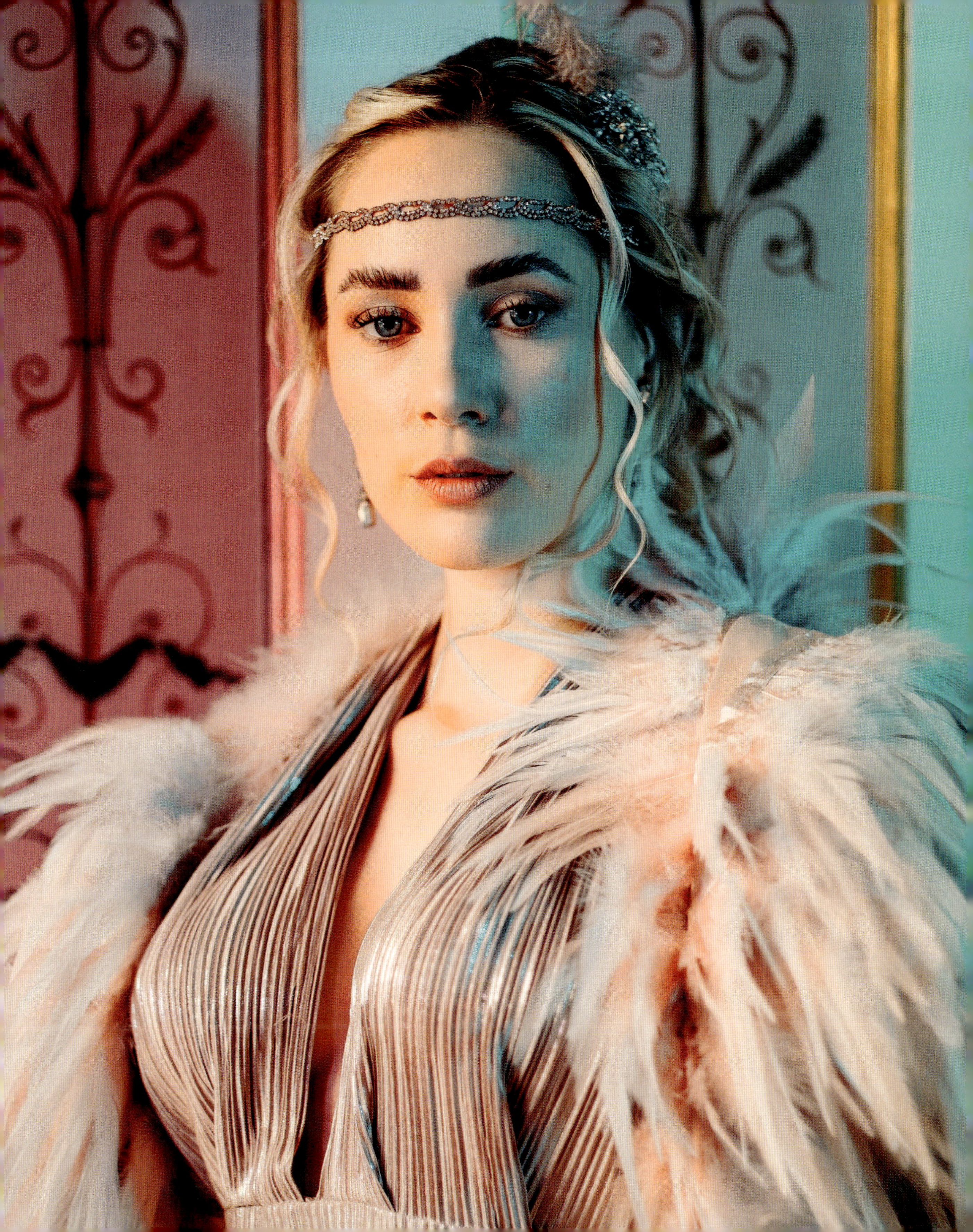

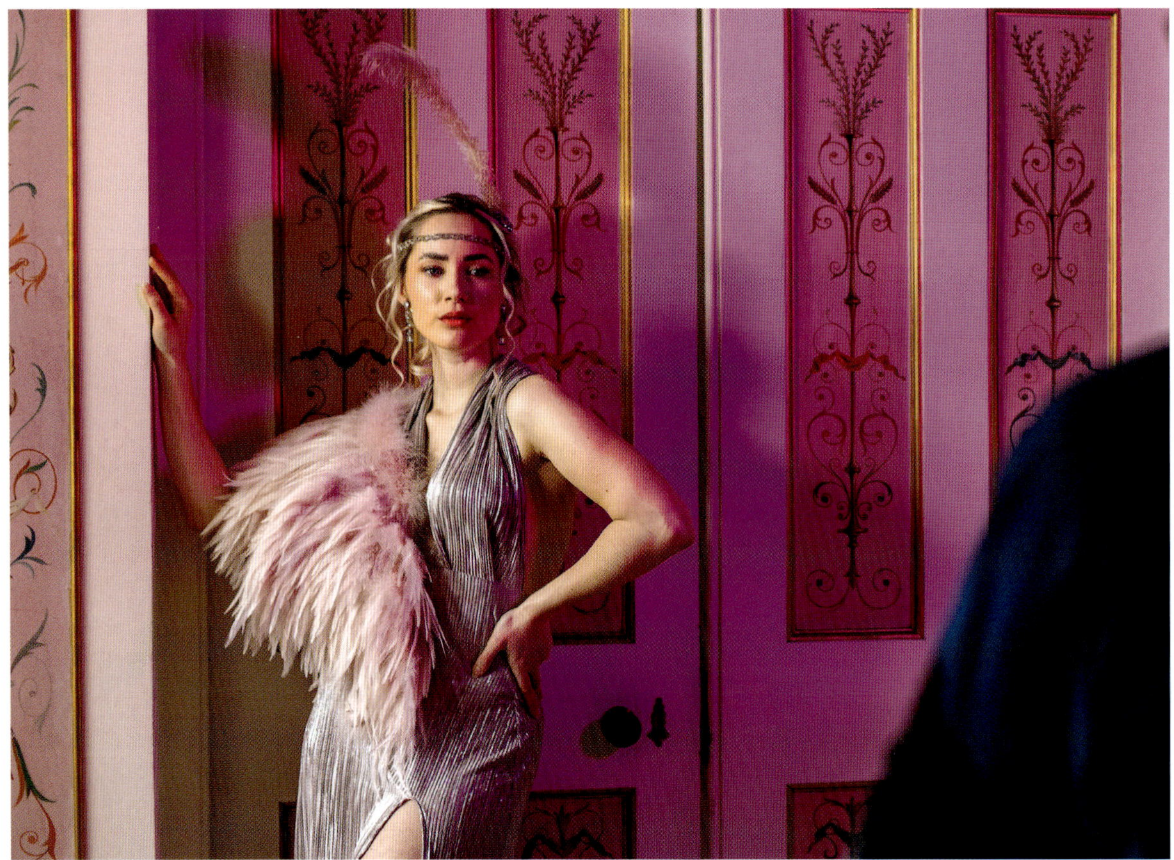

**1 Shoot differently**
Using coloured LED lights, or gel diffusers over a light source, means that you'll need to shoot in a different way. Flash lighting is powerful even when turned right down. You're likely to use a sync speed of around 1/160–1/200 sec, which lets plenty of light in, and continuous lighting allows you to open your aperture for a much shallower depth of field.

**2 Get set to experiment**
The position of your lighting should start with a conventional set-up, with the first ('key') light off to the side, around 150cm from the subject, followed by another ('fill') light in a similar position on the opposite side. Experiment with the light power by reducing it and moving it closer to your subject. Alternatively, bring it further to the front to create a different light fall-off effect on the model's face.

**3 Sense the mood**
Each colour will have a subconscious mood allied to it. Blues can feel cool and modern, while red can feel aggressive and linked to danger. Green and yellow feel calm and relaxed. The combination of colours you choose is just as important as the settings you select on your camera. Most importantly, this can't be reversed during editing.

## Lighting the scene

**When setting up lights, position them at head height or lower, as this makes the whole process easier and safer. Some lights feature built-in colours, but you can also add colour effects by placing plastic sheeted gels over your light sources.**

**First, choose your primary colour. This is a good point to view your model in the light before mixing in the other colour. Sometimes, the light you have selected won't mix well with your background, so pause and review.**

**Now, take your second light and put both lights in roughly the correct height and position – approximately 45 degrees to the side, and above, the subject.**

**Finally, set your colour (or gel) to something you feel will work well with your original colour. For inspiration, refer to the colour wheel and observe how opposites attract.**

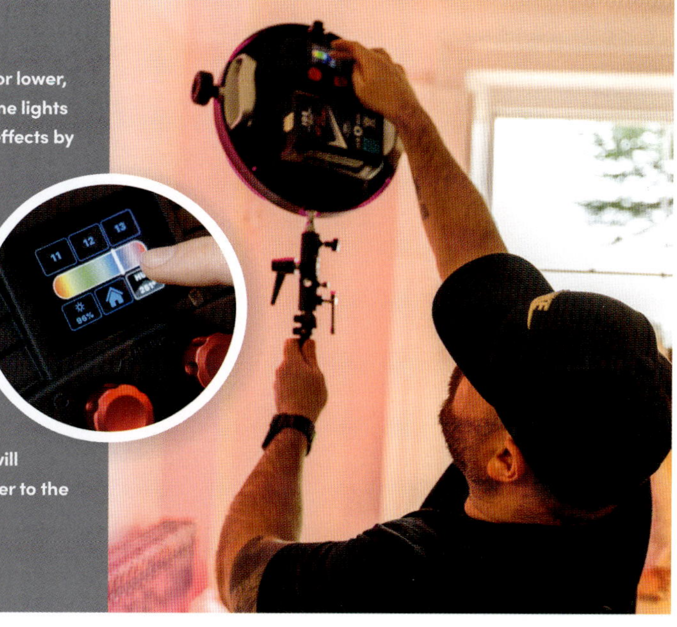

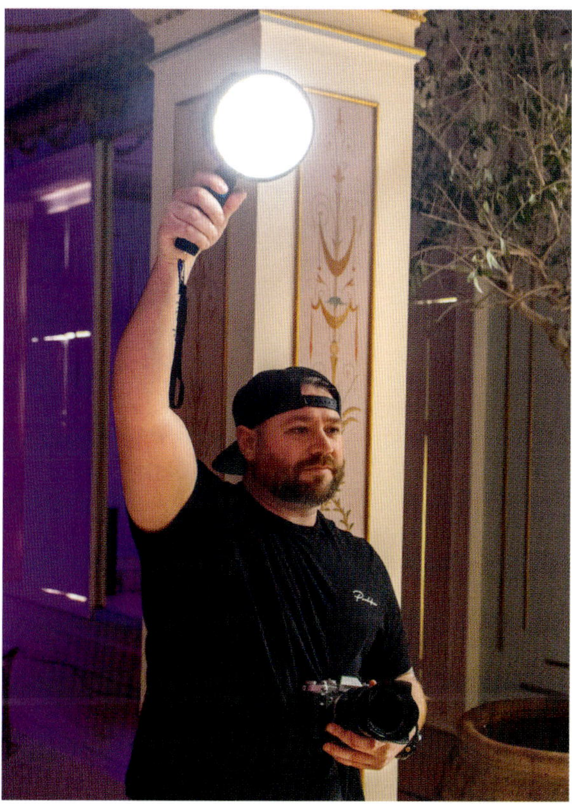

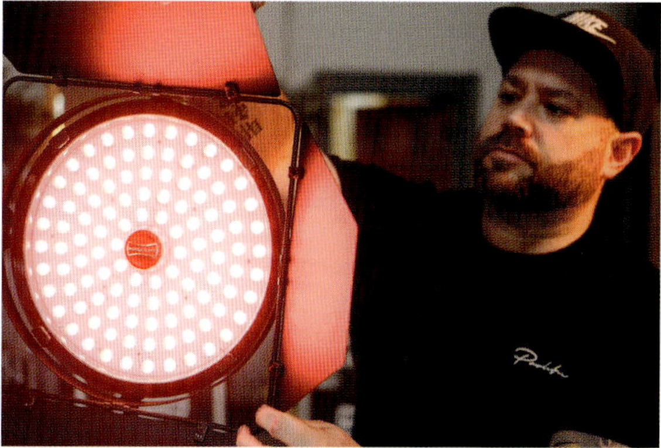

When shooting in more creative ways, you might get carried away with the thousands of colour combinations that are available to you. Sometimes, an image can become dominated by one colour, and more so your model's skin. If you have one available, you could use a smaller third light with a natural white tone of around 5,600K to retain a more natural look. Keep your white balance to 5,600K to match, then experiment by moving this third 'natural' light at the right distance so that it doesn't completely remove the creative combinations you've created.

# BREAK OUT A RING LIGHT

**THE IDEA**
**Shoot portraits with one simple LED light.**

**Time required**: 1-2 hours

**Kit needed**:

- DSLR or mirrorless camera
- 50mm or 85mm lens
- LED ring light

**Camera settings**:
1/1000 sec at f/2, ISO 800

**Skill level**:

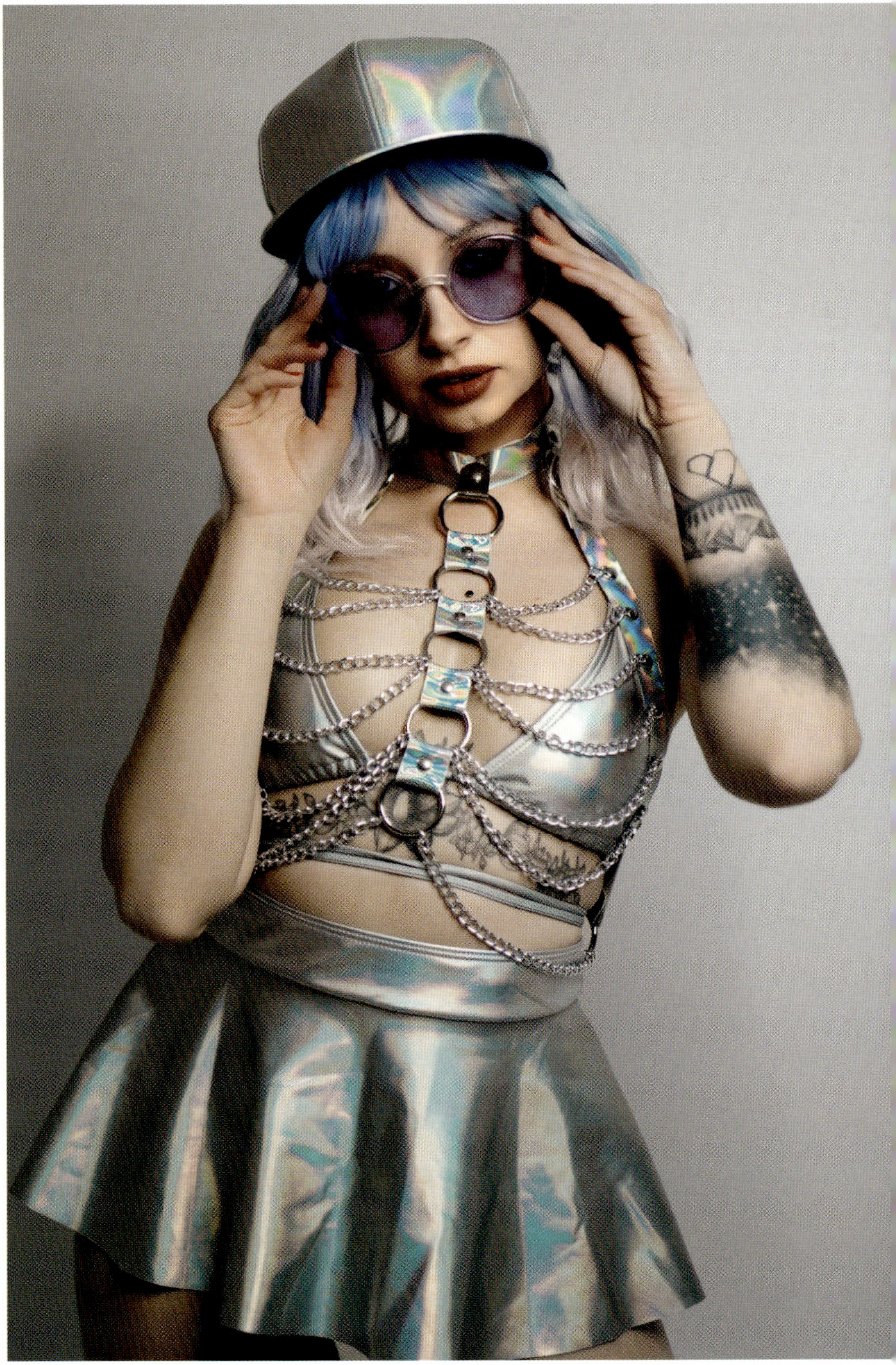

**Portraiture is a photographic genre that is easy to try but difficult to master. Ranging from natural light right through to more complicated four-light set-ups, the choices can sometimes feel overwhelming. Using a single light source, such as a ring light, can simplify a portrait shoot. Place it in front of your model's face – about 45 degrees to one side is always a good default place to start.**

Continuous LED lighting offers another advantage, as it allows you to see in real time how the light falls onto your subject. This is far easier than using a flash or strobe and having to shoot a few test images before finding the ideal shot settings.

An LED ring light eliminates shadows, resulting in simple, flattering lighting over a face, while 360 degrees of illumination helps to give skin a flawless look.

**1 Place your model in the scene**
Find a suitable place for your shoot, with a plain background that won't overpower the model.

**2 Position the ring light**
Place the ring light about 45 degrees to one side – this is always a good default position to start with.

**3 Give the light some height**
Extend the height of the light above the model's face, facing down at an angle of around 45 degrees.

**4 Turn it on and check the lighting**
Power up the ring light and check its effect on your model's face. Dim or brighten the light until you get the effect you're looking for.

**5 Shoot some images**
Take some test shots and check how they're looking on the camera's rear screen. Dial in some adjustments to the lighting power if necessary, or carry on using the current settings. As LED lights don't get hot, you can move the light much closer to your model than usual, allowing you to experiment with lighting intensity.

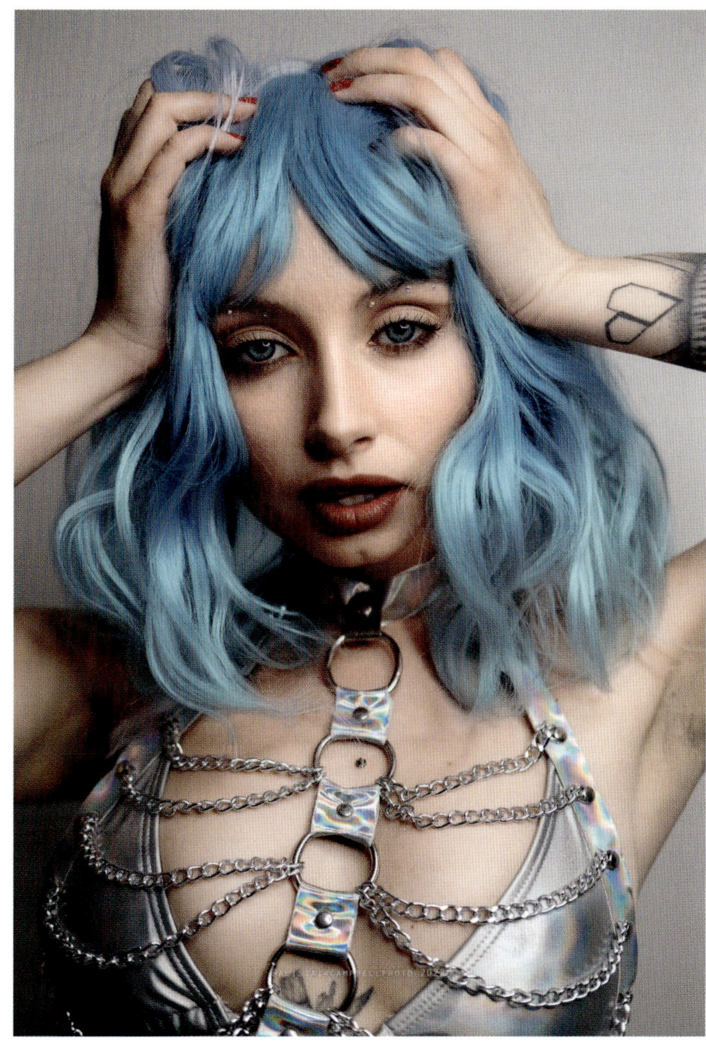

## Lighting the scene

**LED ring lights help to eliminate harsh shadows. Most are dimmable, which is helpful when wanting to change your aperture. Additionally, some lights offer adjustable colour temperature, letting you switch between cool and warm tones to match your shooting style.**

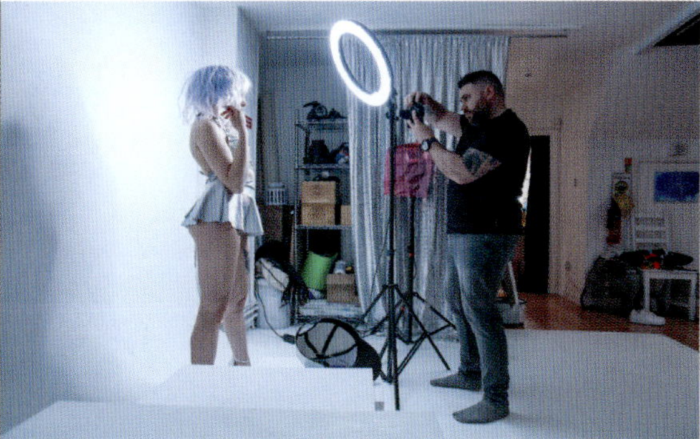

# GET A PRO LOOK WITH GELS

**THE IDEA**
**Use gels on pro LED lights to paint portraits with colour.**

**Time required**: 1-2 hours

**Kit needed**:
- DSLR or mirrorless camera
- 50mm or 85mm lens
- LED lighting
- Lighting gels

**Camera settings**:
1/200 sec at f/1.2, ISO 100

**Skill level**:

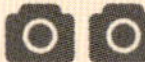  

**Once upon a time, the idea of using LED lights in a professional environment would have been ridiculous. But the technology has now come so far that LEDs aren't just a viable option – they're often the better one.**

Lights such as the Rotolight Neo 3 and Aeos 3 Pro pack serious power, and some even feature built-in gels. This four-light set-up would have been far more difficult with flash but, with the what-you-see-is-what-you-get nature of LEDs and mirrorless cameras, this shot was a breeze to achieve.

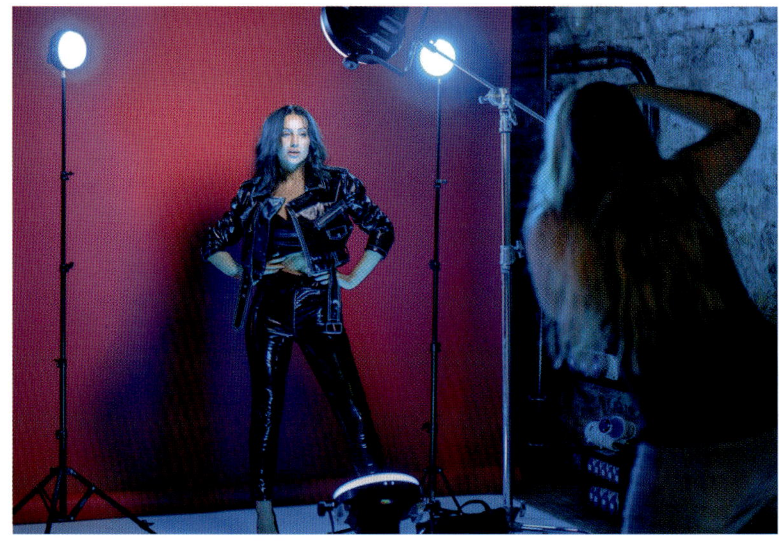

**1 Set up your lighting**
The key light here is an Aeos 3 Pro, which acts like a beauty dish, sculpting the model's cheekbones. Another Aeos with a cyan gel was used as an uplight to fill the shadows with colour, and a pair of Neo 3 Pro lights provided hair and accent light.

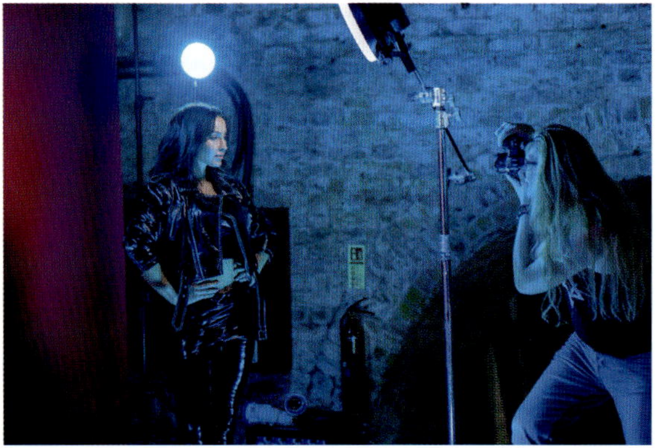

**2 Choose the right lens**
While 50mm is often cited as a perfect portrait focal length, it should only be used for torso or three-quarter shots – used too close, it will distort facial features. For tighter headshots, use an 85mm focal length to flatter the features.

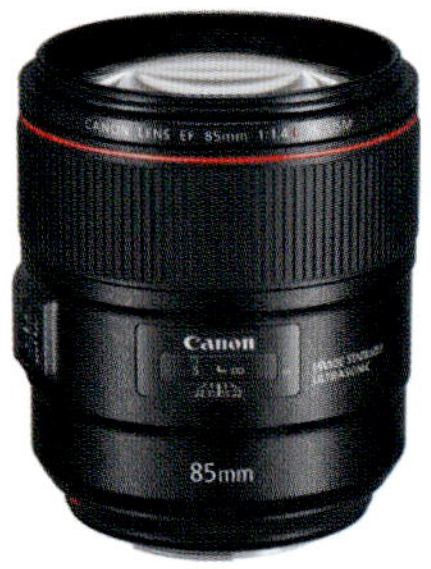

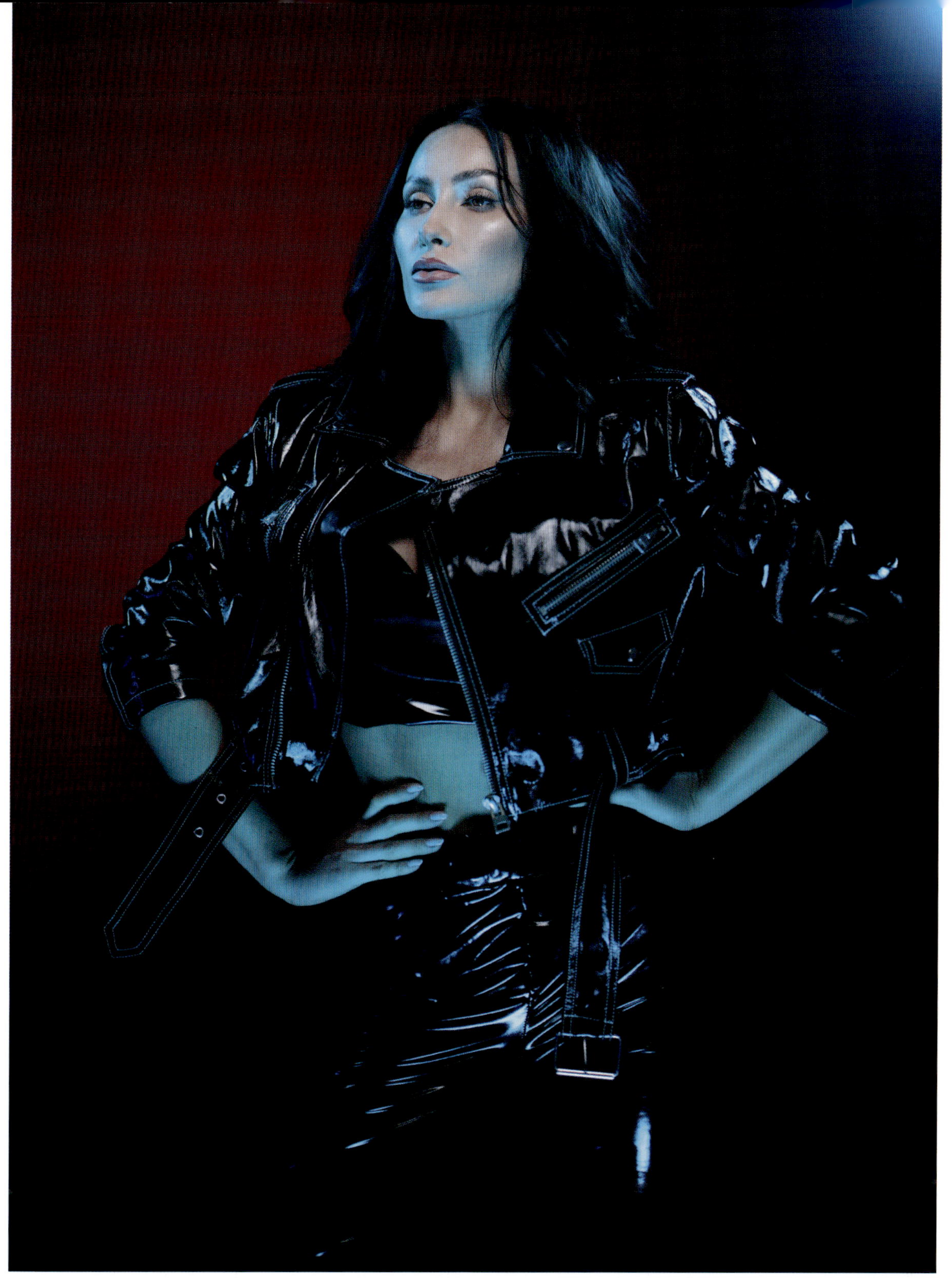

# MASTER MIXED LIGHTING SET-UPS

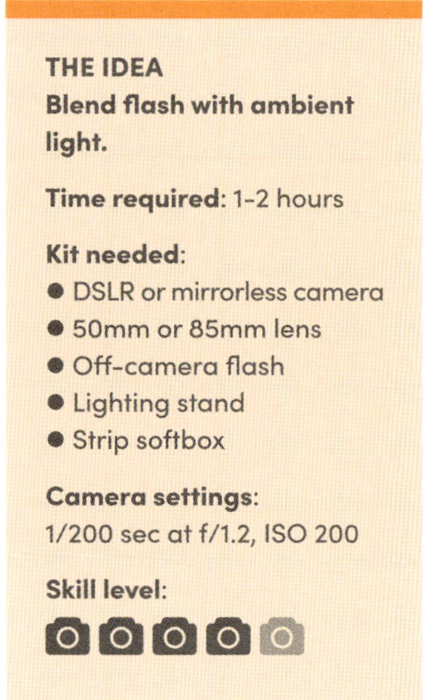

**THE IDEA**
**Blend flash with ambient light.**

**Time required:** 1-2 hours

**Kit needed:**
- DSLR or mirrorless camera
- 50mm or 85mm lens
- Off-camera flash
- Lighting stand
- Strip softbox

**Camera settings:**
1/200 sec at f/1.2, ISO 200

**Skill level:**

**Portraits aren't always just about your subject. Sometimes, their surroundings are just as interesting, and you then have the challenge of balancing the lighting so that you capture both. The subject of this portrait, Alex, was photographed in a bar, which was a maze of rooms, all creatively lit with a soft ambience that gave the place its character.**

Ambient lighting in a bar is designed to illuminate the surroundings, not the guests, so additional lighting was needed to pick Alex out so that he wasn't lost in the shadows. The trick was to light him well enough so that he was clearly the subject of the picture, but without overpowering the ambient lighting.

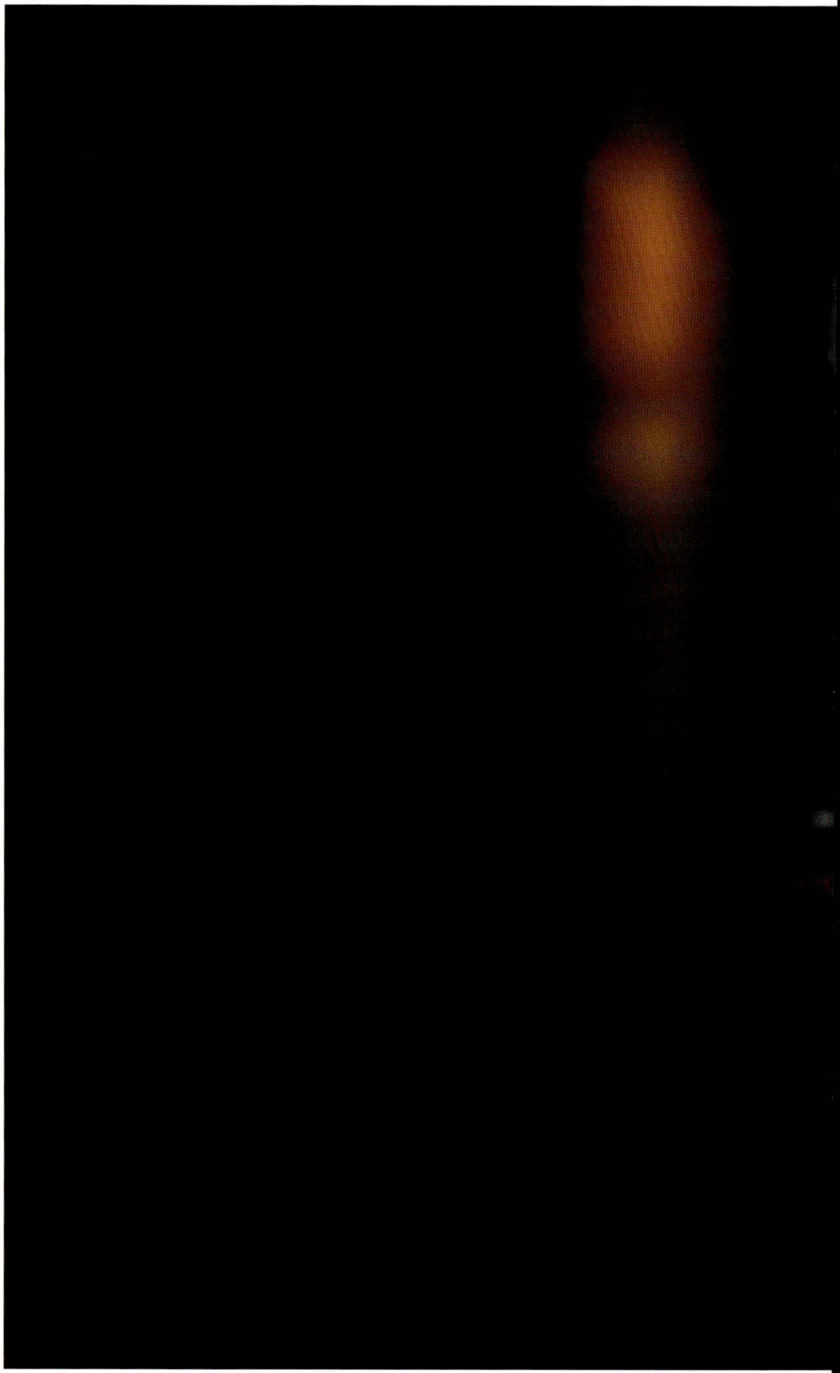

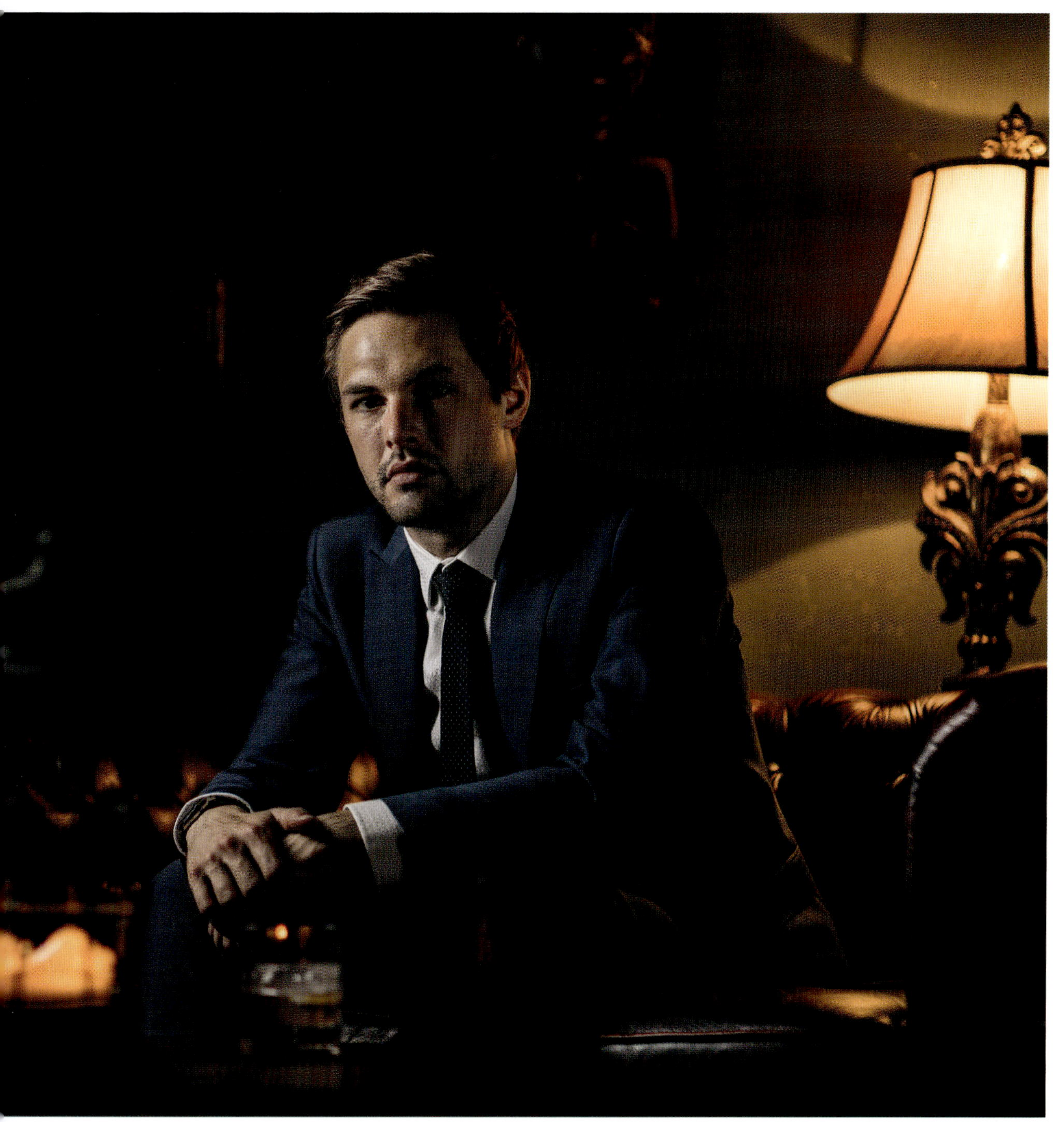

This was all achieved with a single flashgun mounted on a lighting stand, and a silver reflector on the opposite side to bounce some light back into the shadows. Having the flash on a stand means you can change its angle, its distance and the way the light spills onto the surroundings.

There are no hard and fast rules for this kind of location flash photography. Mostly, it's about using your photographer's eye – see what works and what doesn't, and gradually build towards your finished picture by experimenting.

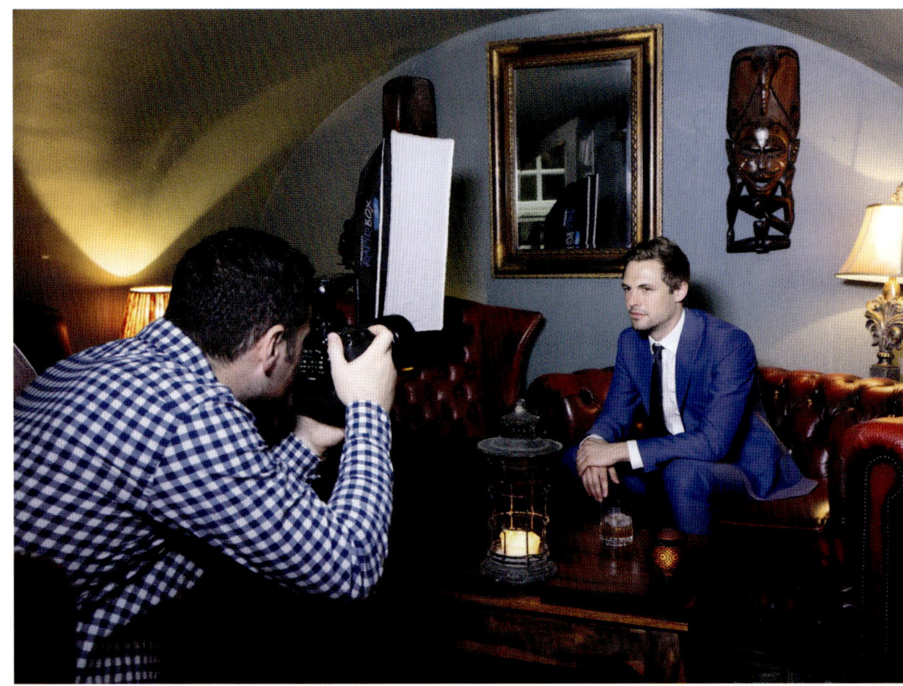

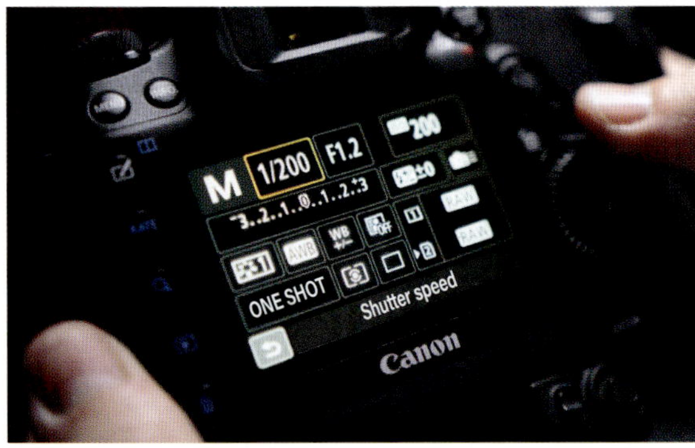


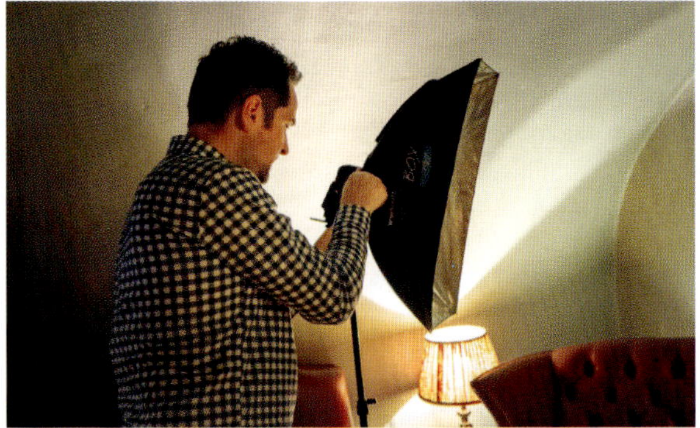

**1 Exposure settings**
The key to balancing flash with ambient light is knowing that the flash strength is governed by aperture, not shutter speed. Choose the aperture you want to shoot at, then set the flash power to provide the right amount of light for that aperture setting. You can then adjust the shutter speed to achieve the right exposure.

**2 Off-camera flash**
If you attach your flashgun to a lighting stand, you can move it around and illuminate your subject from different angles. You'll also need some kind of lighting modifier to restrict the angle of coverage and control any light spill.

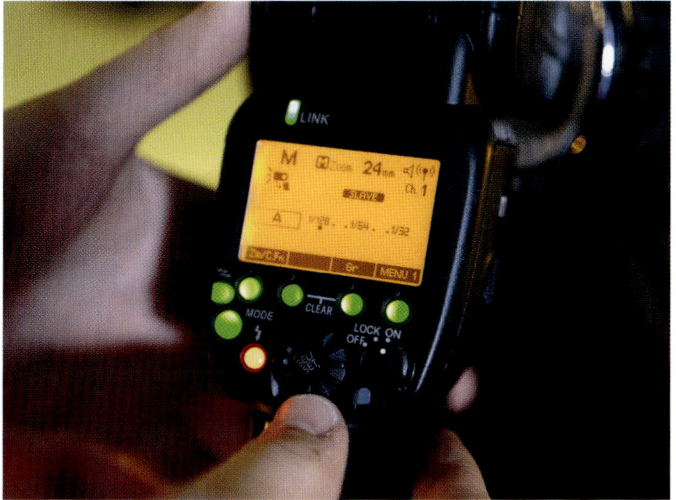


**3 Flash control**

For off-camera flash, you'll need a wireless flash controller such as Yongnuo's 600EX-RT with YN-E3-RT wireless trigger. Don't bother with TTL flash modes – in situations like these, it's simpler to set the flash power manually using trial and error.

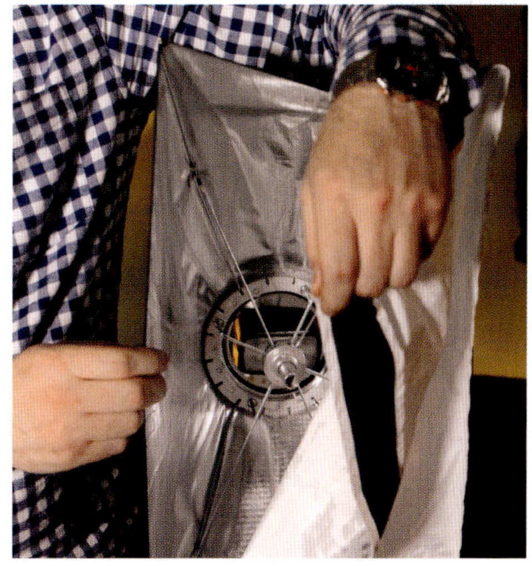

**4 Flash modifiers**

A bare flash head will be no good in these situations, as you won't be able to stop light spilling on to the background. It will also produce a very harsh light. Instead, use a strip softbox. The vertical shape is ideal for portraits, and the narrow reflector will make it much easier to control light spill and illuminate the areas you want.

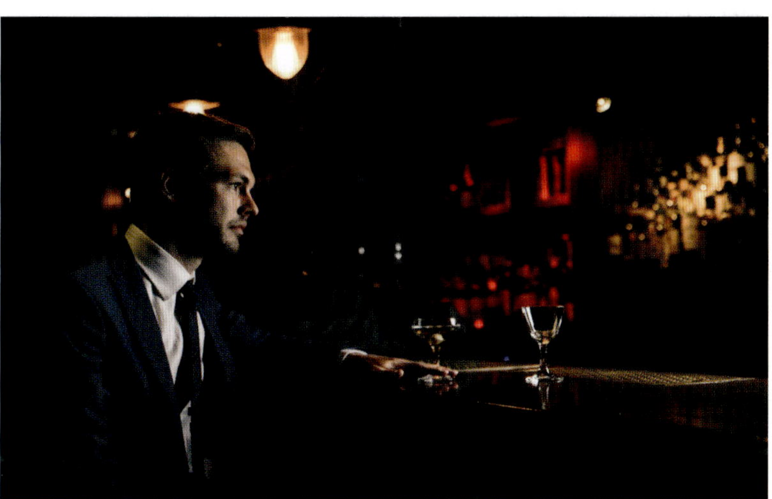

**5 Look for props**

For this second shot, Alex was positioned on a bar stool, with the bar subtly defocused in the background and the flash positioned just off-camera to the right. When you're photographing subjects in their surroundings, you can often find props to connect them. Here, two attractively shaped glasses were used to pick up the lights and add some 'sparkle' to the scene. It's worth spending some time looking at the background, the way the light is falling on it, and the arrangement of props and objects around your subject. Details really do count.

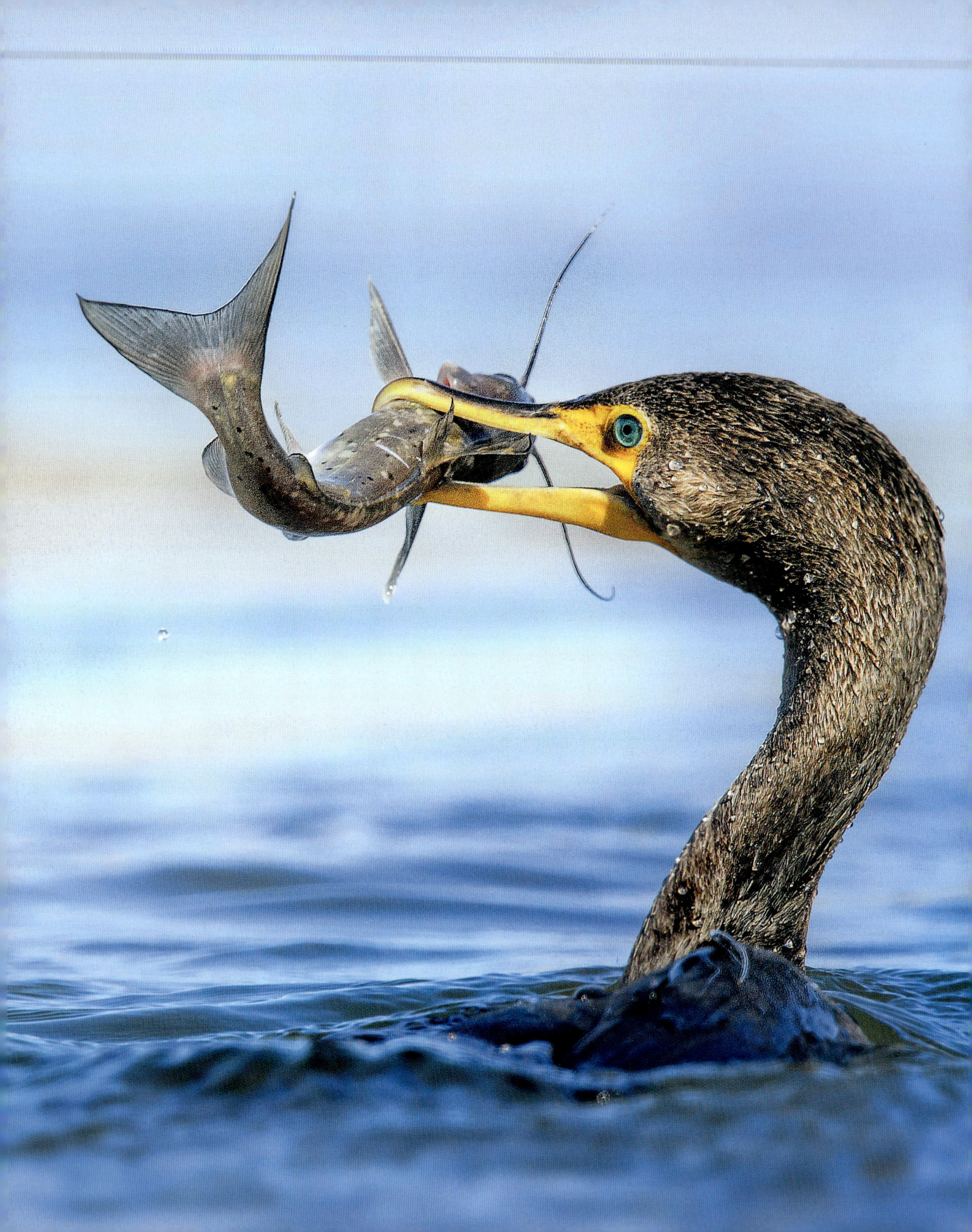

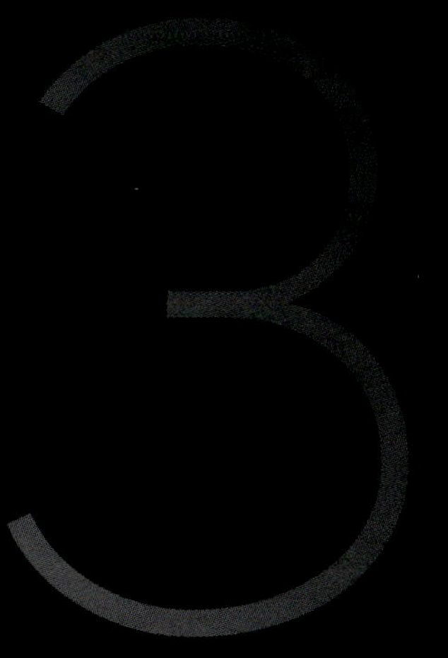

# WILDLIFE AND MACRO IDEAS

**From birds to bugs and much more... learn how to capture creatures in local open spaces or further afield**

# TRY A SIMPLE MACRO SHOT

**THE IDEA**
**Head out with a macro lens to capture the quintessential scene of a bluebell wood in spring.**

**Time required**: 2 hours

**Kit needed**:
- DSLR or mirrorless camera
- Macro lens
- Editing software

**Camera settings**:
1/250 sec at f/2.8, ISO 250

**Skill level**:

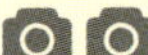  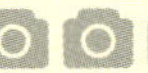

**When spring officially makes its mark, it's easy to get ahead of yourself by planning outdoor shoots, forgetting that seasonal changes can take some time to appear. The bluebell season runs roughly between mid-April and late May in the UK (depending on the weather). If spring is mild, bluebells tend to come out earlier. If you miss them, the advice here can be applied to many other wildflowers found on the forest floor.**

One of harder parts of this project is locating a bumper crop of bluebells in the first place, so check online forums or ask a local wildlife group for recommendations. Many widlife organisations even run bluebell walks, which tend to be perfectly timed for when the woodlands are at their most blue/purple.

It's vital you check the forecast before your shoot to avoid disappointment, as rain and strong winds have the potential to ruin any picturesque vibe in an instant. Once you've found your location and arrive in the right weather and light, you'll no doubt be ready to grab your favourite macro lens and get going. Pick out different specimens and try out lots of locations within the wood to warm up your creative eye. Get low, go wide and try to avoid visual clutter.

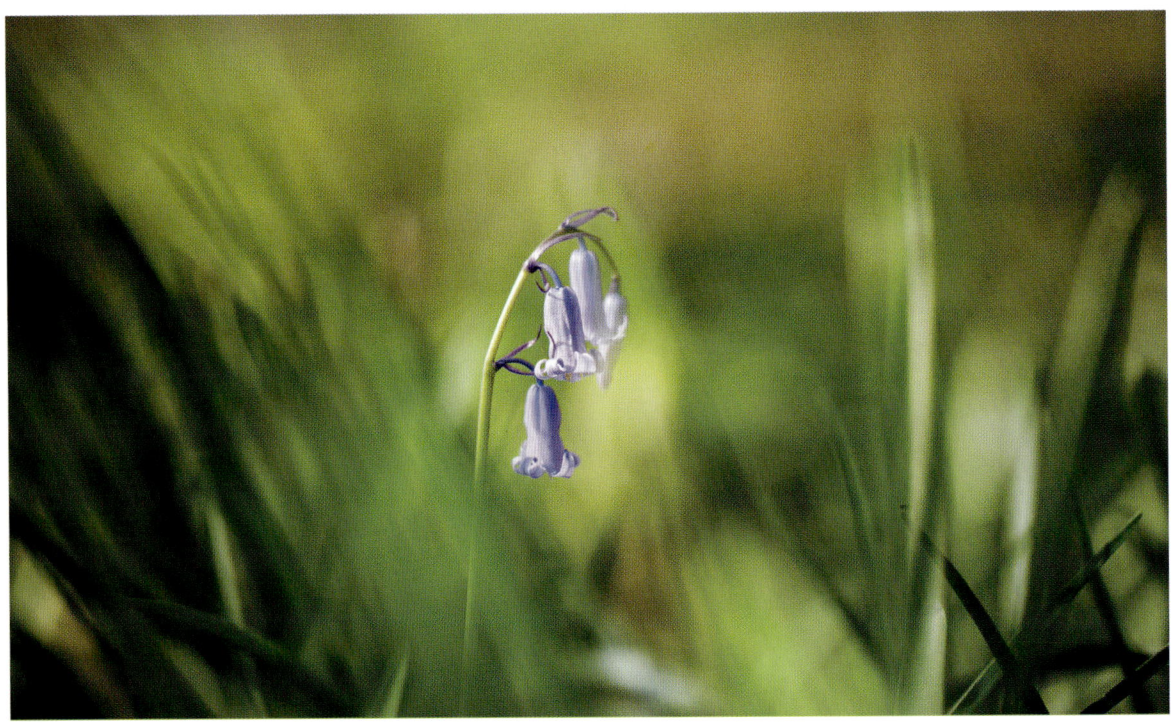

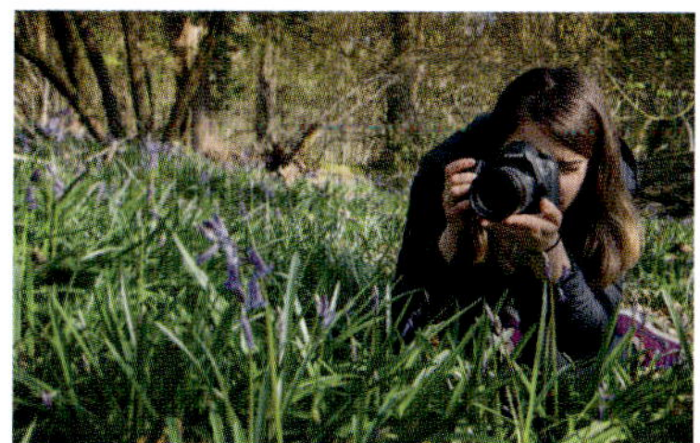

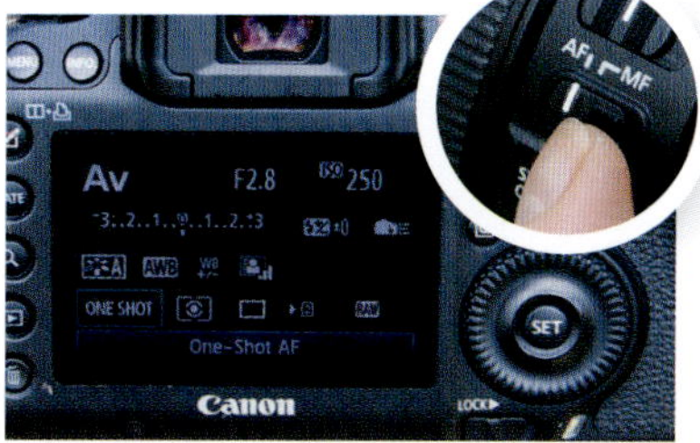


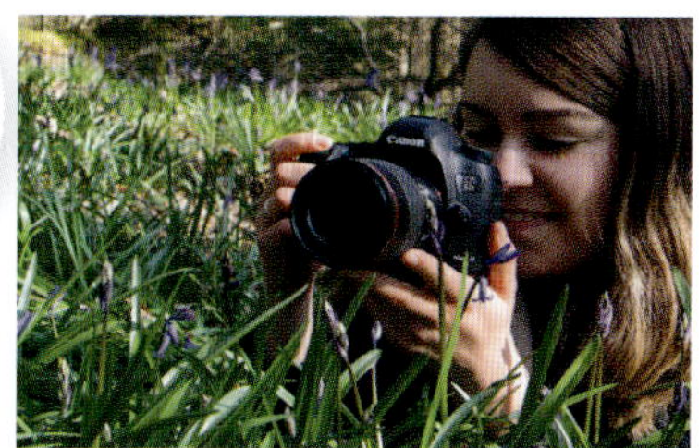

**1 The right place at the right time**
All outdoor shoots rely on the weather, and it's important to check that the conditions match your subject. For a serene and peaceful bluebell wood, this image was taken when there was little wind, as any breeze can blur the flowers in close-up. The ideal time to arrive is just after sunrise (or before sunset), when the low sun illuminates the bluebells more gently than the harsh midday sun.

**2 Gear and settings**
A 100mm macro lens with full autofocus is ideal for isolating single flowers, making use of the f/2.8 maximum aperture to generate a dreamy bokeh in the background. Set your camera to aperture-priority mode, so that the camera tweaks the shutter speed accordingly as the light or composition changes.

**3 Angle up**
Any flaws in a flower become obvious at macro level, so once you've picked a subject, move around it to find the best shooting position and angle. Getting down to a low angle on the ground can create a more immersive view. It's often easier to use Live View, rather than the viewfinder, to compose.

**4 Try different apertures**
While for a wider shot of a bluebell wood, you might want to set a narrow aperture and keep the whole scene sharp, with this macro approach, the key task is to blur the elements around and behind the flower as much as possible. Here, you can see how busy the shot looks with a narrow aperture of f/11 – the main subject gets lost, and the scene loses its focal point. Pay attention to the background of your images, moving around to avoid distracting or busy elements behind the flower.

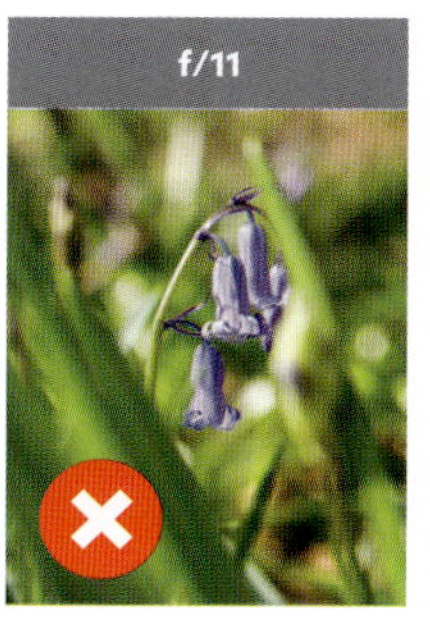


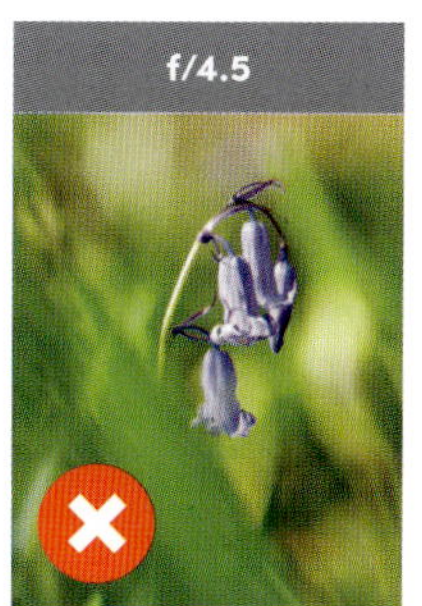


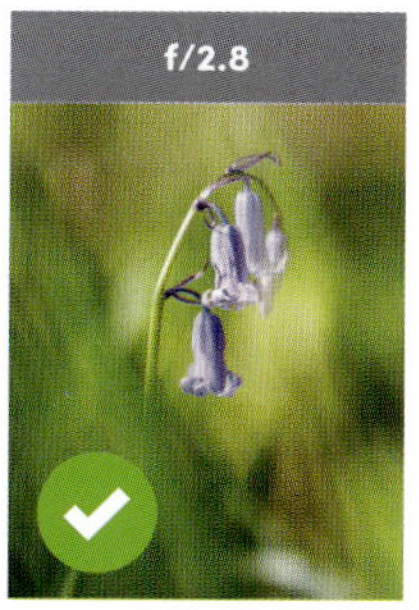


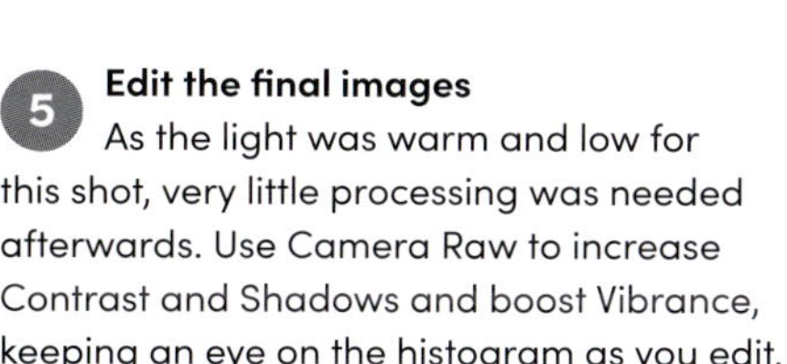

**5 Edit the final images**
As the light was warm and low for this shot, very little processing was needed afterwards. Use Camera Raw to increase Contrast and Shadows and boost Vibrance, keeping an eye on the histogram as you edit.

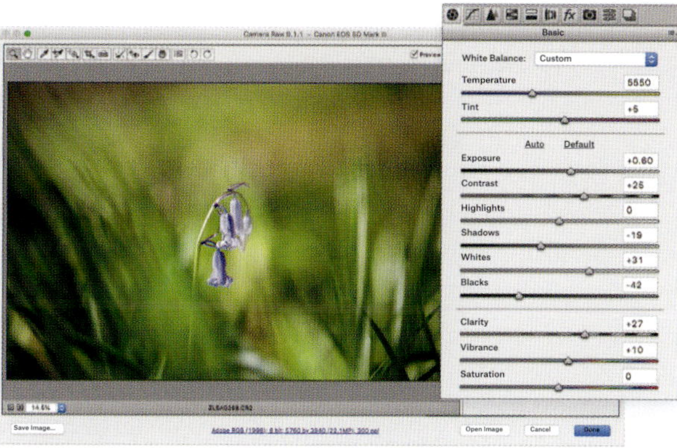

# CREATE STUNNING MACRO BACKDROPS

**THE IDEA**
**Showcase the intricate detail of a flower close-up.**

**Time required**:
30 minutes – 1 hour

**Kit needed**:
- DSLR or mirrorless camera
- Macro lens
- Flashgun
- Reversing ring
- Tripod
- CD and CD case

**Camera settings**:
1/200 sec at f/11, ISO 100

**Skill level**:
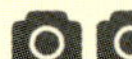   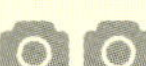

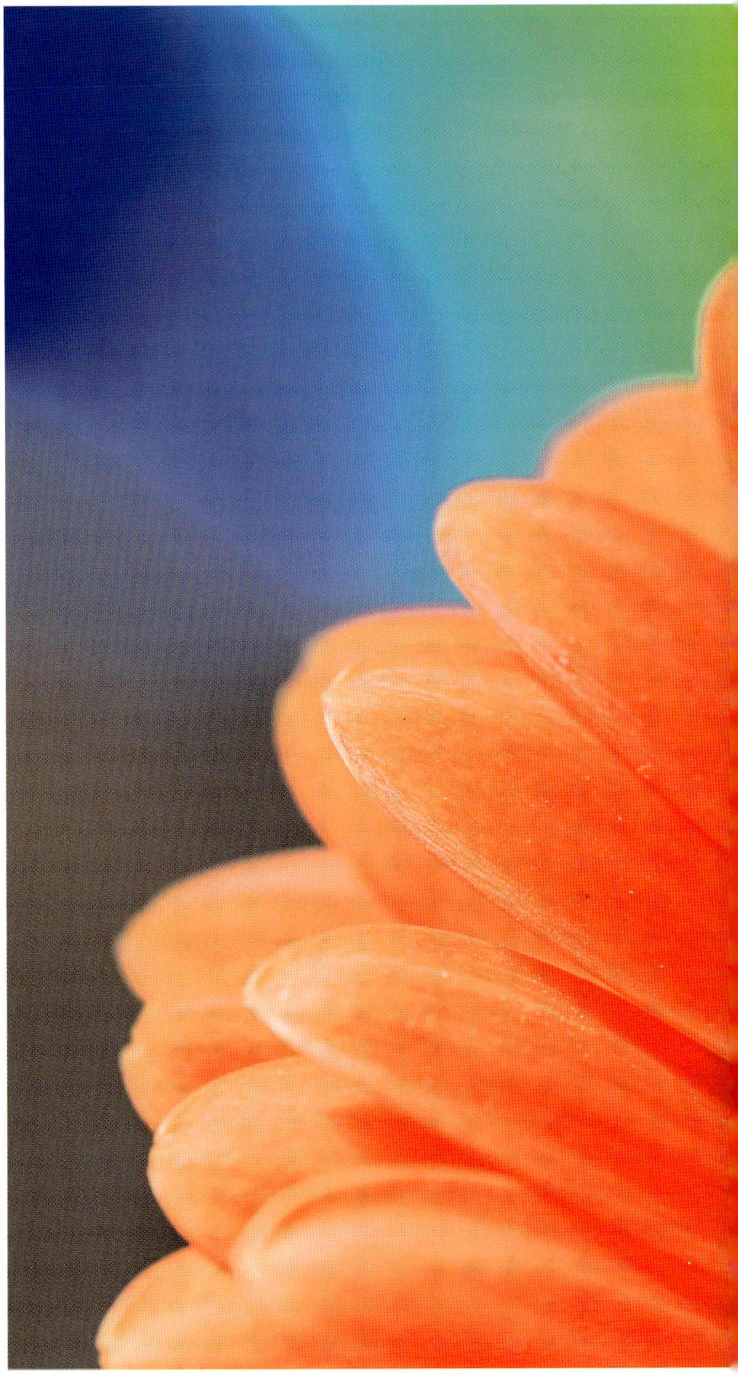

Macro photography and flowers are like two peas in a pod – the two together just simply make sense. Flowers are incredibly intricate and detailed when you view them from a close perspective, and the variety of bold bright colours they provide makes them a popular subject.

Redundant CDs make a fantastic backdrop for close-up shots. If you angle your light source carefully, you can create a rainbow effect from the reflective surface. It's a trial-and-error approach to get it right, but it's well worth the effort.

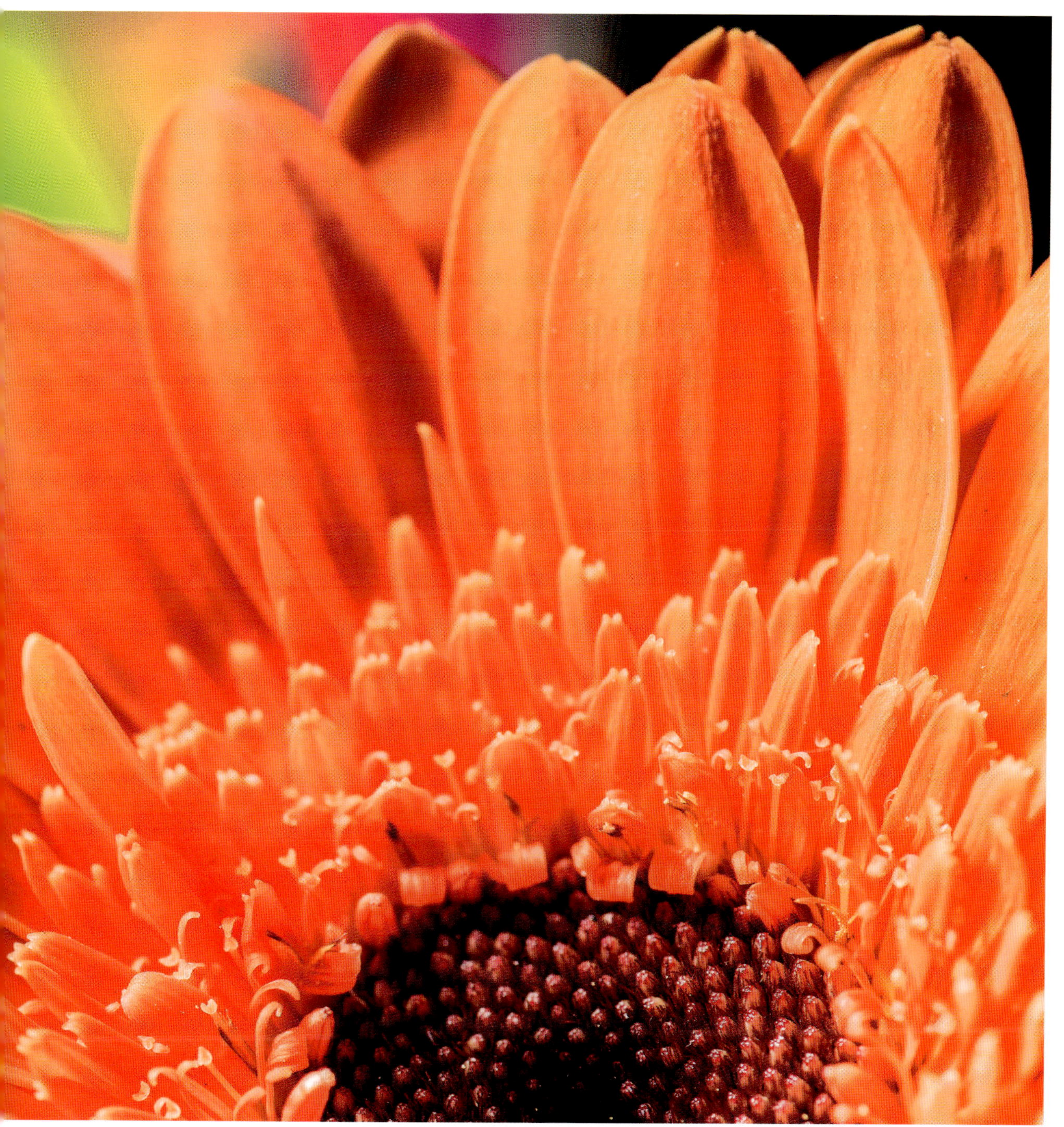

When it comes to setting up this macro flower shot, use a CD as your background, and set up an external flashgun to light it. Put your camera into its manual mode and dial the aperture down to f/11. To sync the shutter speed with the flashgun, set the shutter speed to 1/200 sec, and keep the ISO low at 100. If your flash is positioned close to the flower, balance the flashgun strength at 1/8 power.

After taking a test shot, it's important to check your histogram to ensure your exposure is reading correctly and that the highlights aren't overexposed.

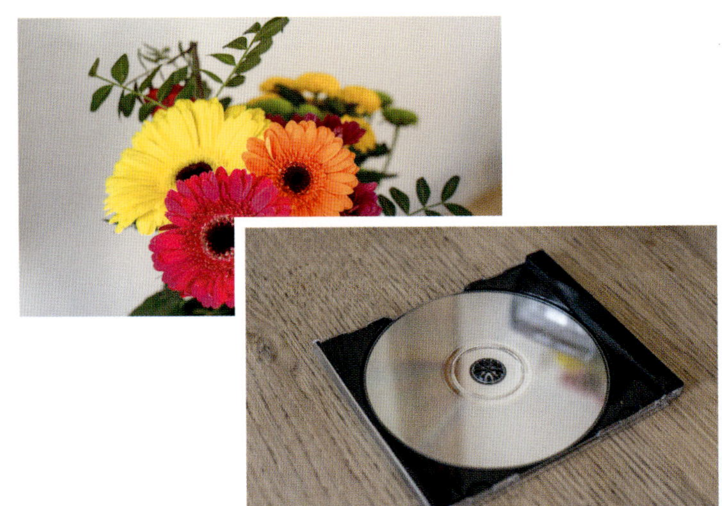

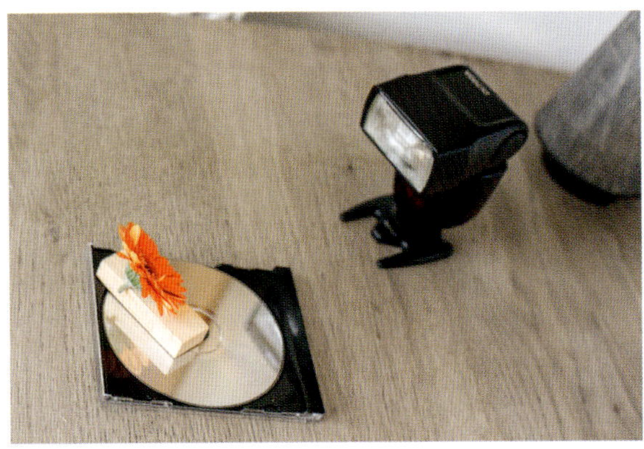

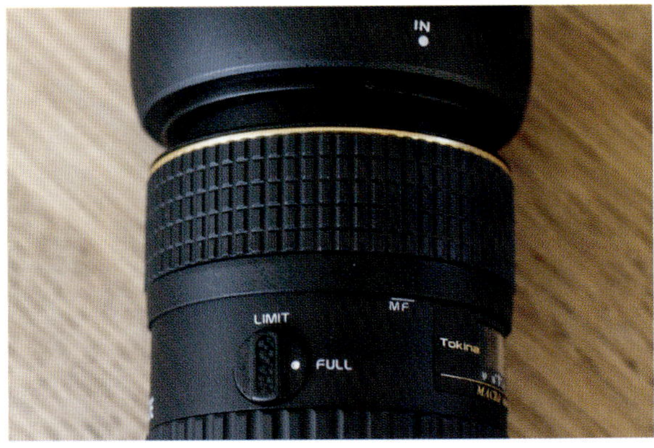


**1 Lighting**
Use an external flashgun pointing directly at the flower and a remote trigger to fire the flash. Set the flash strength to 1/8 power in manual mode. When you shoot with flash, manual mode gives you the most control.

**2 Choose the right lens**
It helps to use a macro lens with a 1:1 magnification ratio to get super close-up shots, but if you don't have one of these, you could use a reversing ring and switch your standard lens around the other way. Set your camera up on a tripod and focus manually. If your flower is positioned at an angle to the camera, consider focus stacking for sharper results.

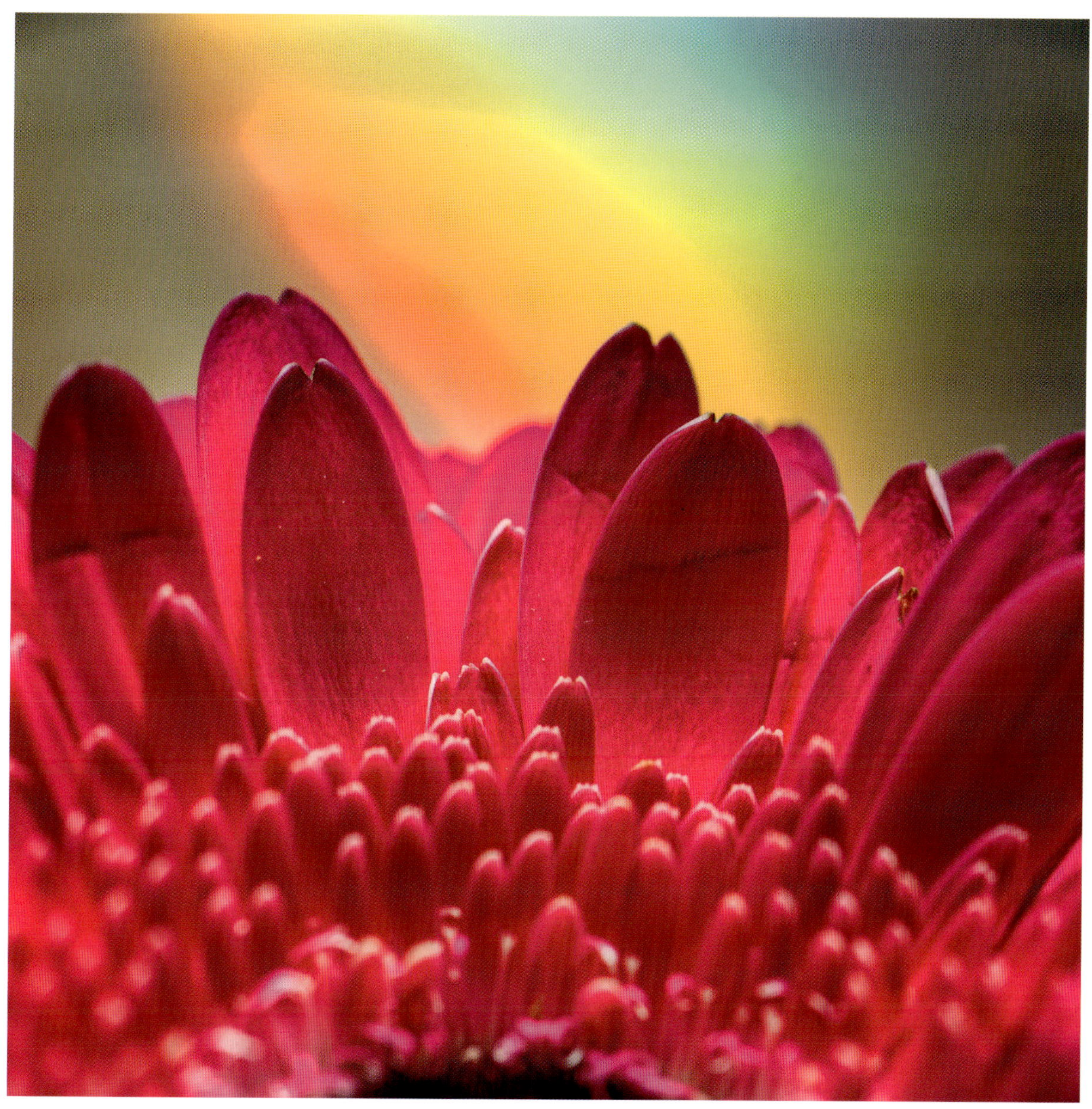

**3 Experiment with different compositions**

The petals of the orange flower make for a striking photo (see page 93), but why stop there? Try introducing some different colours, especially ones that are complementary to the rainbow effect produced by the CD. Search online for a colour wheel that shows the relationship between primary and secondary colours.

# MASTER LONG LENS SHOOTING

**THE IDEA**
**Take colourful portraits of puffins with a long lens and subtle approach.**

**Time required**: 2 hours

**Kit needed**:
- DSLR or mirrorless camera
- 300mm lens
- Teleconverter (optional)

**Camera settings**:
1/1250 sec at f/4.5, ISO 500

**Skill level**:

**Long lenses might be out of reach financially for many of us but hiring them for specific wildlife trips is an affordable way to fill the frame with your subjects, particularly if you're shooting birds and other small creatures.**

When visiting remote wildlife havens, you want to do everything you can to come away with an array of characterful shots of iconic species such as puffins.

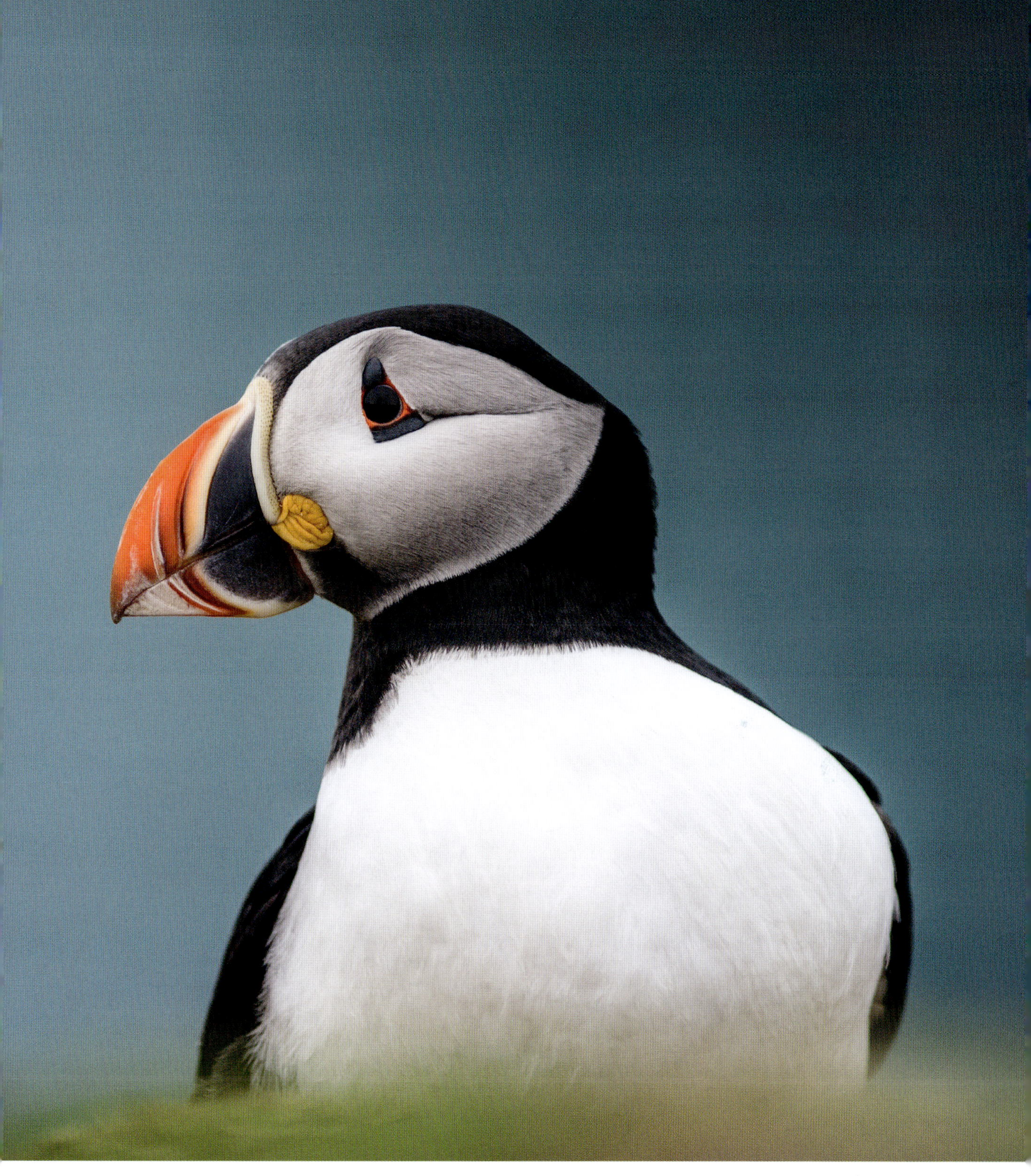

Finding subjects can be a tricky starting point of bird photography, but guides will be able to give you advice on wildlife timings and viewpoints.

For classic portrait shots, a long lens and teleconverter is the obvious choice. But puffins are often undeterred by human presence, which means you may end up taking the teleconverter off, to capture these birds at a closer range.

Getting down to a subject's eye level is generally a key composition point for wildlife portraits, as it creates a connection with the subject and enables you to blur foreground and background details around them in a pleasing way.

If you have time to experiment around the puffins, try shots in portrait and landscape mode, and frame them with different backdrops of sea, foliage and sky.

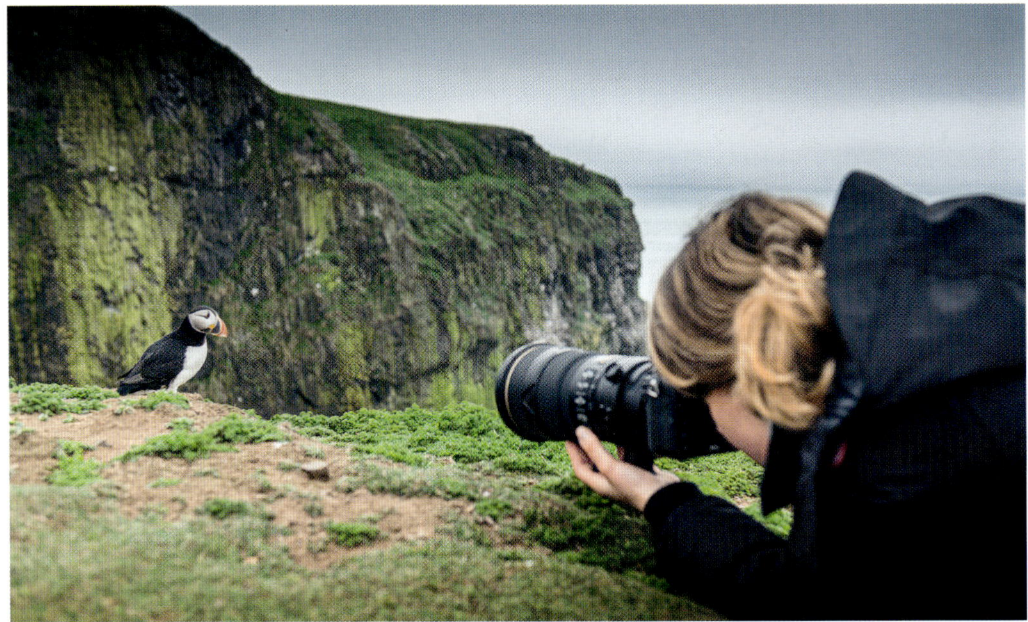

**1 Get down low**
Although lying and crouching down low to the ground means getting covered in mud (and quite possibly puffin excrement), it is necessary to get more immersive images of puffins. If your camera has a vari-angle screen, turn on Live View and make use of it to compose your low-angle shots.

**2 Aperture priority**
Essential for wildlife portraits, aperture-priority mode means you can set your aperture and ISO for the creative effect and available light, then focus more on the composition rather than having to change the shutter each time. If your focus is birds in flight, switch to shutter-priority mode instead.

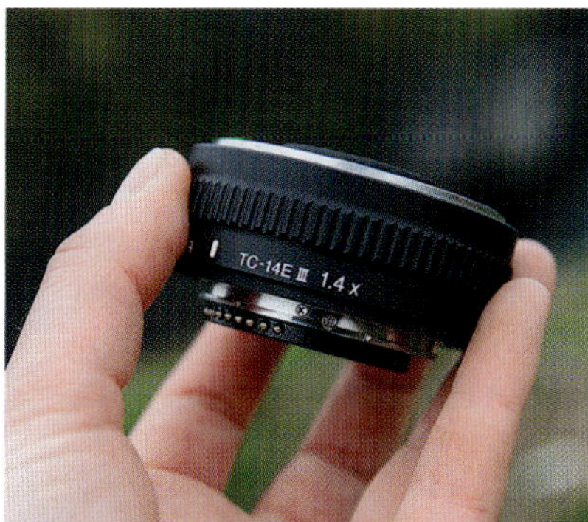


**3 All the gear, some idea**

Long focal lengths are needed for frame-filling bird portraits – a 300mm f/2.8 lens with 1.4x teleconverter is ideal. While using a teleconverter reduces the maximum aperture of a lens (by 1 stop in this case), it also gives you extra focal reach without great expense and bulk in your camera bag.

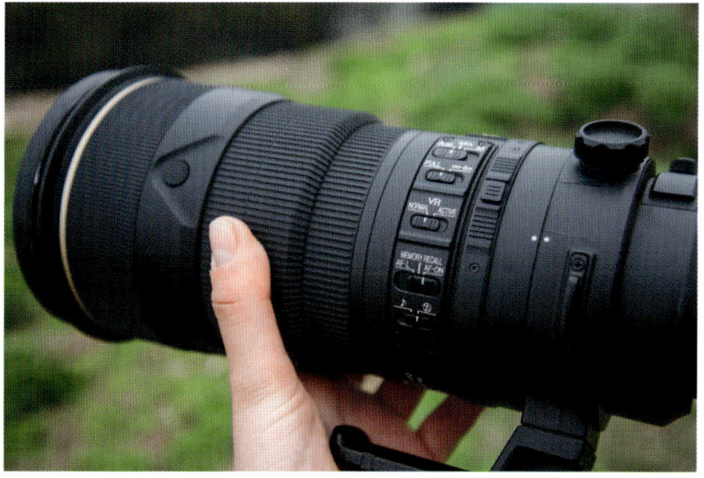

**4 Stabilise long lenses**

In some instances, using a sturdy tripod can help you to shoot sharp bird portraits. In other situations, however, it can be a hindrance. To move around the puffins freely and quickly recompose, stabilise long lenses by holding them underneath, adopting a stable shooting pose to avoid camera shake as much as possible.

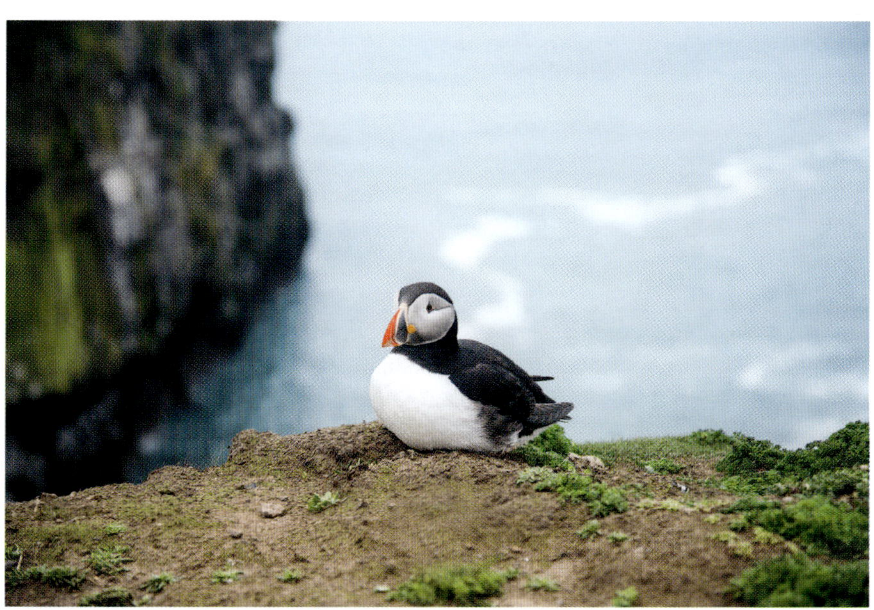

**Once you've captured a few basic portraits, swap the telephoto for a wide-angle lens, and capture some environmental habitat shots. This requires pre-focusing on the subject, then framing to include the landscape beyond.**

# SHOOT ICE CLOSE UP

**THE IDEA**
**Shoot ice close-ups without stepping out into the cold outdoors.**

**Time required**: 1 hour

**Kit needed**:
- DSLR or mirrorless camera
- Macro lens
- LED lamp
- Editing software

**Camera settings**:
1/640 sec at f/13, ISO 400

**Skill level**:

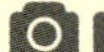 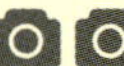  

**Ice is a fantastic substance, with a structure that changes quickly when it starts to melt. For this project, fill a small plastic container with about half a centimetre of water and put it in the freezer. If you want to go one step further, add objects such as flowers or food colouring to your water before it freezes.**

Once your ice is frozen, break it out of the container, either in one piece or as several smaller pieces – the air bubbles inside the middle might be more interesting to photograph.

Select aperture-priority mode and set an aperture between f/13 and f/16 to keep as much of the subject as sharp as possible.

Keep your ISO between 400 and 800 if you're shooting by hand so your shutter fires at a reasonable speed or use a tripod if your camera doesn't perform well at higher ISO settings.

A macro lens is ideal, but if you don't have one, a cheap alternative DIY hack is to get a reversing ring for your standard lens and flip the lens around. A telephoto lens can also deliver decent close-up results.

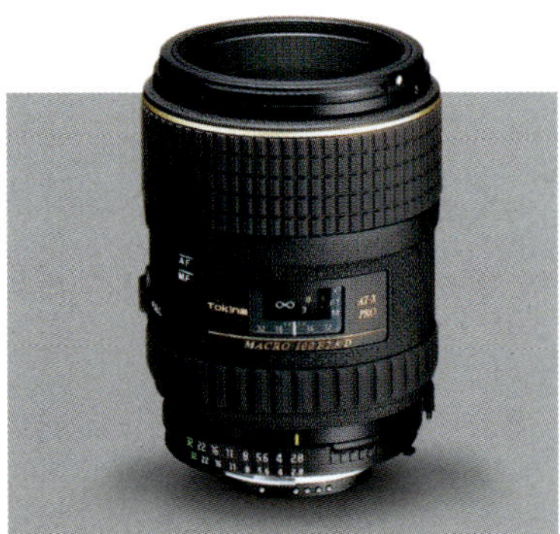


**1 Choose your lens**
Switch the focus setting to manual and turn the focus ring to its closest distance, then move the camera in and out to refine the focus. At this close distance, it's easier to get a good result by moving the camera than by twisting the focus ring.

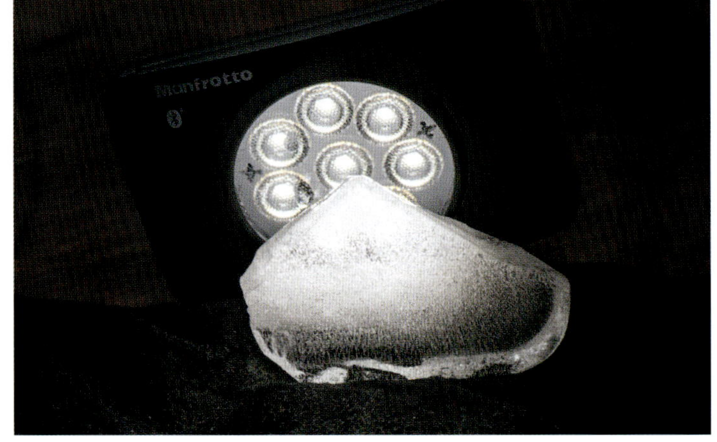


**2 Backlight your subject**
Because ice is transparent, the best way to light it is from behind with a small LED lamp. If you don't have one, use a torch or even place your ice by a window. You'll be surprised how much one small light will illuminate your set-up at this close distance.

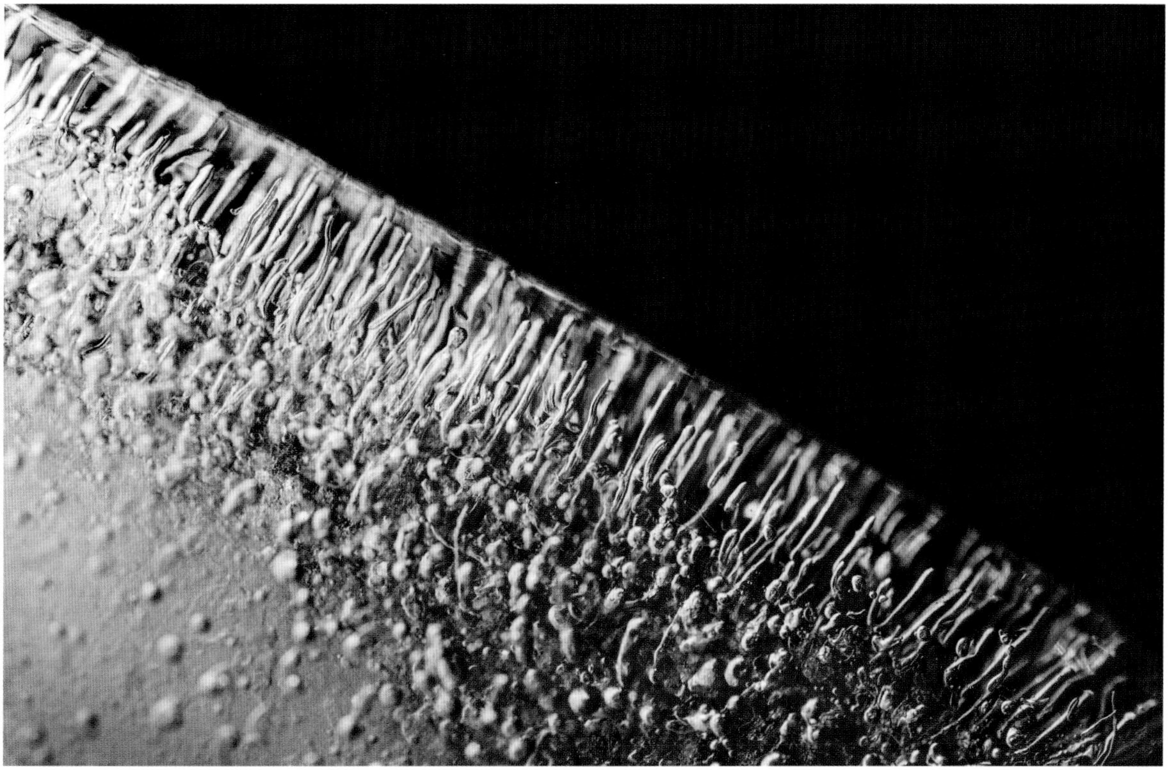

**3 Edit your photo**

The main thing to consider at the editing stage is working towards getting the most out of the textures and shapes in the ice. This image was converted to black and white, and Contrast was increased. Highlights were pulled back to bring detail to a slightly overexposed area and Blacks and Whites were pushed and pulled to refine. Texture and Clarity were also tweaked to enhance detail. The Texture slider accentuates detail but affects blurred areas less than the Clarity slider.

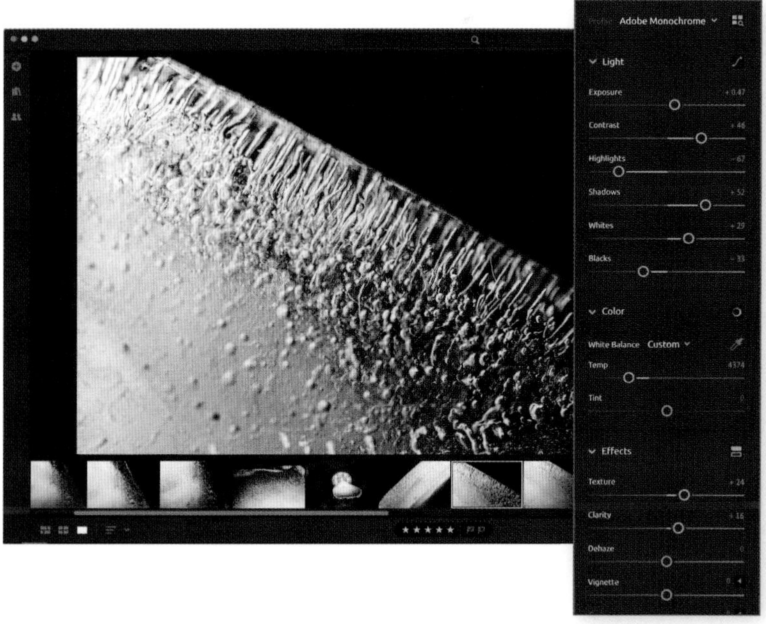

# LEARN TO USE A DOT SIGHT

**THE IDEA**
**Scope out subjects using a dot sight.**

**Time required**: 2 hours

**Kit needed**:
- DSLR or mirrorless camera
- 200–500mm lens
- Dot sight
- Tripod

**Camera settings**:
1/4000 sec at f/5.6, ISO 400

**Skill level**:

**The longer your lens is, the more challenging it is to sight and track your subject. Small movements become exaggerated at higher magnifications, and this can make photographing erratic subjects, such as birds, even more challenging. Dot sights, such as Nikon's DF-M1, are designed to help improve your accuracy when shooting. Although this super-specialist attachment won't appeal to everyone, it's worth looking into if you spend most of your time searching for (or losing) faraway subjects.**

You'd be forgiven for thinking the DF-M1 is a piece of military hardware. The pop-up dot sight slots into the hotshoe of a camera, weighs very little and folds down when not in use. In practice, the sight allows you to pinpoint the centre of your frame without narrowing your vision through the viewfinder, making it much easier to find and track fast-moving or erratic subjects without losing them.

For a dot sight to function properly, you need to calibrate the position of the reticle, so it matches the framing of your viewfinder or rear display perfectly.

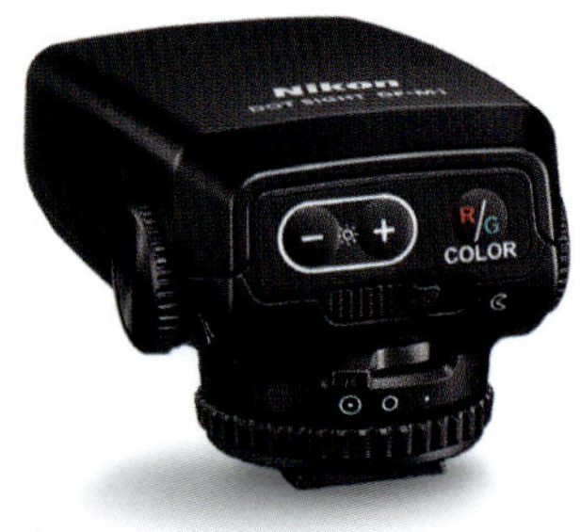

Dot sights are common in optics for hunting but are scarcer in photography. Nikon's DF-M1 is designed for the P1000 bridge camera but will also work with other Nikon cameras. OM System offers the EE-1 for Micro Four Thirds cameras.

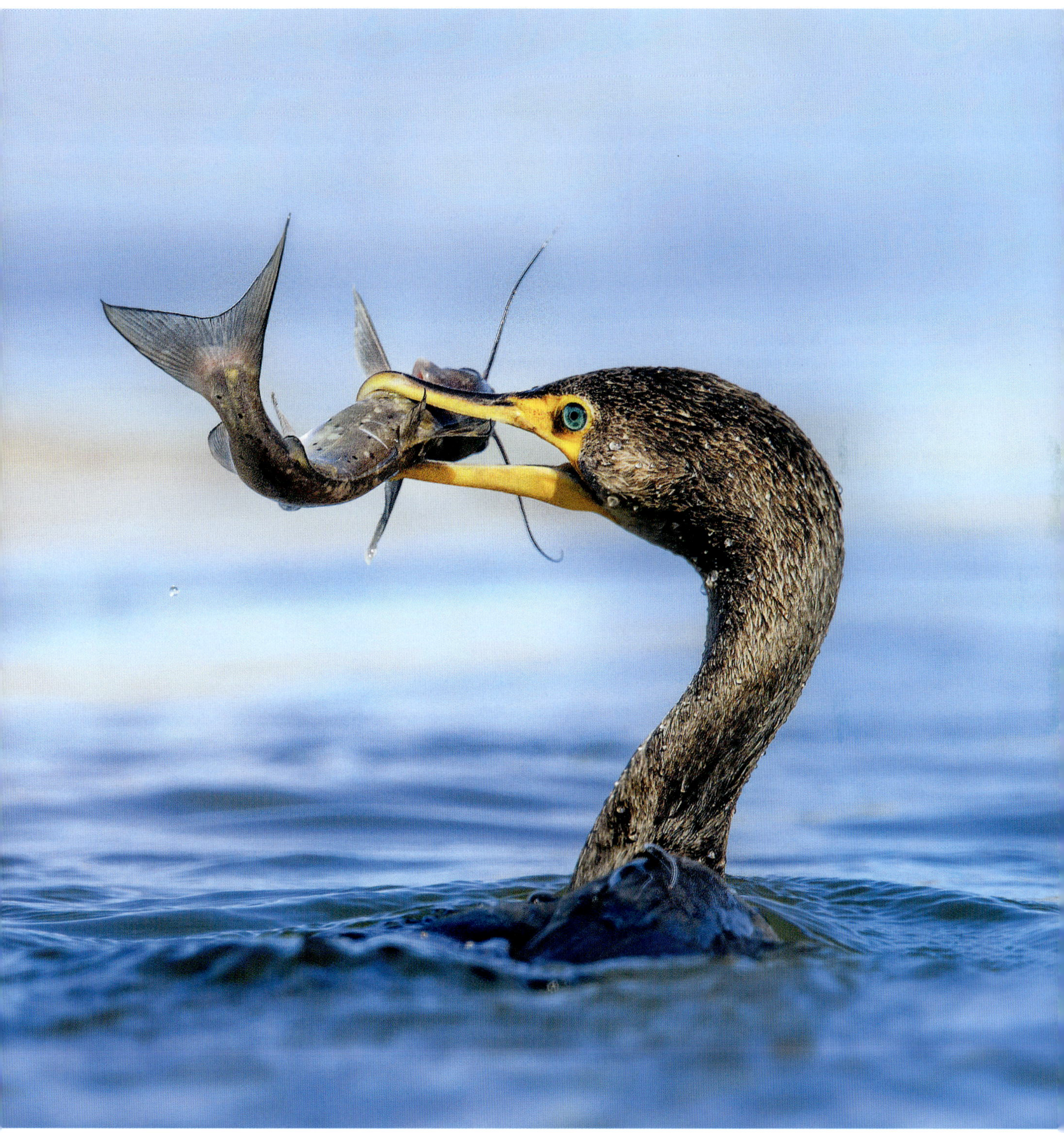

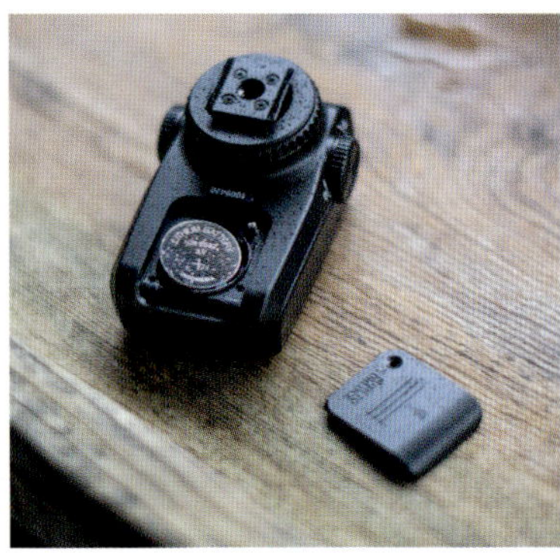

**1 I've got the power**

The DF-M1 uses a CR2032 battery. A thin implement is needed to push down the lock pin and access the battery slot. Power is used when the sight pops up. If left inactive for four hours, or by holding the colour selection or brightness buttons, it'll switch off.

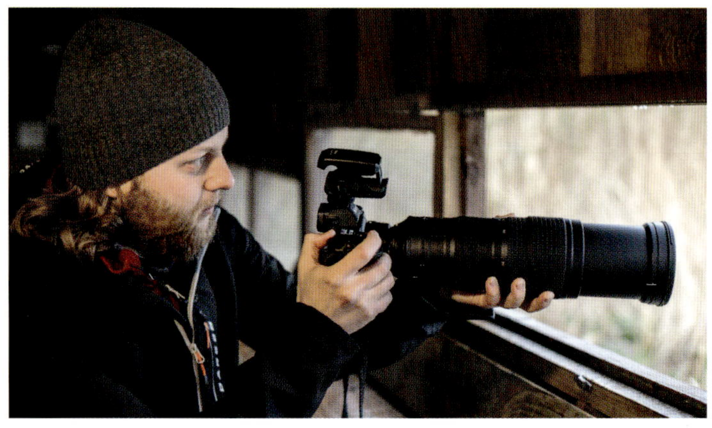

**2 If the shoe fits**

The dot sight mounts on top of a camera's hotshoe and screws into place. The DF-M1 is officially designed for use with the Nikon Coolpix P1000 and P950 bridge cameras. However, it also works fine with most D and Z-series cameras. It comes with a small, branded pouch, so you can stow it safely in your bag when not in use.

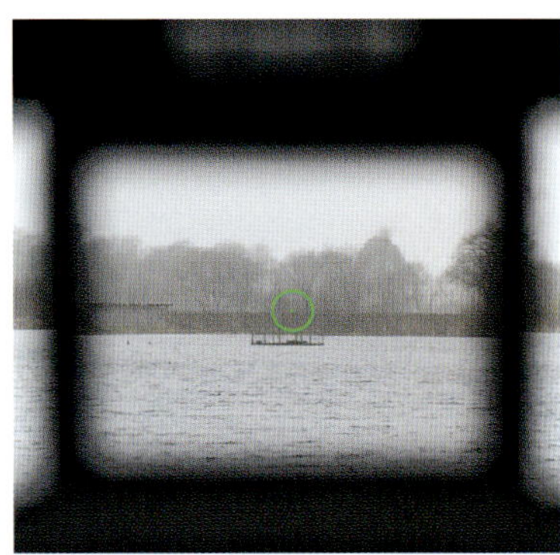

**3 Custom settings**

You can customise the DF-M1 to suit your preferences. A colour selection button allows you to choose between a green or red reticle, brightness buttons let you change the intensity of the dot, and a small clickable lever allows you to cycle through three different reticle designs.

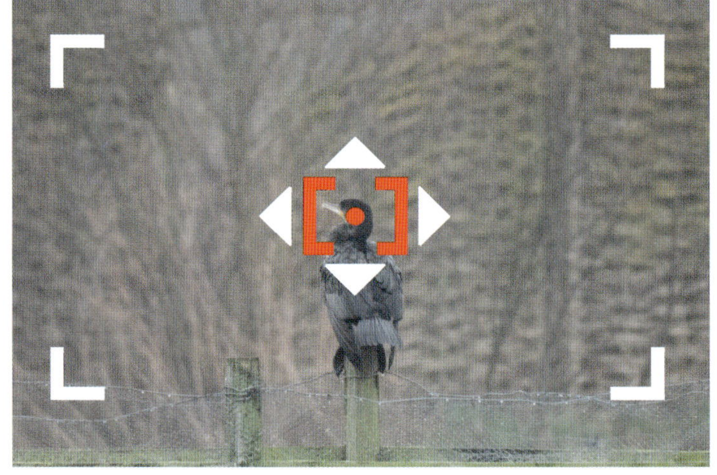

**4 In your sights**

To calibrate the dot sight, you first need to place your camera on a tripod. Find and sight an object (ideally, something that's roughly the same distance as your subject) and centre it in the frame. Use a single AF point as a guide to ensure the frame is centred perfectly.

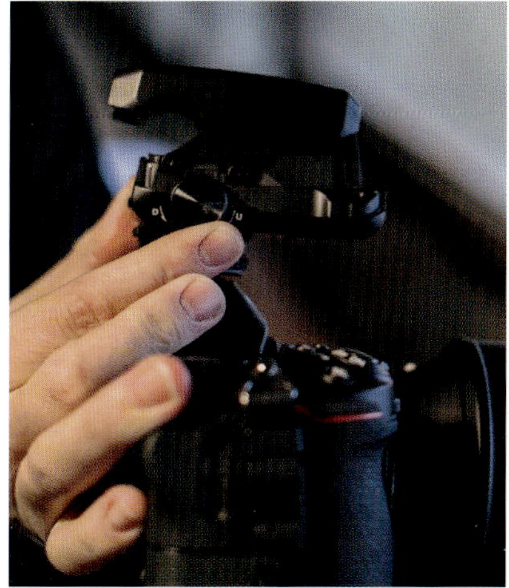

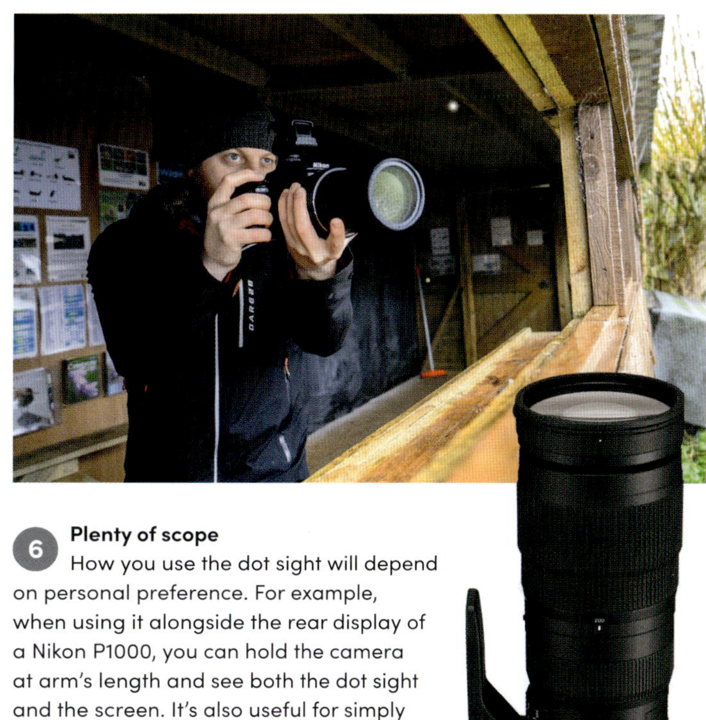

**5 Reticle readjustments**
Look directly through the sight and turn the two dials either side of the device to place the reticle precisely over your object. Rotate the right dial clockwise to move the reticle up and anticlockwise to move it down. Turn the left dial clockwise to move the reticle left and anticlockwise to move it right.

**6 Plenty of scope**
How you use the dot sight will depend on personal preference. For example, when using it alongside the rear display of a Nikon P1000, you can hold the camera at arm's length and see both the dot sight and the screen. It's also useful for simply sighting a faraway subject, as the dot sight gets you in the vicinity before switching over to the viewfinder.

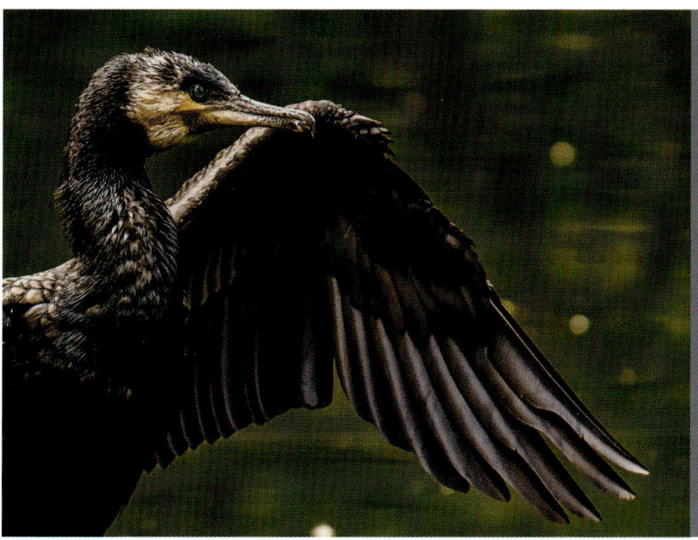

## Spot meter, continuous shutter and Raw

**Your camera settings can be the difference between a great photo and a mediocre photo while shooting wildlife in action, such as these cormorants diving and catching fish. Use spot metering to get a good exposure of your bird. Don't worry if the background is a little bright, as shooting Raw will allow you to retrieve that in post-processing. It's easy to miss the action if you're not prepared, so switch your shooting mode to continuous, where you can shoot between 5–30 frames per second (fps).**

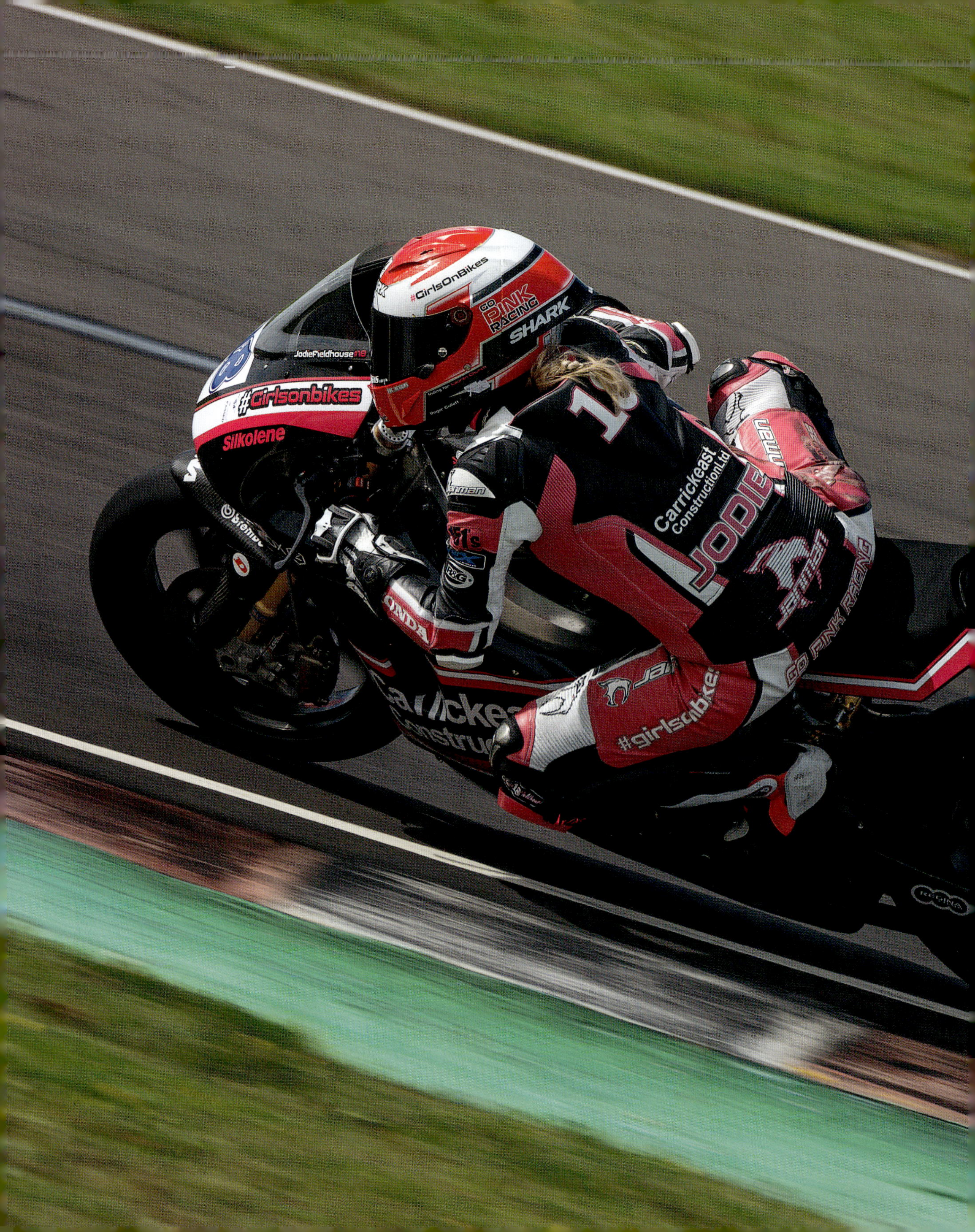
#GirlsOnBikes
GO PINK RACING
SHARK
#Girlsonbikes
Silkolene
Carrickeast ConstructionLtd
JODIE
GO PINK RACING
#girlsonbikes
HONDA

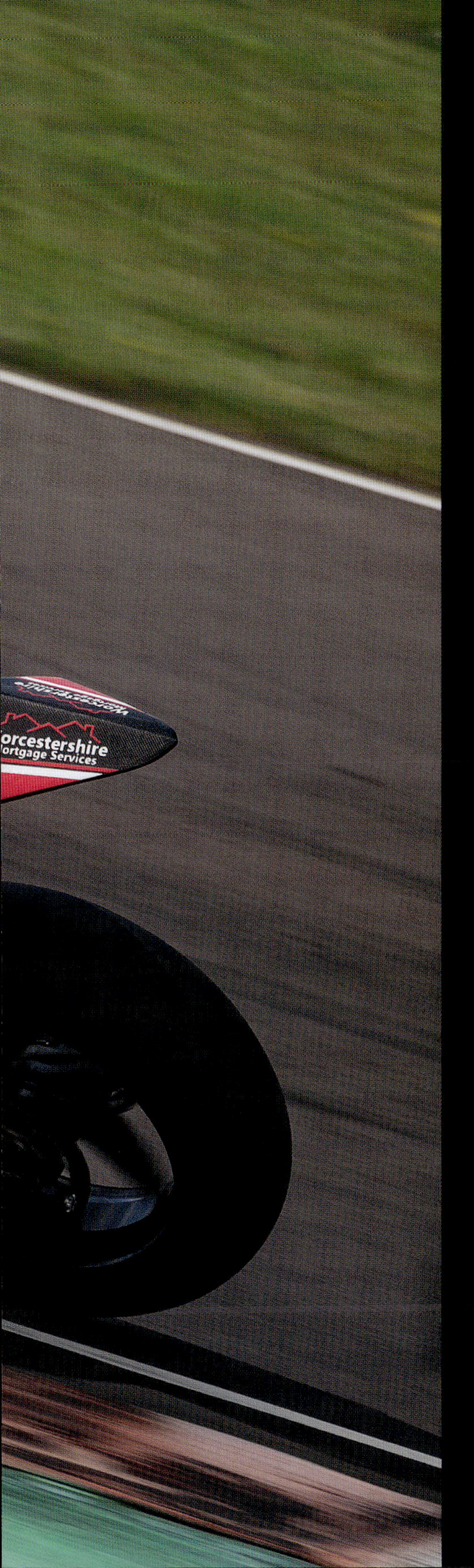


4

# ACTION IDEAS

**Strategies for developing the quick-thinking camera skills needed for capturing split-second thrills and spills.**

# FREEZE A DANCER MID-LEAP

**THE IDEA**
**Step up to the challenge of dance photography in a rural location.**

**Time required**: 2 hours

**Kit needed**:
- DSLR or mirrorless camera
- 24–70mm lens

**Camera settings**:
1/6400 sec at f/3.5, ISO 200

**Skill level**:

   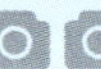

**Although the studio is a safe and comfortable environment to work in when it comes to dance photography, there is something magical about being in the great outdoors and capturing those impressive ballet moves in a wide-open space.**

This image was taken in the wilds of Dartmoor in Devon, UK. Despite the area being a vast, open space, it can get rather busy at the popular landmarks. When shooting in a scenic tourist area, be sure to do your research and choose a quiet spot away from the crowds.

Before you head out the door, it's important to plan, plan, plan. This means you'll both be getting what you want from the shoot, and it's important to understand what each person's capabilities are. For example, while leaping across rough terrain looks great, make sure there is plenty of space and that your dancer is in their comfort zone. It's amazing what the camera can make look dynamic without having to put anyone at risk.

**1 Collaboration**
This project is an artistic collaboration between dancer and photographer. As a photographer, you need to ensure you are directing your dancer to stand in the right spot, count them into jumps and be ready to fire the shutter at the optimum moment. It helps to have a practice in a more comfortable environment, so you know what your dancer is capable of.

**2 Camera kit and settings**
All you need is a typical 24–70mm zoom and camera body. Having a simple set-up means you can give your full concentration to working on composition and ensuring that a feeling of movement is captured. Switch the AF setting to tracking and shoot using the burst mode. Keep showing shots to the dancer to make sure they're happy with the form of their body.

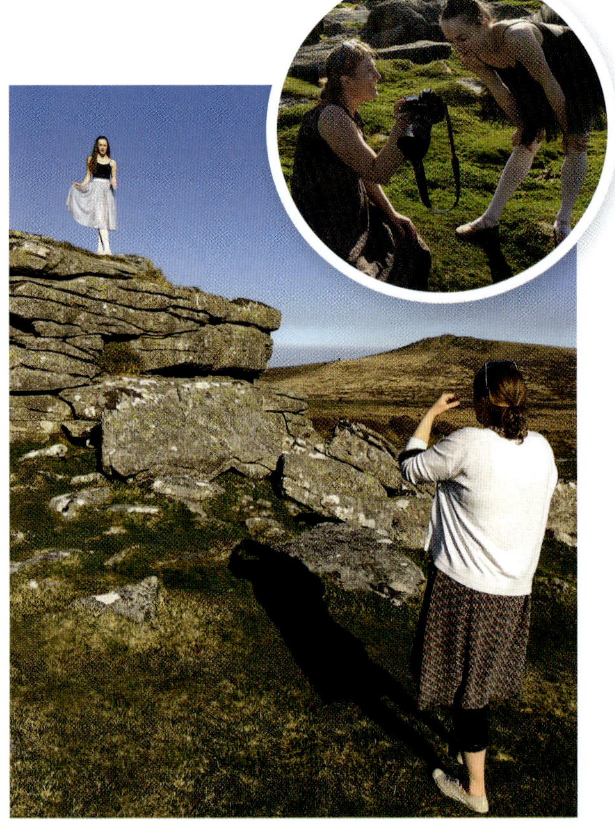

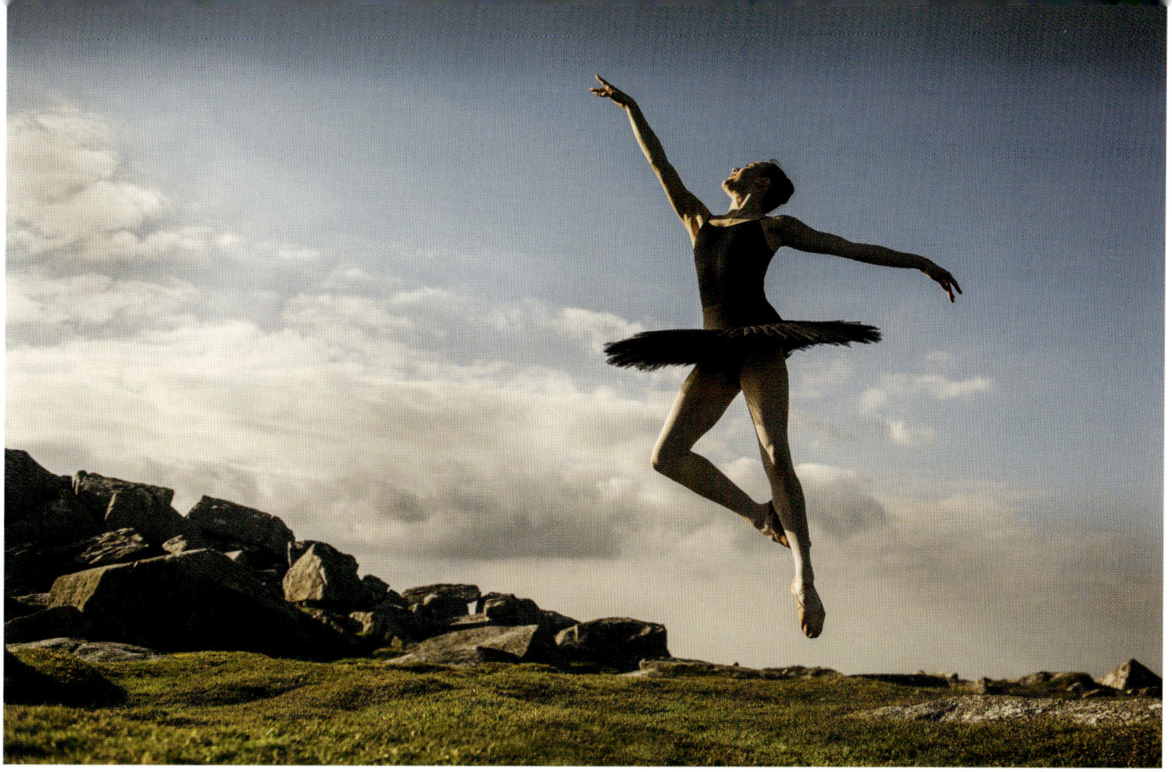

### 3 Working with the light

Natural light at the latter part of the day becomes much easier to work with, as it will soften and create a warm glow around your dancer. Shooting into the sun also offers an opportunity to play around with silhouettes. Different types of clothing will play a role. Lace or mesh can create intricate patterns of light and dark, whereas silk or chiffon can create softer, delicate shadows.

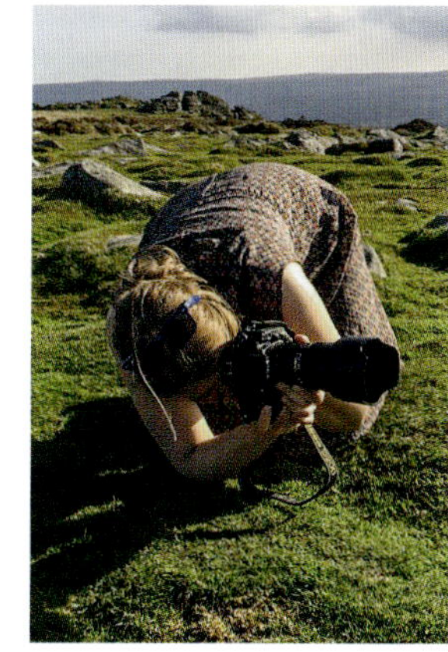

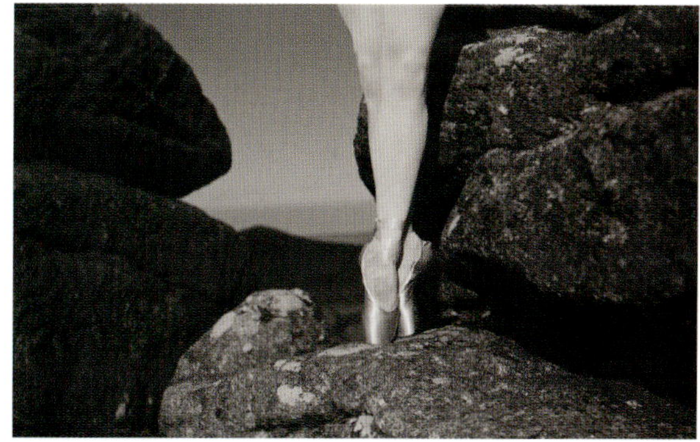

### 4 Tippy toes

Experiment with different ideas and don't be afraid to crop in tight. To finish the image, convert it to black and white, which is a classic technique for bringing out the details and textures in a scene. Here, it also helps to highlight the dancer's legs and feet against the rocks.

To keep your dancer sharp in the frame, select a fast enough shutter speed. If your subject is jumping, a setting of 1/500 sec or faster is necessary. It's important to get the right amount of movement, otherwise your subject may look slightly blurry.

# PAINT WITH SPARKLERS

**THE IDEA**
**Bring your low-light scenes to life with sparks.**

**Time required**: 1-2 hours

**Kit needed:**
- DSLR or mirrorless camera
- 50mm lens
- Tripod
- Sparklers
- Editing software

**Camera settings:**
30 secs at f/8, ISO 100

**Skill level:**

  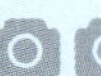 

**This project is all about having a creative spark – literally! Sparklers look fantastic in low light and dramatically illuminate your subject as you trace around its outline.**

A bike with a kickstand is a convenient subject, and you can also see through the spokes. Having a friend to help you with the 'painting' while you operate the camera is ideal, though not essential. If you're flying solo, set a long self-timer to give yourself enough time to get into position and light the sparkler once you've set up the shot and pressed the shutter button.

Safety is paramount, so wear protective clothing and gloves, carry a bucket of water, sand or a fire extinguisher if you have one, and never bring a sparkler close to flammable sources. This means the technique is not safe for motorcycles or cars, as sparks and petrol or oil are not a good combination.

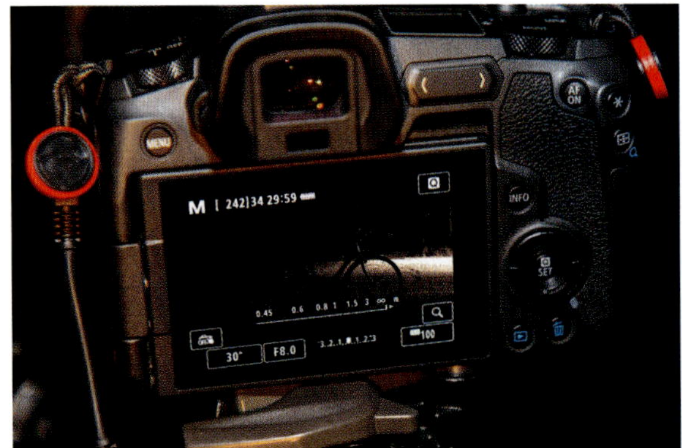


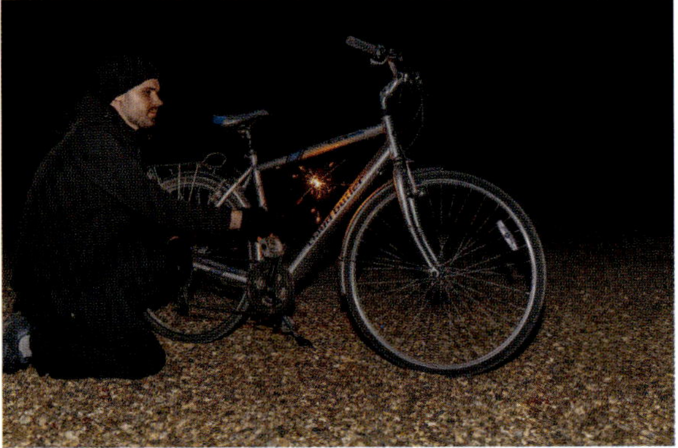

**1 Set up the shot**
Prop up your bike on its kickstand and, from a tripod, frame your composition. Switch to manual mode and shine a light on the bike so that your camera can autofocus on it, then lock the focus setting in manual-focus mode. Set the exposure to 30 sec at an aperture of f/8, and ISO 100.

**2 Paint with your sparkler**
Trigger the camera's self-timer and move into position in front of the bike with your sparkler lit. When you hear the exposure start, begin tracing around the bike and make sure that you've gone around all of it within a single exposure.

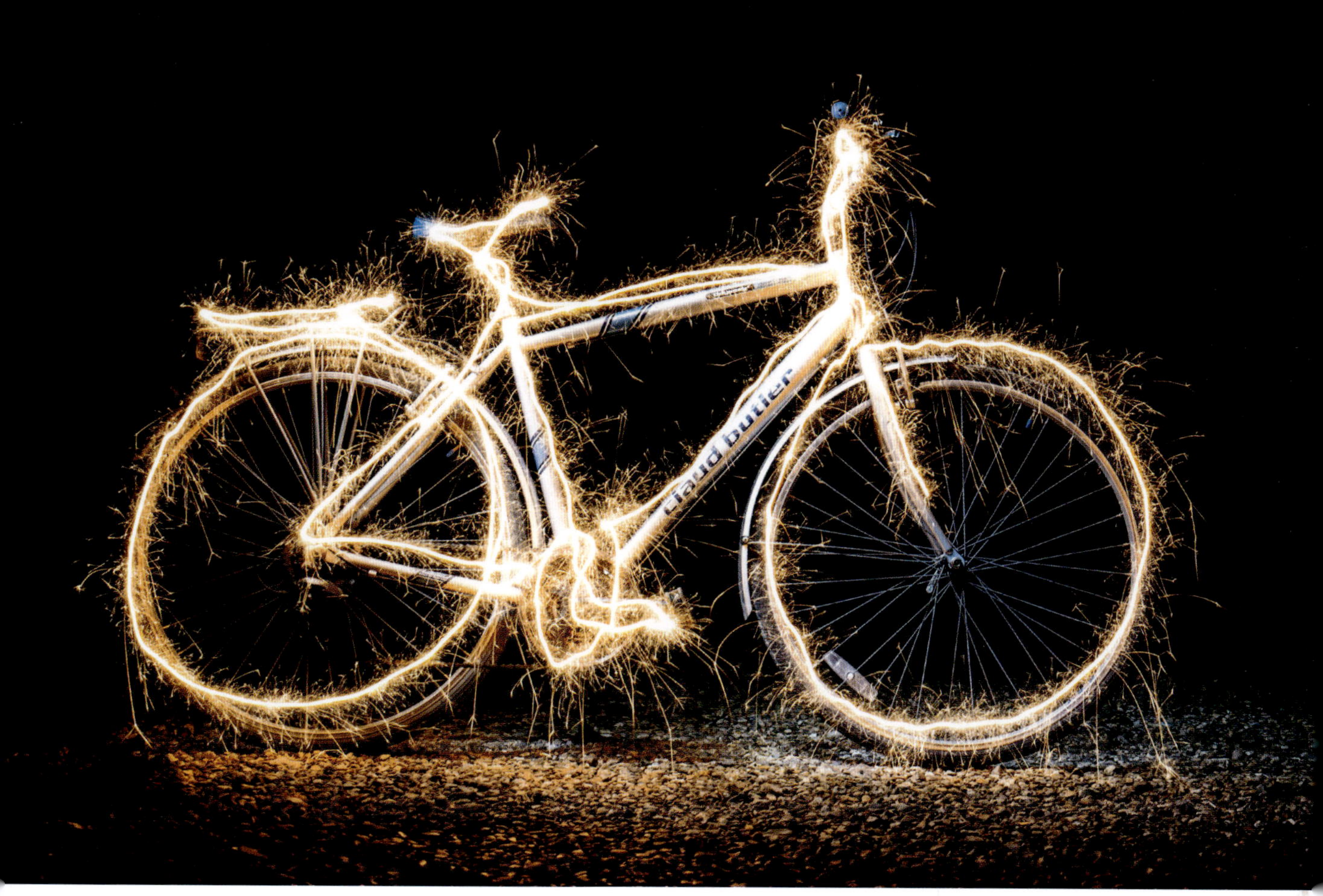

**3 Finish off in Photoshop**

To get a clean, distraction-free background, remove your face if it appears in the final image. In Photoshop, grab the Clone Stamp Tool, hold Alt and click on an area of clean background to source it, then paint over areas to darken them down and clean up the shot.

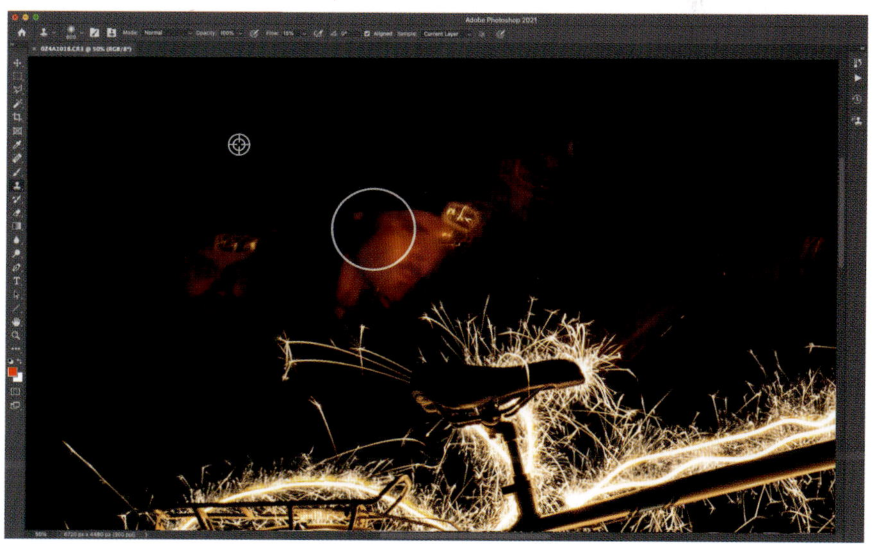

# SHOOT INDOOR LIGHT TRAILS

**THE IDEA**
**Slow down the shutter speed to create indoor light trails.**

**Time required**: 1-2 hours

**Kit needed**:
- DSLR or mirrorless camera
- 50mm lens
- ND filter (optional)
- Tripod
- String
- Torch or small light

**Camera settings**:
13 secs at f/16, ISO 64

**Skill level**:

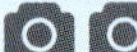
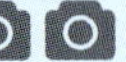

**On those rainy days when you don't want to venture outdoors, photographing indoor light trails are a fun mini project. All you need is a piece of string, a torch or small light, and a tripod. What you use as the main subject to cast your light trails around is up to you, so experiment with objects such as glass vases.**

Taking the image is all about using a long shutter speed to record the swirling, twirling light patterns. To avoid any camera movement, securely fasten your camera to your tripod. You may also want to use a remote shutter release (or self-timer if you don't have one) and the mirror lock-up feature.

Finally, keep moving when making the twirling motions. If you do pause, you will have an unwelcome patch of light in your frame.

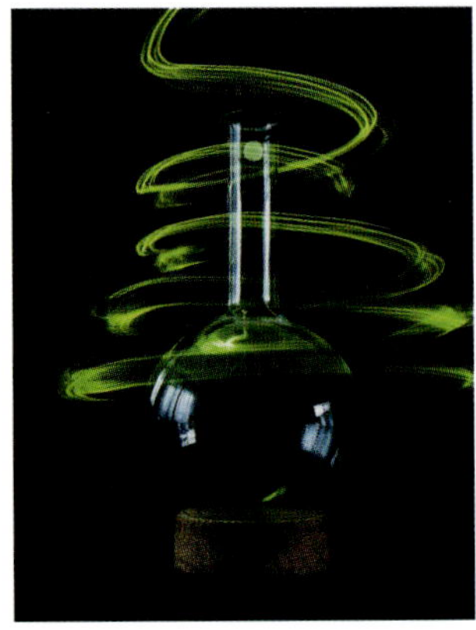

For an alternative result, wrap a piece of coloured cellophane over the torch. You could also use a brighter and larger light source. There really are no limits, so make your indoor light trails unique.

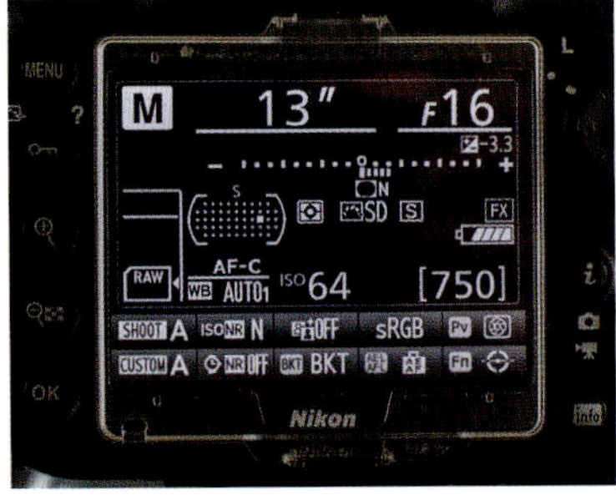


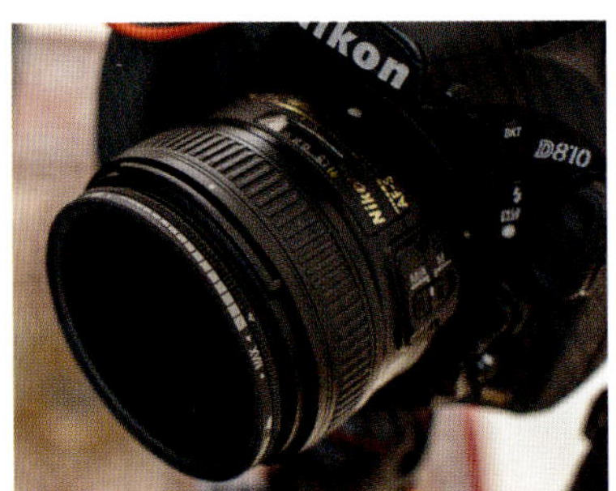


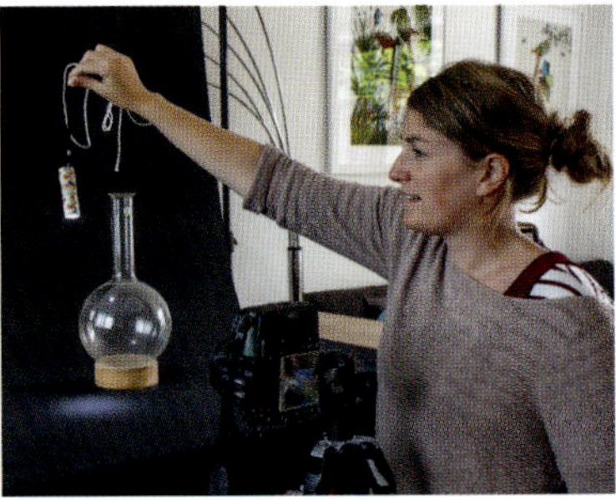

**1 Camera set-up**
Aim for an exposure of around 13 secs, reducing the aperture and ISO as needed. You won't need an ND filter if you shoot in a completely dark room, but may do if shooting in the middle of the day in a dark but not completely black room.

**2 Light on a string**
To create the swirling, twirling effect, attach a small torch to the end of a piece of string, focus on the vase, then open the shutter and make small circular motions with the light around the object. Review each shot and adjust the exposure accordingly – this is a process that requires experimentation.

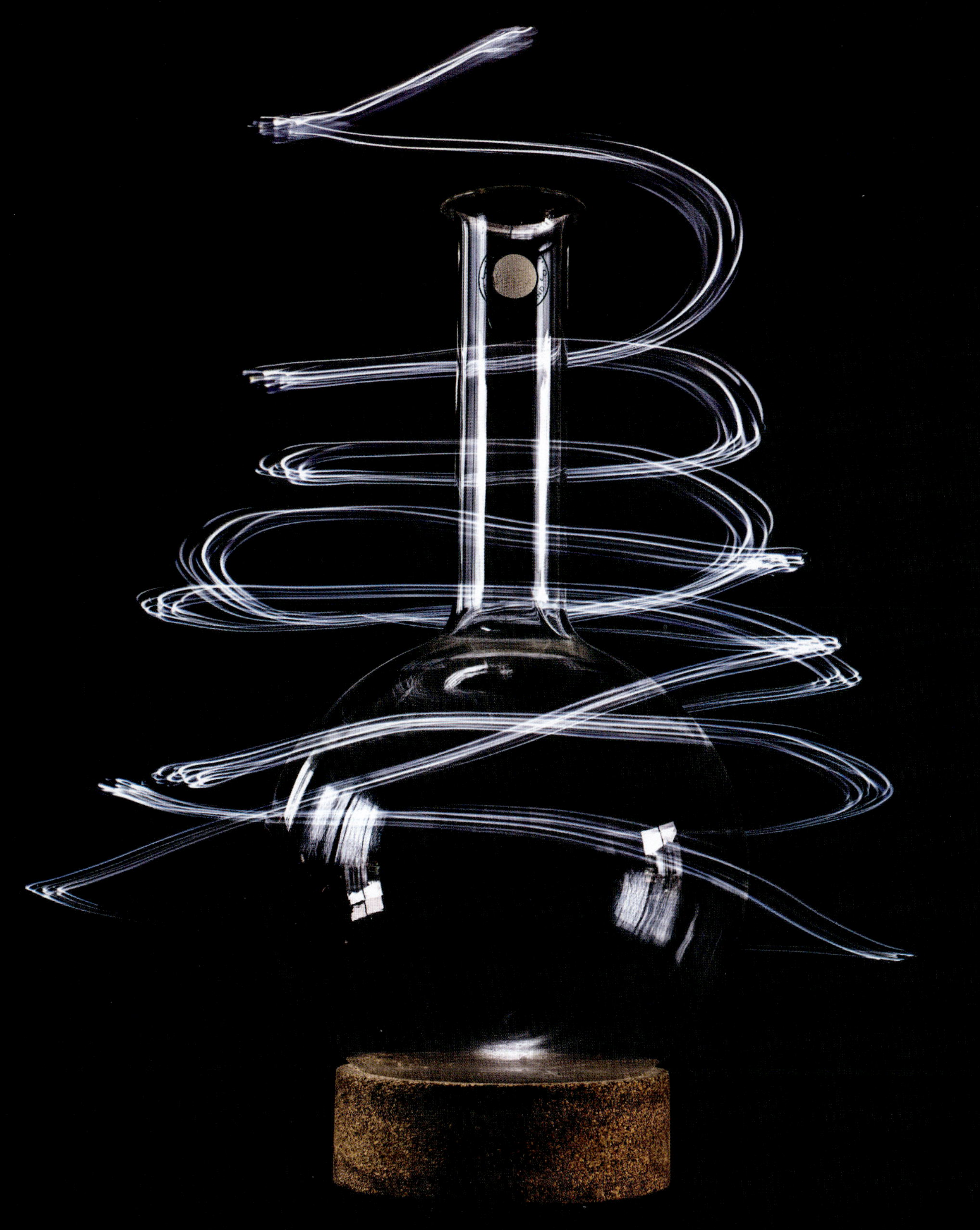

# GO WILD WITH SPARKLERS

**THE IDEA**
**Create an arty sparkly image using some indoor sparklers and a touch of bokeh.**

**Time required**: 1 hour

**Kit needed**:
- DSLR or mirrorless camera
- Short telephoto lens
- Sparklers
- Editing software

**Camera settings**:
1/320 sec at f/2, ISO 800

**Skill level**:

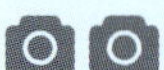

**If you enjoyed painting with sparklers on page 110, why not try and get even more creative and shoot some festive low-light images using some sparklers and a bokeh effect?**

In terms of kit, all you need are some small sparklers, a lighter, two small models as helpers (these can be any size or age over five), a camera and lens, Lightroom (to tone and style our image) and Photoshop (to blend multiple images together).

As this is a trial-and-error type of project, have some spare sparklers to hand. It's amazing how quickly they burn through, so make sure you're ready to shoot as soon as they are lit. Also, to reduce the risk of injury, safely extinguish the sticks in a bucket of cold water immediately after use.

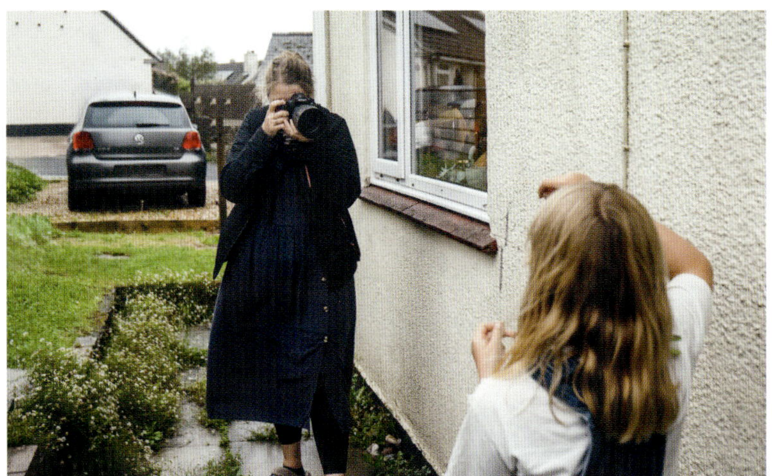

Always have an adult present when using sparklers, and remember, children under the age of five are not allowed to handle sparklers. Hold the sparklers at arm's length, away from the body, and have a bucket of water close to hand so you can put the hot end of the sparklers into it once they have been used.

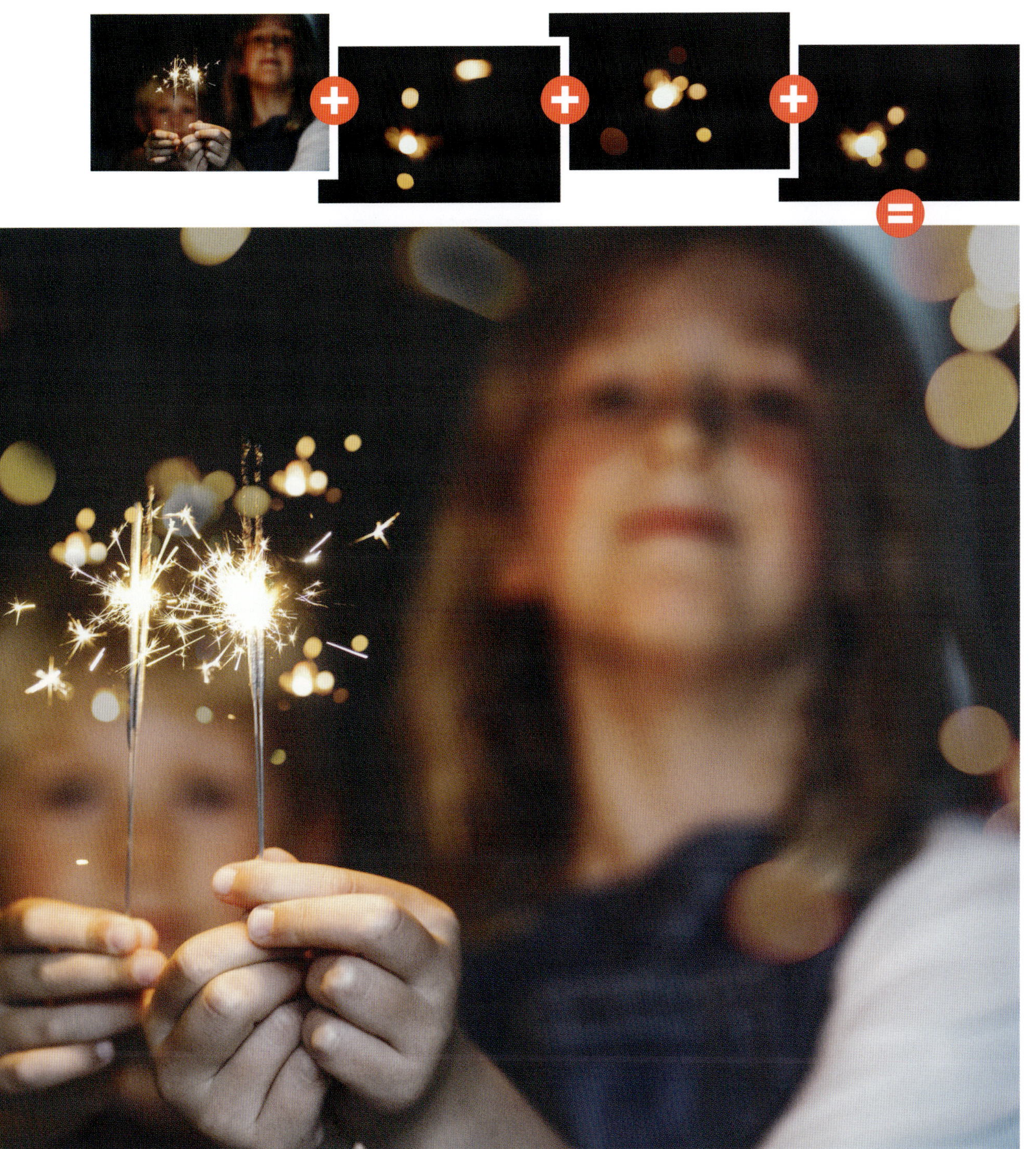

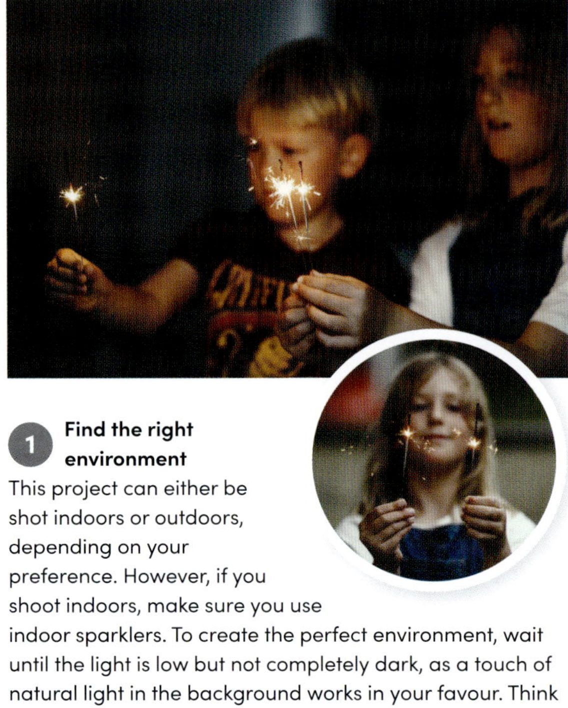

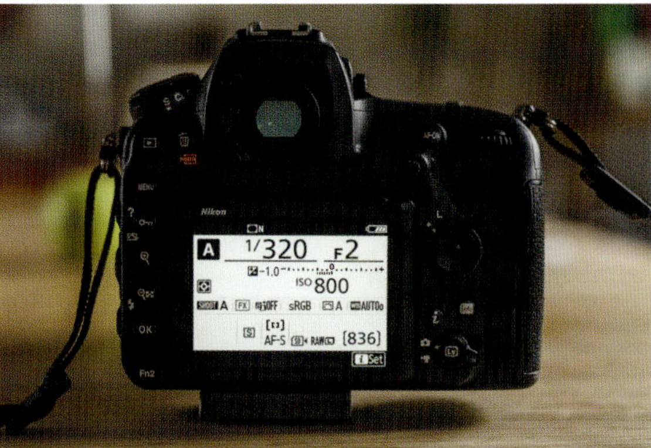


### 1 Find the right environment

This project can either be shot indoors or outdoors, depending on your preference. However, if you shoot indoors, make sure you use indoor sparklers. To create the perfect environment, wait until the light is low but not completely dark, as a touch of natural light in the background works in your favour. Think about your background and how it will frame your subject – a plain background often works best.

### 2 Dial in your camera settings

The most important setting to take into account is the aperture of the lens. Put your camera into aperture-priority mode and set aperture to around f/2 for a shallow depth of field. To ensure shutter speed is fast enough (ideally over 1/200 sec), set ISO to between 400 and 800. This is so you can handhold your camera, but it also keeps the sparks pleasingly sharp. You may need to do some light tests to determine the right camera settings.

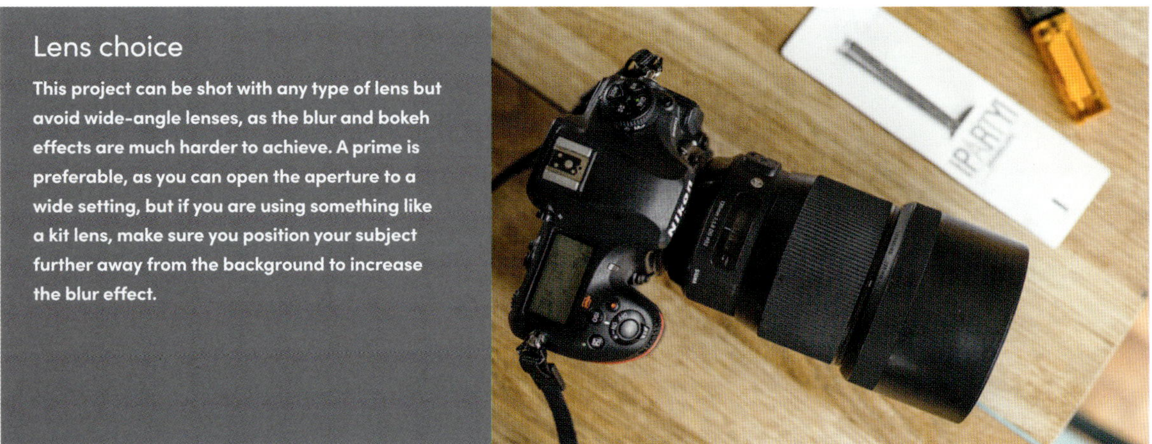


## Lens choice

**This project can be shot with any type of lens but avoid wide-angle lenses, as the blur and bokeh effects are much harder to achieve. A prime is preferable, as you can open the aperture to a wide setting, but if you are using something like a kit lens, make sure you position your subject further away from the background to increase the blur effect.**

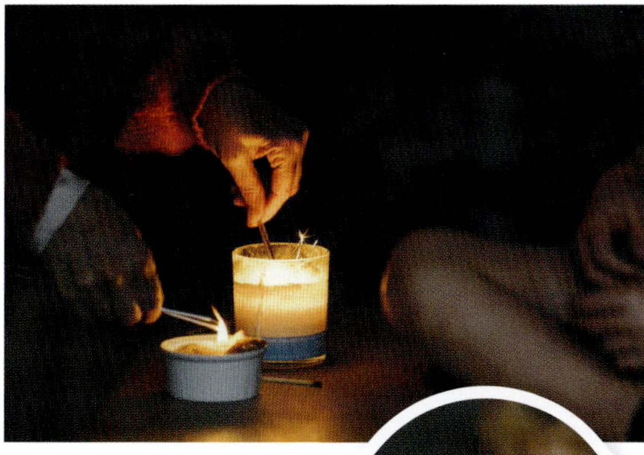

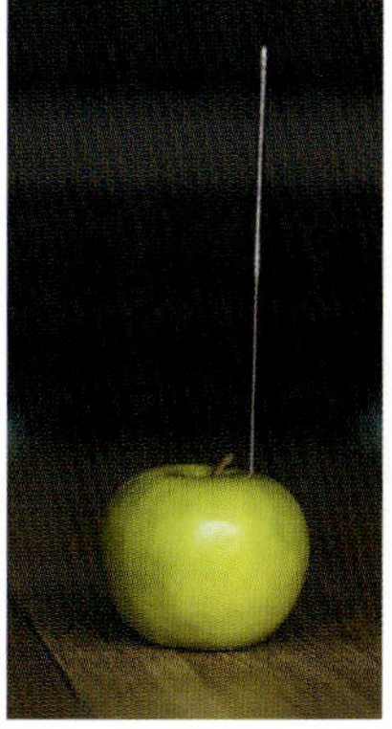

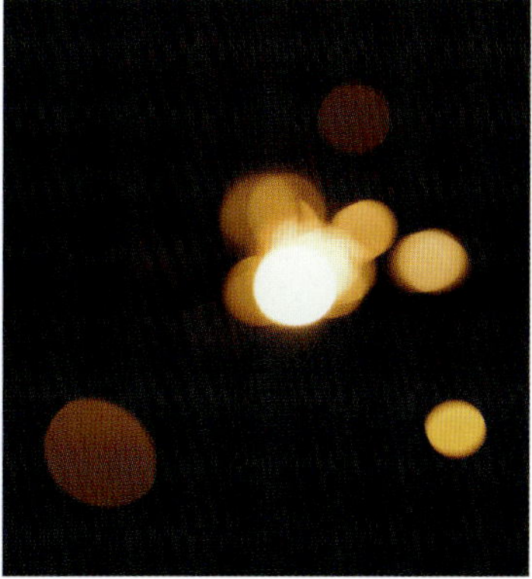

### 3 Light the sparklers

Once you have your camera ready, get the sparklers out. Ask your subject to hold the sparkler at arm's length, and slightly raised, to create the shallow depth-of-field effect. Run through the technique before you light anything to ensure everybody knows what they are doing. Focus should be on the sparkler and the hand. Keep shooting as the sparkler burns down the stick.

### 4 Capture the bokeh image

Next, shoot your bokeh image. Keep the same camera settings as before but instead of using AF, switch your lens to manual focus and knock the focus out to create those round bokeh dots. Shoot again from the start of the sparkler until the end to get a selection of images, using an apple as an inanimate sparkler holder.

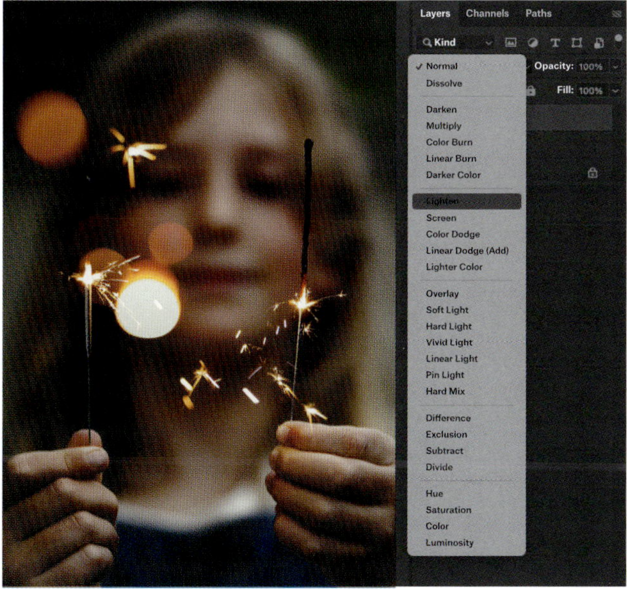


### 5 Style and combine the two images

Tone and stylise your images in Lightroom. Keep the background cool and use warmer tones for the bokeh and foreground so the two contrast well against each other. Once you're happy with the style of your images, export these files into Photoshop. To layer your bokeh images on top of your original, import each bokeh image one at a time and change the blending mode to Lighten. Experiment with turning down the opacity of the bokeh layers. Adjust the size and position of each bokeh image (for example, place some small bokeh effects around the sparkler and larger bokeh effects in the corners) to create a final look that you're happy with.

# GET PERFECT PANNING

**THE IDEA**
**Capture pin-sharp and speedy motion blur for pro-style photos at your local racetrack.**

**Time required:** 2 hours

**Kit needed:**
- DSLR or mirrorless camera
- 400mm lens

**Camera settings:**
1/320 sec at f/5.6, ISO 200

**Skill level:**

**Many of the best motorsport photos have one thing in common: a sense of speed. We're taught that fast shutter speeds will freeze moments of action, so why would the high-octane energy of motorsport be any different? At a shutter speed of 1/320 sec, you can capture a crisp shot of a motorbike zooming around a circuit, but you'll also freeze the background and wheels, removing any traces of motion. For all the viewer knows, your subject was stationary on a racetrack. To retain a sense of velocity, you need to shoot at a much slower shutter speed. However, this will blur the entire subject.**

The answer is to sight and track your subject through the viewfinder, matching its speed while engaging continuous focus, and press the shutter when everything is perfectly framed. This is called panning. Do it in one fluid movement and you'll end up with spinning wheels and a tack-sharp subject surrounded by smooth lines of blur. Faster subjects and slower shutter speeds result in more motion, but it's harder to keep the subject in focus.

Depending on the speed of your subject, a shutter speed of around 1/320 sec is a good middle ground that provides decent motion blur and a high hit rate of sharp subjects. To start with, try shooting at faster shutter speeds and slow it down as you get more confident.

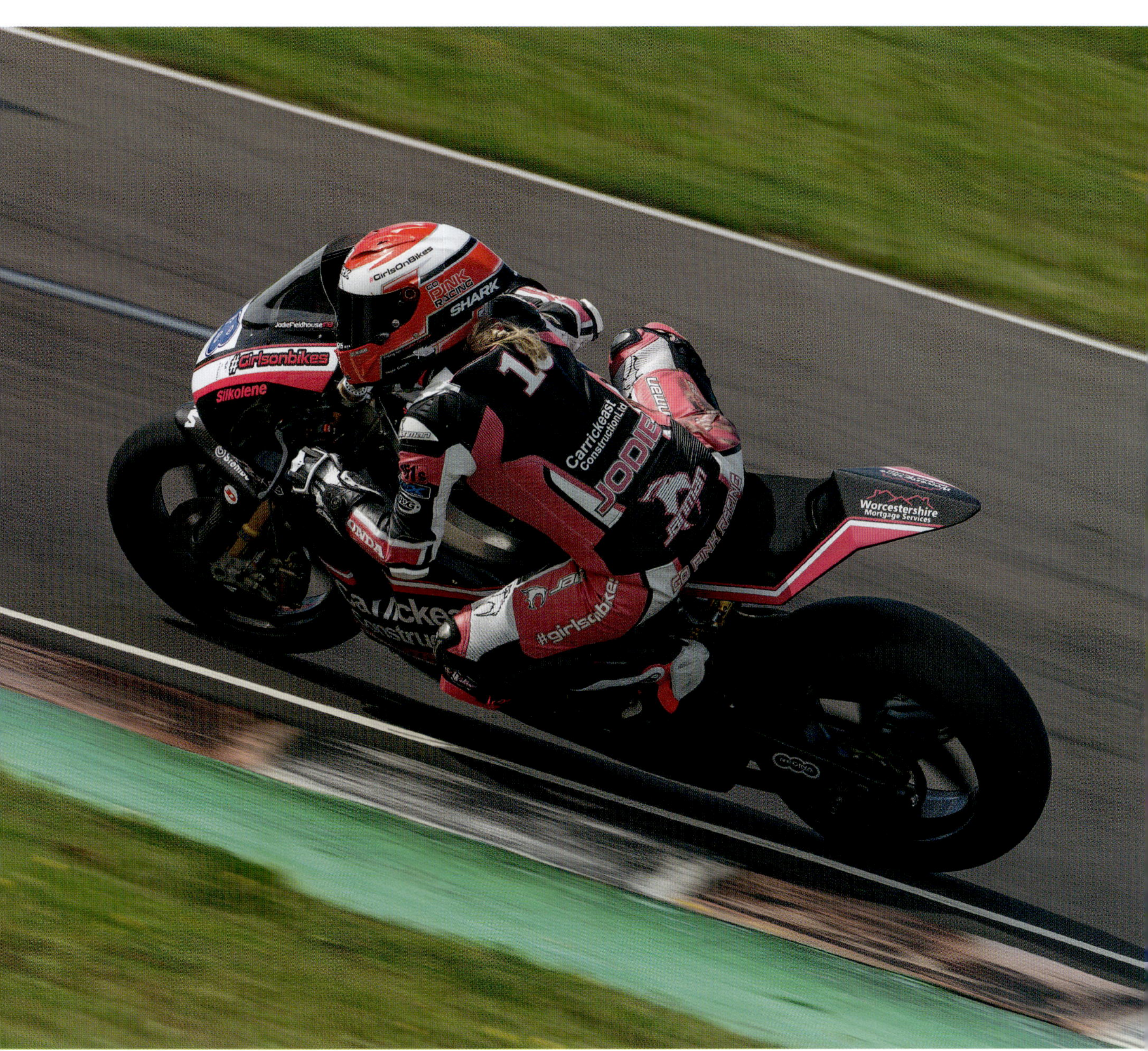
#GirlsOnBikes
GO PINK RACING
SHARK
#Girlsonbikes
Silkolene
Carrickeast Construction Ltd
JODIE
Worcestershire Mortgage Services
#girlsonbikes

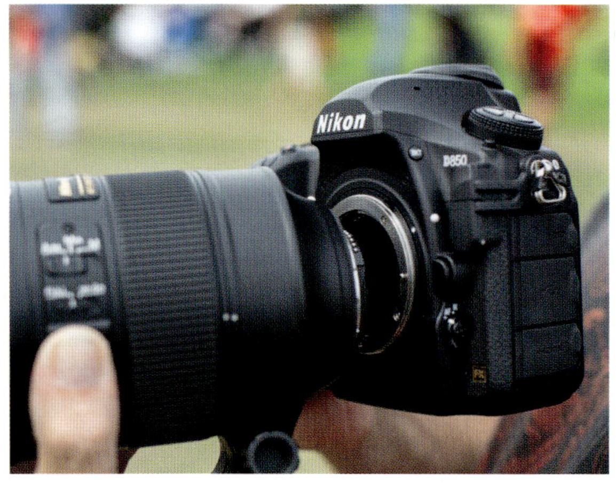


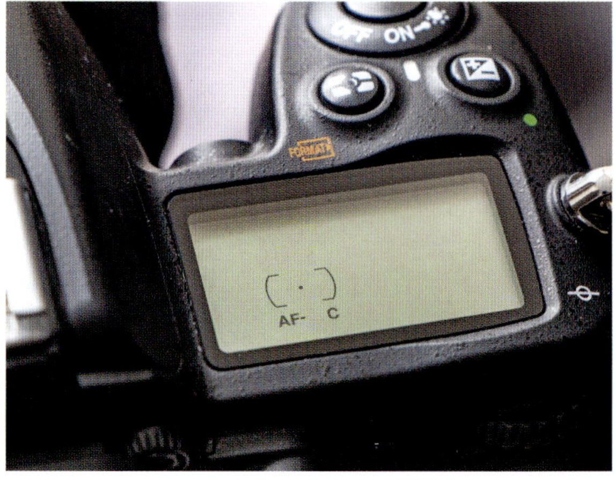


**1 Use a long lens**
A lens with a large zoom range is preferable, as this will give you enough reach when you're positioned far from the track but is also suitable for when you get a little bit closer to the action.

**2 Switch to continuous focusing**
Set your AF mode to continuous and your AF-area mode to single-point to allow you to target a rider's helmet. If you're struggling to find focus, use a 'dynamic' AF-area Mode. A cluster of AF points will appear, and the camera will identify the most suitable point to focus on.

**3 Get your stance straight**
Panning is the most physical technique in photography. Plant your feet shoulder-width apart and point them in the direction you intend to frame your subject. Switch to manual mode, look through the viewfinder and frame as if photographing a stationary shot to receive an accurate meter reading.

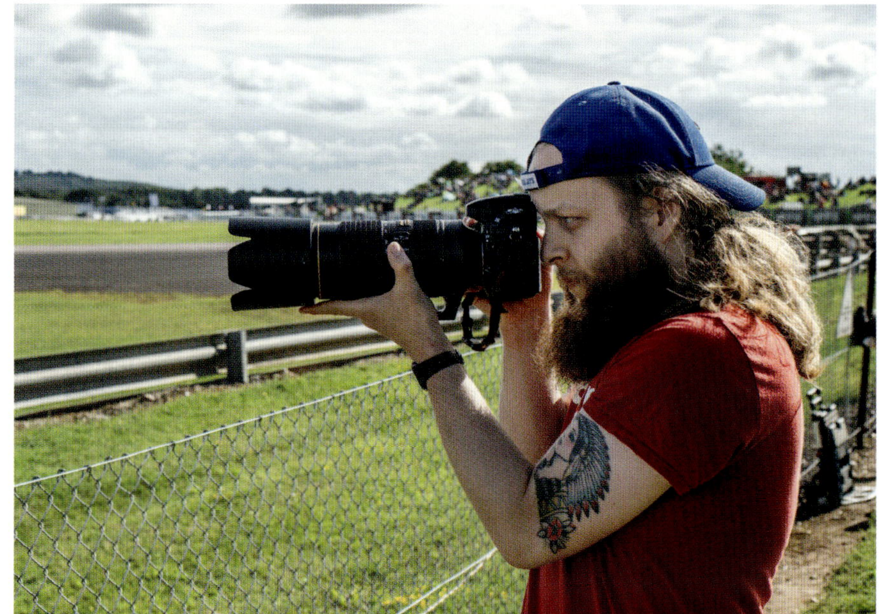

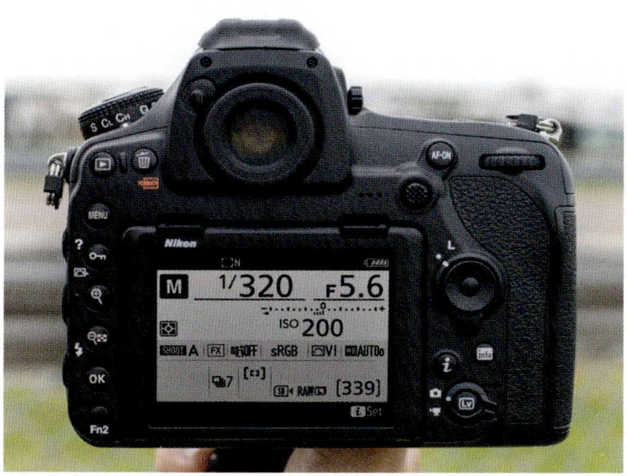


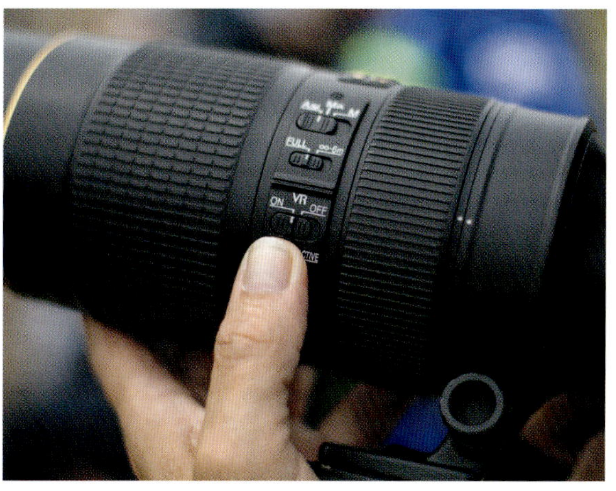

**4 Dial in the right settings**
Unless you're at a night race, you shouldn't need to push ISO too high. The range of apertures available will depend on the speed of your lens, but anything between f/4 and f/8 should work well. Your shutter speed will depend on how much motion blur you want to include.

**5 Slow and steady will win**
Try to keep your shots as sharp as possible by maintaining good form when panning. Vibration reduction should always be turned on (if you have it) and this is especially true when you are using shutter speeds of 1/15 sec or slower.

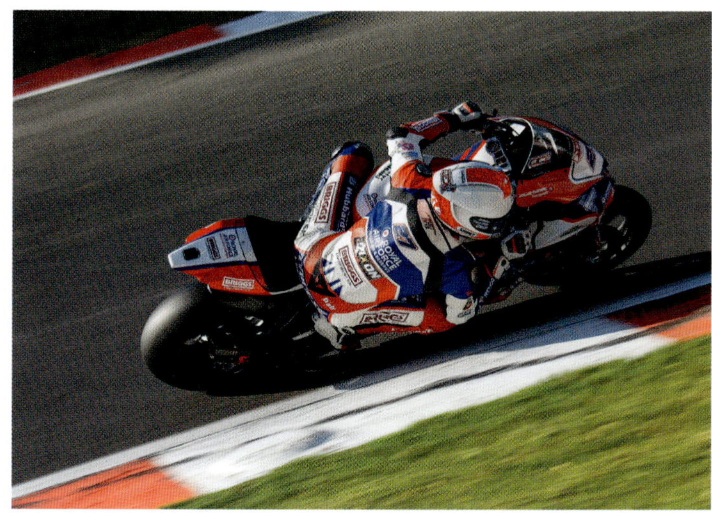

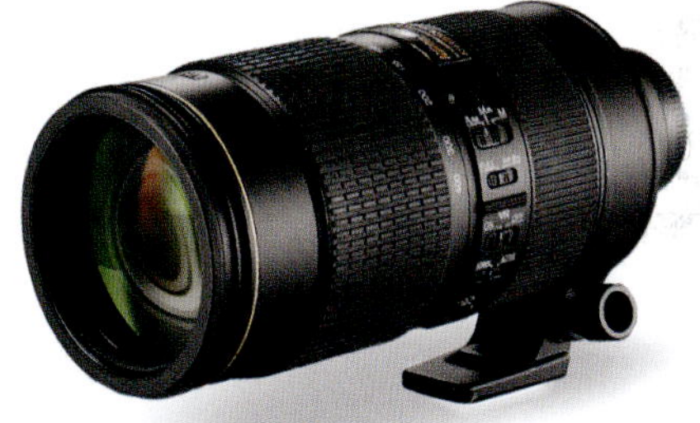

Invest in a 'workhorse' super-telephoto zoom that's fast enough for daytime track-side photography, capable of capturing crisp images and light enough to use handheld.

# GO POP!

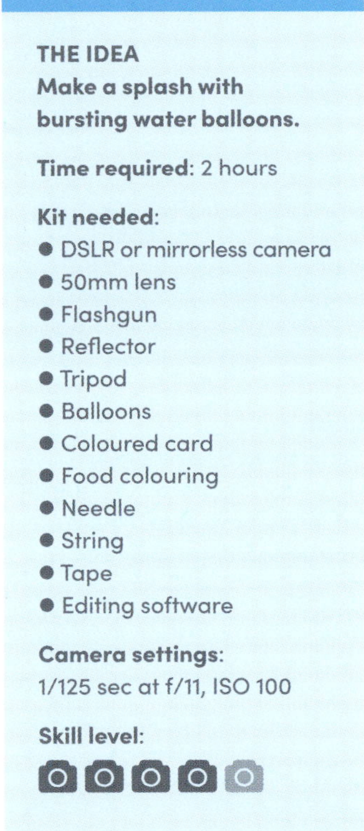

**THE IDEA**
**Make a splash with bursting water balloons.**

**Time required**: 2 hours

**Kit needed**:
- DSLR or mirrorless camera
- 50mm lens
- Flashgun
- Reflector
- Tripod
- Balloons
- Coloured card
- Food colouring
- Needle
- String
- Tape
- Editing software

**Camera settings**:
1/125 sec at f/11, ISO 100

**Skill level**:

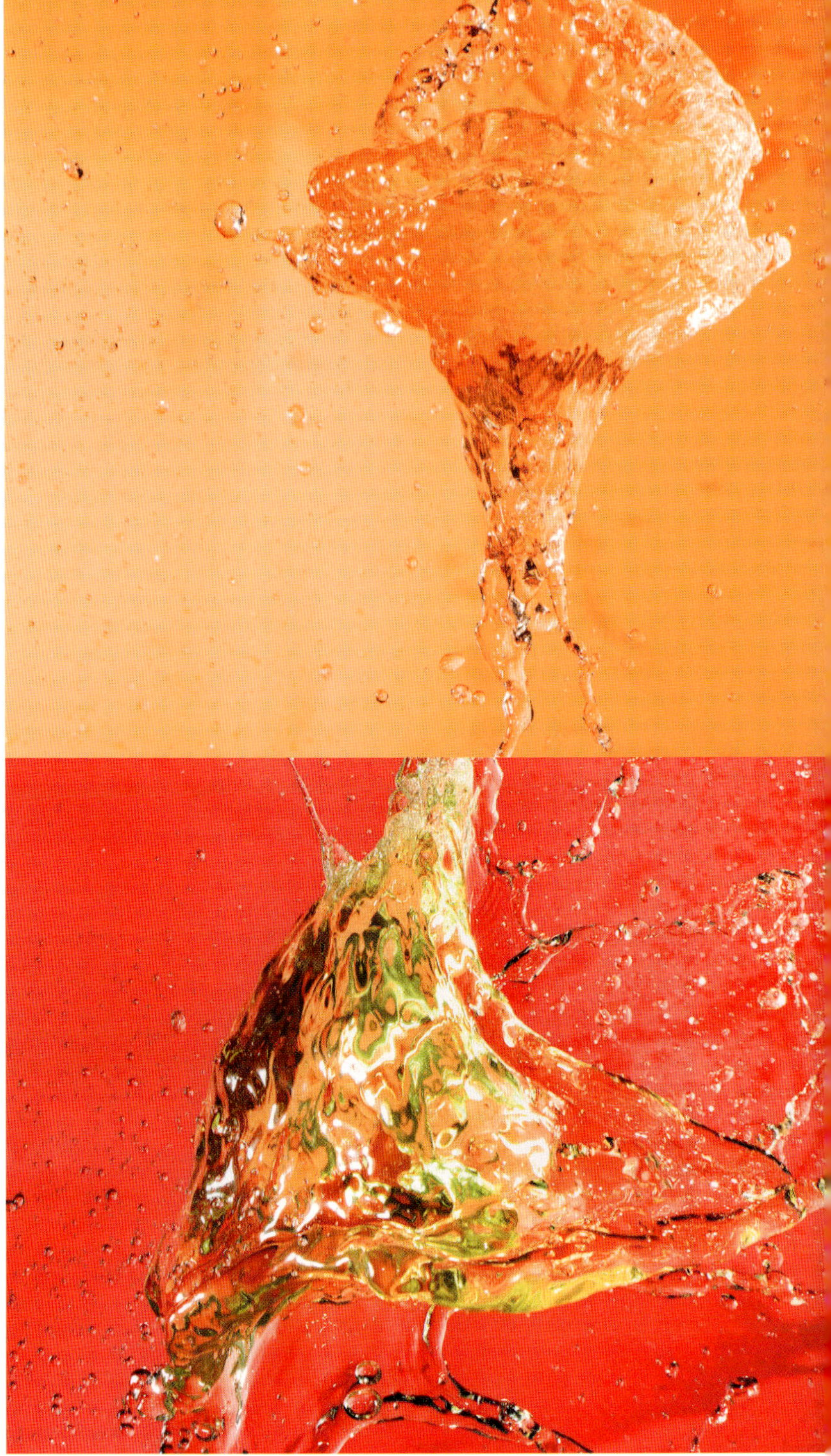

**This project is all about capturing a water balloon bursting. The main items you need are some balloons, food colouring, a needle, a tripod, additional lighting (a flashgun is ideal), and a bright backdrop such as coloured card.**

Although many photographers apply this technique using a movement or sound trigger, you just need to be good with your timing – and be prepared to try it a few times.

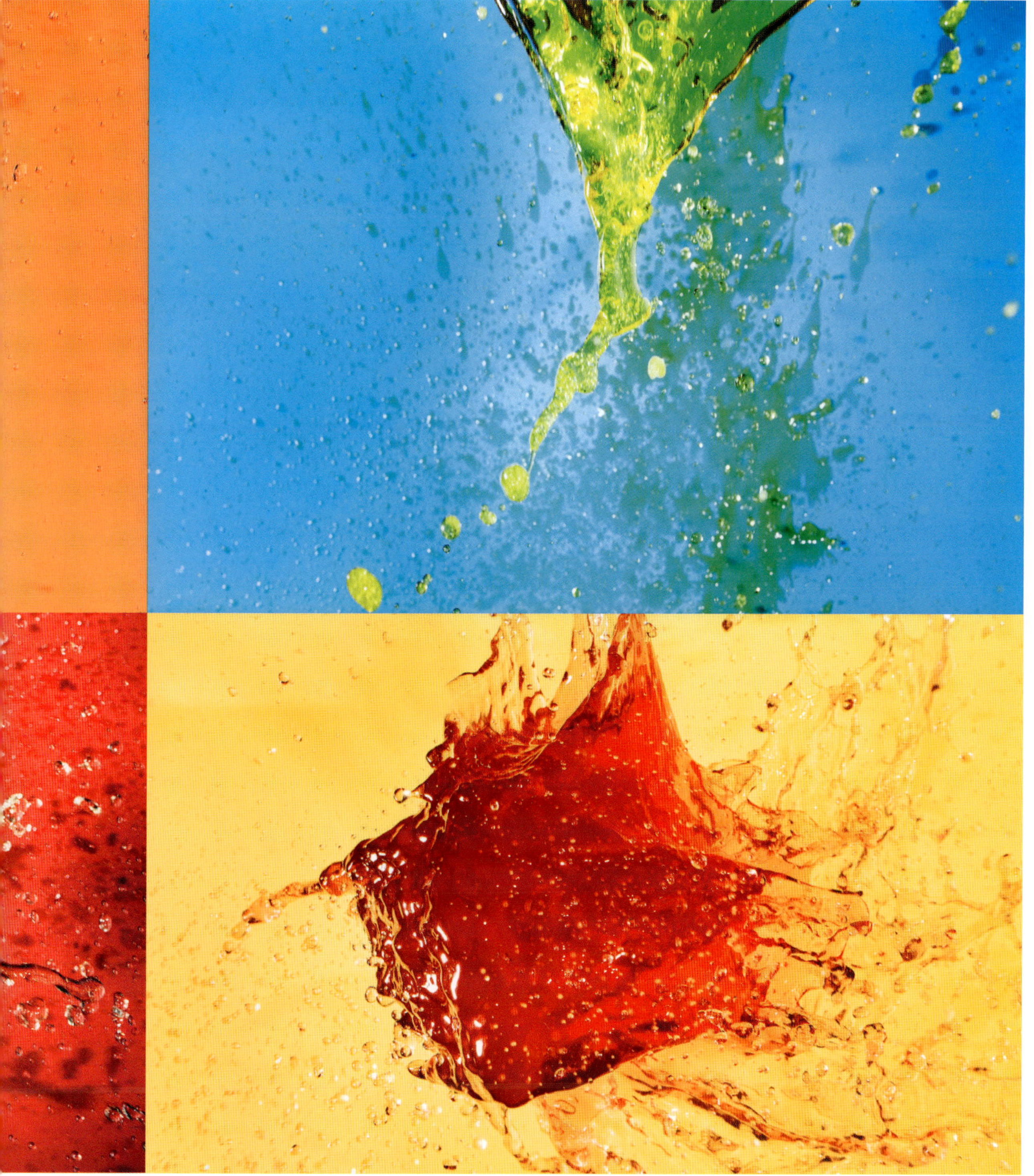

If using flash, set the shutter speed below 1/250 sec to sync with the light. If not using flash, set the shutter speed to at least 1/500 sec (faster if possible), and increase ISO to compensate if shooting in lower light. You might want to add some form of extra lighting to your set-up, such as a reflector and LED lights, to add a degree of 'lift' to the water. Select your camera's burst mode (not an option for flash-lit images), so you can get the entire sequence and pick the best from the bunch.

This project can get messy, so is a great one to try in your garden, but shoot indoors if the wind is too strong and the balloons are flying around.

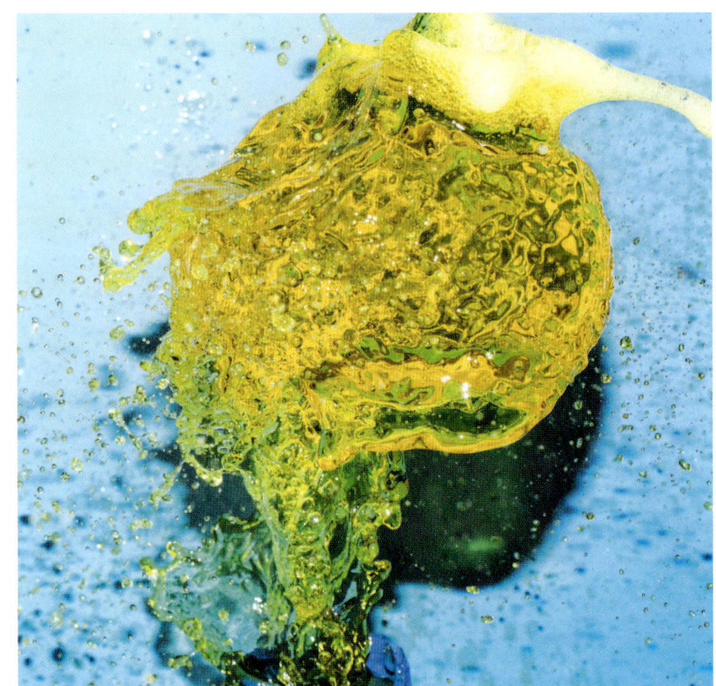

**1 Props you will need**
Use a range of coloured cards to form the backdrop, and add food colouring to the water in the balloons. The card will get wet after each try, so you will need to change it after each shot. If you use food colouring, put a few drops in the balloon first before you add the water. The more food colouring you use, the stronger the colour. It can also help to burst the balloon if you blow a little air in once the balloon is filled with water. Have some duct tape to hand for securing the backdrop in place.

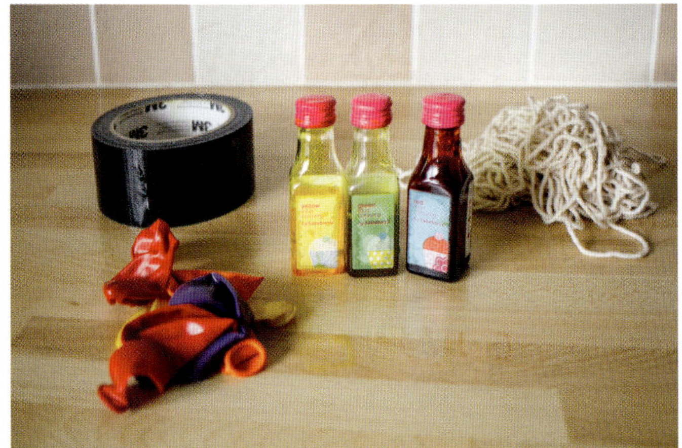

**2** **Use a pool**
If shooting outdoors, you don't need to worry about catching all the water, but if shooting indoors, a children's paddling pool is the perfect solution. You may also want to keep a towel around to wipe down your equipment.

**3** **Lighting set-up**
Position the on-camera flash to illuminate the balloon and water, and place an external flash to the right to light the backdrop. Set the on-camera flash to 1/8 power to trigger the external flash, which should be set to 1/2 power. A reflector will bounce some light back into the scene.

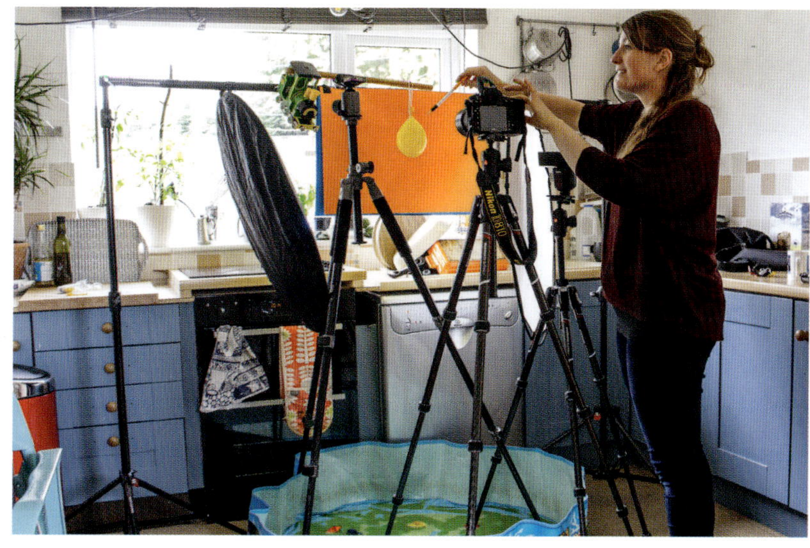

**4** **Camera settings and timings**
To sync with the flash, switch your camera to manual mode. This image was lit purely by the flashgun, so exposure had to be accurate. Count down then open the shutter and pop the balloon at the same time. You may have to try it a few times to get it right.

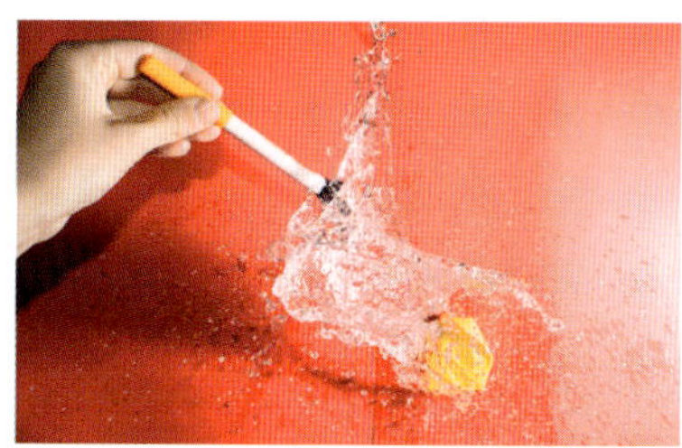

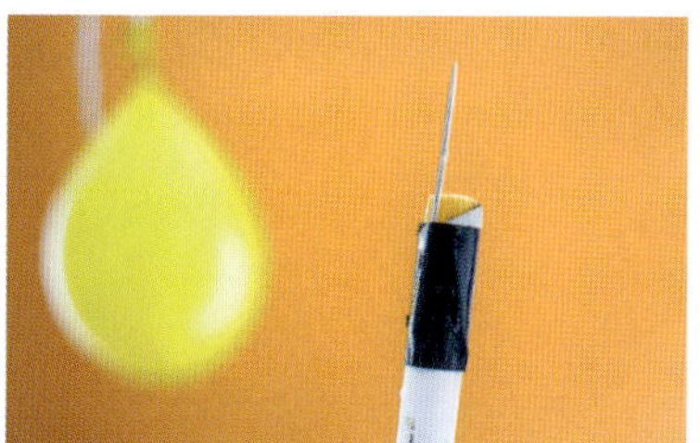

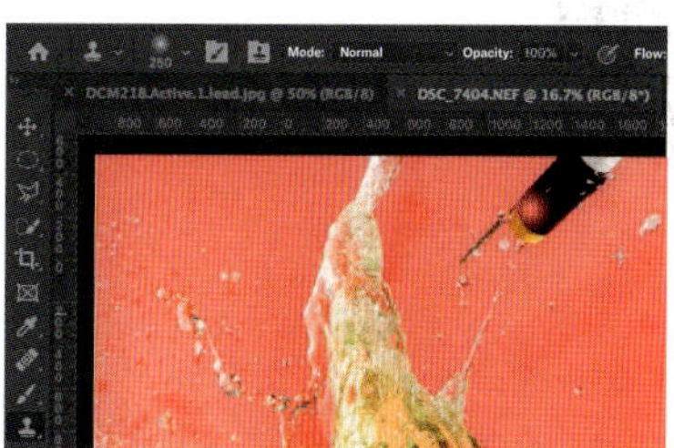

Be aware of which side you need to burst the balloon from to avoid casting a strong shadow with your hand. The aim is to achieve a nice, flat light, and then to source a point to copy, and paint the cloned area over the unwanted part.

As you will need to edit out the needle in your image, instead of holding the needle by hand, tape the needle to a pen. This makes it a far easier editing job.

To clone out the needle in Photoshop, select the Clone Stamp tool, Alt-click to source a point to copy, and paint the cloned area over the unwanted part. Boost the contrast to make images jump from the page.

# CREATE FALLING FOOD

**THE IDEA**
**Throw food into the frame and shoot it using flash.**

**Time required**: 3 hours

**Kit needed:**
- DSLR or mirrorless camera
- 50mm lens
- Tripod
- Backdrop
- Reflector
- Two flashguns
- Diffuser panel
- Food and props
- Editing software

**Camera settings:**
1/200 sec at f/16, ISO 100

**Skill level:**

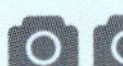

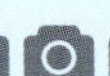
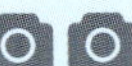

**If you enjoy setting up shots in the comfort of your own home, this is the perfect project for you. Not only will it test your technical skills, but it's also a fun, creative challenge that will push you to be experimental with your photography.**

To try this yourself, you will need a few essential items. Firstly, prepare a backdrop, which could be a simple piece of card or a sheet. You will also need two flashguns, though if you only have one, you can substitute the second for another light source, like a lamp, to illuminate the backdrop. A reflector is also useful, but you can improvise by wrapping tinfoil around a piece of card. A diffuser panel will help to spread and soften light. If you don't have one, then some greaseproof paper over a cardboard frame will do the trick. Finally, pick some food and props that you think will work well in your photos.

Fire your flash units with a remote trigger, but if you don't have one of these, use on-camera flash. Fire the flashes through two separate channels if they are set to different strengths. Finally, a word of warning: as you are throwing food around, it can get messy, so cleaning supplies are essential after your shoot.

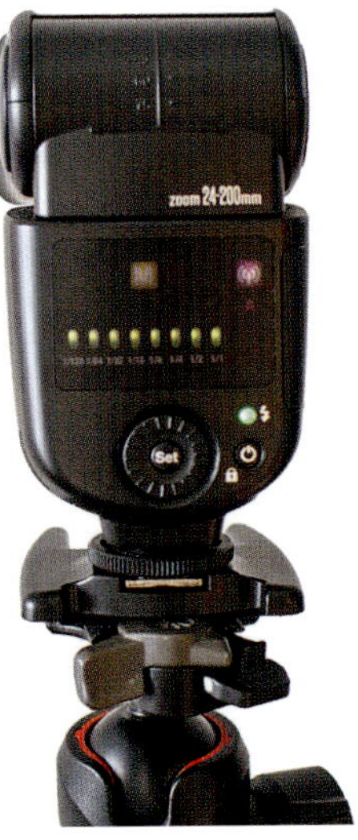


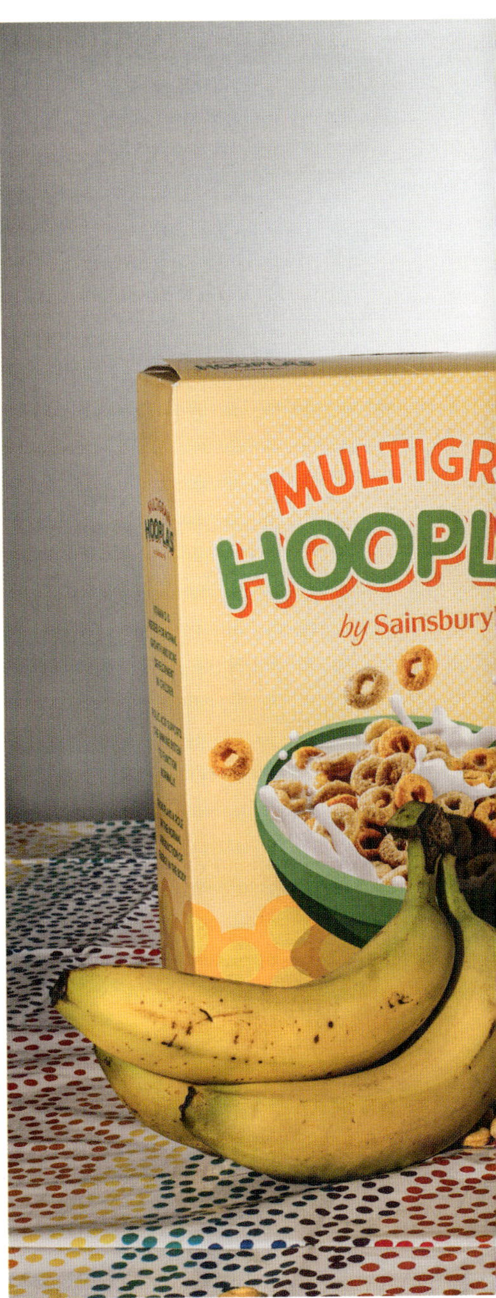

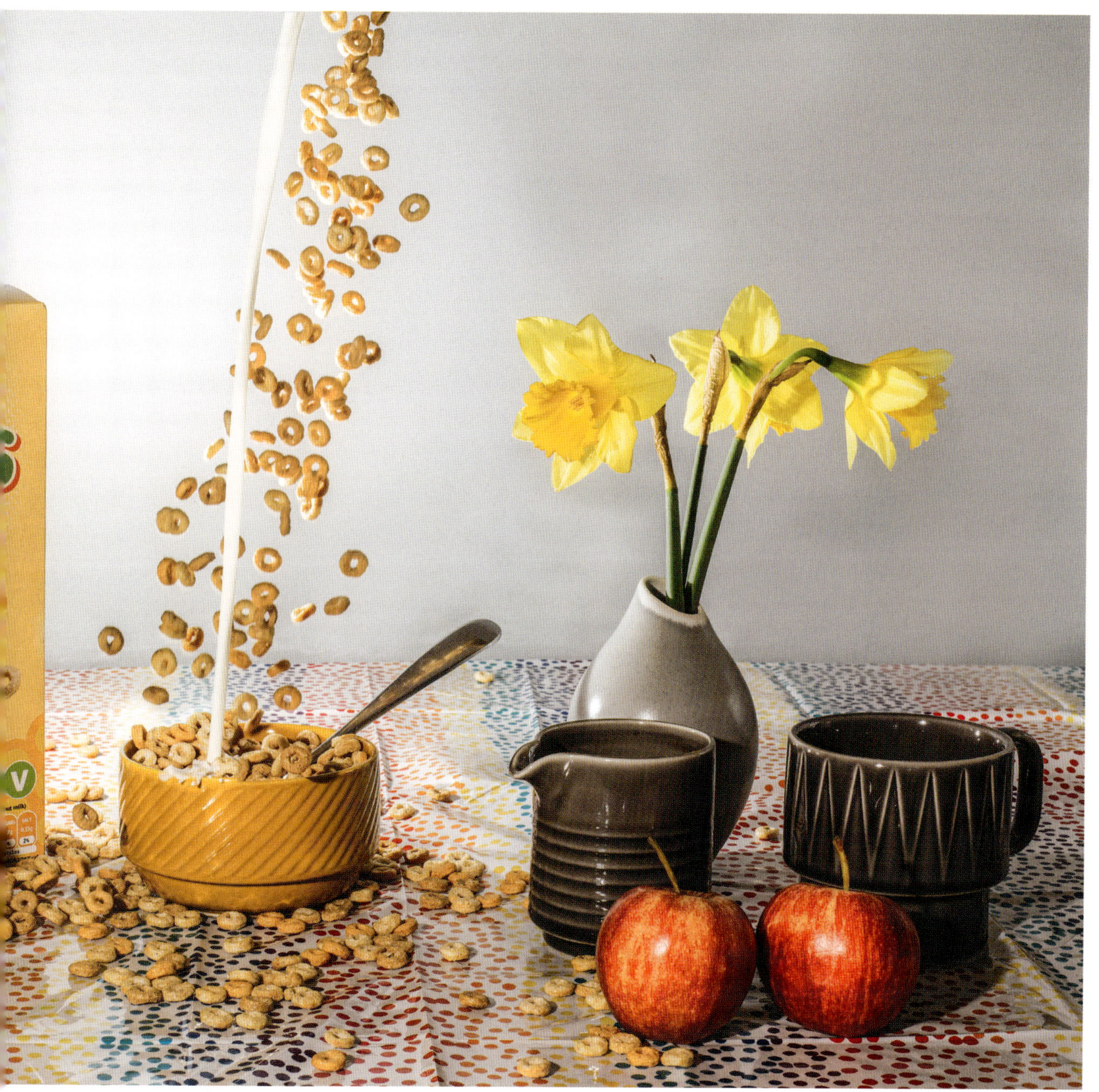

## 1 The setting

To create the set-up, hang up a neutral backdrop and drape a colourful tablecloth over the table. Position a breakfast bowl in the middle of the frame and fill it with cereal. To add colour, strategically position flowers or fruit around the frame. Mount your camera onto a tripod and keep tweaking the composition and the positioning of objects in the frame until you're happy.

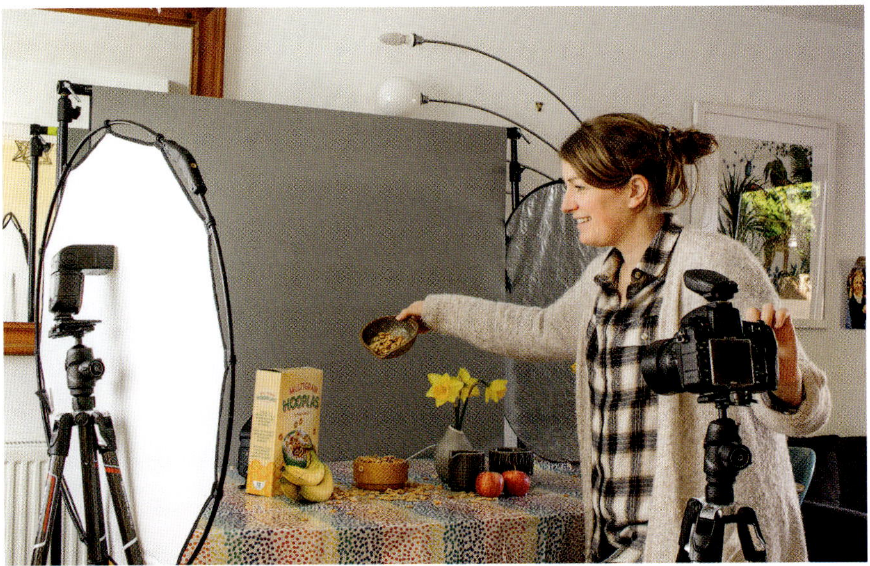


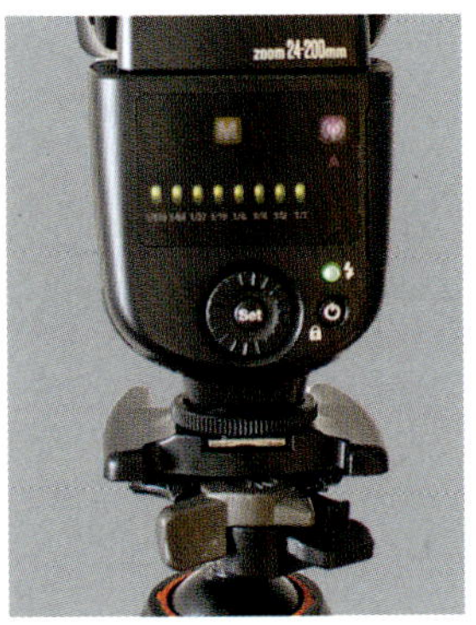


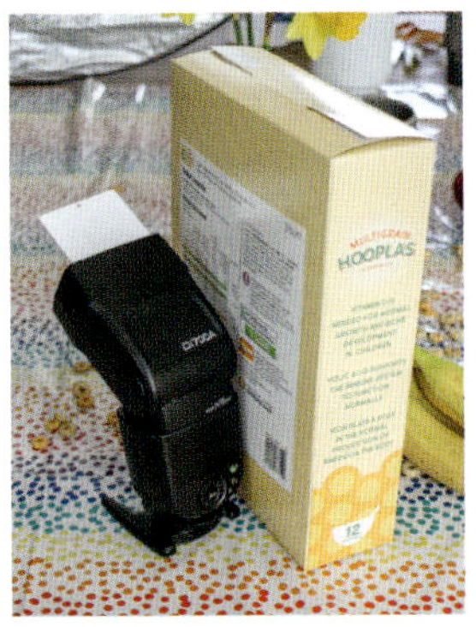


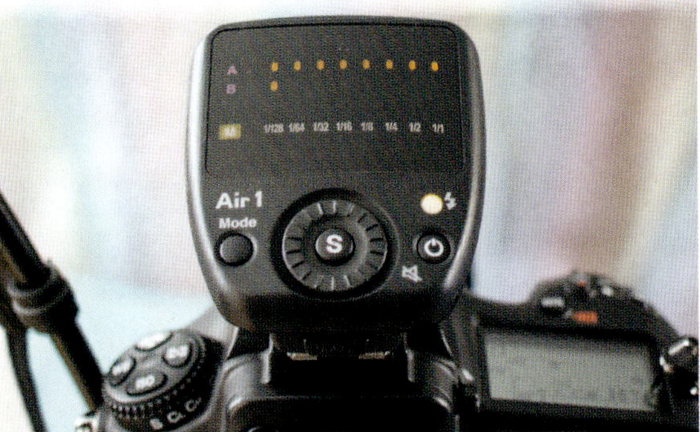


## 2 Lights

It's easier to build your lighting set-up one light at a time, as this allows you to see where the light is falling and tweak the positioning for perfect results. Place the key light at the front of the set-up and use a diffuser panel to spread the light more evenly. To light the background and remove most of the shadows there, place one of the flashguns behind the cereal box. Position the reflector to the side of this flashgun, to bounce light back onto the backdrop.

## 3 Camera and flash settings

Put the camera into manual mode and sync the shutter speed to the flash. Select the lowest ISO and an aperture of around f/16. To balance the flashlight to the camera settings, set the front flash to channel A at full power, and the flashgun at the back to channel B at its lowest setting.

## 4 Getting the timing right

Achieving the falling cereal is simply a case of dropping it into the frame and experimenting with the timing and quantity. The best method is to drop a bowlful at once, and to fire the shutter straight after the release. You will have some mistakes and some keepers, so keep trying. To make it easier, shoot two separate exposures of the milk and the cereal. If you have an extra pair of hands, you could try and shoot them together, but it might be trickier.

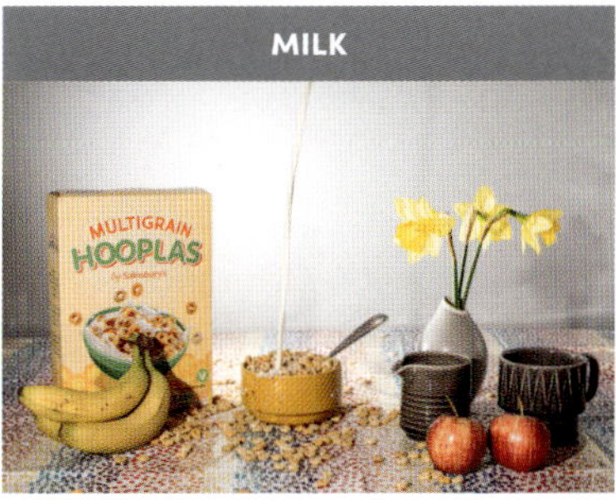


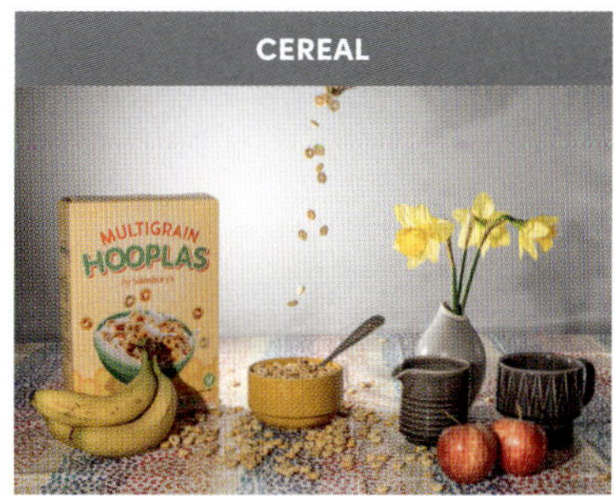


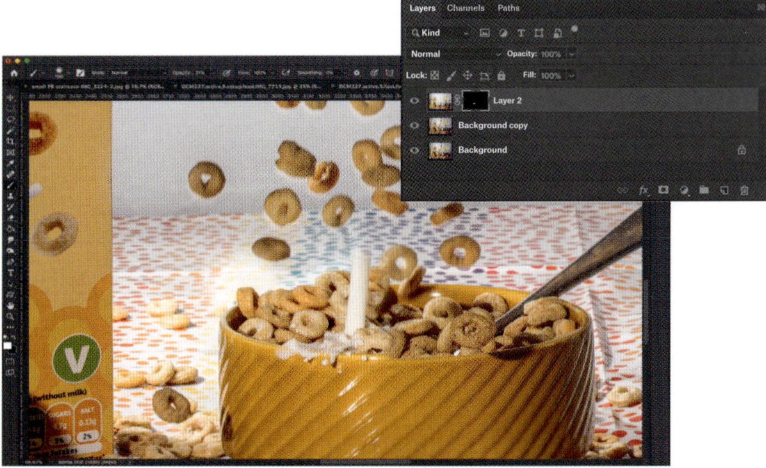


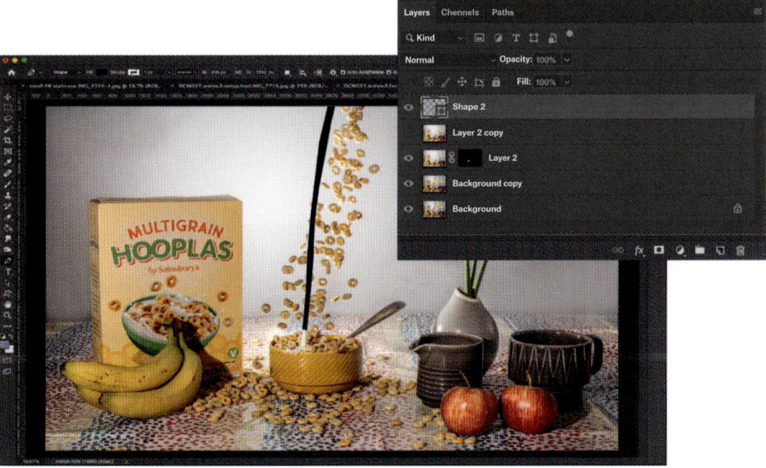


## 5 The final edit

Edit the two images (cereal and milk) together in Photoshop. Bring both images over into one document, with the milk layer on top. To cut out the milk, use the Pen Tool for accurate results. Zoom into the picture and place markers around the falling milk. The Pen Tool will create a new Shape Layer. Once you're happy with your selection, move the milk layer above the Shape Layer in the Layers Panel, right-click on the top layer, and select Create Clipping Mask to paste the milk into the shape.

If the milk has made a splash at the bottom of the bowl, duplicate the milk layer, add a black layer mask and use a white brush to paint back the parts you want to reveal. Finally, on a merged top layer, use a grey paint brush at a reduced Opacity (around 20%) to smooth out the background for a flawless result.

# GET SMASHING RESULTS

**THE IDEA**
**Drop a wine glass to create a cracking image.**

**Time required**: 3 hours

**Kit needed**:

- DSLR or mirrorless camera
- Wide-angle lens
- LED light pane
- Reflector
- Tripod
- Glasses of coloured liquid
- Slate plate
- Wallpaper lining

**Camera settings**:
1/800 sec at f/4, ISO 1600

**Skill level**:

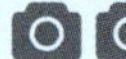 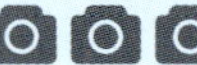

**There are many ways to capture glass breaking on a hard surface. Many professionals use flash and a trigger system that is activated by the sound of the glass smashing, but if you don't have this high-tech gear to hand, here's an easy hack. You will need a strong continuous light source – and be prepared to clean up when you're finished, as this is going to get messy.**

Let's highlight some safety procedures. First, lots of glass will fly everywhere, so wear shoes and clean up properly afterwards. It is recommended to wear protective eye gear and have an assistant to help drop the glass, although it's possible to do it single-handed.

When dropping one glass on top of another, release the top one at a slight angle. This creates the biggest break and splash, which although messy, leads to the best effect.

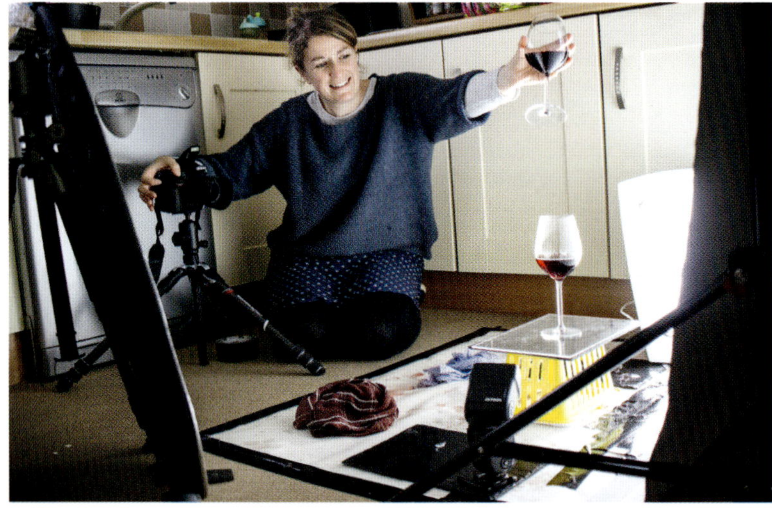

**1 Tape cardboard/paper to floor**
The kitchen floor is the best place to set up, as it's easy to clean up afterwards. Tape some wallpaper lining over a large area to roll the glass up once finished. This will also keep most of the liquid off the floor. Place a slate plate on a raised area, and over the top of this place a sheet of Perspex to make a reflective surface.

**2 Camera settings**
To capture the sequence unfolding, select your camera's fastest burst mode. Before dropping the glass, position the focus point over the sitting glass. Make sure you have a fast enough shutter speed to capture the action. Start at 1/800 sec and increase if necessary.

**3 Lighting tips**
To light your setup, use a large continuous LED light panel that illuminates the glasses and the backdrop. Watch out for unwanted shadows. Place a reflector to the other side of the glass to bounce some light back into the darker areas. If you don't have an LED panel, use natural light – set up by a window or even outside if the weather allows.

**Red wine is expensive and a nightmare to clean up. Instead, mix a few drops of red food colouring in with some water and pour a small amount into each glass. After each take, wipe down the backdrop and surrounding area to get it back to pristine white.**

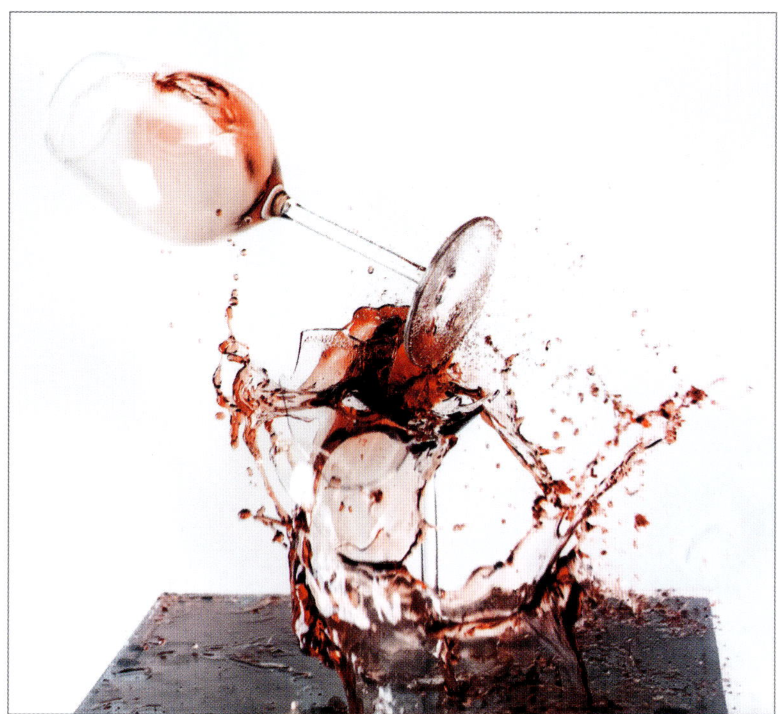

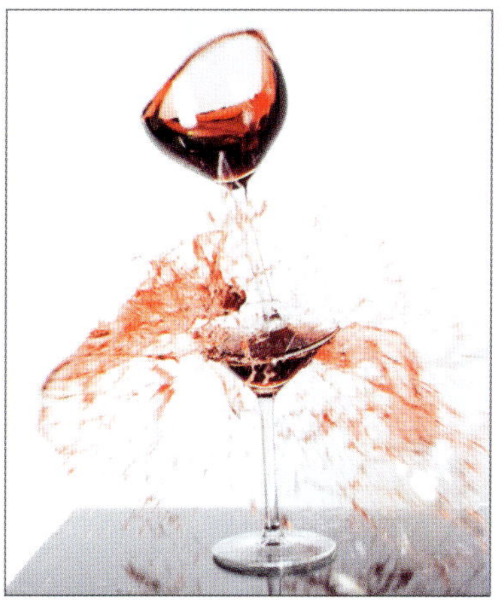

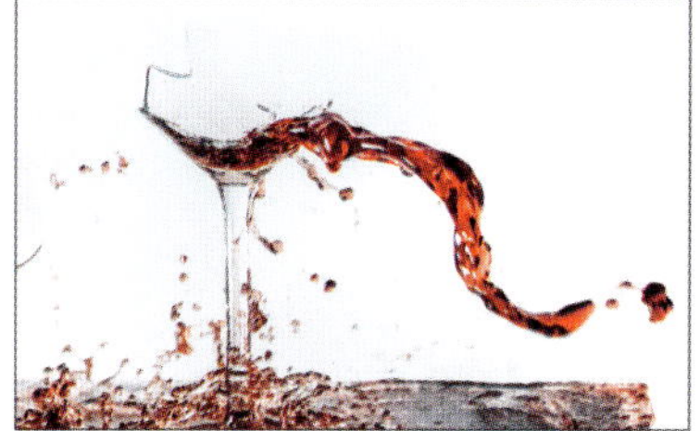

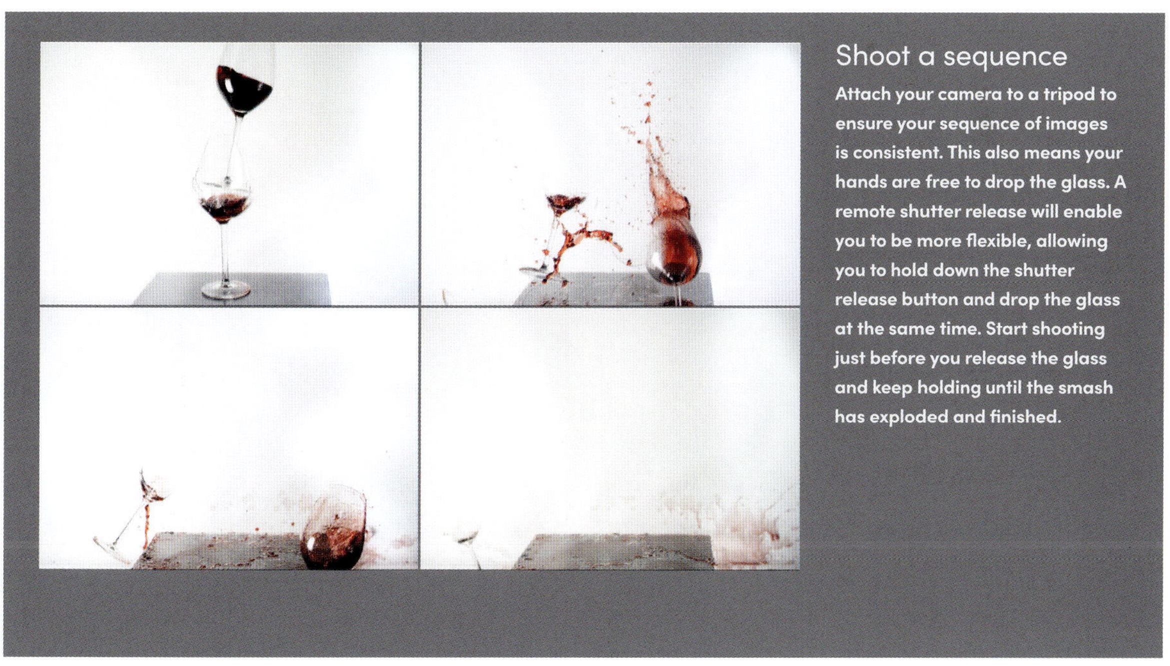

## Shoot a sequence

**Attach your camera to a tripod to ensure your sequence of images is consistent. This also means your hands are free to drop the glass. A remote shutter release will enable you to be more flexible, allowing you to hold down the shutter release button and drop the glass at the same time. Start shooting just before you release the glass and keep holding until the smash has exploded and finished.**

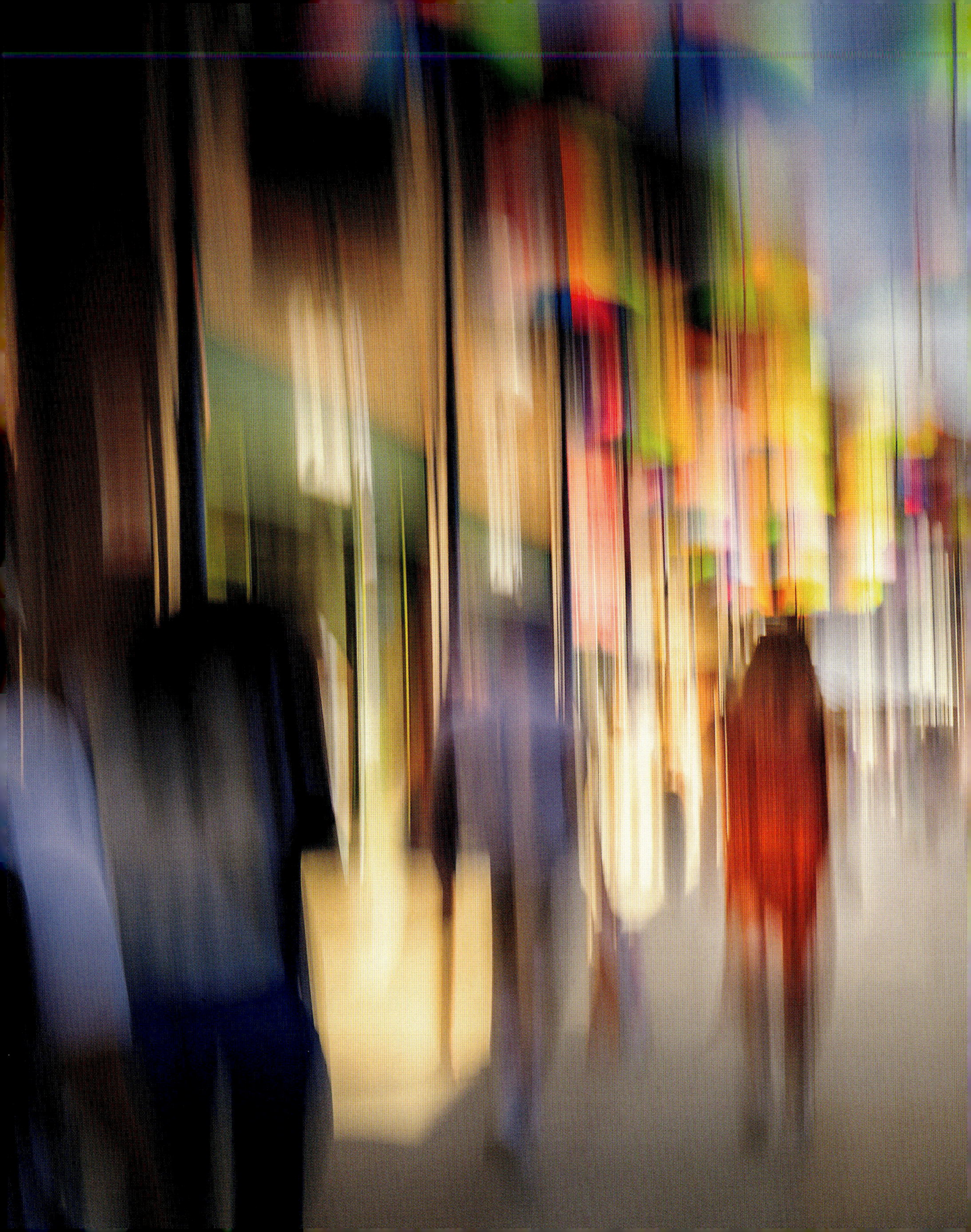

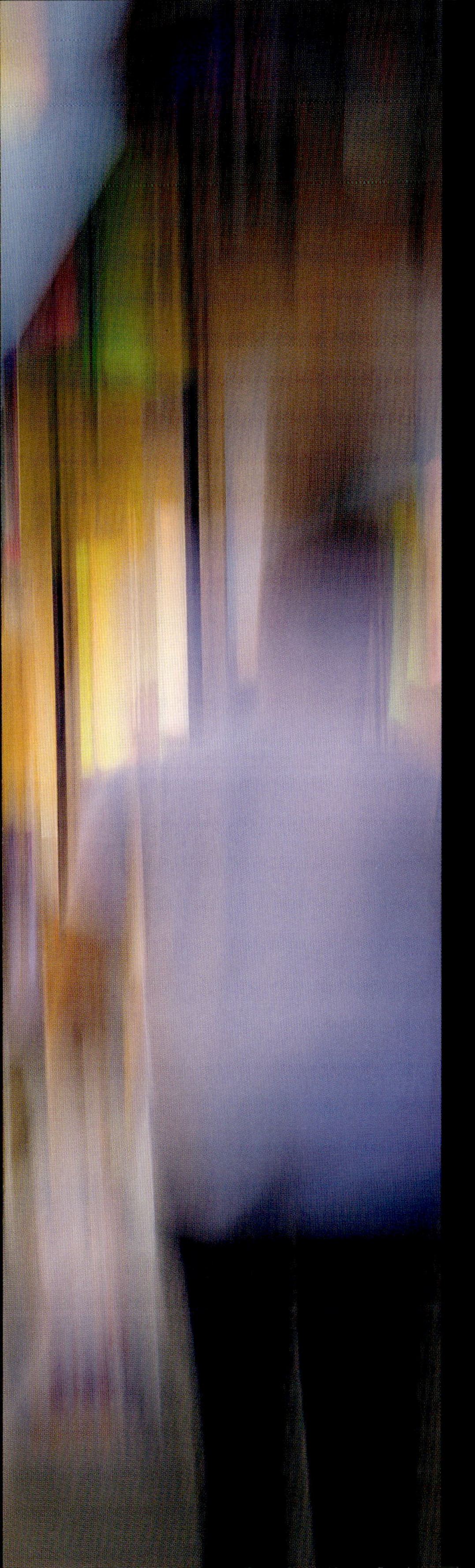

# 5

# STREET AND DOCUMENTARY IDEAS

**Whether achieved in an abstract way or captured faithfully, this type of photography is all about telling stories**

# PLAY HUNT THE ALPHABET

**THE IDEA**
**Head out with your camera and hunt for every letter between A and Z.**

**Time required**: 3 hours

**Kit needed**:
- DSLR or mirrorless camera
- Short telephoto lens
- Editing software

**Camera settings**:
1/200 sec at f/5.6 ISO 200

**Skill level**:

**For this challenge, create your own photo alphabet. This idea sounds simple, but it's a great way to train your photographic eye and see everyday objects differently.**

In terms of kit, you'll probably find a flexible telephoto lens is easier to work with, as it'll enable you to zoom in and out and isolate letter shapes more easily. Leave the tripod at home.

Set your camera to aperture-priority mode, select an aperture of around f/5.6 and a low ISO of 100–200. This will enable you to concentrate on looking for shapes and strong compositions.

Once you've found every letter, compile them into one shot using Bridge. Select all your letters, then go to Tools > Photoshop > Load Files into Photoshop Layers. Once all the images have loaded in Photoshop, size and drag them around the canvas until you're happy with the final collage. It's (almost) as simple as ABC.

For this project, shoot in an urban area that offers plenty of different shapes, objects and stimuli. Look for letters in the parks and green spaces dotted around the city, too. You don't have to shoot the letters in order (or on the same day). You might just want to keep the project in mind every time you head out onto the streets with a camera.

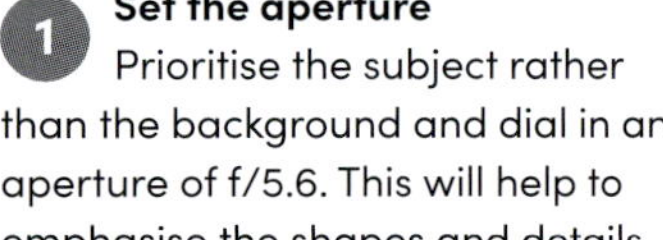

**1 Set the aperture**
Prioritise the subject rather than the background and dial in an aperture of f/5.6. This will help to emphasise the shapes and details you are photographing.

**2 Dial in the ISO**
Keep the ISO value low to get maximum image quality.

**3 Look for shapes**
You'd be amazed by everyday objects that have shapes which resemble letters of the alphabet. As you can see here, a crane can make an A, a pair of door handles an O, and a pavement chair looks like an R.

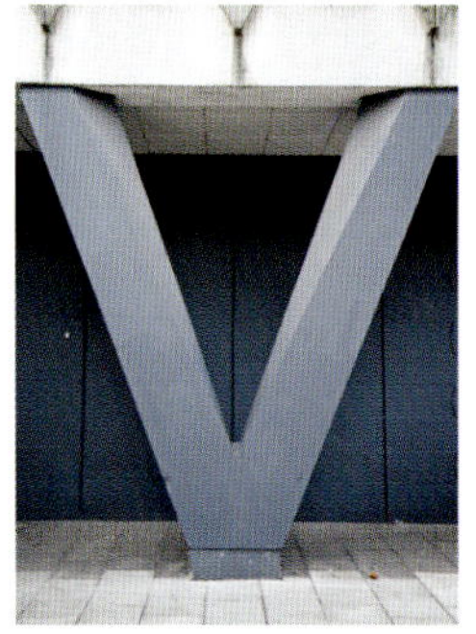

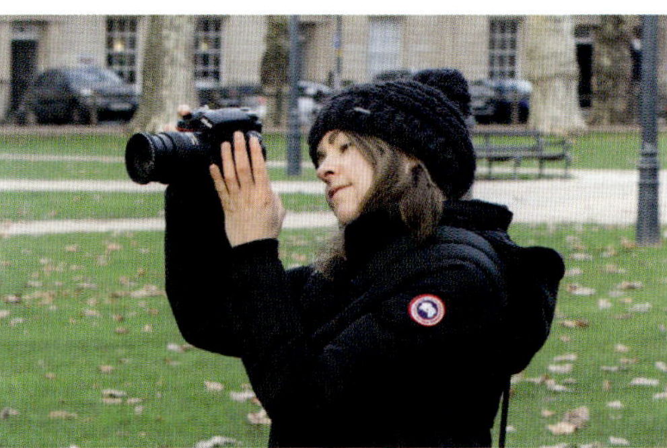

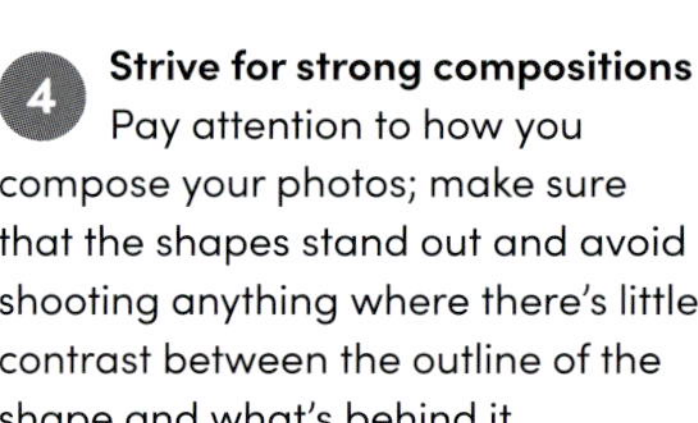

**4 Strive for strong compositions**
Pay attention to how you compose your photos; make sure that the shapes stand out and avoid shooting anything where there's little contrast between the outline of the shape and what's behind it.

**5 Edit as you go**
As you will need to make a composite image once you've captured 26 suitable photos, save time afterwards and cull any frames that aren't suitable as you go along.

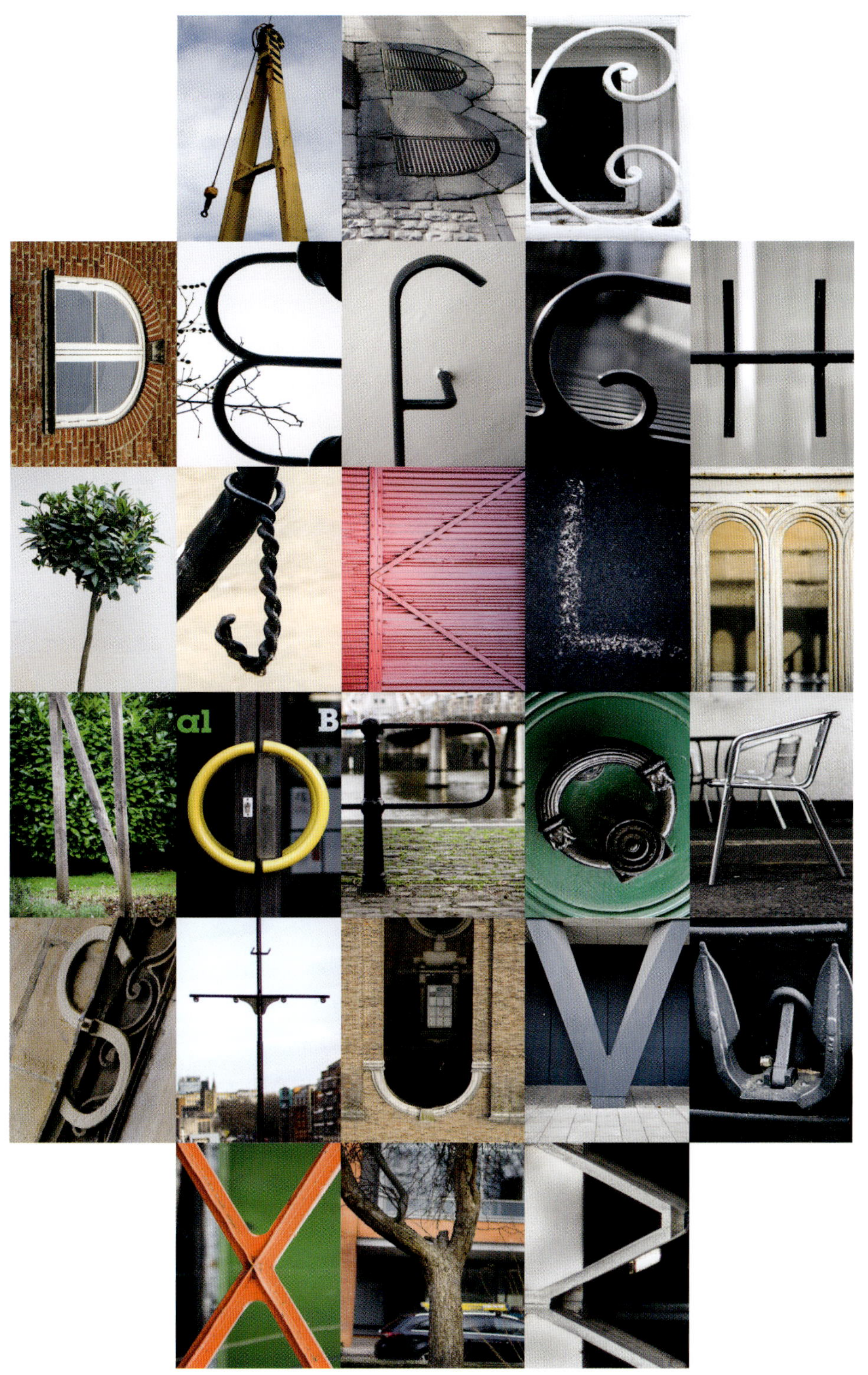
al
B

# EXPLORE A BYGONE ERA

**THE IDEA**
**Capture the spirit of a bygone age by taking a trip to a heritage railway.**

**Time required**: 1–2 hours

**Kit needed**:
- DSLR or mirrorless camera
- Standard zoom lens

**Camera settings**:
1/400 sec at f/5.6, ISO 400

**Skill level**:

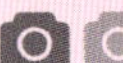  

**Taking a heritage railway offers not only a nostalgic journey through some wonderful countryside, but it also provides you with an opportunity to capture the ambience of steam trains and a bygone era, producing a diverse array of images for your portfolio.**

**Many heritage railways show their railway locomotives off on special charter tours throughout the world.**

It will give you a good opportunity to practise all types of photography skills, including experimenting with tripods and slow shutter speeds.

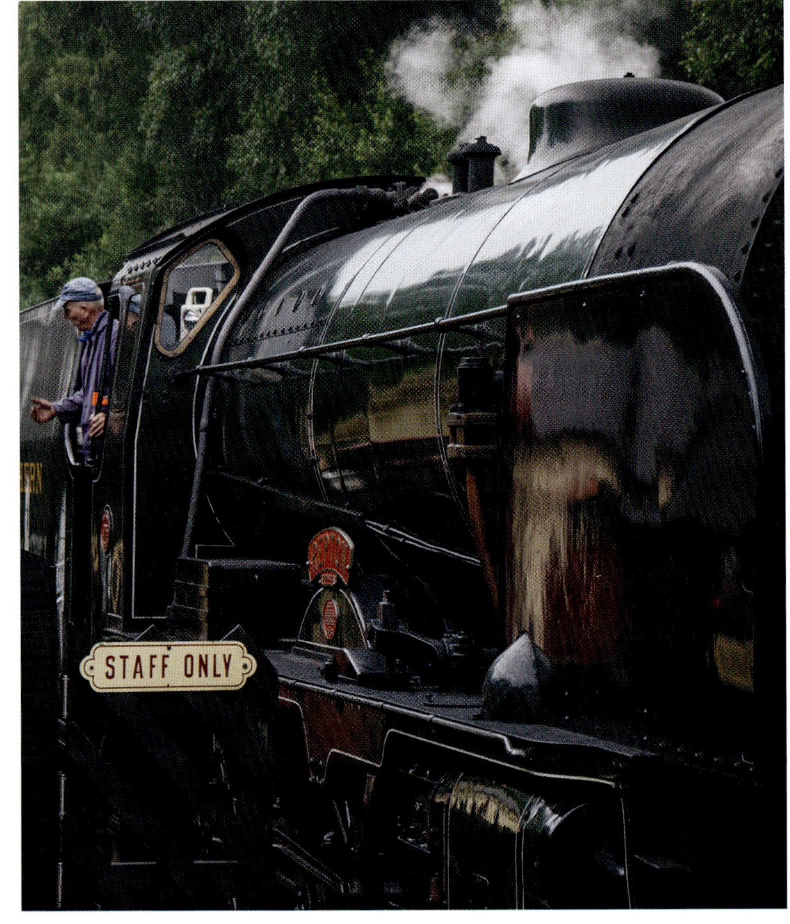


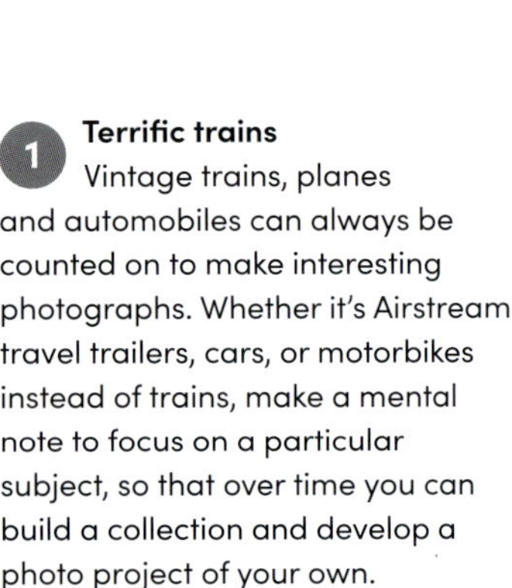

**1 Terrific trains**
Vintage trains, planes and automobiles can always be counted on to make interesting photographs. Whether it's Airstream travel trailers, cars, or motorbikes instead of trains, make a mental note to focus on a particular subject, so that over time you can build a collection and develop a photo project of your own.

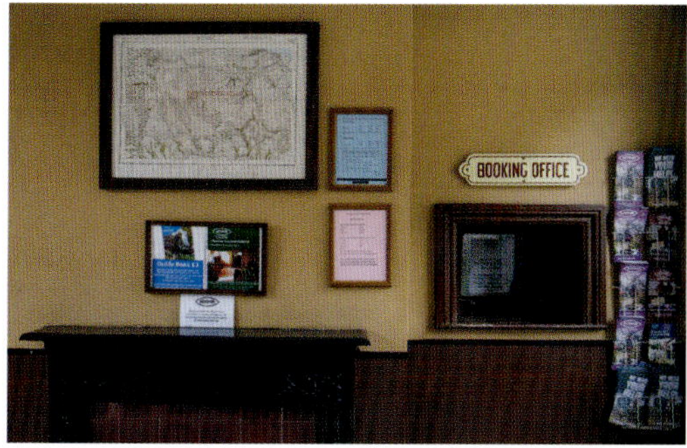


**2 Shoot interiors**

Heritage railway station interiors never fail to make interesting photographs: the styles might not have changed for nearly 100 years. You'll get more pleasing results if you use natural light where possible, so find a well-lit office and take a shot without flash, to avoid flash bouncing off any reflective surfaces.

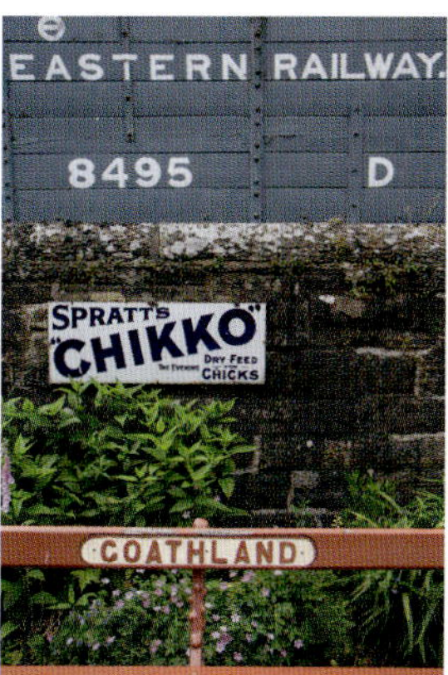


**3 Signage**

Many historical stations feature objects and signage from bygone days. These are rewarding to capture and, usually because they include old forms of advertising, come in different shapes and colours. Here, some signage against a wall was shot straight on, capturing contrasting elements within the shot, all of which fell into three distinct layers.

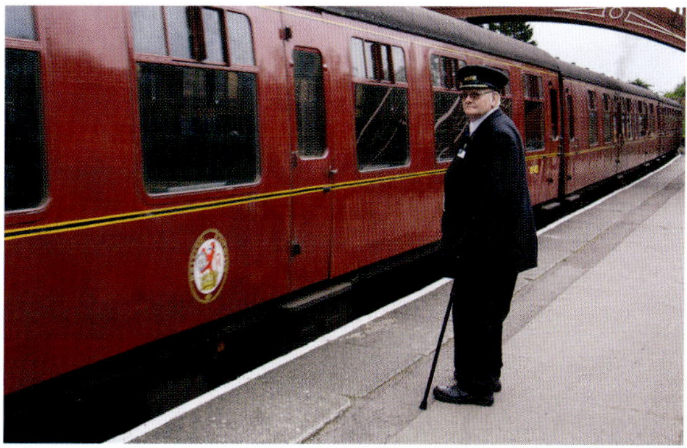

**4 Capture people**

You often meet a lot of interesting people at vintage locations, and they're usually dressed accordingly. This railway volunteer watching the train depart was wearing period attire. Don't overlook your backgrounds – a person shot against a solid background, like this train, adds context and makes for a better image.

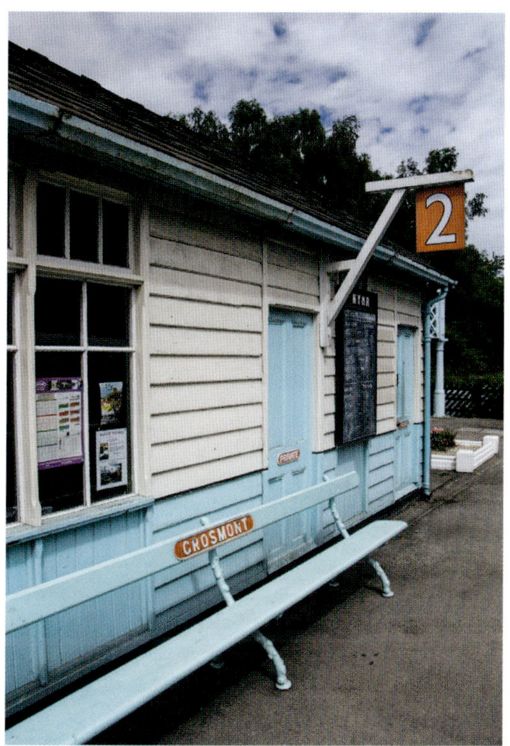


**5 Perspective**

Shot close on the platform towards the wide end of the lens, this original renovated building was striking in colour, and the blue contrasted well with the orange accents. Shooting the building and the railway seat at an angle gives a good sense of perspective, drawing the eye from left to right. Using lines in your shots is a good way to produce better compositions.

# SHOOT THROUGH A WINDOW

**THE IDEA**
**Use a polariser to avoid reflections and capture stunning scenes through windows.**

**Time required:** 2 hours

**Kit needed:**

- DSLR or mirrorless camera
- Telephoto lens
- Circular polarising filter
- Editing software

**Camera settings:**
1/500 sec at f/5.6, ISO 400

**Skill level:**

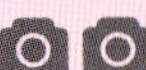

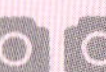

**Have you ever been presented with a stunning view, but struggled to photograph it because it was behind a large sheet of glass? No matter where you are – think shops, the zoo, museums – windows can be tricky to take photographs through. Fortunately, there are ways to eliminate, or at least minimise reflections and take a clearer shot.**

One approach is to position your lens as close and square to the glass as possible. If your lens has a lens hood, attaching it and pressing the hood right up to the glass pane will block out light around it.

While effective, this method means that you can only photograph what's directly in front of the lens, rather than any interesting angles. Instead, approach this photo challenge with a polarising filter in hand.

A circular polariser is a piece of optical glass with a linear polarising film, which only passes light moving in one linear direction. With the polarising filter attached to your lens, there is a slight reduction in exposure, but this can be easily compensated for by adding a few positive stops of exposure compensation.

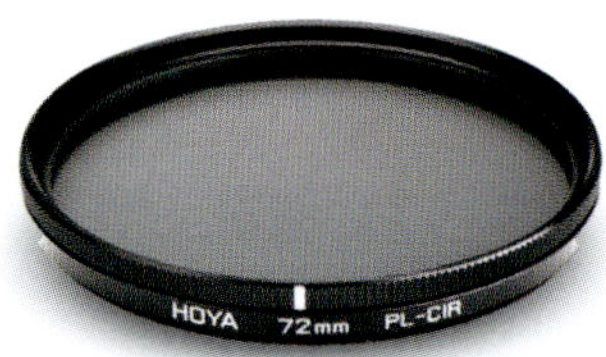


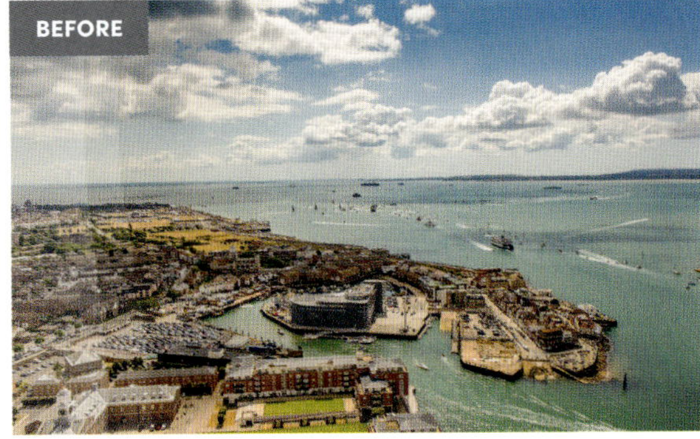


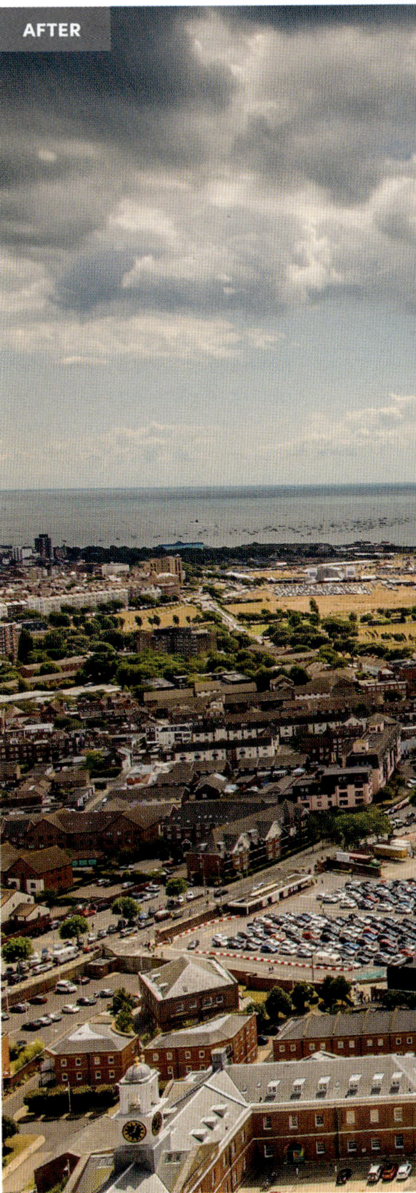

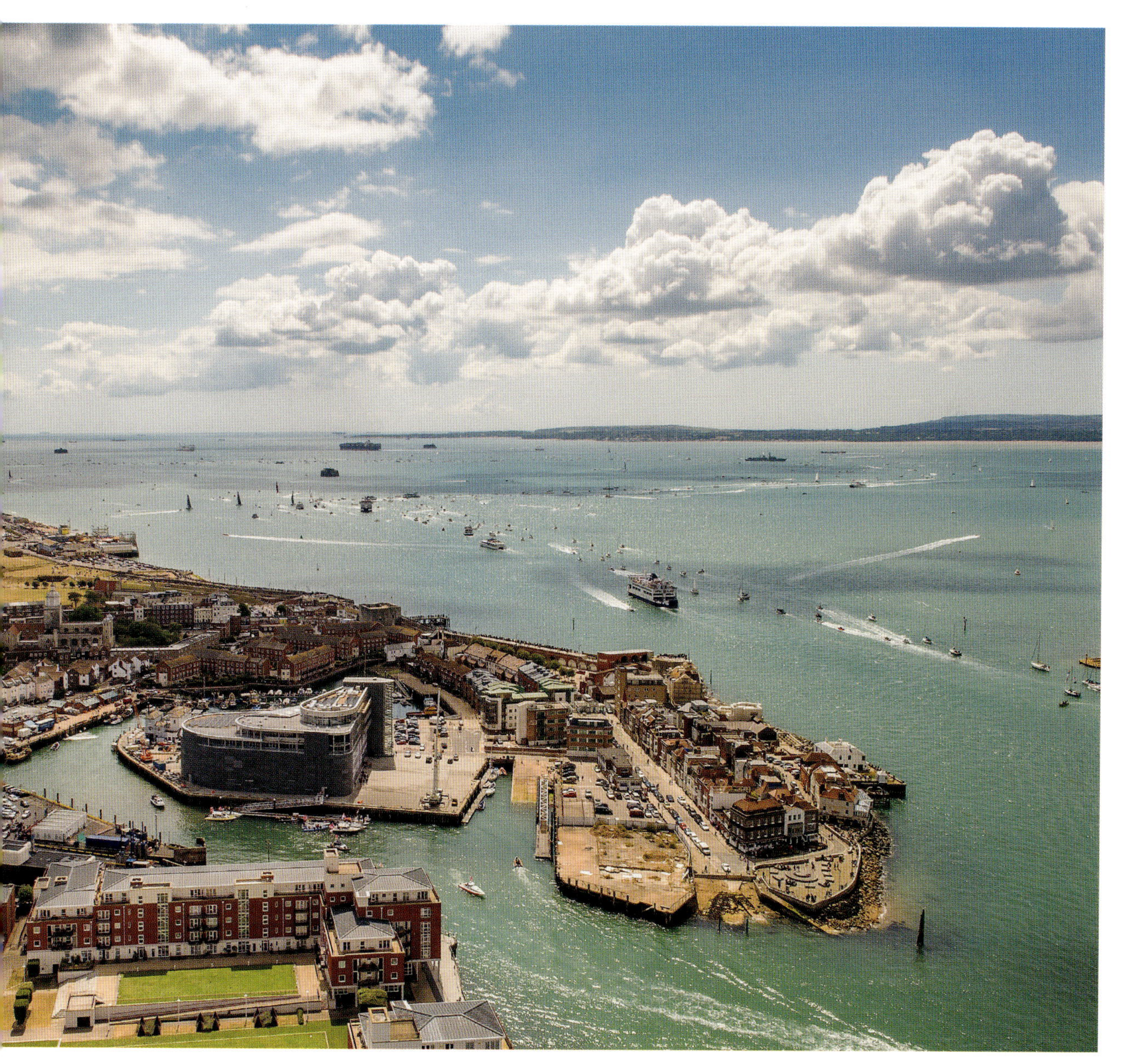

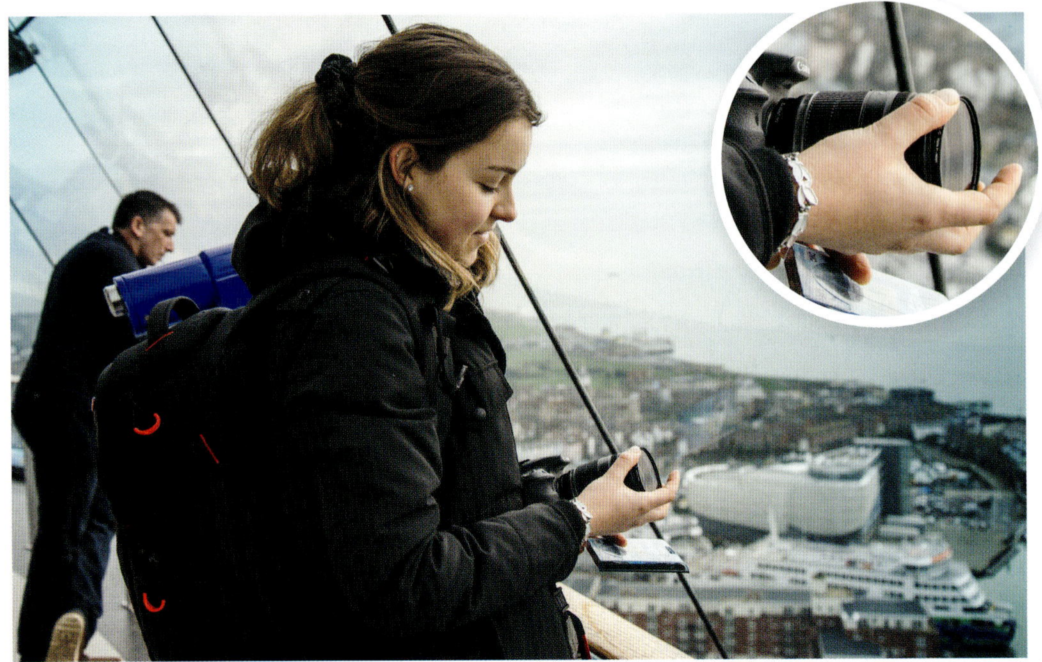

1 **Find a setting**
To take this technique to new heights, an observation platform such as the Spinnaker Tower in Portsmouth, UK, will give you amazing aerial views. Fitting a polariser will minimise distracting reflections in the glass. This technique can be used for an array of scenes, such as cityscapes from tall buildings.

2 **Filter fitting**
You'll need a circular polarising filter that fits the size of your lens filter thread. Screw it on and compose your shot using Live View, then rotate the filter until you see the reflections disappear (or reduce). A telephoto zoom lens will make it easy to recompose around unwanted people or objects in the frame, and hone in on details.

3 **Camera settings**
Switch to aperture-priority mode and select a wide aperture of around f/5.6. This means you can handhold the camera and minimise motion blur. (Tripods are often unwelcome in cities and tourist destinations.) With the filter attached, there will be a slight reduction in exposure, but this is easily remedied by applying a few positive stops of added exposure compensation.

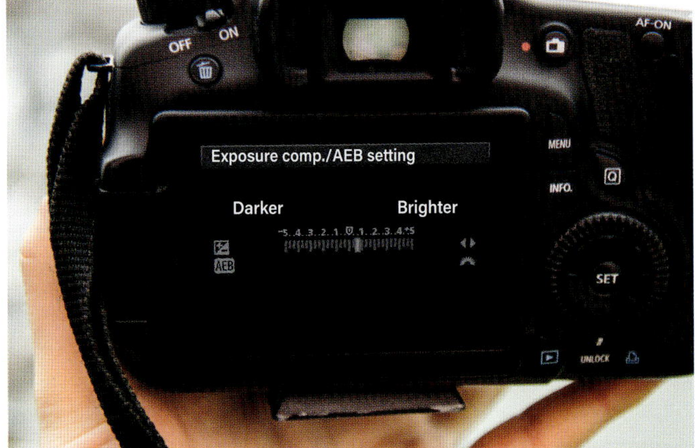

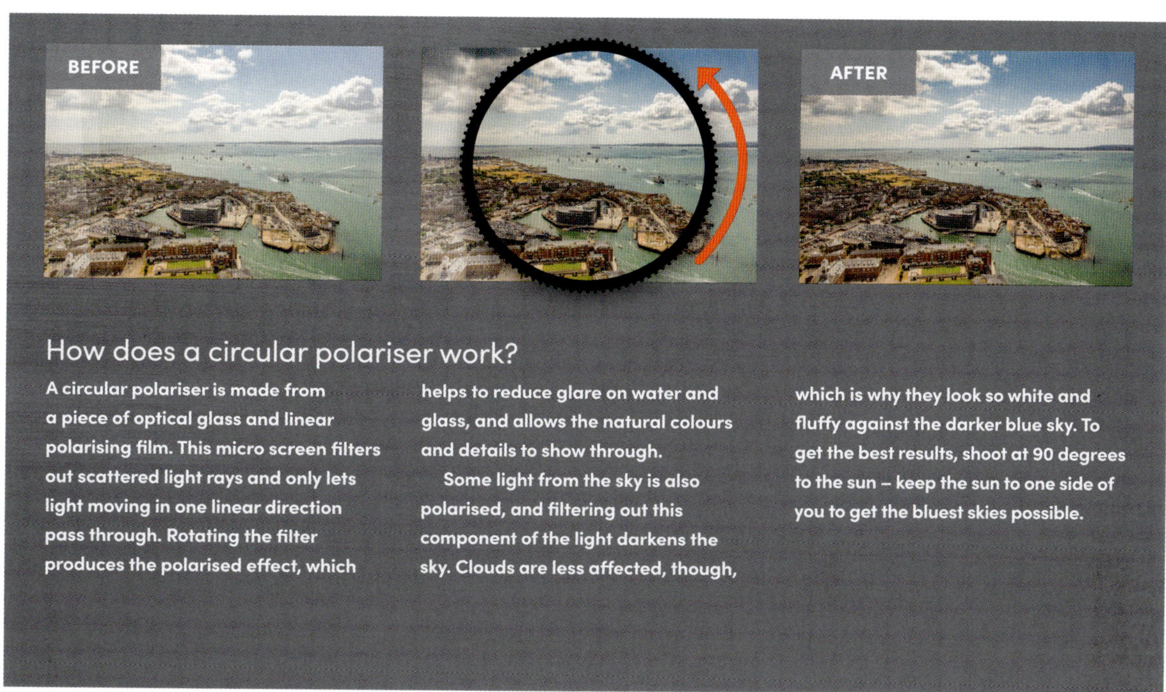


## How does a circular polariser work?

A circular polariser is made from a piece of optical glass and linear polarising film. This micro screen filters out scattered light rays and only lets light moving in one linear direction pass through. Rotating the filter produces the polarised effect, which helps to reduce glare on water and glass, and allows the natural colours and details to show through.

Some light from the sky is also polarised, and filtering out this component of the light darkens the sky. Clouds are less affected, though, which is why they look so white and fluffy against the darker blue sky. To get the best results, shoot at 90 degrees to the sun – keep the sun to one side of you to get the bluest skies possible.

**4 Colour it right**

Windows are hard to photograph, as they often leave you with an intense colour cast – in this case, a blue hue made everything look as if it was underwater. In Camera Raw, use the Temperature setting to warm the hues and push the Tint setting slightly to the right. Use white or neutral objects such as clouds to guide you.

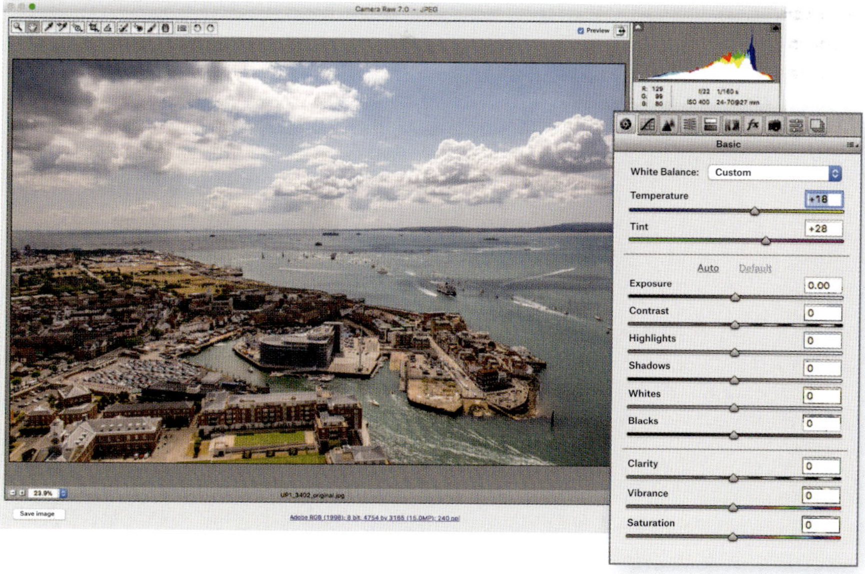

# ARTY STREET SCENES

**THE IDEA**
**Turn an urban streetscape into abstract art with camera tricks.**

**Time required:** 1–2 hours

**Kit needed:**
- DSLR or mirrorless camera
- 50mm lens

**Camera settings:**
1/15 sec, f/22, ISO 100

**Skill level:**

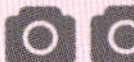 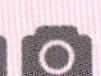 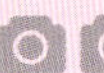

**Urban environments can be a frenetic mass of contrasts – vibrant or mundane, lively or eerie, beautiful or drab. For a photographer, it's easy enough to capture how places like this look, but it's more of a challenge to convey how they feel. To create a sense of a place without the distractions of detail, we can turn to abstract techniques. Intentional blur, multiple exposures, unusual camera angles and digital mash-ups can all help us emphasise the emotion of the place and create wall-worthy art that feels more in touch with the work of impressionist painters than it does with 'conventional' photographic techniques.**

There is a range of techniques that you can try out on the streets. Camera skills are often about eliminating shake, keeping scenes in focus and preventing wonky horizons but, here, throw all of that out of the window. Instead, celebrate the blur and the softness. When you think about it, streets and buildings are rather simple geometric shapes and lines, dotted with people and lights and, as such, they're ripe for an abstract treatment. You can reduce the elements down to blurry strokes of colour, impressions of people and flowing shapes, while still retaining the spirit of the scene.

You don't need any special equipment or lenses for this. In fact, even the cheapest lens can produce results just as good as premium optics. What's more, you can try this in all conditions – sunny, overcast, rainy, even at night.

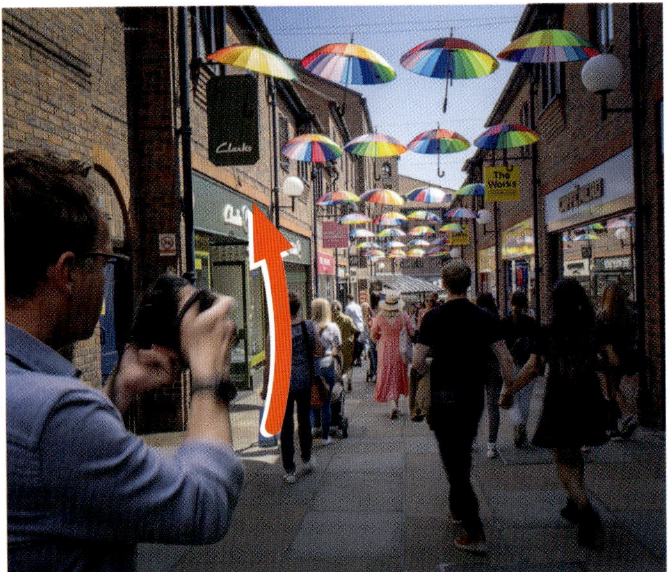


**1 Camera motion**
Intentional camera movement can transform scenes into streaks of blur while still retaining an impression of the place. Move the camera up, down, left, right or swivel it during the exposure. There's a real skill in doing this – for a smoother motion, it helps to press the camera against your forehead or use a tripod.

**2 Slow shutter speed**
You need to slow the shutter speed down so that the camera movements register in the exposure. Try setting your camera to shutter priority at 1/15 sec and ISO 100, then see what kind of blur you get. For a stronger blur effect, either experiment with a longer shutter speed or make quicker camera motions.

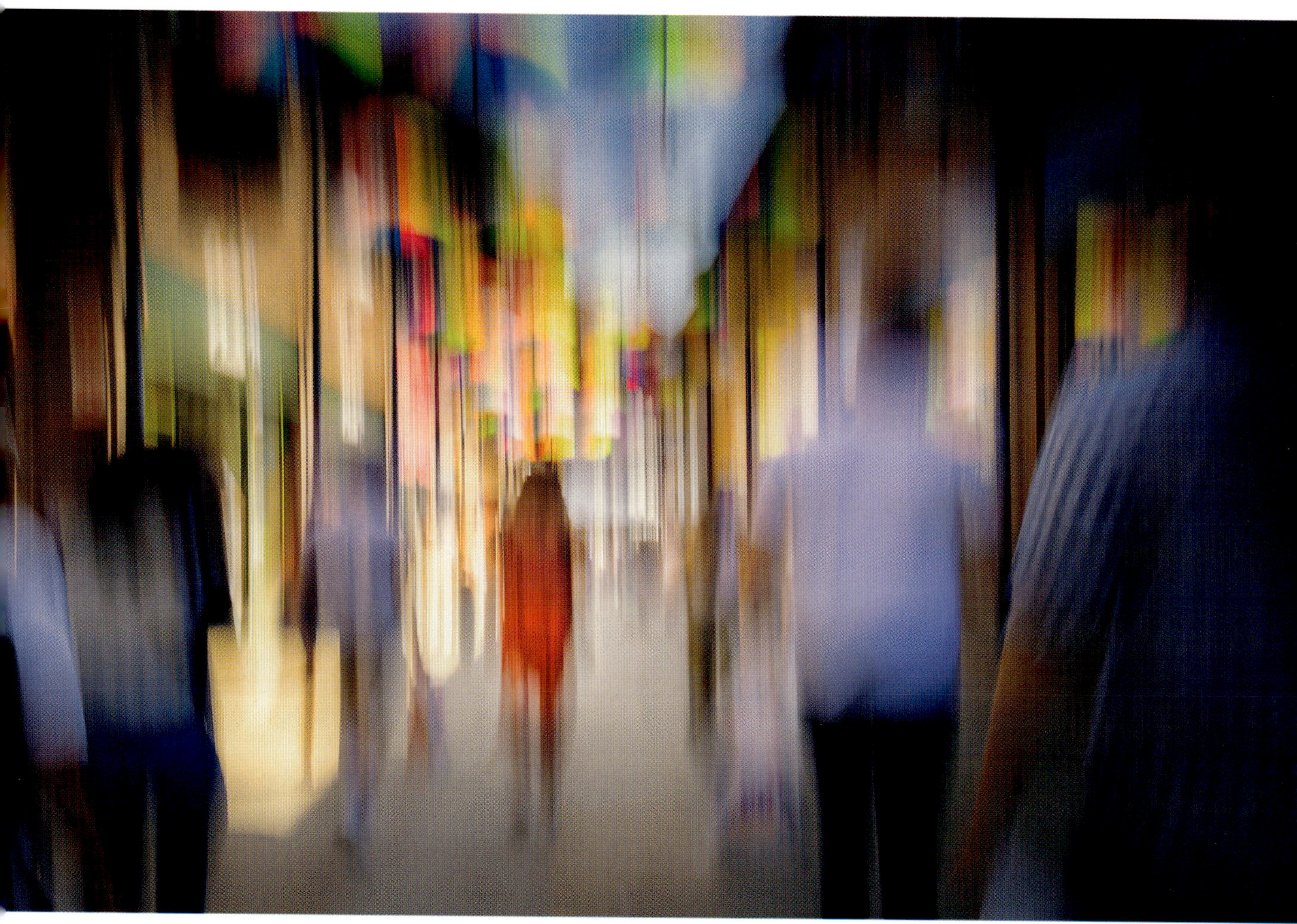

**3 Look for bold colours**
One of the main reasons why this scene works for the intentional camera movement technique is because of the colourful rainbow umbrellas hanging over the street and illuminated from behind by sunlight. When blurred by dragging the camera downwards, these offer beautifully bold highlights that filter into the street below.

**4 Use the right focal length**
This has an impact on the camera motion: the longer the lens, the more exaggerated the camera motion will be, so with wider lenses, you might need a longer shutter speed or faster camera movement. With a wide angle, the blur is more exaggerated in the centre than at the edges.

**5 Compose the shot**
Even though you're intentionally blurring the scene, it helps to choose a street with recognisable shapes and simple geometry, so that the viewer's eye can still make sense of the abstract shapes. Here, the shot was composed centrally so that the two sides converge in the centre and the shoppers recede into the distance.

## SIX MORE IDEAS TO GET THE BEST OUT OF YOUR ABSTRACTS

**Turn your urban streetscapes into abstract art with these camera tricks.**

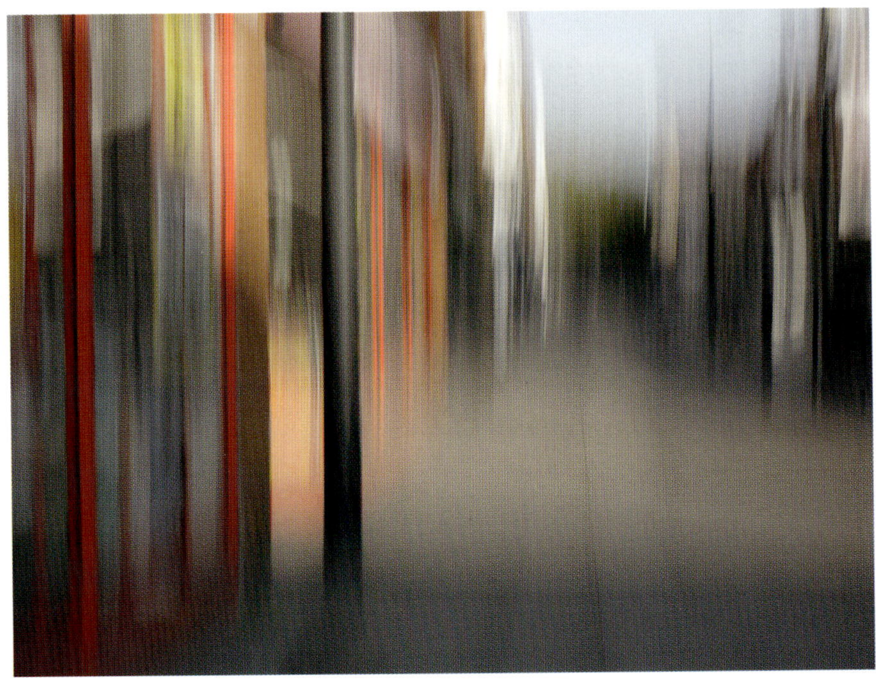

**1 Camera movements** There's beauty in every urban area if you look for it. Search out bold colours and the vertical lines of shop windows or lamp posts, then try an up-down camera movement over a 1/15 sec exposure to create streaks of blur. A side-to-side movement, or even a camera swivel, can also lead to some interesting results.

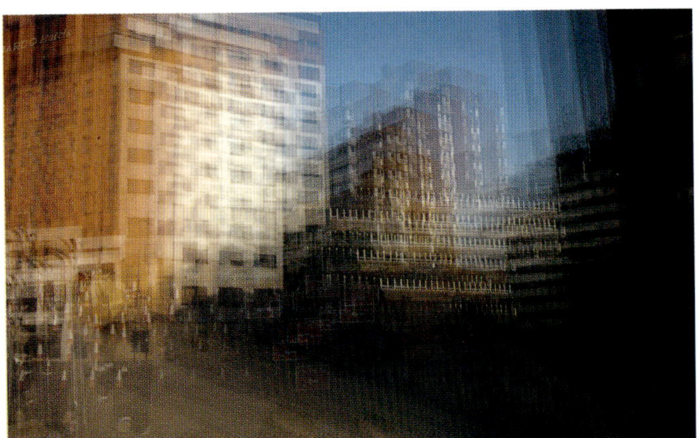

**2 Multiple exposures** This is a multiple exposure with the number of frames set to around nine. Shoot a building or object while varying the position, framing or zoom. Images will overlay to form an abstract. You may need negative exposure compensation to control the brightness.

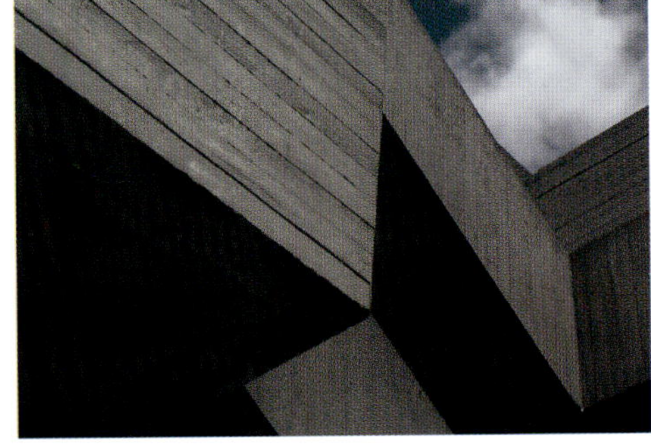

**3 Picking out details** When taken out of context from their surroundings, little details, interesting shapes and blocks of colour can be used to striking effect in your an scene. Look for these details and you'll start to notice them all around you. Use a tight crop and frame with lines, textures and shapes in mind.

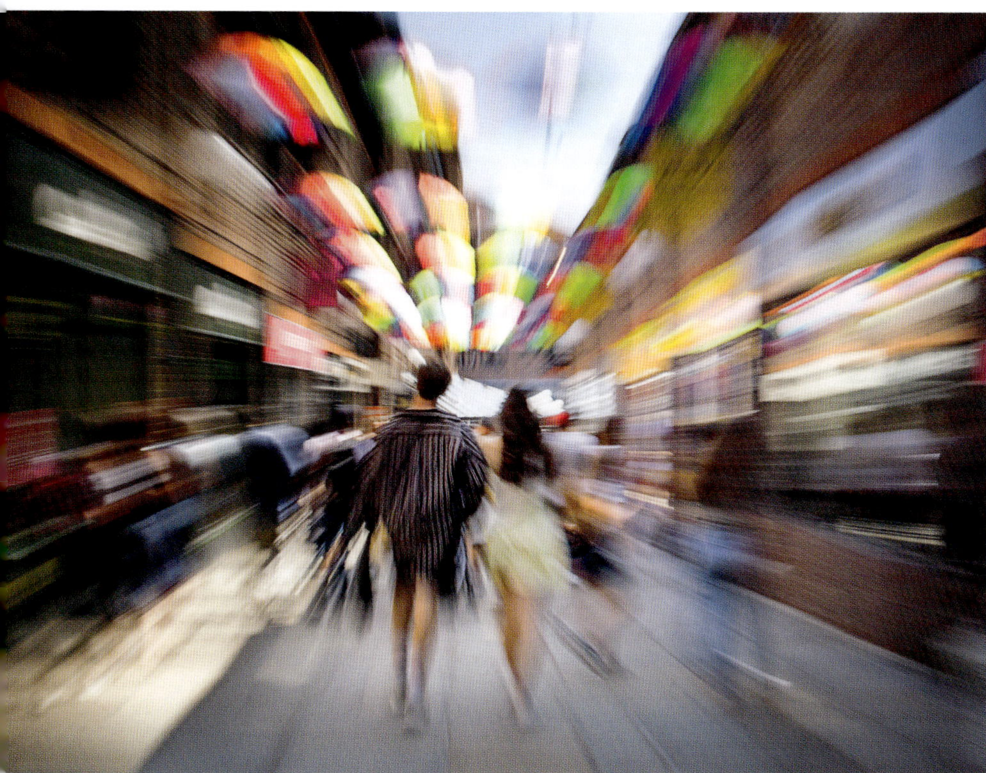

4 **Zoom bursts**
A zoom burst is similar to intentional camera movements, but with a twist. Over the course of a long exposure (try 1/10 sec to begin with), use a zoom lens and quickly zoom in or out during the exposure. The edges of the frame will be transformed into streaks of blur.

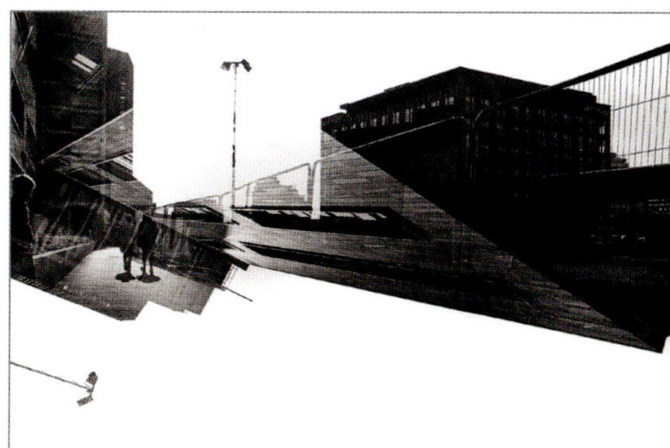

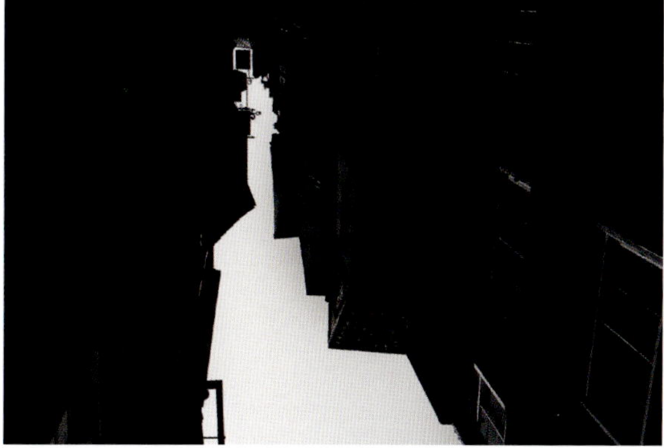

5 **Double flips**
For in-camera double exposures, enable the mode in your camera's menu, set the blending mode to Add and set the number of frames to two. Shoot a skyline, positioned slightly above the centre of the frame, then flip the camera upside down and shoot another skyline.

6 **Upside-down shots**
Look up from the street and you might see how buildings form a jagged edge against the sky. On a clear day, the sky will be much brighter than the buildings below. Use negative exposure compensation to expose for the sky and the street will go dark. Try flipping the image upside down.

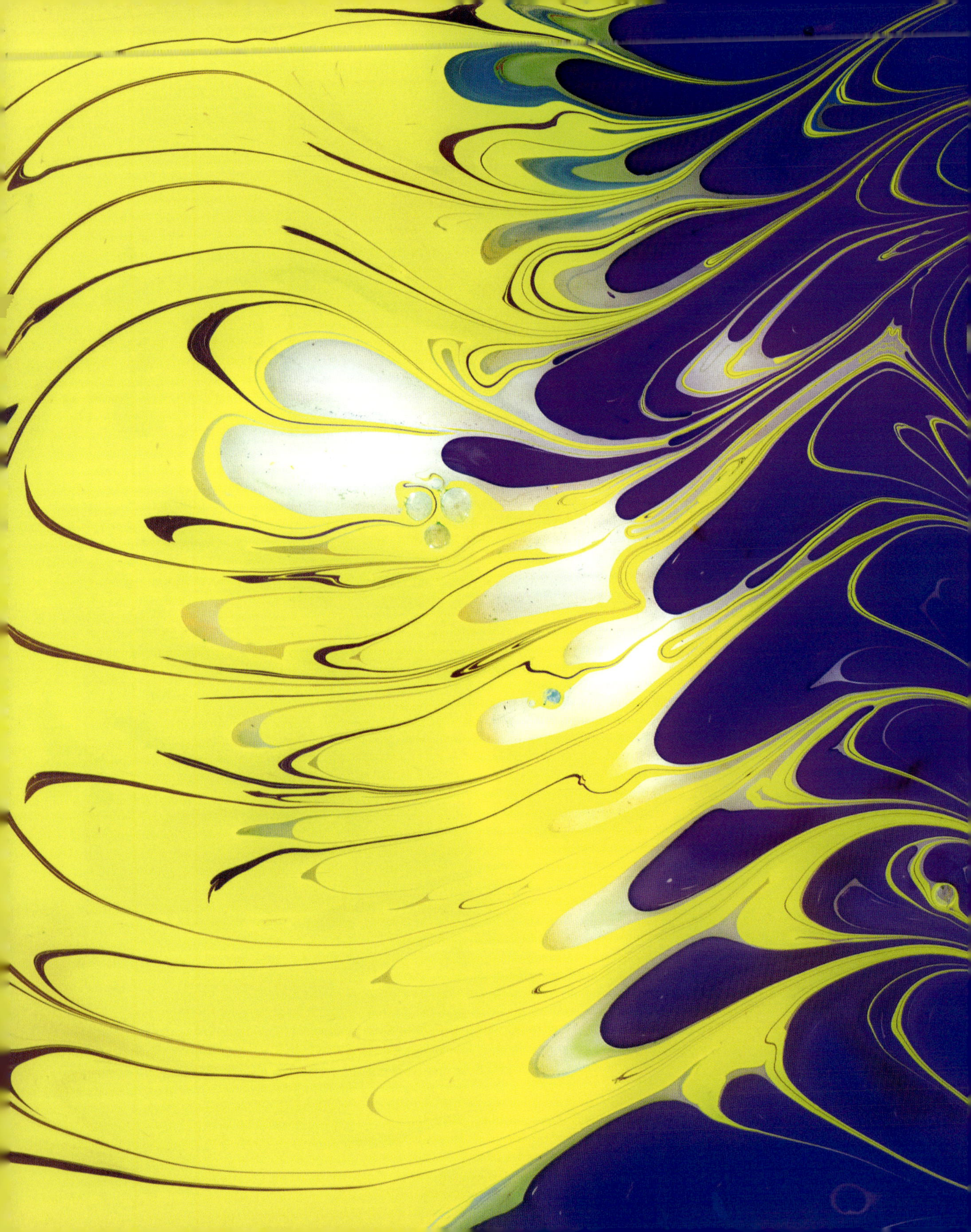

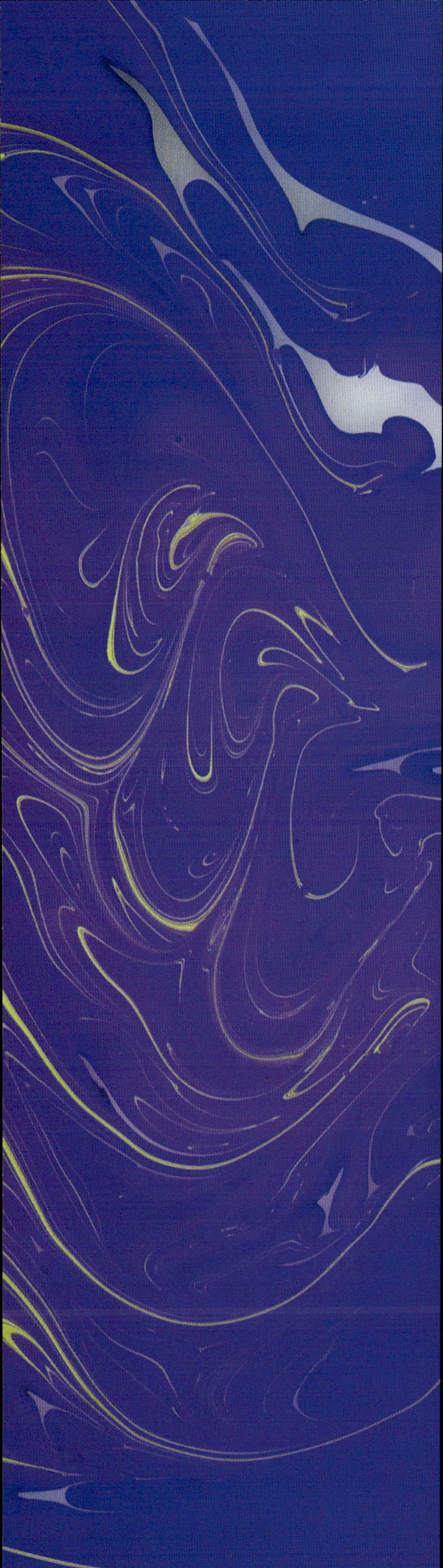

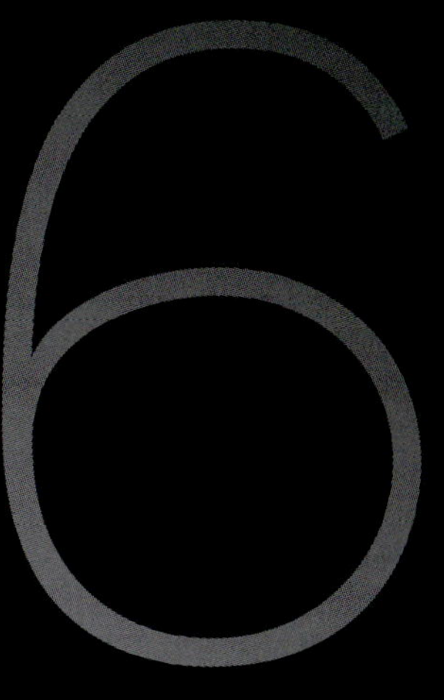

# STILL LIFE AND CREATIVE IDEAS

**Give your photography a fine-art feel with these projects that you can enjoy creating in the comfort of your own home**

# MAKE A SEAMLESS BACKDROP

**THE IDEA**
**Create a seamless background for shooting on a tabletop.**

**Time required**: 1 hour

**Kit needed**:
- DSLR or mirrorless camera
- 50mm lens
- Flexible poster board
- Tape
- Two A-clamps
- Two metal brackets
- Two pieces of foam board

**Camera settings**:
1/160 sec at f/2.8, ISO 1400

**Skill level**:

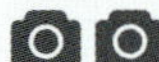  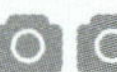

**When you try to shoot still-life objects head-on, you'll notice an unsightly line where the backdrop joins the tabletop. Fortunately, it's easy to get around this problem by creating what's called a 'sweep' – essentially a seamless background – using a flexible, curved backdrop.**

In this project, you'll discover how easy is it to create this set-up at home, whatever the size of your space. It's best to arrange everything near a large window, so that you've got plenty of light to work with.

The sweep will save you time in Photoshop cloning out the seam, and the result is a much more professional look for small tabletop products. Once you've had a go at a plain white background, try taping fabric such as linen to your board (even napkins will do) to create a textured sweep effect.

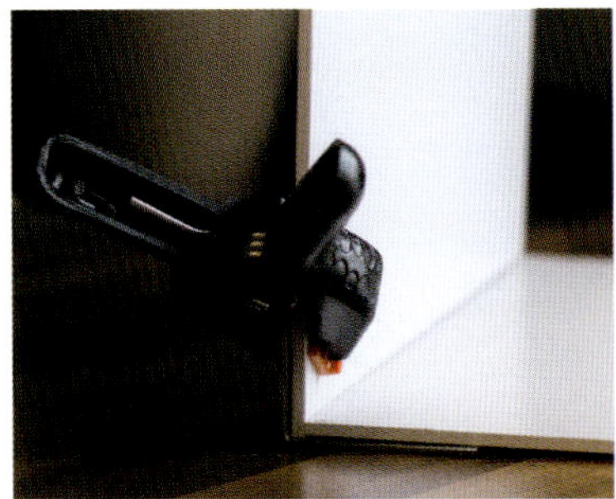

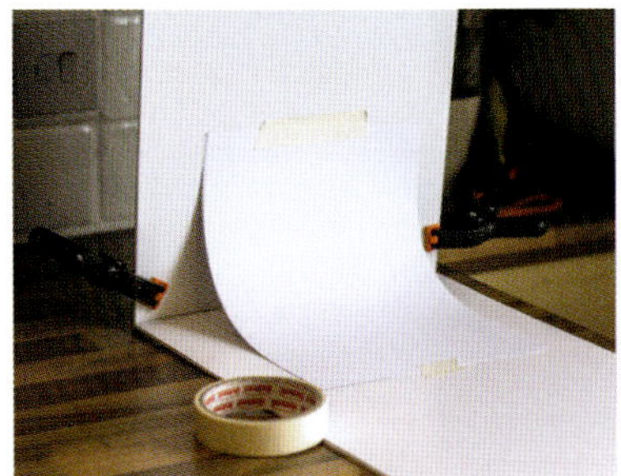

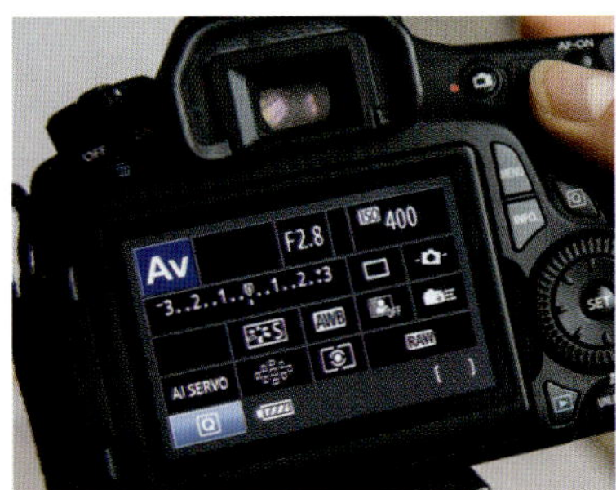


**1 Setting up**
Attach the foam boards to the metal brackets with the clamps. You want an arrangement of two foam boards that meet at a 90-degree angle to each other.

**2 Secure the curve**
Tape the flexible poster board, card or your chosen fabric to the vertical board. You want to create a sweeping curve shape, without any noticeable dents.

**3 Time to shoot**
In aperture-priority mode, set a wide aperture such as f/2.8. Get down to the height of your subject (tripod or hands-free), focus, then shoot.

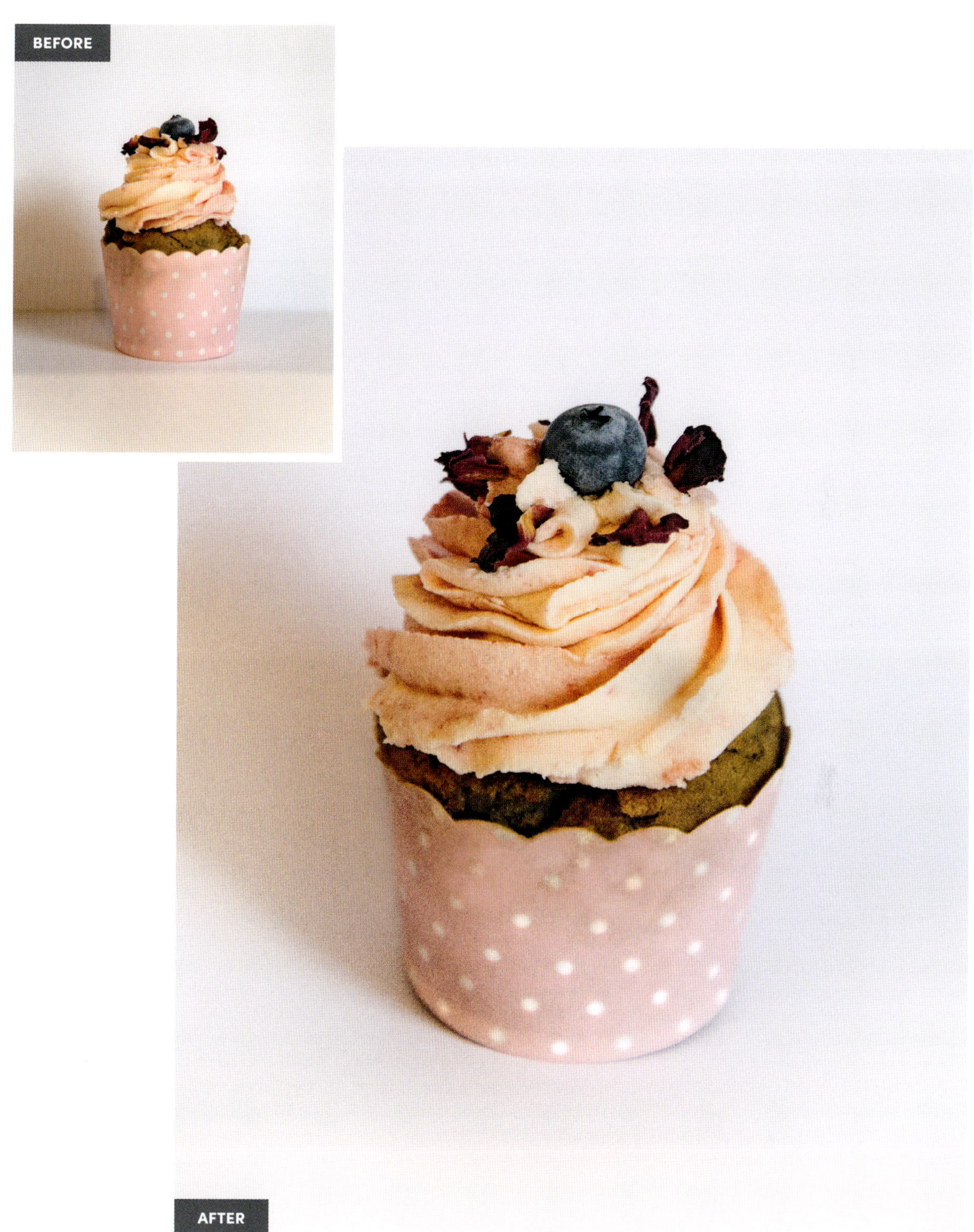
BEFORE
AFTER

# ADD LIGHT STREAKS TO A STILL LIFE

**THE IDEA**
**Light your subject using only your mobile phone.**

**Time required**: 1-2 hours

**Kit needed**:
- DSLR or mirrorless camera
- 50mm lens
- Smartphone
- Tripod
- Black background
- Sheet of transparent plastic

**Camera settings**:
8 secs at f/16, ISO 100

**Skill level**:

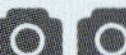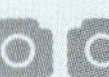

**You don't need loads of fancy lighting kit to get great results when it comes to product photography. For this set-up, all you need is a black background, a sheet of transparent plastic, a main subject, a tripod and a mobile phone as your lighting.**

First, darken a room using blinds or dark curtains (or shoot at night and turn all the lights out). It doesn't need to be pitch black, but you want to get an exposure time of at least 5sec, so keep making it darker if your shutter speed isn't reducing. The idea is to create light streaks around your subject with your phone, so you need enough time with the shutter open to ensure you get all the way around your subject.

When it comes to pressing the shutter, a remote release is preferable. If you don't have one, use the self-timer on your camera. You can also put the camera into Live View mode to lock the mirror up – this will help prevent any camera shake and blurring of your image.

The great thing about this technique is that there really are no limits, and everything is experimental, so no two shots will be the same.

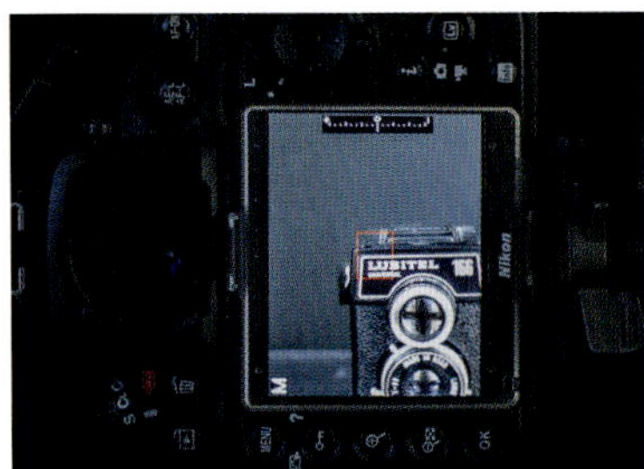


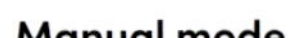

**1 Manual mode**
Darken a room. Put your camera into manual mode, set the ISO to the lowest possible setting and stop down the aperture to f/16). Underexpose your shot by a few stops to keep the blacks, black. (If your meter is reading on the line, drop it by three stops.) Try a shutter speed of 5–10 secs and focus manually on the subject to ensure it's pin-sharp.

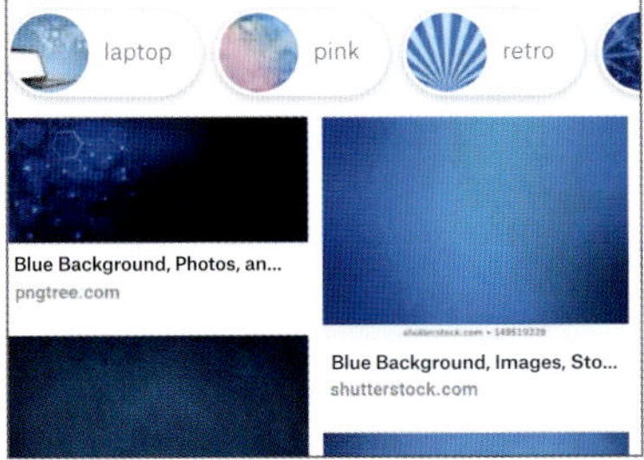


**2 Download a colour**
Go to your phone and search the web for a colour or pattern to use in the background of the scene. Think about how the colour image will look when in motion. Strips can be effective, as can plain colours with a strip of white along the bottom. It really can be anything, so keep experimenting with this aspect.

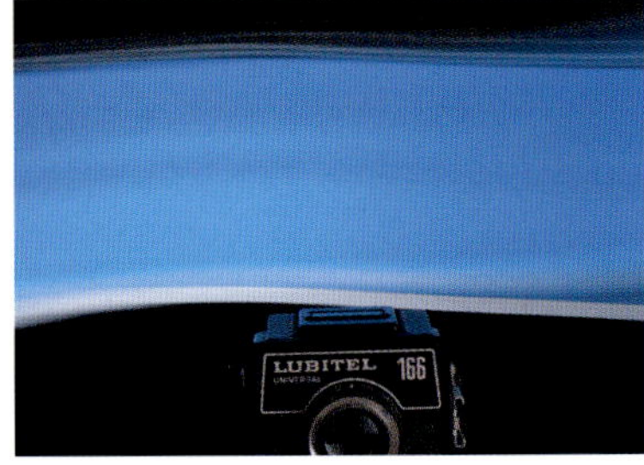


**3 Moving light**
Once you have some images downloaded on your phone, open the shutter and get creative. If you run the phone around the back of your set-up, you'll get a band of light. You can also tint your subject with the colour by shining the phone forward. Just keep the phone moving so you don't get your hands in the shot.

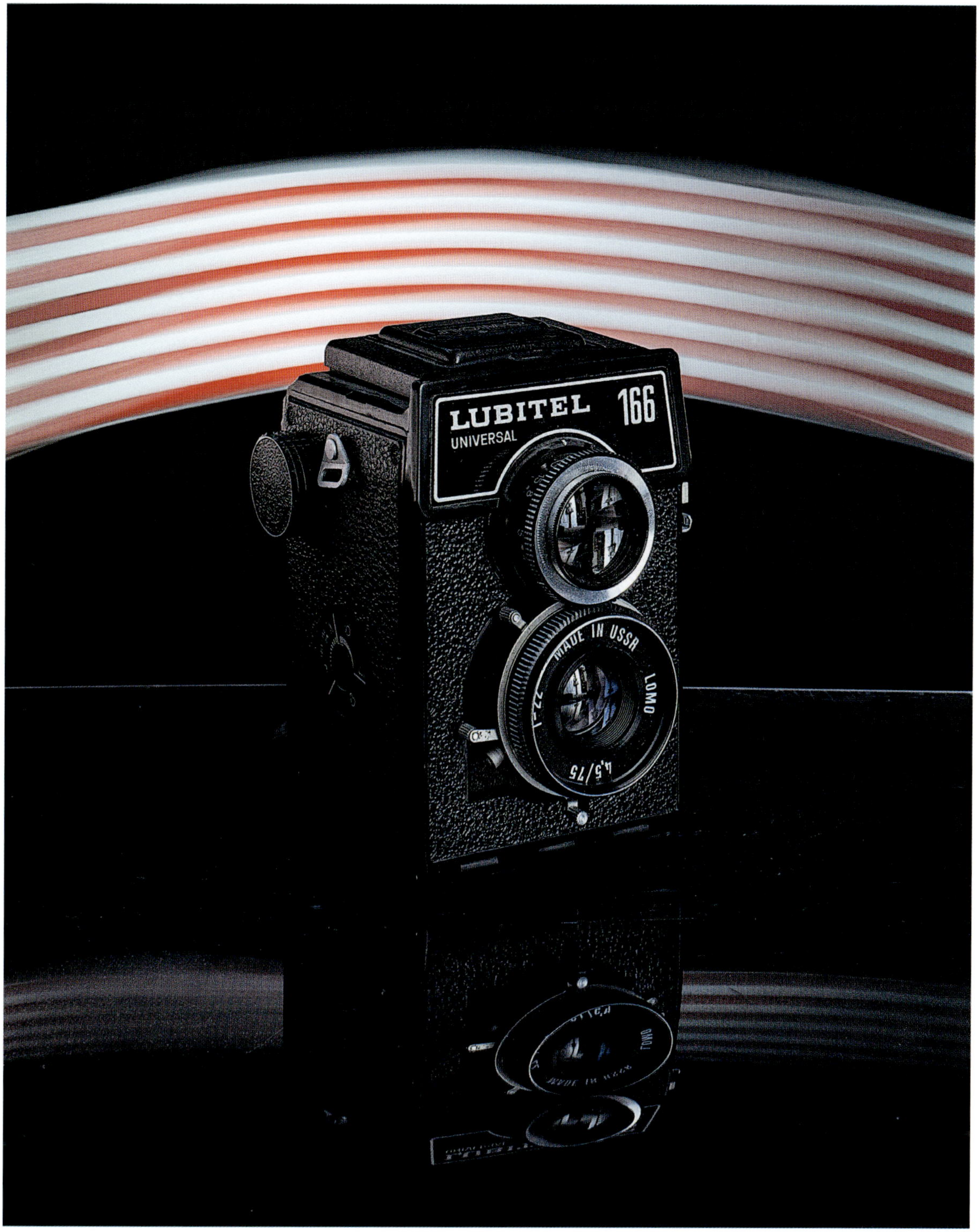
LUBITEL 166
UNIVERSAL
MADE IN USSR
LOMO
4,5/75

# SHOOT CUTLERY CREATIVELY

**THE IDEA**
**Use a polariser to create quirky abstracts.**

**Time required**: 1–2 hours

**Kit needed:**
- DSLR or mirrorless camera
- Macro lens
- Polarising filter
- Taplet or laptop
- Tripod
- Plastic cutlery

**Camera settings:**
1/80 sec at f/5.6, ISO 400

**Skill level:**

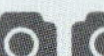

**There are some things that just can't be replicated in Photoshop, and this is certainly the case when using a circular polarising filter. This tool, a favourite among landscape photographers, is essential for cutting down reflections in water or glass, and has the power to reduce scattered light, making blues in the sky look punchier.**

These wonderfully affordable and useful accessories can also be used to change the appearance of polarised light emitted by computer screens. If you have a laptop, tablet or even a smartphone in your pocket, the chances are it's throwing out some polarised light.

In this project, take advantage of this special light to achieve the vibrant, almost radioactive-looking abstract in the transparent plastic cutlery you see here.

The trick is to use a polarising filter on your DSLR or mirrorless camera and twist it to change the amount of polarisation. When you twist it to the sweet spot, the screen of your electronic device will appear entirely black, leaving the plastic cutlery lit up in all sorts of strange and wonderful colours.

As it is possible to get closer to still-life subjects, a macro lens will make this job easier when shooting your knives and forks. While you can still get great results with entry-level kit such as a DSLR or CSC (compact system camera) with a kit lens and a tripod, your framing might be a bit wider. Most modern screens are scratch-resistant but it's still worth taking care when placing your cutlery on your screen.

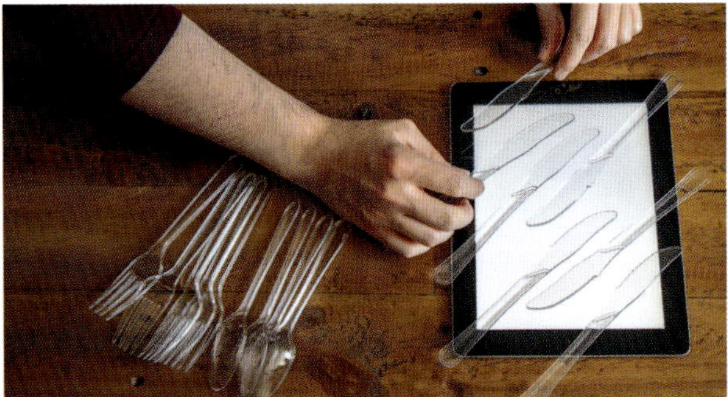

**1 Position your cutlery**
Position a large tablet, computer monitor or laptop on its side, and set it up so the entire screen is bright white – this can be most easily done by making a blank white document in Photoshop and entering full-screen mode. Remember to set your device to maximum brightness, then carefully position the plastic cutlery in an interesting pattern on the screen.

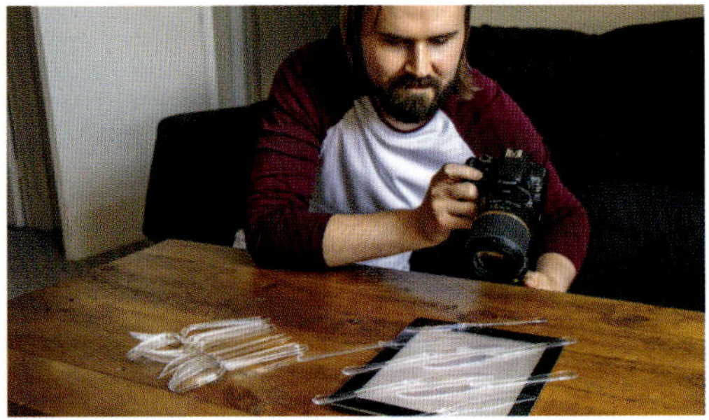

**2 Compose your shot**
Set up your DSLR or mirrorless camera on a tripod looking down towards your still-life set-up. Zoom in to the long end of your lens if necessary and re-adjust the tripod legs until you get a frame-filling shot where just the plastic cutlery can be seen. Focus on the piece of cutlery that you want to be sharpest and switch to manual focus to lock it off.

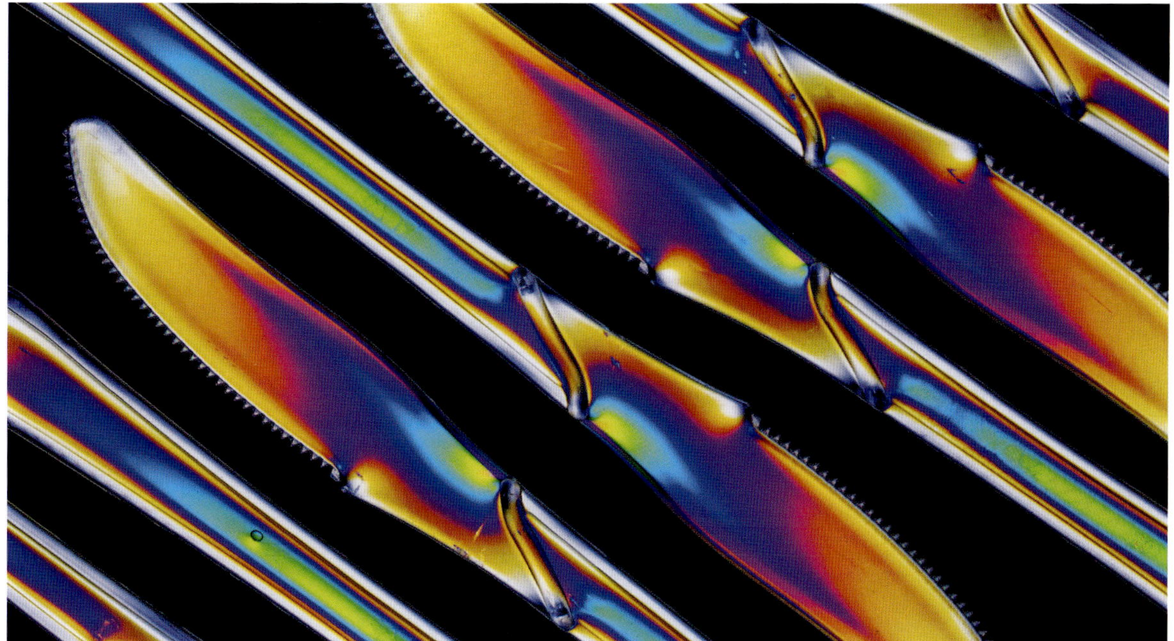

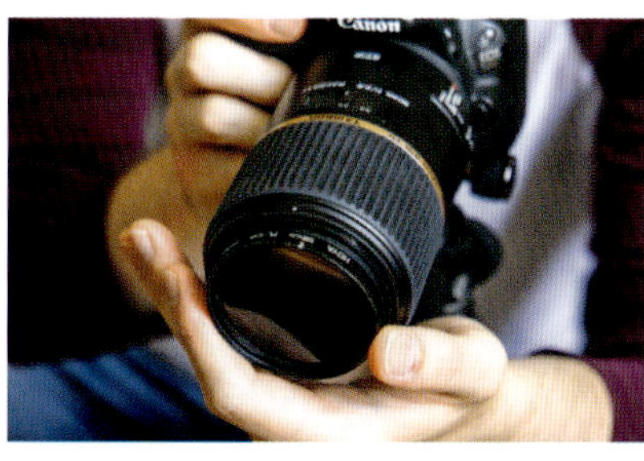

### 3 Twist and shoot

Attach your polarising filter, being careful not to knock the focus, and then twist the polariser ring until it blocks out the polarised light emitted by your electronic device. This will leave the plastic cutlery eerily illuminated with wonderful colours. In aperture-priority mode, dial in the depth of field required and enable the self-timer to avoid camera shake.

## Understanding polarising filters

**Polarisers are an essential accessory in any photographer's kit bag, as they let you dial in the exact amount of polarised light coming in through the lens and hitting your camera's sensor. The light that bounces off reflections in water and the blue in the sky are polarised, so twisting a circular polarising filter lets you control them with ease. The light that is emitted by computer screens is also polarised, so you can use this to get a quirky abstract result with plastic cutlery.**

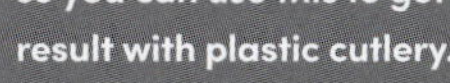

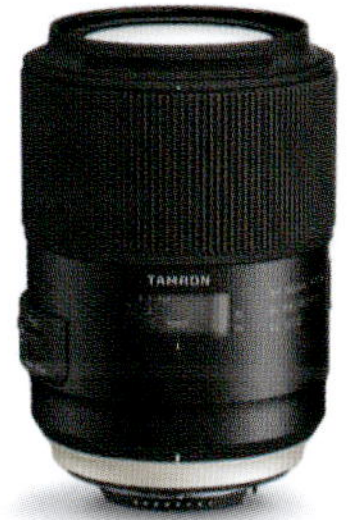

Macro lenses are perfect for this type of work. They allow you to get closer to your subject for a frame-filling shot, which will help you get an even more abstract view. Typically available in focal lengths of 50mm, 100mm and 180mm and often sporting wide apertures, they can also double up as fantastic portrait lenses.

# GET FESTIVE WITH NATURAL LIGHT

**THE IDEA**
**Use natural light to get creative Christmas shots.**

**Time required:** 2 hours

**Kit needed:**
- DSLR or mirrorless camera
- 50mm lens
- Tripod
- Extending arm
- Fairy lights
- Editing software

**Camera settings:**
1/13 sec at f/8, ISO 100

**Skill level:**

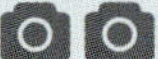 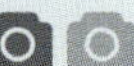 

**Food is a wonderful subject to photograph. It doesn't move, you can arrange and rearrange it until it is exactly how you want in the frame, and it tastes delicious after you have finished photographing it.**

This festive food photo shoot is all about creating a Christmas tree design from mince pies, or any other type of festive treats. If you don't have time (or the skills) to bake your own, visit a bakery or supermarket. However, if you're a keen baker, use this to your advantage and make your image really stand out.

Soft, diffused light is great to work with, as it falls evenly over your subject, meaning you don't get unwanted harsh and distracting shadows in your image.

A lens with a focal range between 40–70mm is ideal, but avoid using a lens that's too wide, as you may encounter image-distortion issues.

When you photograph food, use a tripod so you can spend time arranging your composition. A steady camera also means you can keep your aperture narrow and your ISO low, which is desirable for this type of set-up. Switch to aperture-priority mode and, if using fairy lights, underexpose by a stop so the fairy lights don't pop the highlights. Use the camera's self-timer or a remote shutter release.

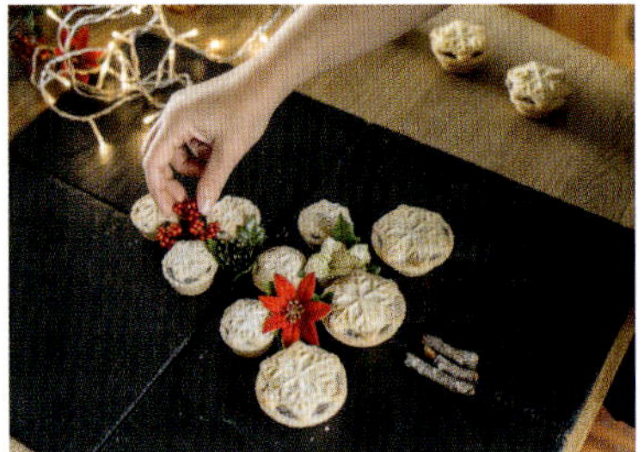

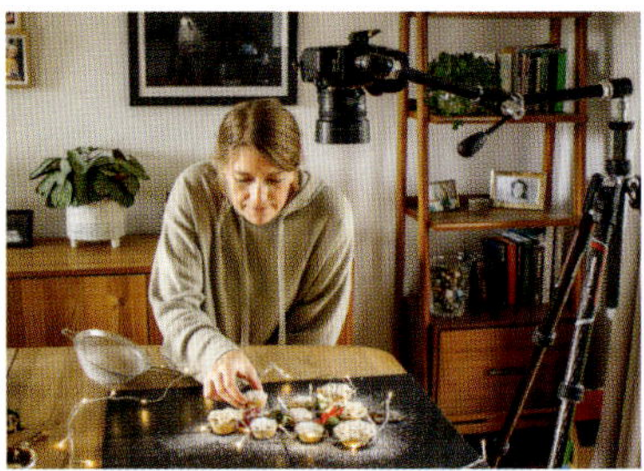

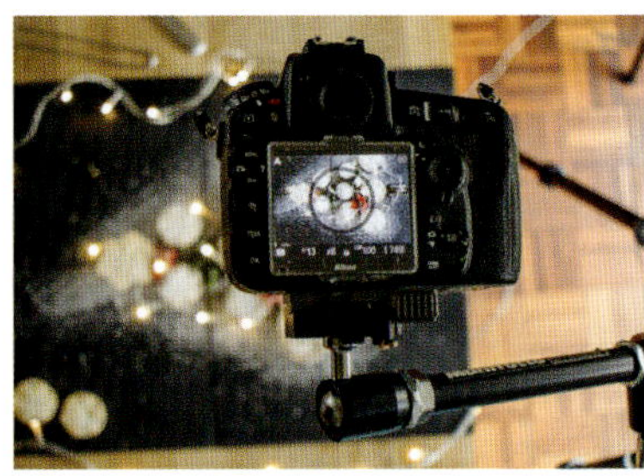

**1 Arrange the food**
Build your set-up next to a large window or natural light source. Think about your background and how the food will appear in the frame – these mince pies were arranged into a tree formation on four dark slate placemats. To bring in a touch of colour, scatter some Christmas decorations around.

**2 Add atmosphere**
To enhance the festive feel, add some fairy lights. Weave them in and around, as you would if you were decorating a normal tree. Make sure the lights are small and warm in colour to produce a glowing festive hue. Finally, a sprinkling of icing sugar helps to transform the scene.

**3 Shoot from above**
This type of shot works best from a bird's-eye view. If necessary, use an extending arm attached to the tripod to frame up the composition. Switch your camera to Live View to compose your shot. Experiment with adding or removing a mince pie from the frame – the sprinkled icing sugar creates a silhouetted shape, which can also look effective.

**4 Tone and feel**
At the editing stage, tone and stylise your image. Lift the shadows, boost Clarity and Texture, and warm up the overall effect of the image. Make some isolated exposure adjustments using the new Auto Mask feature to bring out some of the detail in the middle of the Christmas tree.

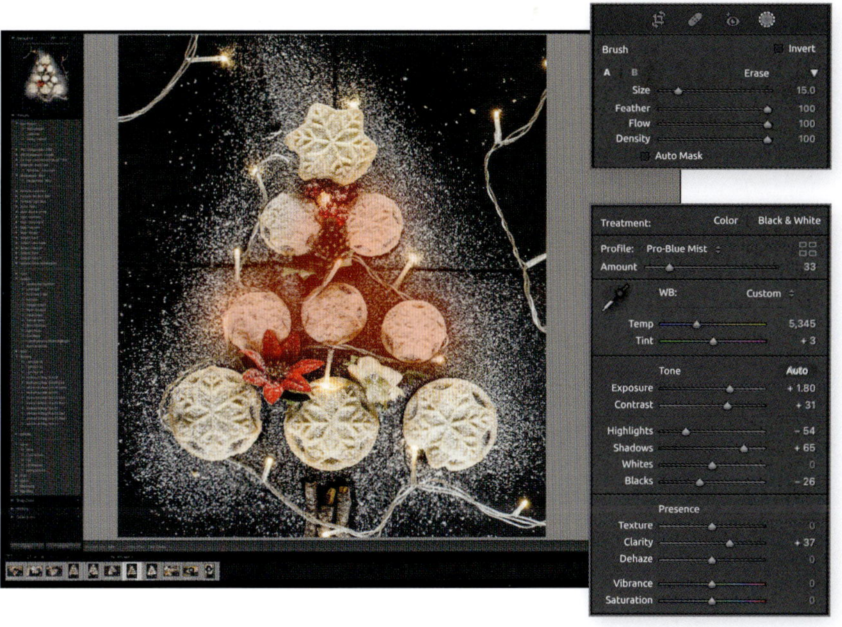

# CAPTURE A CLASSIC CAR

**THE IDEA**
**Take a picture of an old car using multiple exposures to create a gritty HDR effect.**

**Time required:** 1-2 hours

**Kit needed:**
- DSLR or mirrorless camera
- Wide-angle lens
- Tripod
- Editing software

**Camera settings:**
1/125 sec f/8, ISO 100

**Skill level:**

 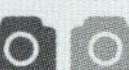  

**HDR stands for 'high dynamic range' and is a photographic technique that enables you to capture a greater range of luminosity. It works by taking three or more separate exposures of the same scene that expose for the shadows, highlights and midtones.**

Old classic cars are a great candidate for the HDR treatment, and they are such a pleasure to photograph with their lovely curves and iconic features. When you are trying to find the right model, there are a few key features that help enhance the HDR effect. The first is rust, as rusty cars create an even better result.

The next key aspect to consider is the background. Look for textures such as mossy, faded cladding or another old vehicle, and objects of interest to bring that extra layer to your frame. Avoid showing any new cars in the background, as they will detract from the appeal of your classic subject.

The only items you need to accompany your camera are a tripod, to keep the camera still, and a wide-angle lens. You will also need some sort of photo-processing software to merge your final images together and create the HDR effect. There are several alternatives to Photoshop that are specifically designed to process only HDR effects, such as Photomatix Pro, Photomatic Essentials and EasyHDR.

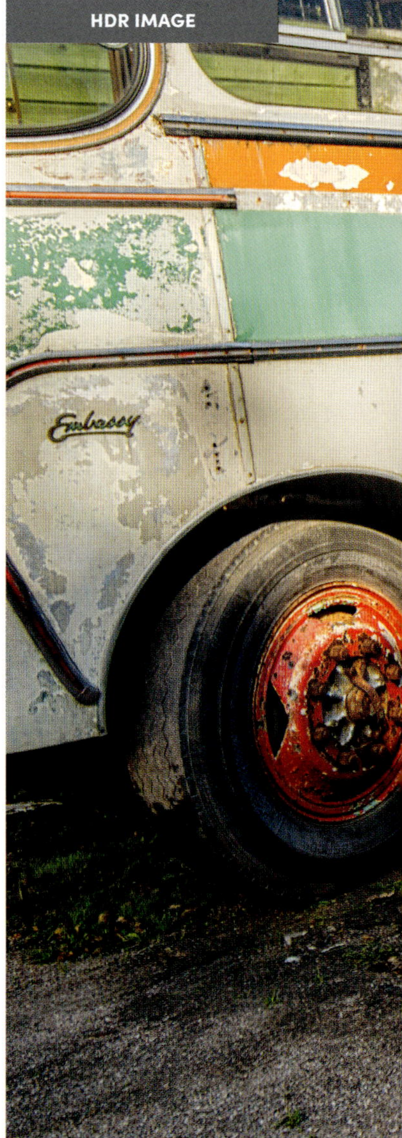

HDR IMAGE

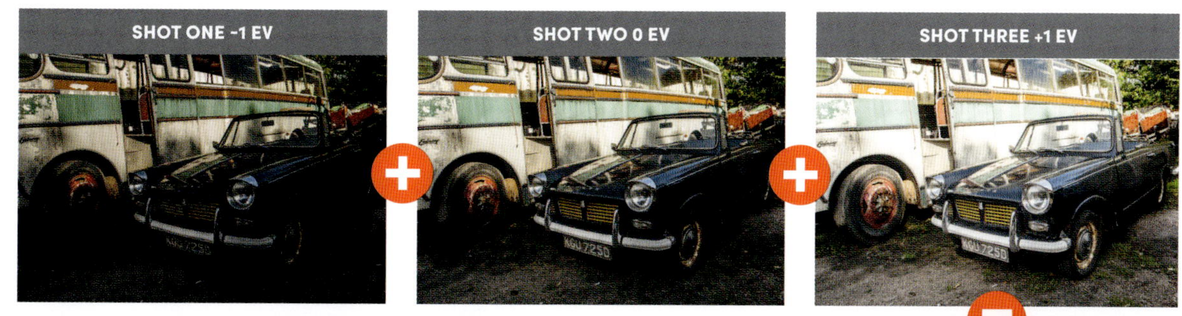
SHOT ONE -1 EV
SHOT TWO 0 EV
SHOT THREE +1 EV

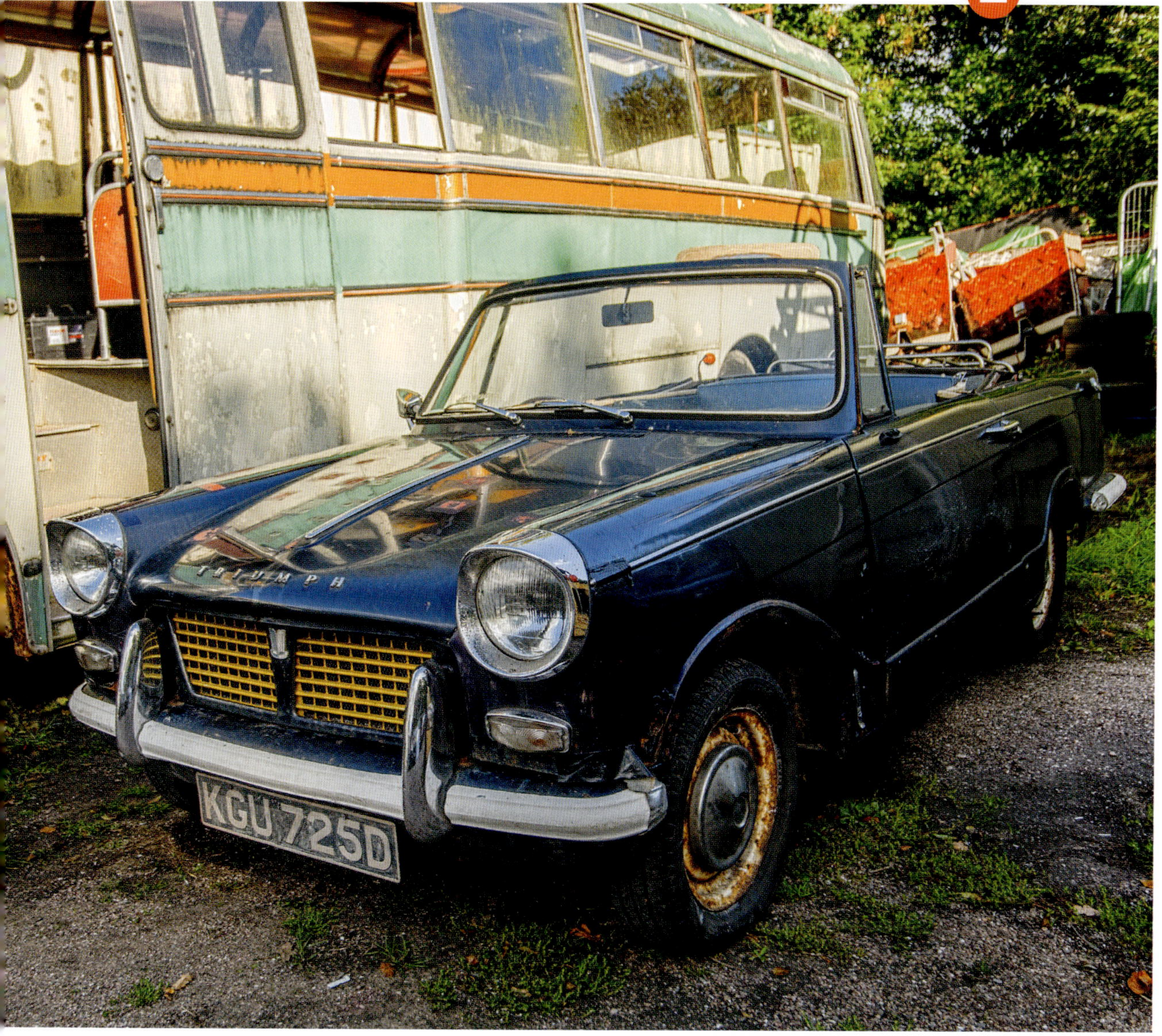

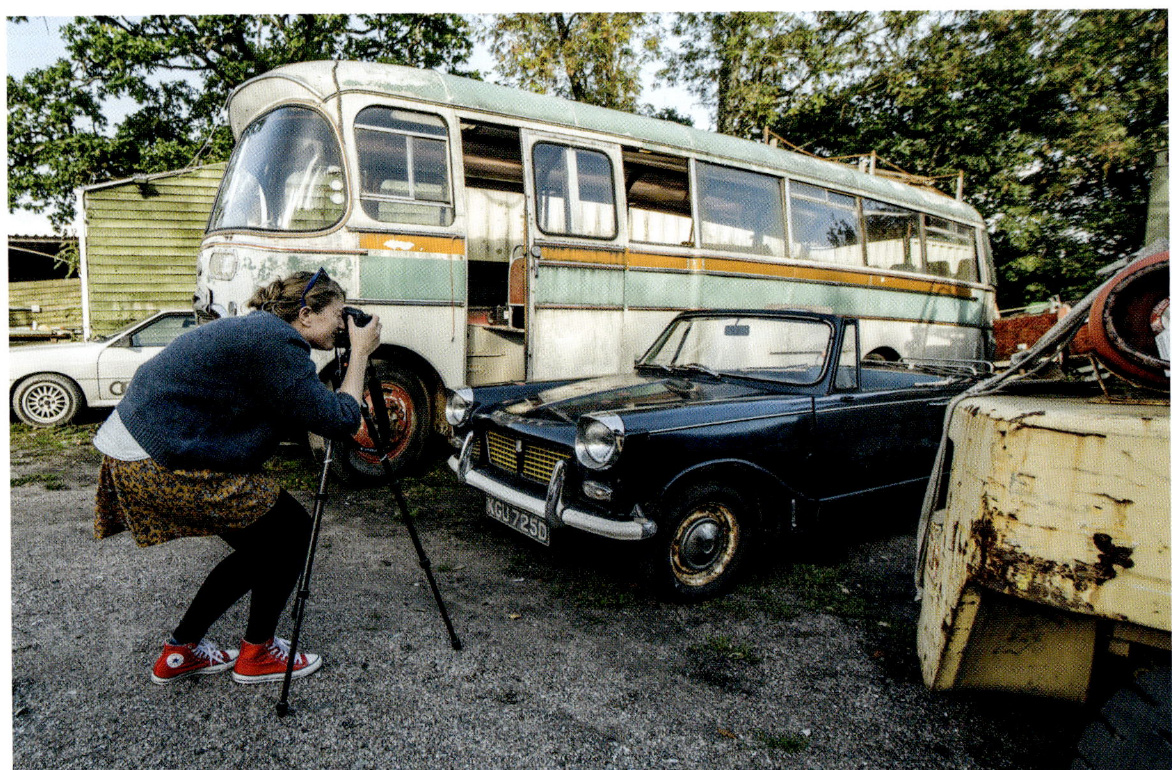


### 1 Camera on a tripod

Set your camera up on a tripod. It might be easier to experiment with compositions without having your camera attached at first, but after reviewing your shots, use a tripod to take three separate exposures of the best composition.

### 2 Bracket exposing

Bracket exposing is simply taking three shots of the same scene at different exposure settings. Use aperture-priority mode and set your aperture to f/8 and ISO to 100. Take the first shot with the camera giving an average reading, then use the exposure compensation button to take one shot a stop over (+1), and another a stop under (-1).

### 3 Go wide

A wide-angle zoom lens will enable you to fit the whole car easily into the frame. Be careful not to get too close to your vehicle, as this kind of lens makes close-up objects appear to bend and distort. If you do encounter distortion on a smaller scale, you can fix it in post-production, but it's easier to look out for this issue while shooting.

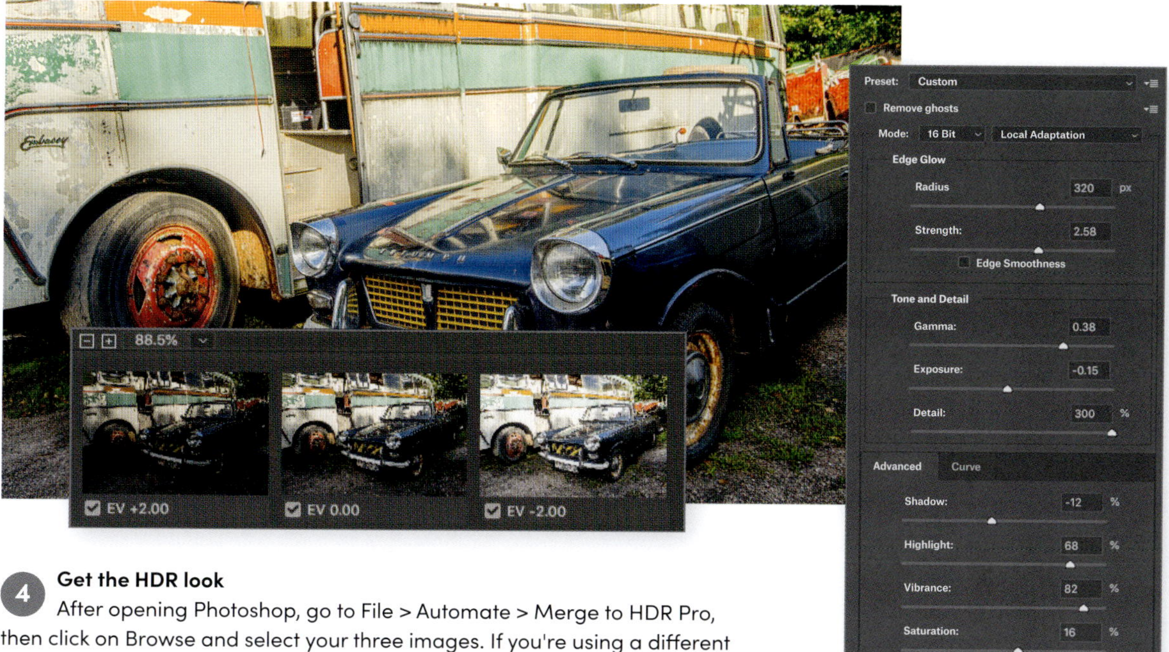


## 4 Get the HDR look

After opening Photoshop, go to File > Automate > Merge to HDR Pro, then click on Browse and select your three images. If you're using a different photo-processing software, the steps might vary slightly, but the general process should be similar. Once the HDR Pro window opens, you can tweak the effect to your liking. Select a preset option as a starting point, then boost Highlights to 100 and reduce Strength and Radius under the Edge Glow setting. Play around with the settings until you're happy and click OK. Process the correctly exposed image in Camera Raw, boosting Clarity and reducing Highlights. Place this image over your HDR-processed one and reduce Opacity to 65%. This will give you a gritty effect without it being too strong.

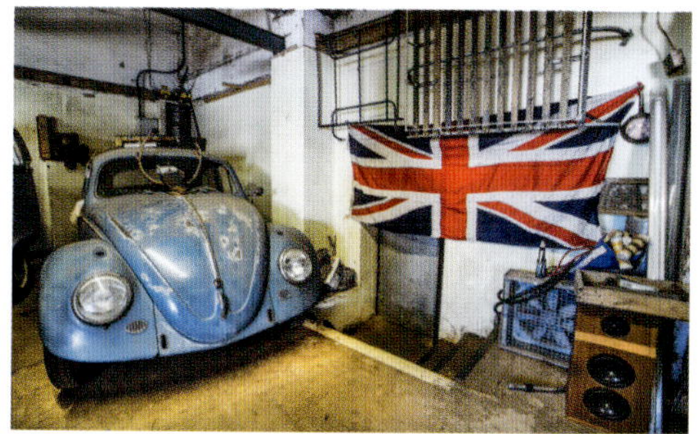

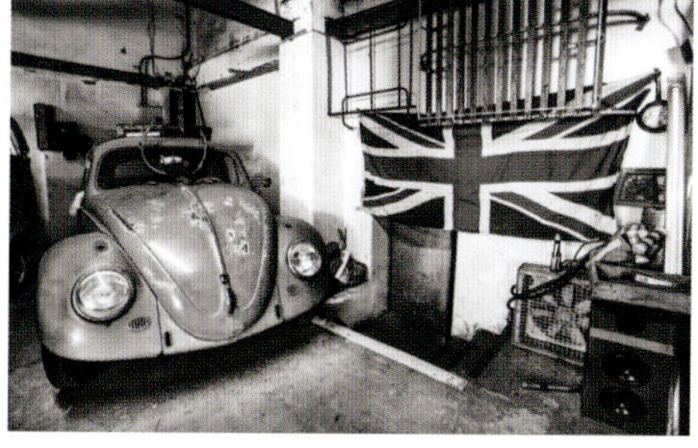

Try processing your images in colour and black and white to see which you prefer. The HDR effect works great for both. In this example, the colour image shows the rich reds of the flag, although the lighting in the workshop was very orange and there is a bit of a funny colour cast. The black-and-white version gets rid of this problem and emphasises the tones and textures in the scene.

# MAKE SMOKE SPIRALS

**THE IDEA**
**Capture spirals of smoke to make surreal images.**

**Time required:** 1-2 hours

**Kit needed:**
- DSLR or mirrorless camera
- 50mm lens
- Off-camera flash
- Black background
- Incense stick
- Editing software (optional)

**Camera settings:**
1/125 sec at f/8, ISO 400

**Skill level:**

**When the weather is unsuitable to venture outdoors, a great DIY photography project to try in the comfort of your own home is smoke art. For this project, use a black background, incense sticks, a spoon (to shape the smoke formation into jellyfish-style shapes) and an external flashgun.**

The flash helps illuminate the smoke formation and separates it from the background. If you don't have a flashgun, it is possible to use a reflector and natural light, but in this type of project you will get more reliable and consistent results with flash. Incense sticks offer the easiest, safest and most effective way to create the smoke. Be careful, though, not to place anything flammable nearby or underneath, and have the incense stick attached in a sturdy holder.

When it comes to the editing part of this project, there are a few different options you can take. The first is to leave the shots as they came out of the camera. You may want to boost the tone and contrast a little, but they can look effective just as they are. The other option is to bring colour into your smoke formation. This is simple to do using Photoshop or other image-editing software. Try using a Hue/Saturation Adjustment Layer and play around with the results to create a surreal effect.

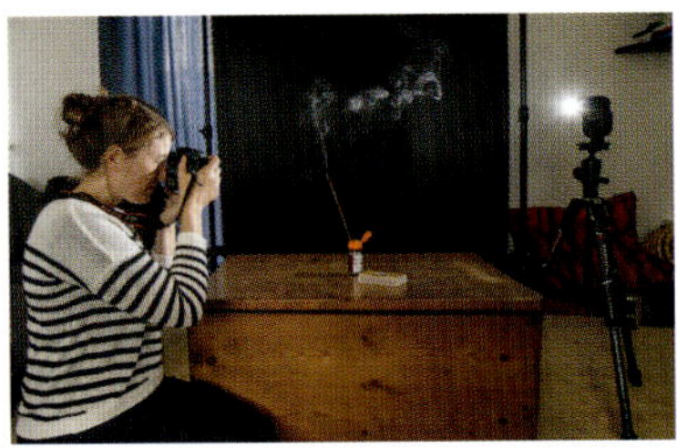

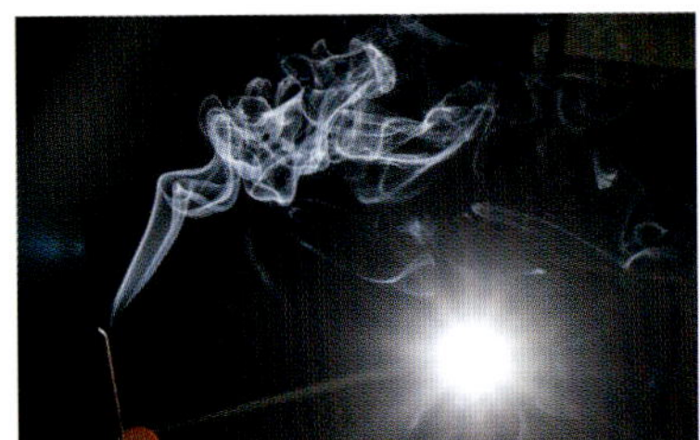

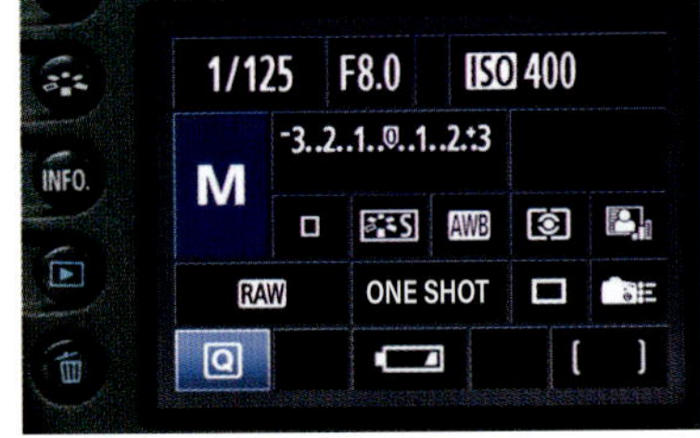


**1 The set-up**
To capture the best smoke formations possible, shoot against a black background. Ensure there is some separation between the background and the light, so bring your incense stick forward if need be. You want your background to be as black as possible, so ensure no light is hitting it. We positioned our flashgun behind and to one side of the smoke.

**2 The right smoke**
Your best option for creating the smoke is lighting an incense stick. Make sure you choose a smell you like as it can hang around for a few days afterwards. When you take the shots, keep the air around the incense as still as possible, and don't open the window. Any of your movements will affect the smoke too, so keep still.

**3 Camera and flash settings**
When it comes to setting up your camera, put your camera into manual mode and select a shutter speed of 1/125 sec. This means you can handhold your camera while also syncing the shutter with the flashgun. As you want the smoke to stay sharp, use a mid-range aperture setting of around f/8. Set ISO to 400 and balance this with the flashgun, firing at 1/16 of maximum power in manual mode. Finally, use the continuous AF tracking setting on your lens to make sure your focus remains sharp.

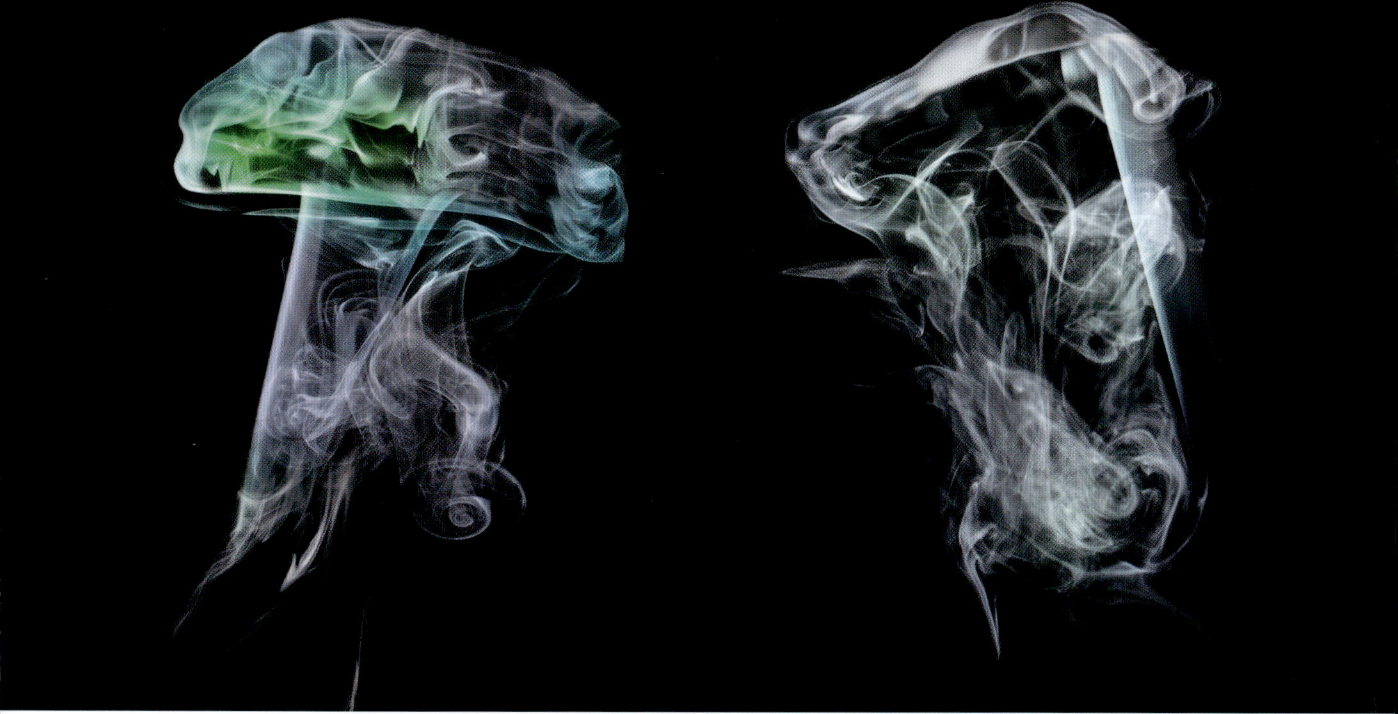

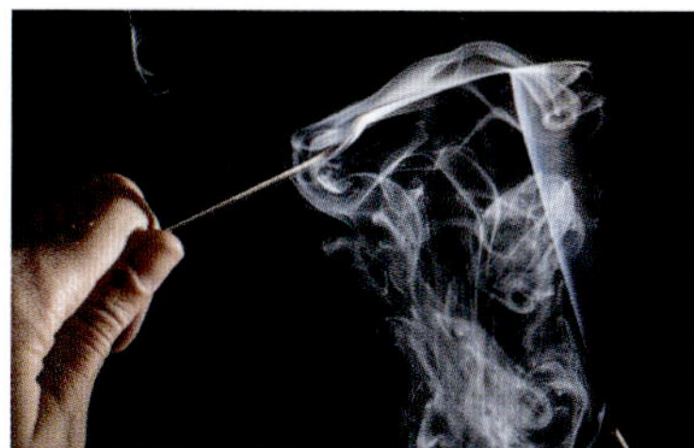

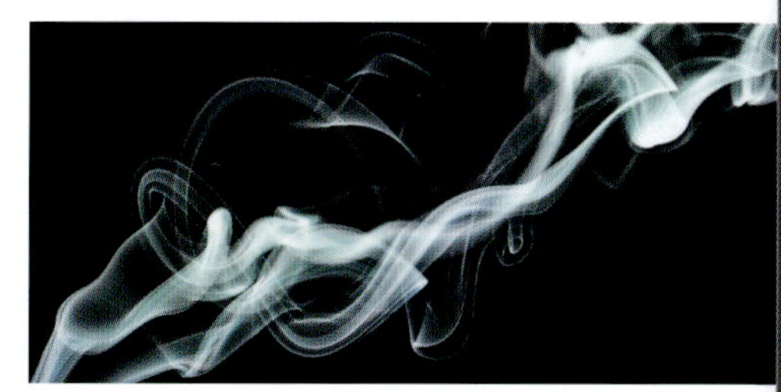

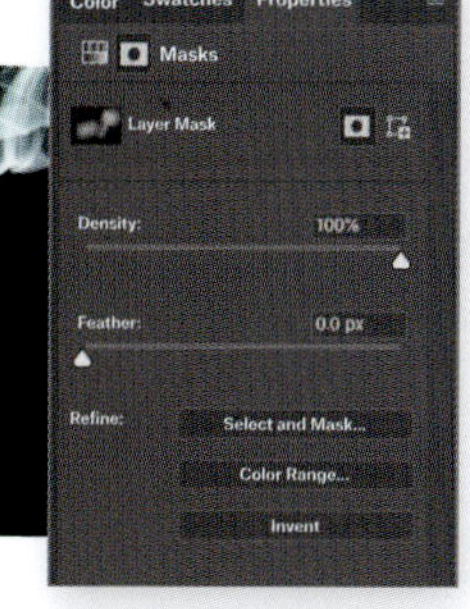


### 4 Bend the smoke

If you simply let the incense stick burn, you get a lovely straight flume of smoke. If you're after more twirls and curls, you want to focus on the area where the flume starts to break. You can also interfere with the smoke formation using objects. To bend the smoke to resemble jellyfish floating around in the sea, place a spoon where the smoke starts to break, so it bends into a curved shape.

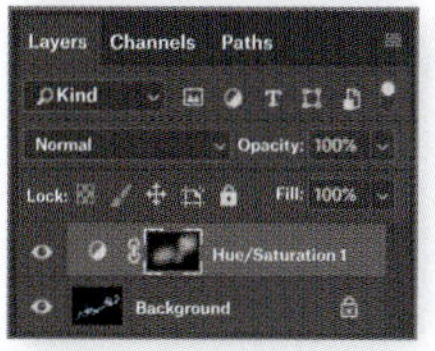


### 5 The editing part

When it comes to editing your images, there are a few options. First, open them up into Camera Raw and boost Clarity and Contrast. You can also push the Black slider a touch to darken the background further. Once you're happy, open your image in Photoshop and add a Hue/Saturation Adjustment Layer. Push the Hue slider to alter the colour. To create the two-tone effect, invert the Hue/Saturation Layer Mask and, using a white brush at 50% Opacity, paint over parts of the smoke formation to add bits of colour to isolated areas.

# THE MAGIC OF MARBLING

**THE IDEA**
**Combine photography with the art of marbling.**

**Time required**: 3 hours

**Kit needed:**
- DSLR or mirrorless camera
- 50mm lens
- Tripod
- Marbling kit
- Editing software

**Camera settings:**
1 sec at f/8, ISO 100

**Skill level:**

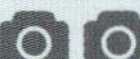 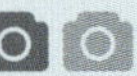 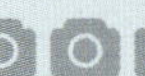

**Marbling has been around for many years, and we see it in lots of different places – from pillars on old buildings to artworks, wrapping paper, book covers and even tiled surfaces in the home. There are many different ways you can marble and the fun and unique appeal of marbling is that no two effects are ever going to be the same.**

The marbling technique in this tutorial uses a water solution and coloured paint. This was part of a marbling paint kit, which can be purchased online. Alternatively, you can experiment with household products including oil-based paints, food colouring, milk, nail polish and even shaving foam.

With our marbling kit, we were also able to lift and record our final marbled images onto paper; however, we opted to shoot the effect while it was still in the tray. We chose to do this so that we could shoot a sequence of images but we also liked the 3D appeal of the paint floating on the surface of the liquid.

Finally, as with any paint-based project, things can get a little messy. So make sure you have some kitchen roll to hand, and you may also want to put down a protective cloth before you begin.

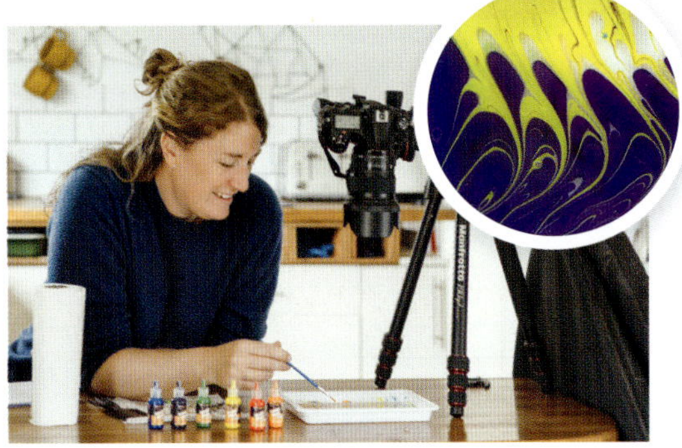

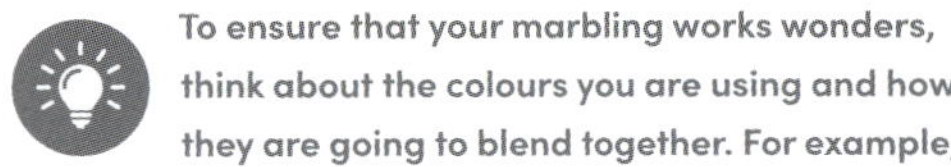

To ensure that your marbling works wonders, think about the colours you are using and how they are going to blend together. For example, a warm and bright colour such as yellow will provide a good contrast when paired with a cooler, darker colour such as purple. Again, blue and orange will work well together, or green and red are also complementary colours. You can introduce more than two colours if you want, but bear in mind that sometimes less is more and it's easy to go one step too far and have to start all over again, so embrace some failure along the way!

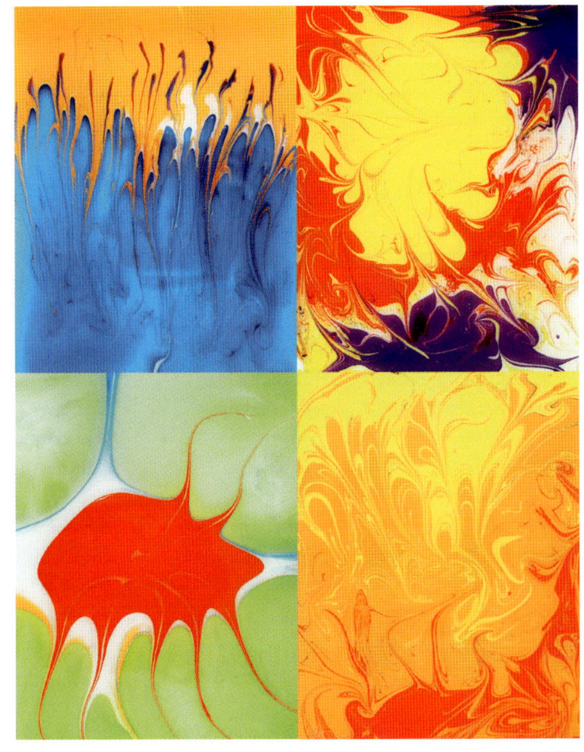

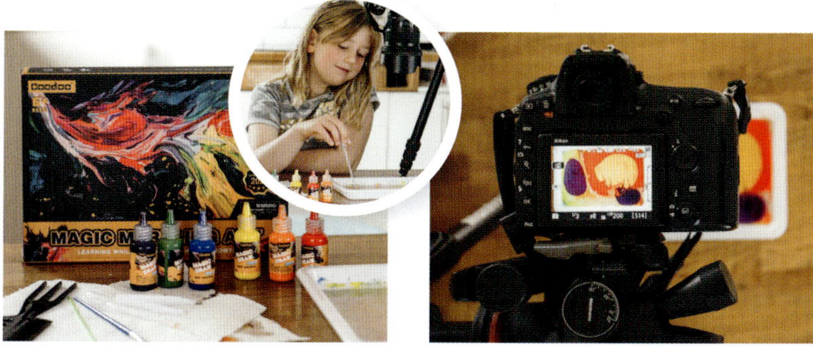

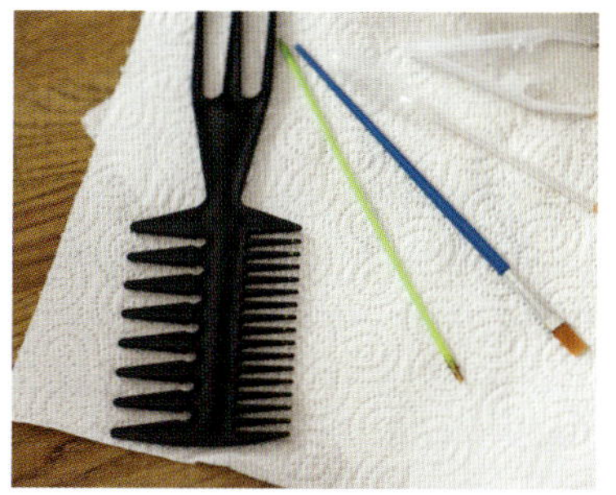

**1 Get started**
Following the instructions in our marbling kit, we made a solution around six hours in advance, mixing together 250ml of water with a sprinkle of powder (safe and non-toxic). To start, we placed the solution on an even surface and set up our camera overhead. This project is great fun to do with children, and we had a little helper on standby.

**2 Dial in the camera settings**
We took our images using natural light from a bird's-eye view, which meant our camera needed to be mounted on a tripod. We set the ISO at 100 and the aperture to f/8 to keep everything sharp. Our shutter speed was reading around one second so to ensure we had no camera shake, we used the self-timer to fire the shots.

**3 Get creative and experiment**
Once everything is set up, get creative. Our marbling kit came with some tools, but sticks and combs are effective. We experimented with techniques and colours until we were happy with the result but found it best to shoot throughout the different stages, so that if we overdid the marble effect, we still had our earlier efforts to work with.

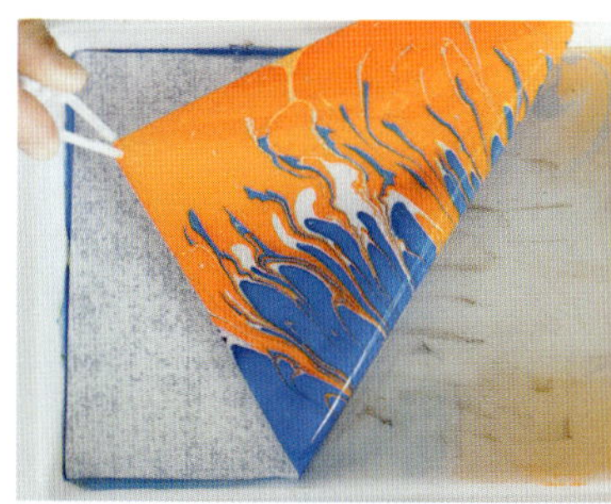

**4 Record the final results**
If you are using a marbling kit, you can record your final images on paper. Place a piece of paper over the paint, carefully lift a corner and peel back. Leave your paper to dry for an hour before you move it and a few more hours to ensure it is dry. If you don't want to use your camera, you could scan in your final marbled images instead.

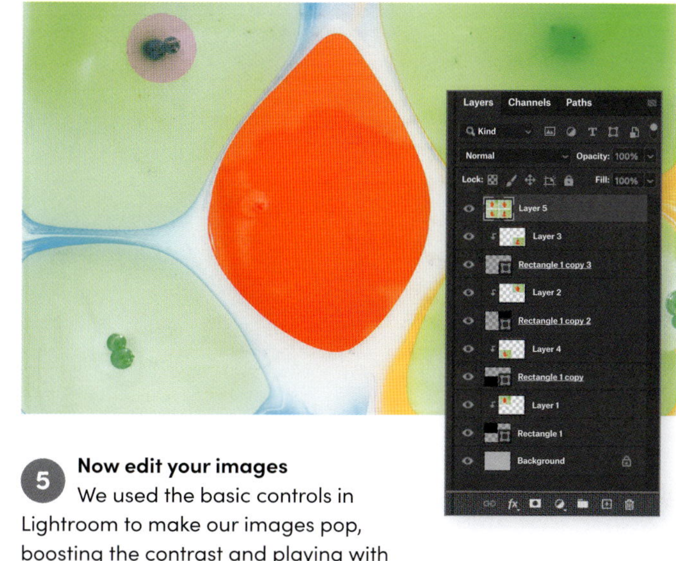


**5 Now edit your images**
We used the basic controls in Lightroom to make our images pop, boosting the contrast and playing with the Black and White sliders. We also cleaned up any bubbles and other distracting elements in Photoshop using the Remove and Spot Healing tool. Finally, we experimented with different presentation ideas to combine the images.

# USE MOODY LOW-KEY LIGHTING

**THE IDEA**
**Shoot a still-life with a Renaissance painting feel.**

**Time required**: 1-2 hours

**Kit needed**:
- DSLR or mirrorless camera
- 50mm lens
- Tripod
- Props, including candles
- Table lamp
- Editing software

**Camera settings**:
2.5 secs at f/11, ISO 64

**Skill level**:

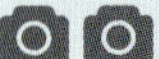 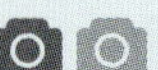 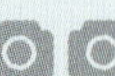

**Low-key lighting is a soft lighting scheme that retains dark tones and shadows and is atmospheric and moody in appearance. To achieve the low-key effect, use three candles, a table lamp and a bit of natural light. Shoot on a day and mix the cool daylight tones with the warm orange tungsten cast from the candles for a visually pleasing effect.**

Do some online research first, searching for 'still life renaissance' to see how the objects are arranged and what types of props will work.

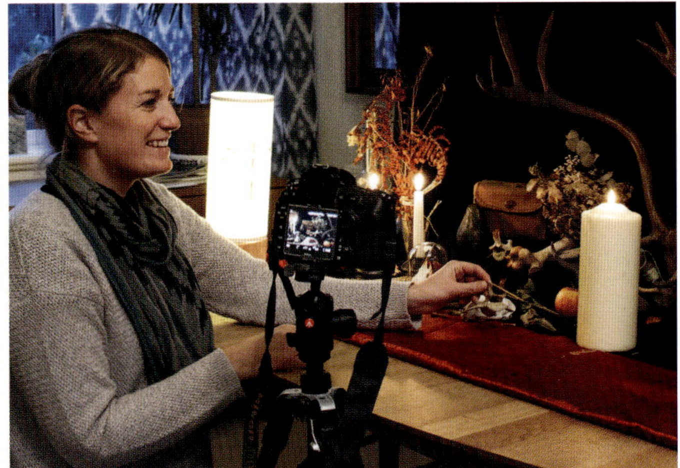

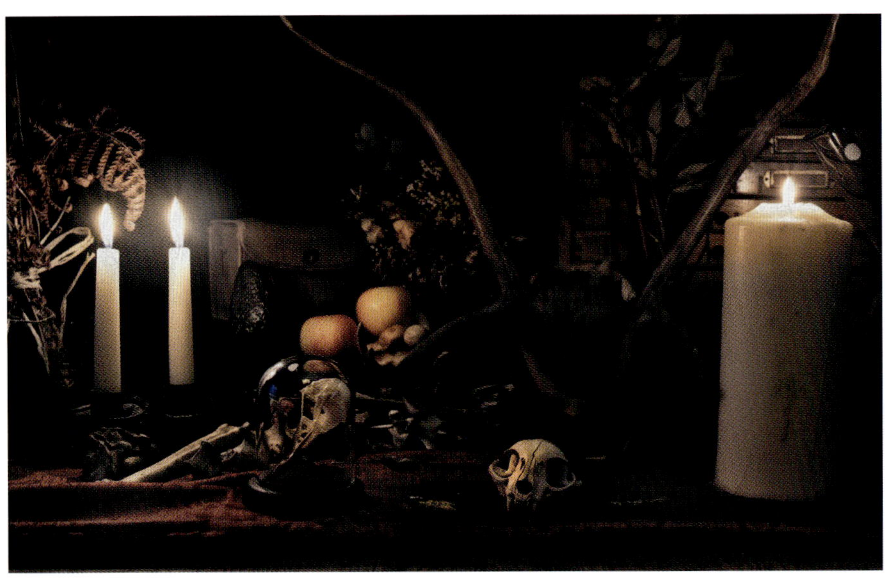

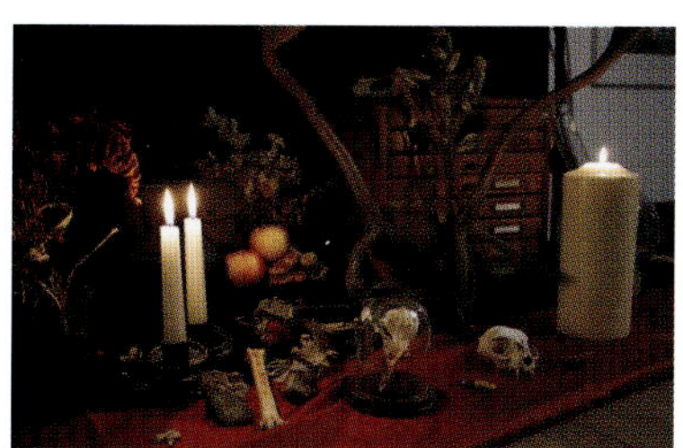

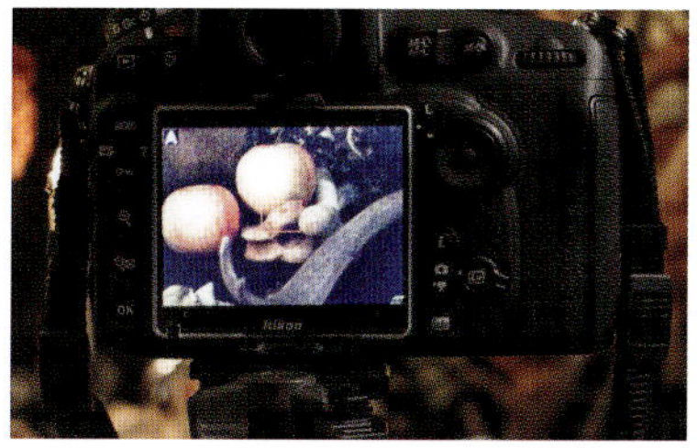

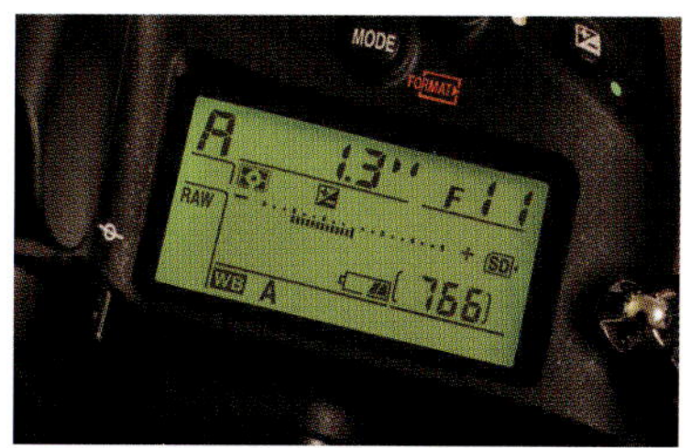


**1 Props and getting set up**
Hang a black background behind the table and place a couple of boxes underneath a black blanket to create a raised area. To add some subtle colour, lay a coloured scarf along the front of the composition. Position your props. For this image, skulls, candles, dead bugs, antlers, glass cases, fruit, a camera, a small wooden drawer set and dead flowers were used. Of course, you don't need to go as macabre as this – jugs, fruit bowls and flowers work just as well.

**2 Manual focus and Live View**
It can be easier to compose your shot through your camera's Live View feature to get a strong composition and the best positioning of your props. It will take a lot of tinkering, so don't expect to get it right first time. Once you're happy with your composition, switch to manual focus and zoom in, turning the focusing ring by hand to make sure your image is sharp.

**3 Camera set-up**
Place your camera on a tripod. Switch to aperture-priority mode at f/11 to keep all the objects in the scene sharp, and set ISO to 100 to retain maximum image quality. To ensure the black parts remained black, underexpose the scene by 2 stops. Finally, set the camera to self-timer mode, to avoid camera shake.

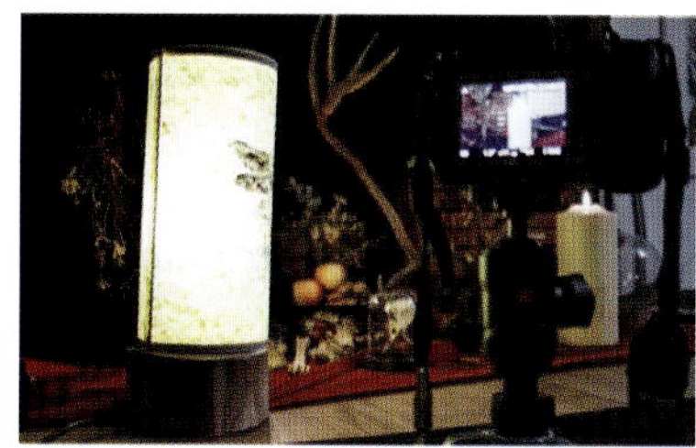

**4 Lighting tips**
Although the candles and natural light from the window light the scene, there will be a few areas that are still a little dark. Hold a warm table lamp (with a diffused cover) overhead to pick out details on the objects. If you use candles and dried flowers, be very careful – the latter will catch fire very easily, so never leave the exposed flames unattended.

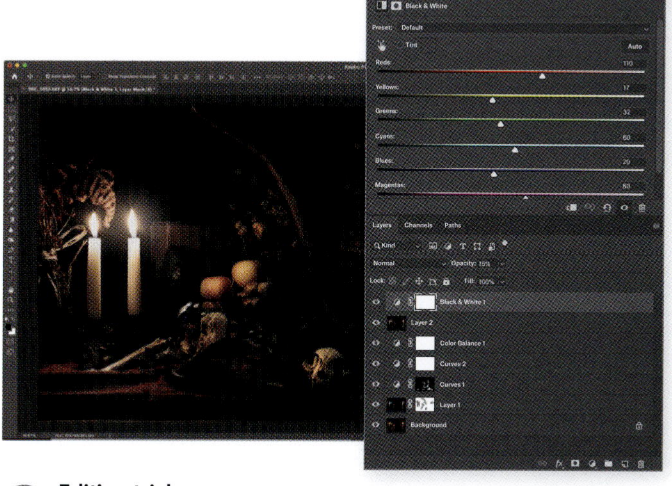


**5 Editing tricks**
To get the final look of your Renaissance-inspired still-life set-up, process the Raw file twice, once in a cooler tone and once in a warmer temperature, then blend them. Add a Curves Adjustment Layer to tweak the contrast and exposure. For a more painterly feel, add an Oil Paint filter (Filter > Stylize > Oil Paint), and use the Burn Tool (set Range to Shadows) to manually darken areas, so the objects appear like they're coming out of the shadows.

# SHOOT A SCIENCE EXPERIMENT

**THE IDEA**
**Capture a science experiment in a sequence.**

**Time required:** 1–2 hours

**Kit needed:**
- DSLR or mirrorless camera
- 50mm lens
- Flashgun
- Tripod
- Food colouring
- Old glass bottle
- Pipette or eye dropper
- White background
- Editing software

**Camera settings:**
1/200 sec at f/8, ISO 100

**Skill level:**

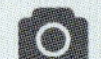  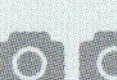

**Fill an old glass bottle halfway with water. Into this, add a few drops of food colouring at a time using a pipette or eye dropper, building the effect slowly. You will gradually see a change in the vessel, which you can then photograph in a series of images.**

The aim of this project is to create a grid of images, and you can display and shoot as many as you like and play around with this aspect. Set up your camera on a tripod to ensure all the images match, so they can be edited flawlessly together.

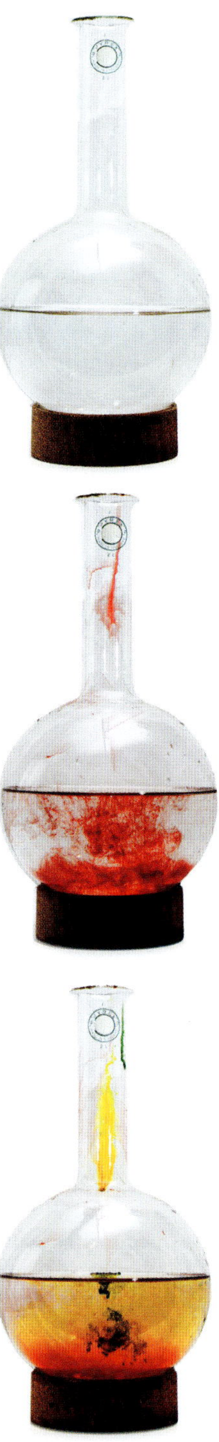

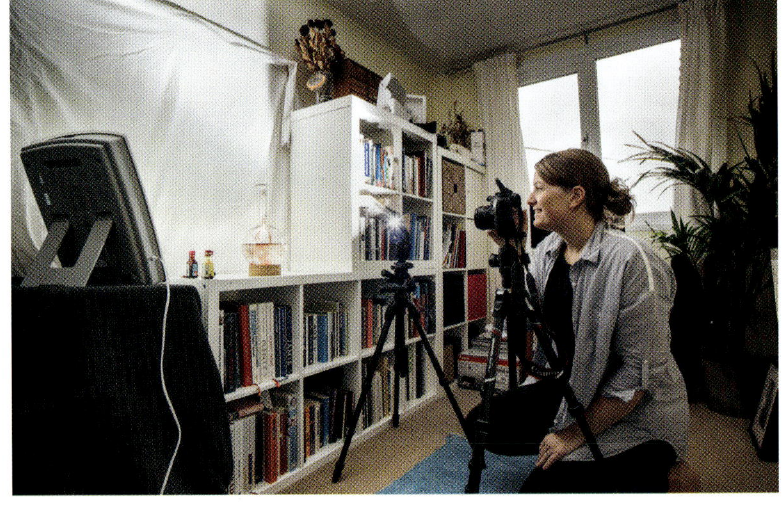

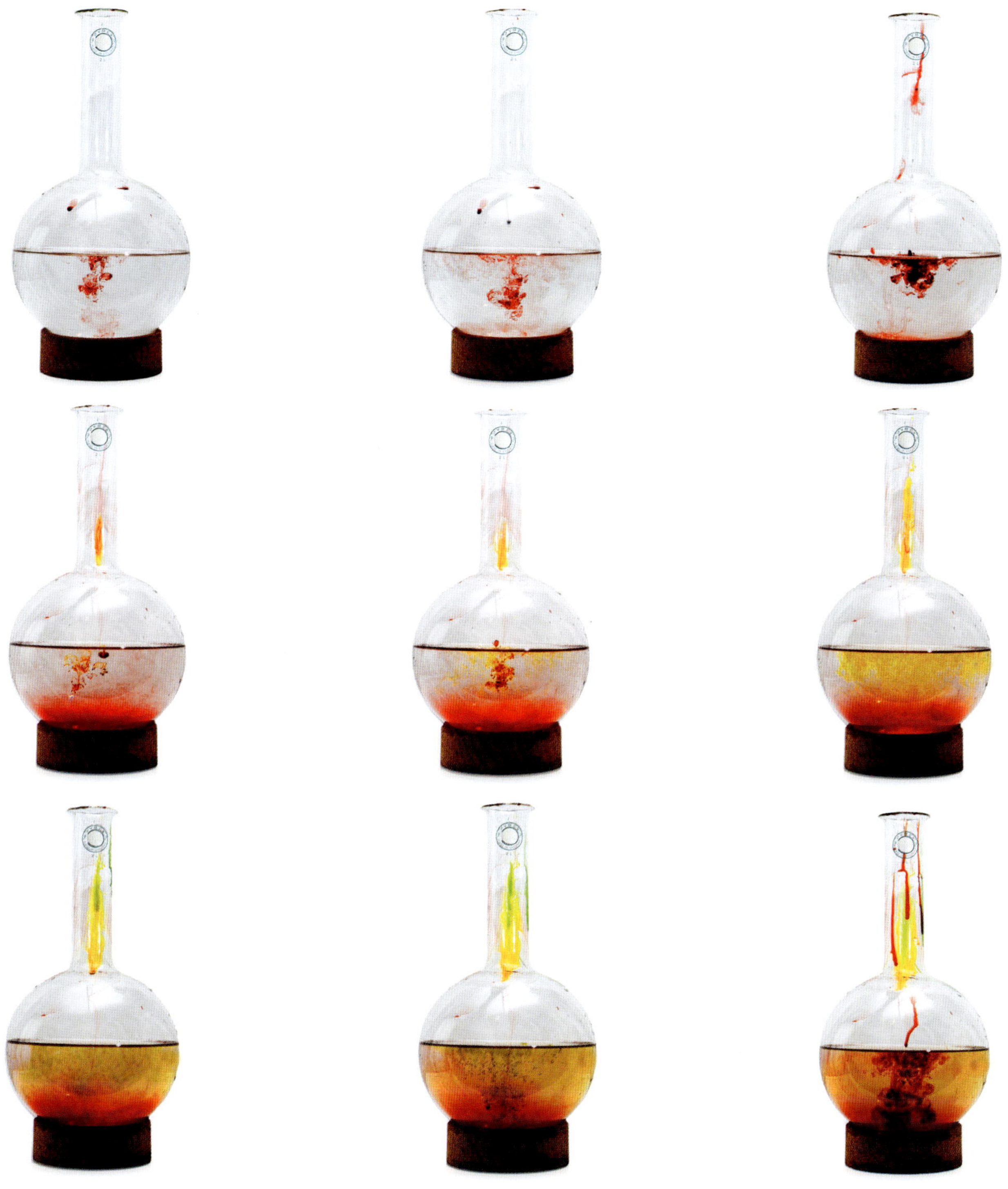

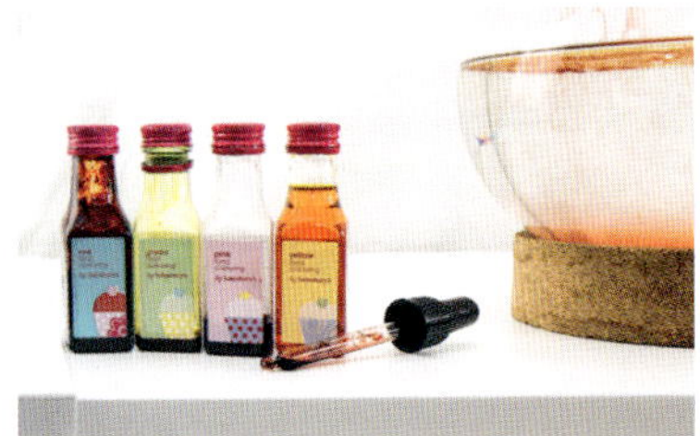

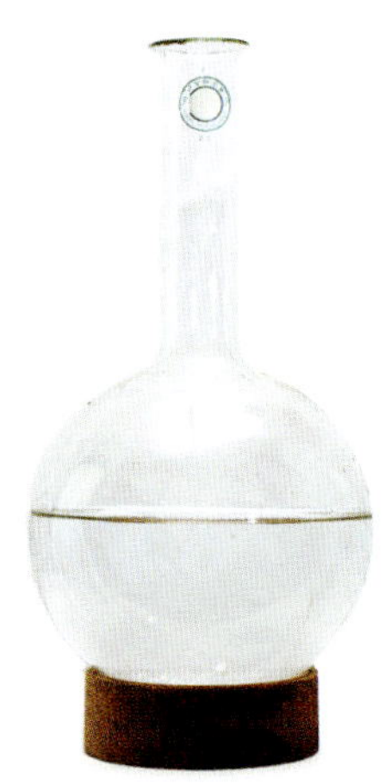

**1 Props**
Fill an old glass bottle halfway with water. Have a few bottles of food colouring to hand to add to it. Using an eye dropper means you can build the effect slowly.

**2 Background**
To create a clean white backdrop, pin an old sheet to the wall and drape it behind your bottle. To avoid creases, iron the sheet first, but if you have a roll of paper or a piece of card, this can look cleaner and save you time editing in post-production.

**3 Time it right**
Once you've got your lens focused and camera settings selected, it's time to get shooting. You can either use a remote control or press the shutter button by hand and squirt some food colouring drops into the water. Your camera's burst mode can be useful for capturing the dynamic movement of the colours as they disperse. Start with a clean bottle as your first image, then build slowly from there.

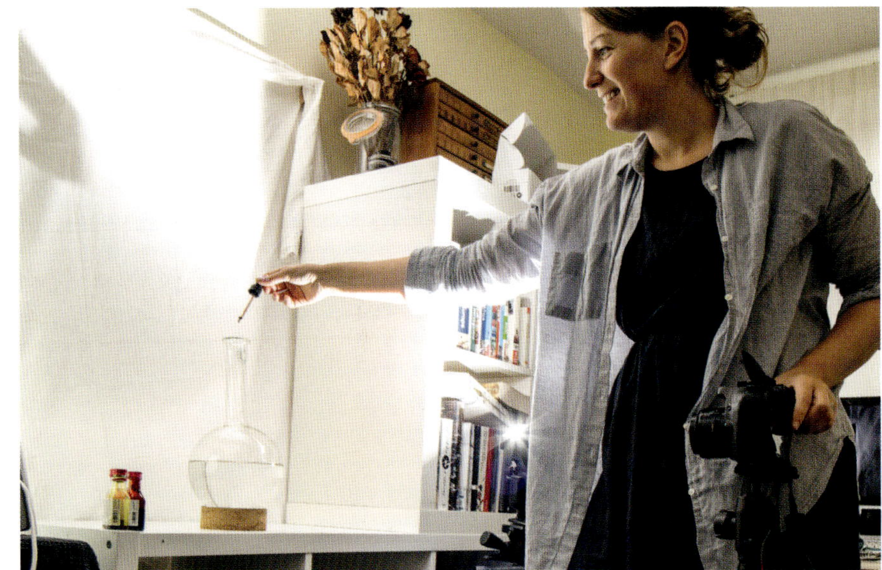

## 4 Flat lighting

Use flashlight to light your bottle and liquid. To ensure an even distribution of light, bounce the flash off the ceiling at a high-power setting. To do this, simply point the flash head upwards, but consider how high your ceilings are and try a few test shots, balancing the aperture and ISO (set shutter to 1/200 sec to sync with flash) to get the right exposure. Use your histogram to check your exposure setting.

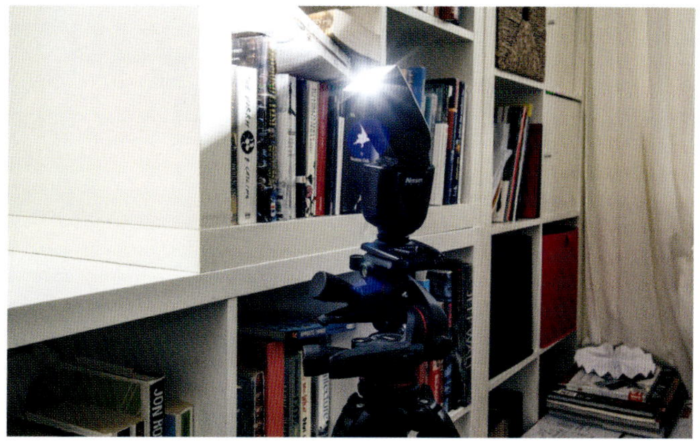

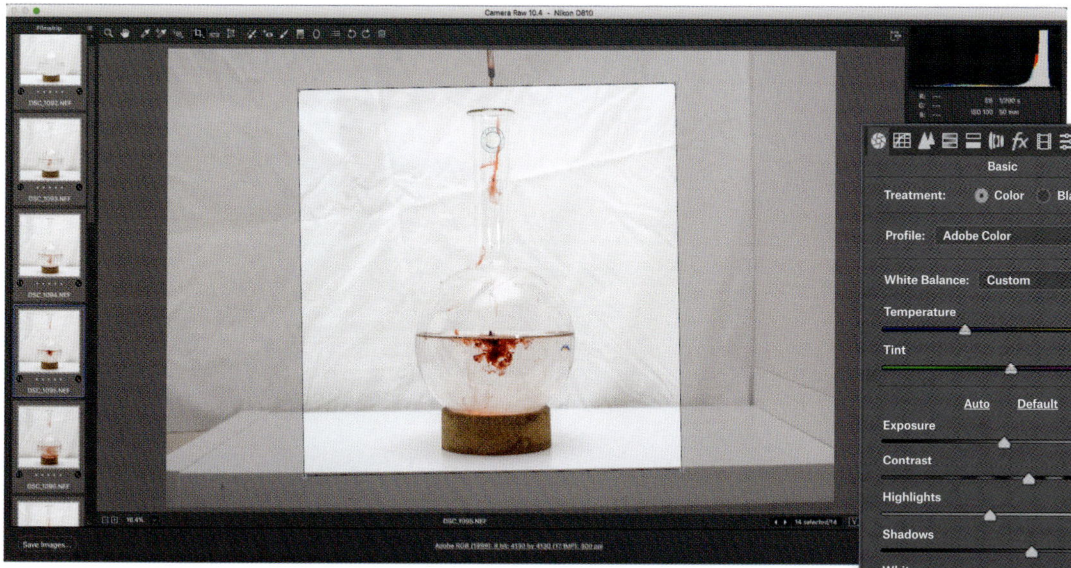

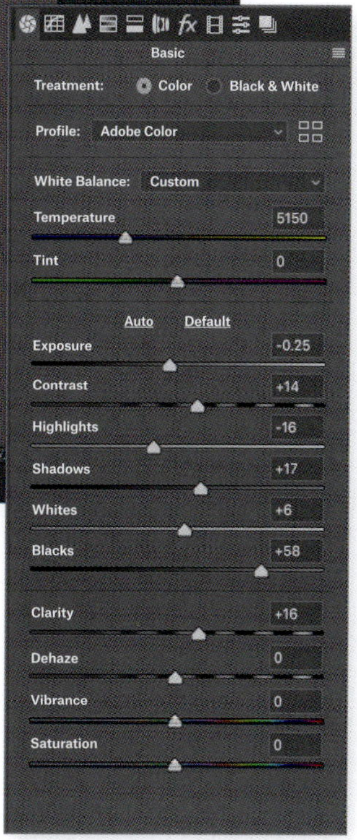

## 5 End with an edit

At the editing stage, select all the images from the sequence and open them into Camera Raw. From here, Select All then adjust all the settings at once, so the images match in tone, exposure and contrast. You could also crop each image (again in a batch edit) into a square using the Crop Tool at the 1:1 ratio setting. Once you're happy, take all your images into Photoshop then experiment with your grid formation and display.

# HAVE FUN WITH FOOD

**THE IDEA**
**Build a cupcake clock.**

**Time required**: 1 hour

**Kit needed**:
- DSLR or mirrorless camera
- 35mm lens
- Tripod
- Reflector
- Food and drink props
- White background

**Camera settings**:
1/50 sec at f/8, ISO 100

**Skill level**:

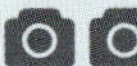 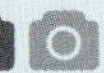  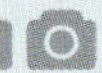

**DIY photography projects are a great way to get creative and try out new techniques and shooting styles from the comfort of your home.**

A cupcake clock could be made with a range of food or drink (or both). Think of a theme and how you could make it work – chopsticks as the hands, spices with cinnamon sticks, the process of brewing a cup of tea... you get the idea. Elements such as the clock hands – for this image, they were made from a small sieve and whisk – help bring the whole concept together.

When it comes to creating your clock, making it a bit messy really helps. However, you don't want to go so far that it looks chaotic. It's more like a bit of stylised mess, such as a dribble of icing, a sprinkling of flour or a cracked eggshell. It helps to have a cloth to hand so if it does get too messy, you can bring it back.

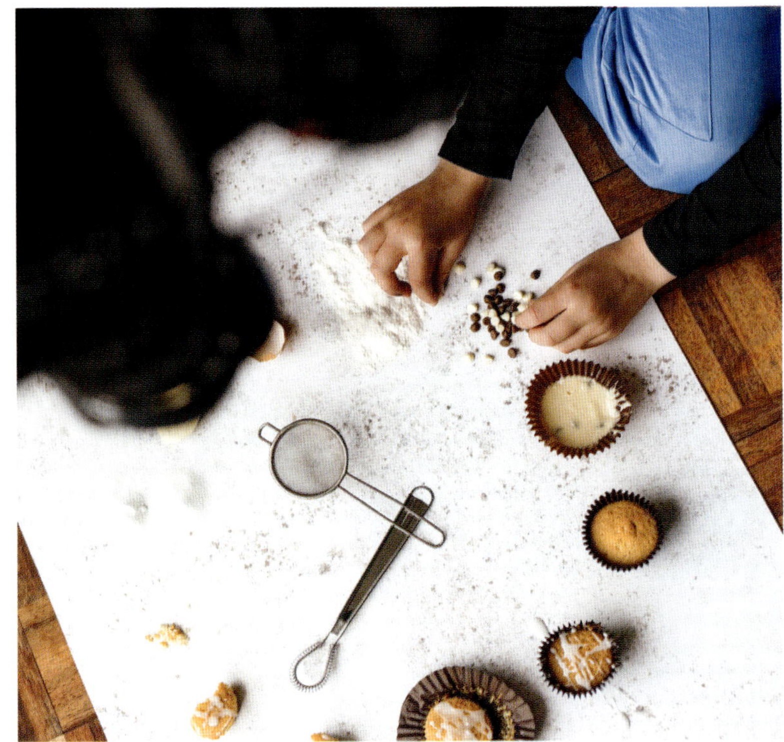

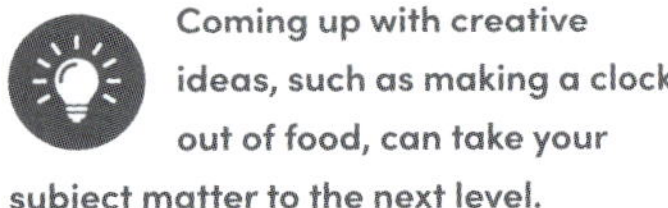

Coming up with creative ideas, such as making a clock out of food, can take your subject matter to the next level.

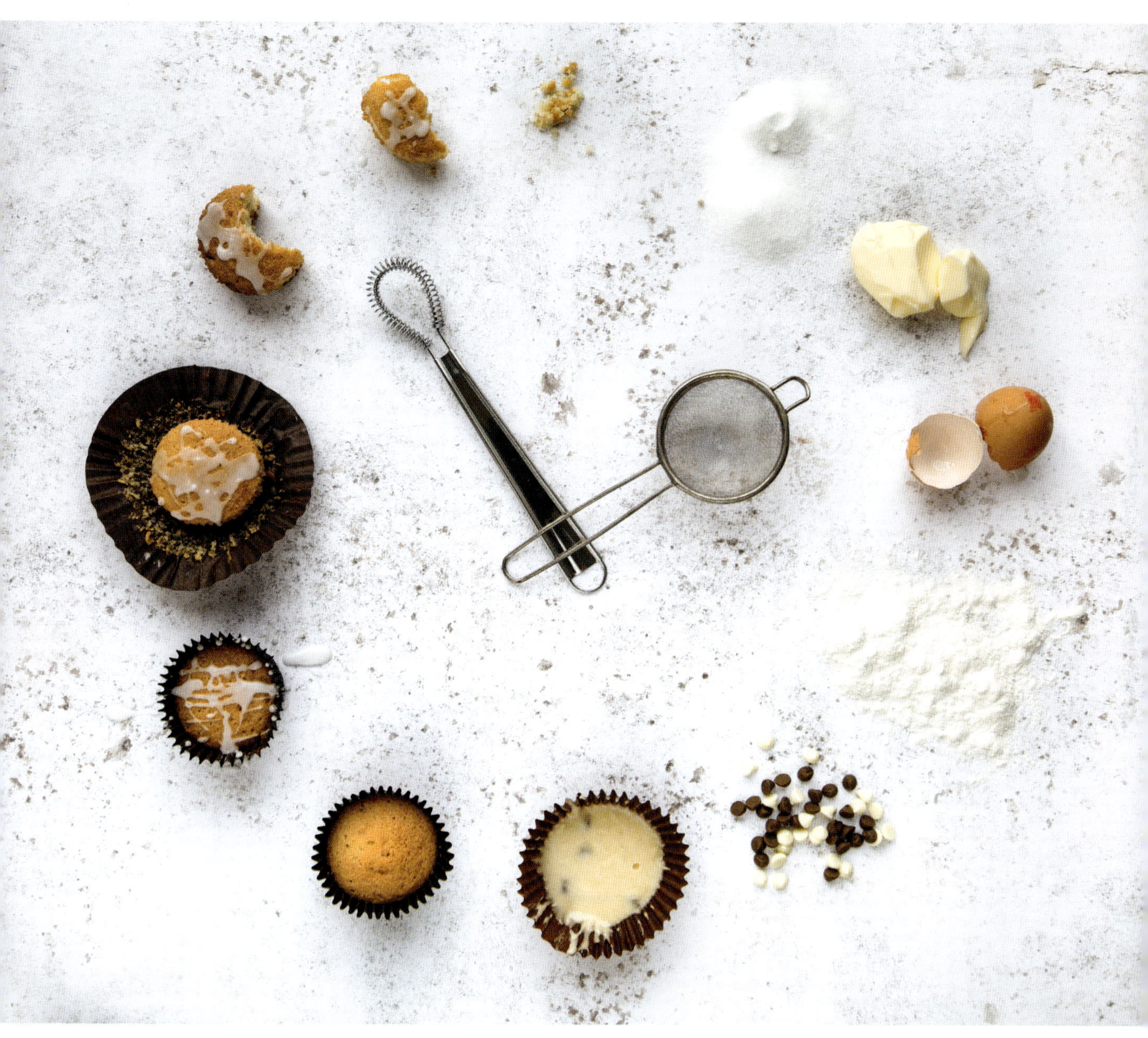

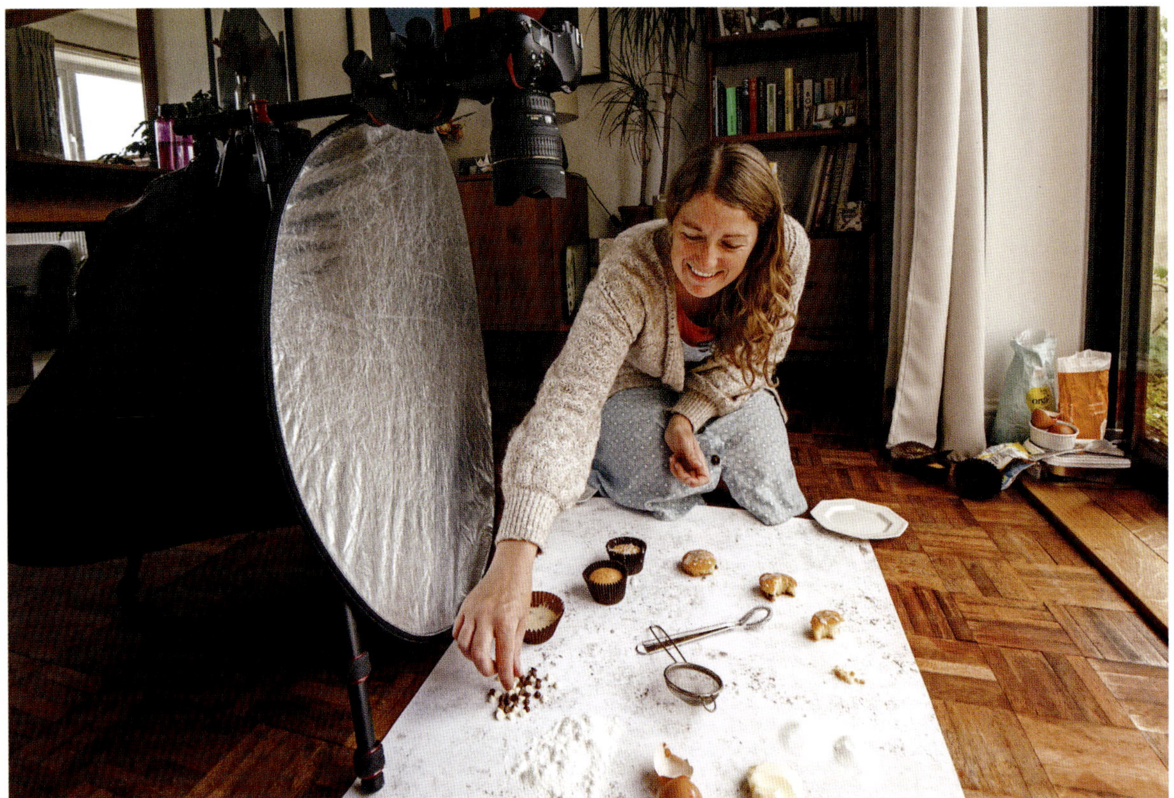

## 1 Prepare and plan

Plan your shoot using pen and paper, so you know which elements to use and in which space. Here, empty cupcake cases were used to build the clock face, so the photographer knew where to place each ingredient. Then, a batch of cupcakes was baked, with a cup of the raw mixture kept aside for the number six on the clock face.

## 2 Choose a background

The choice of background is critical to making the shot work. Here, a light-textured vinyl backdrop was used. Of course, you don't have to buy anything especially for your photography shoot, as you could use a table surface, a piece of material or whatever options you have at home. Your background will set the tone of your shots, so experiment with different textures and materials.

## 3 Mount your camera

A bird's-eye view works well for this set-up, so extend your tripod's centre column. Although you could shoot this project handheld (make sure you have a fast enough shutter speed), a tripod will help you take time composing the perfect shot. Keep tweaking the elements until you are happy with the composition and placement.

### 4 Fine-tune your camera settings

Put your camera into aperture-priority mode and set the aperture to f/8 to keep the image sharp from front to back. Reduce the ISO to 100 for high-quality results. As your camera is on a tripod, it doesn't matter what the shutter speed is reading. Adjust the exposure compensation if your image is underexposing slightly. Use the self-timer.

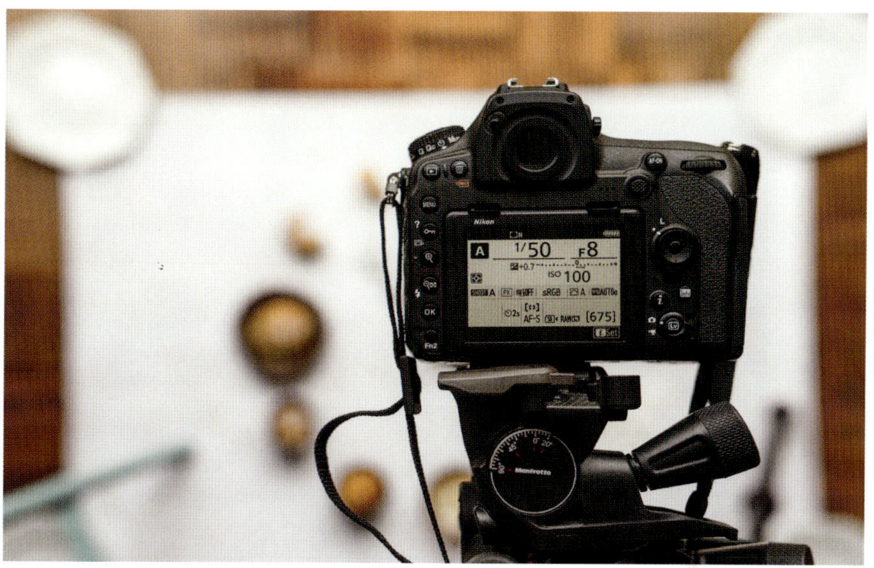


## Natural light

**You don't need any fancy studio lighting or flashguns for this project. Instead, set up your shot next to a large window and bounce the light back into any unwanted shadows using a reflector.**

# CREATE A CYANOTYPE

**THE IDEA**
**Discover Sunprint paper and develop cyanotypes.**

**Time required:** 1–2 hours

**Kit needed:**
- Sunprint kit
- Leaves and stems
- Tray of water

**Camera settings:**
See Sunprint kit instructions

**Skill level:**
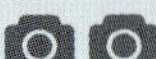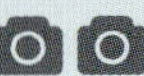

**The historic cyanotype process was used well into the 20th century as a simple and cheap way to produce copies of drawings and photos, known as blueprints.**

Today, you can replicate this bold cyanotype process using Sunprint paper, which is a specialist material coated with light-sensitive chemicals. The paper is both safe and fun and can be used to make 'sun art' using leaves, flowers or any other objects you choose. Those with a recognisable outline tend to work best.

To make a Sunprint, place the object on the paper, leave it in a bright spot for a few minutes, then remove and rinse it in tap water for a minute to fix the chemicals. The stronger the sun, the quicker the paper develops, though you don't need full summer sun to make a print. A bright windowsill or overcast daylight works too, just leave it out a little longer.

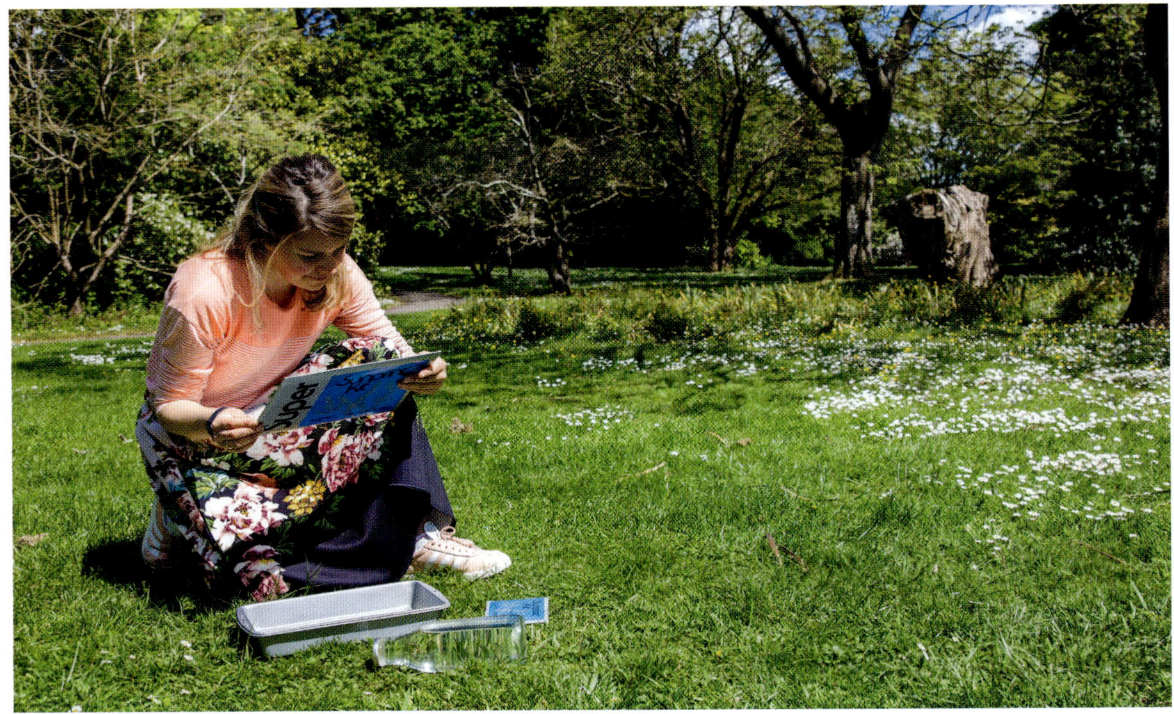

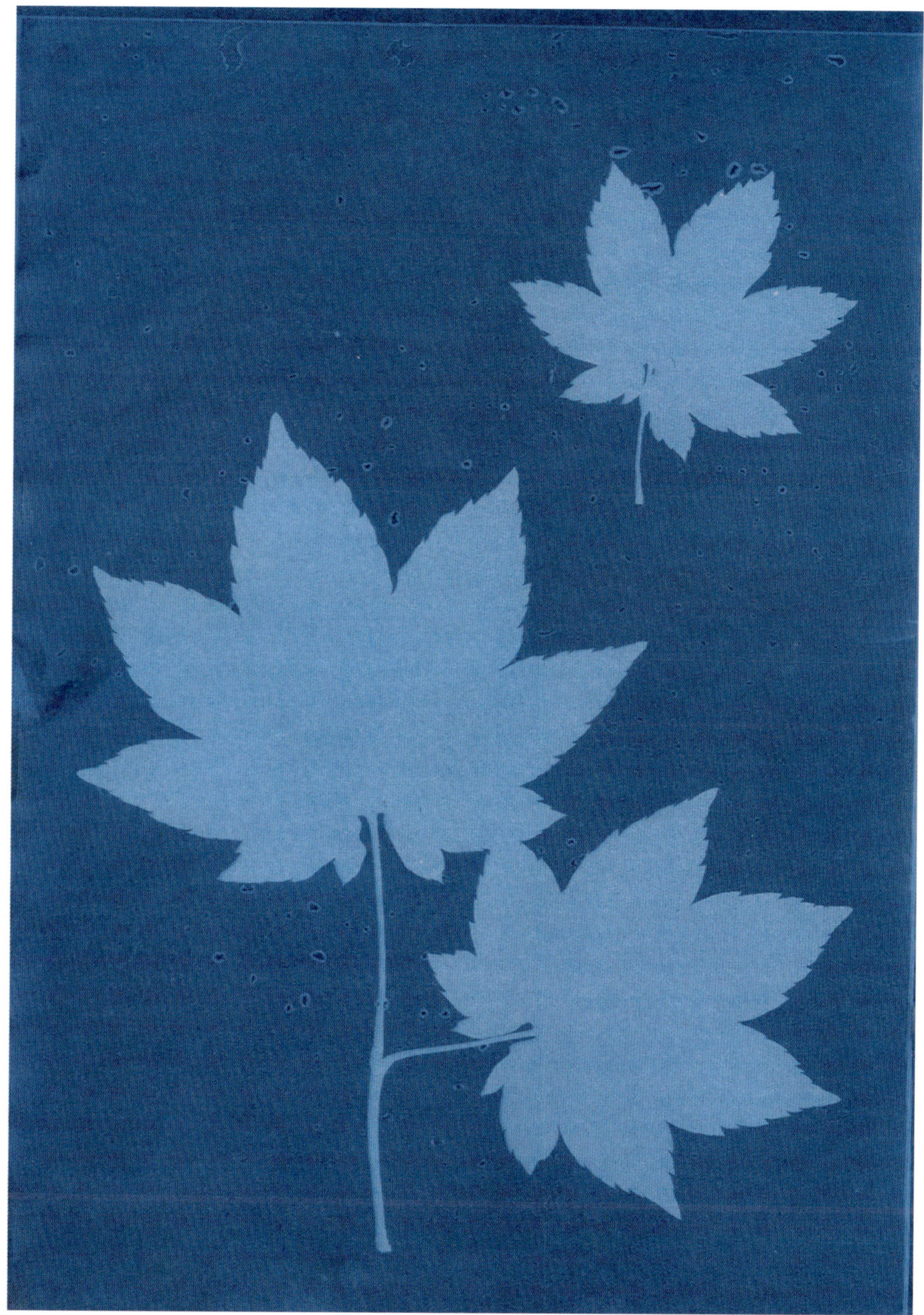

## How does it work?

**Exposed areas of the Sunprint paper fade from blue to white in ultraviolet light. This is because two molecules in the paper interact to form a new molecule. The new molecule is colourless, and so when the blue molecules are converted, the white of the paper base begins to show through. Areas of the paper covered by objects still contain the original blue molecule, so they remain blue.**

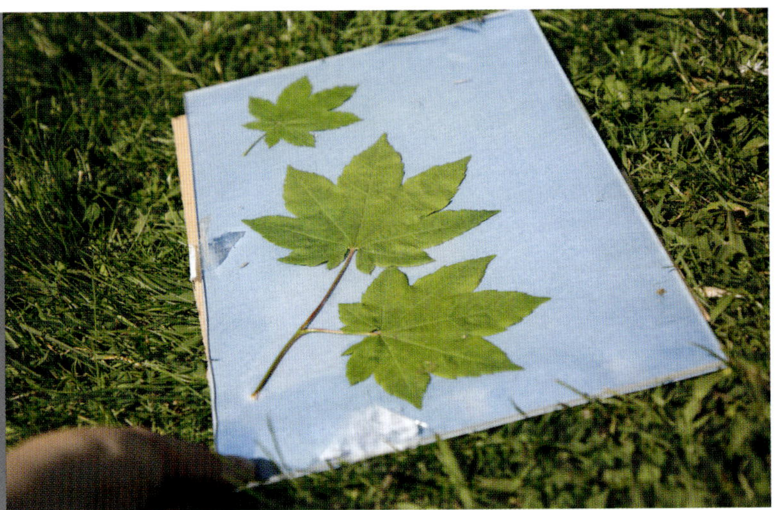

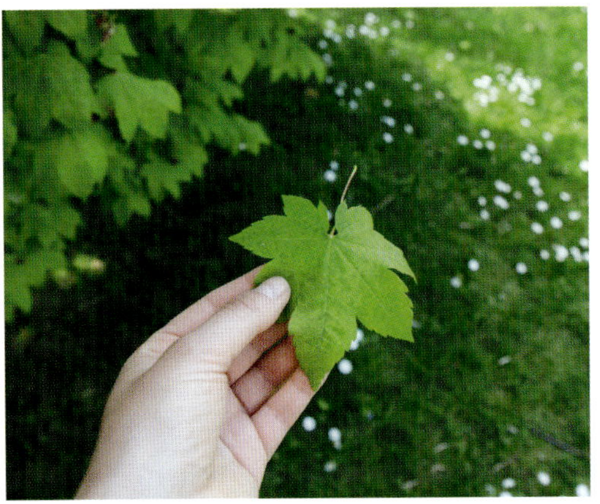

**1 Gather objects**

Decide what you're going to lay on your paper for printmaking. Head outside and pick leaves and stems with clear outlines – the final print is two-tone, so interesting silhouettes are best. You could press your own flowers, or use keepsakes that are personal to you, and frame the final prints for wall art or gifts.

**2 Assemble and expose**

Grab your Sunprint kit (available online or at big craft shops), plus a tray of water. Arrange the objects on a piece of Sunprint paper out of the reach of the sun, either inside or just in the shade. Next, place the acrylic sheet on top to flatten and hold your items to the Sunprint paper. Leave your set-up in the sun to develop until most of the colour disappears from the paper and it turns from blue to white.

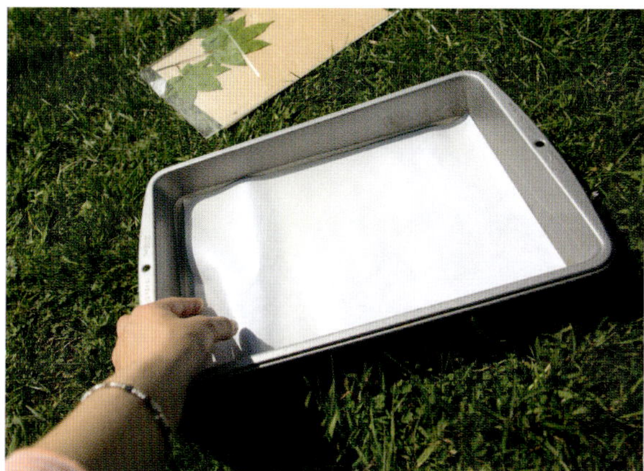

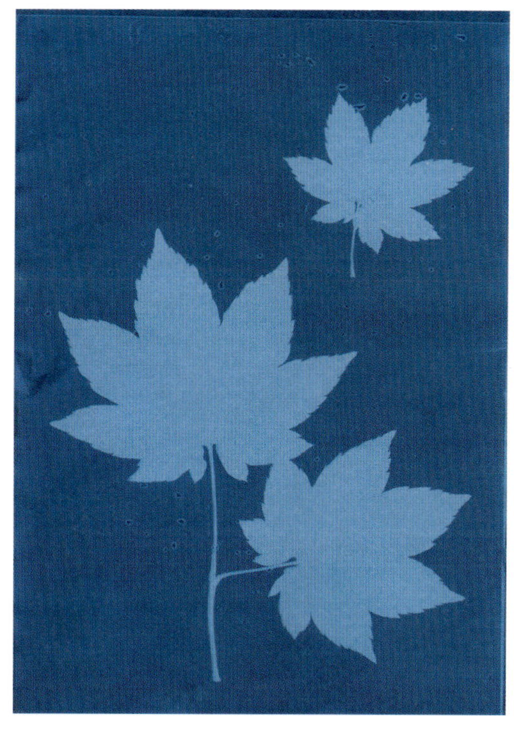

### 3 Rinse, fix and dry

Once exposed, rinse your Sunprint in water and watch the white tones turn into blue and the blue to white. To get the deepest tones the paper can give, leave it in water for 1–5 minutes. Just as the sun's light stimulated a chemical change in the previous step, the water stimulates another here. Lay your Sunprint flat to fully dry (use the acrylic sheet for this) and you're finished.

## How long should the exposure be?

**A Sunprint is ready to fix when the paper has turned almost white, but how long does it take for this to happen? The back of the kit suggests leaving the paper exposed for one to five minutes, depending on the sunlight intensity. In practice, most prints take the full five minutes, sometimes longer – under cloud cover (or on a windowsill), the process could take up to twenty minutes. Light intensity varies hugely and there's no exact timing, so use your creative judgement. Why not experiment with different timings? If the blue tone isn't strong enough in your final print, leave the next print exposed for longer. Use a phone timer to help you.**

# PLAY WITH SHADOWS

**THE IDEA**
**Shoot fine-art images during golden hour.**

**Time required:** 2 hours

**Kit needed:**
- DSLR or mirrorless camera
- 50mm lens
- Editing software

**Camera settings:**
1/125 sec at f/2.8, ISO 400

**Skill level:**

 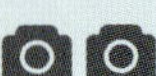 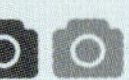

**When taking photographs, the light at the beginning and the end of the day is some of the best to work with. To get the most out of it, you might think you have to go out and shoot stunning vistas, but this simply isn't the case. In this project, you will shoot during what's known as the golden hour in the comfort of your own home and create some incredible fine-art results in the process.**

If you're not lucky enough to get good light through your windows at the start or end of the day, search close to home and select another location nearby.

For example, the garden or the garden shed could also be viable, as you don't need much to make it work – just some natural light, a plain background and a subject to frame.

For your main subject, aim to pick something that creates interesting shadows, so form and structure are important aspects to consider.

When it comes to kit, a 50mm prime is ideal, but you could always use a wide-angle lens or a long lens. Experiment and find the right optic that matches your style of shooting.

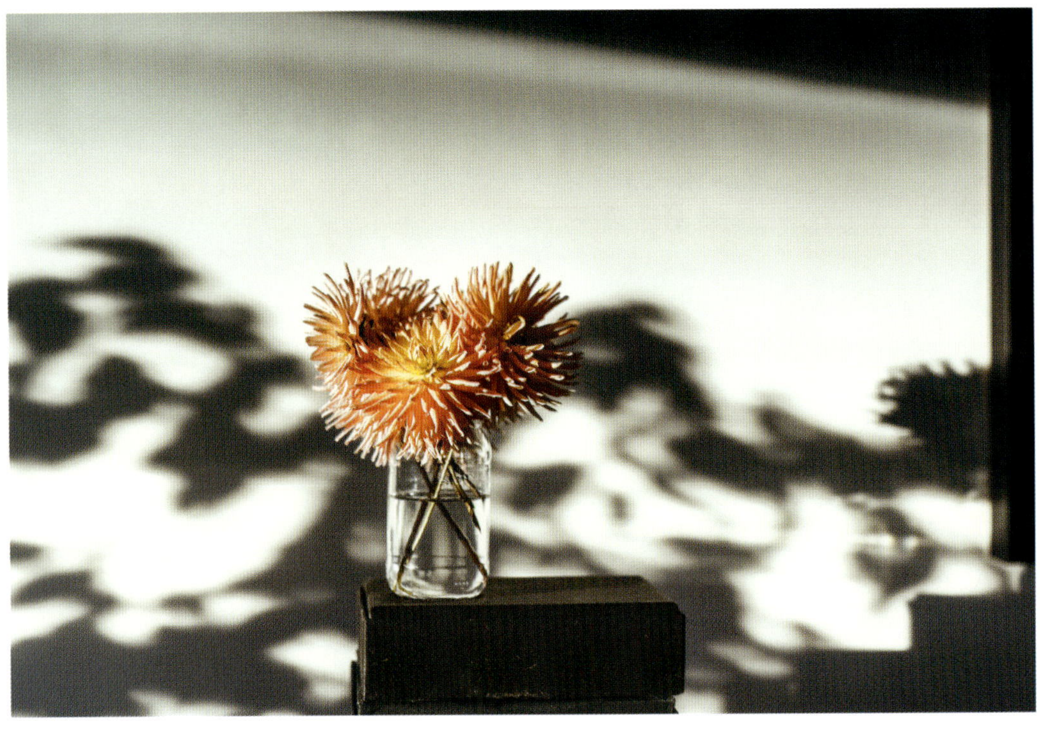

**1 Get set up**

For this project, you can either shoot handheld or use a tripod. If you want to slow down and build your composition, then a tripod is a great aid. However, in terms of the camera settings, a tripod isn't necessary. Because of the light, your shutter speed setting should be reading relatively fast but open your aperture to a wider setting too.

**2 Underexpose by a stop**

You don't want your highlights to be overexposed so take your meter readings from the lighter part of your image and not the shadowed areas. Put your camera into aperture-priority mode and dial in -1 stop of exposure compensation to make sure that you are exposing for the main subject and for the lighter parts of the image.

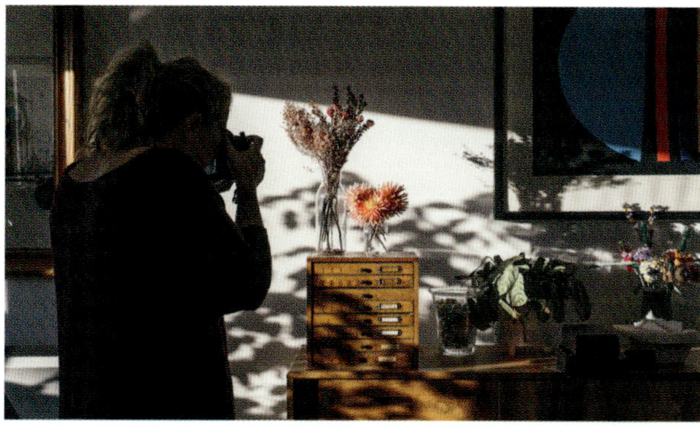

**3 Be experimental**

To make the most of the scene and get that fine-art appeal, look for shapes in the shadows and think about your composition. It could be that you shoot from a different angle or adjust your scene to the light. You may even need to use some plain boxes to raise the main subject into a better position.

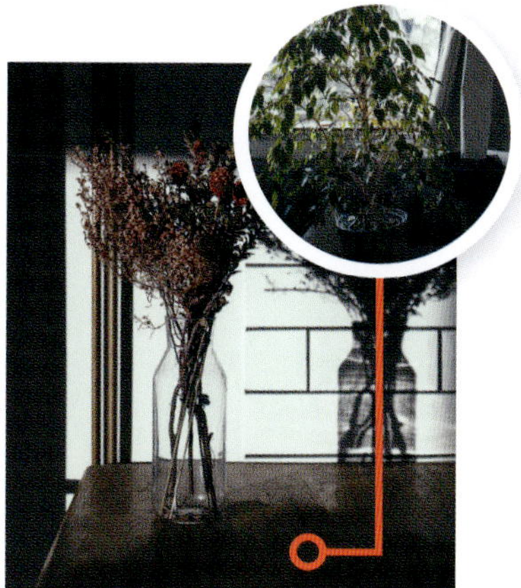

**4 Create additional shadows**

To enhance your still-life image further, you can create additional interesting shadows to fall in the background. For example, a large house plant next to the window will create some softer leaf shadows. A mixture of lighter and darker shadows will add to the overall impact in the final image.

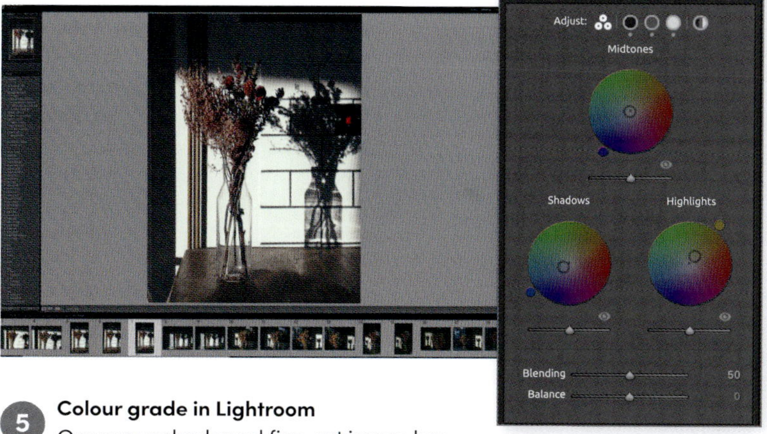


**5 Colour grade in Lightroom**

Once your shadowed fine-art image has been shot, think about the tone and styling. One of Lightroom's best tools for stylising is the Color Grading option. You can either create a global adjustment across the whole image or adjust the colours in the shadows, midtones and highlights separately. The latter gives you a more precise result (click the three-circle icon for this option). Here, the Shadows and Midtones were set to a cool tone and then the Highlights to a warm tone to contrast with each other. Note that the closer the circle is to the middle of the Color Grading circle, the more subtle the colour. You don't want the colours to be overpowering – just a hint is enough. Experiment with the different effects, strengths and tones to see how they impact your image.

# GO TO THE INFRARED

**THE IDEA**
**Use an infrared filter to get out-of-this-world results.**

**Time required**: 2 hours

**Kit needed**:
- DSLR or mirrorless camera
- 50mm lens
- Infrared filter
- Tripod
- Viewfinder blocker (if using DSLR)
- Editing software

**Camera settings**:
5–10 minutes at f/4, ISO 1600

**Skill level**:

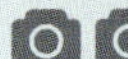

**The human eye can see an extraordinary amount of colour and detail, but the world that we see every day is only part of the wavelength spectrum. Just outside of the visible light range is ultraviolet at one end and infrared at the other.**

We can't see infrared light, but you can take a picture with it. You'll need a DSLR or mirrorless camera and an infrared filter. This will ensure that only infrared light is coming through the lens and hitting your camera's sensor. Inexpensive options are available online – just make sure you get one that fits the filter thread of your lens.

Most modern digital camera sensors have a filter on top of the sensor to virtually cut out infrared light. This means you'll need to use a long exposure, generally 5–10 minutes long, to get a good exposure.

You can get cameras converted to shoot permanent infrared photography, but this method is a more affordable way of getting infrared results. It's also a brilliant way of getting some unique images and making use of a slow shutter speed.

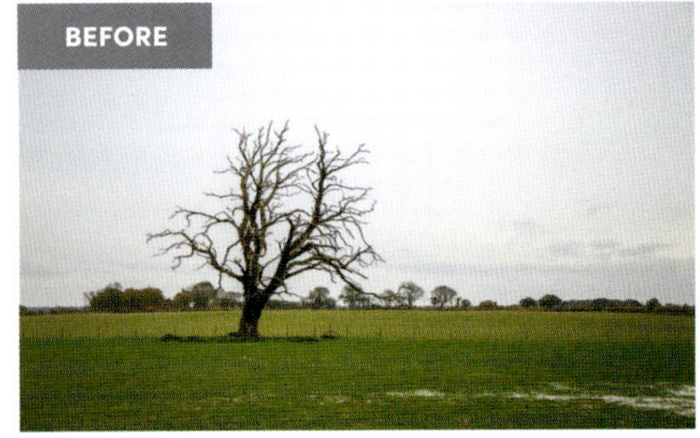
BEFORE

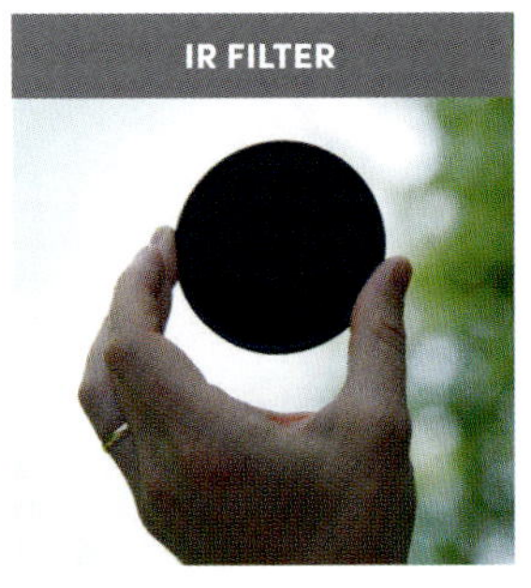
IR FILTER

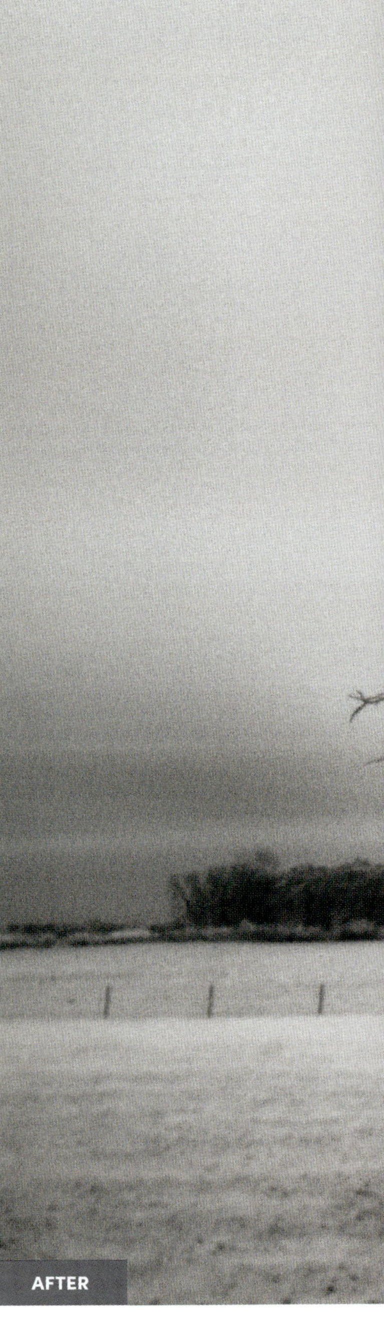
AFTER

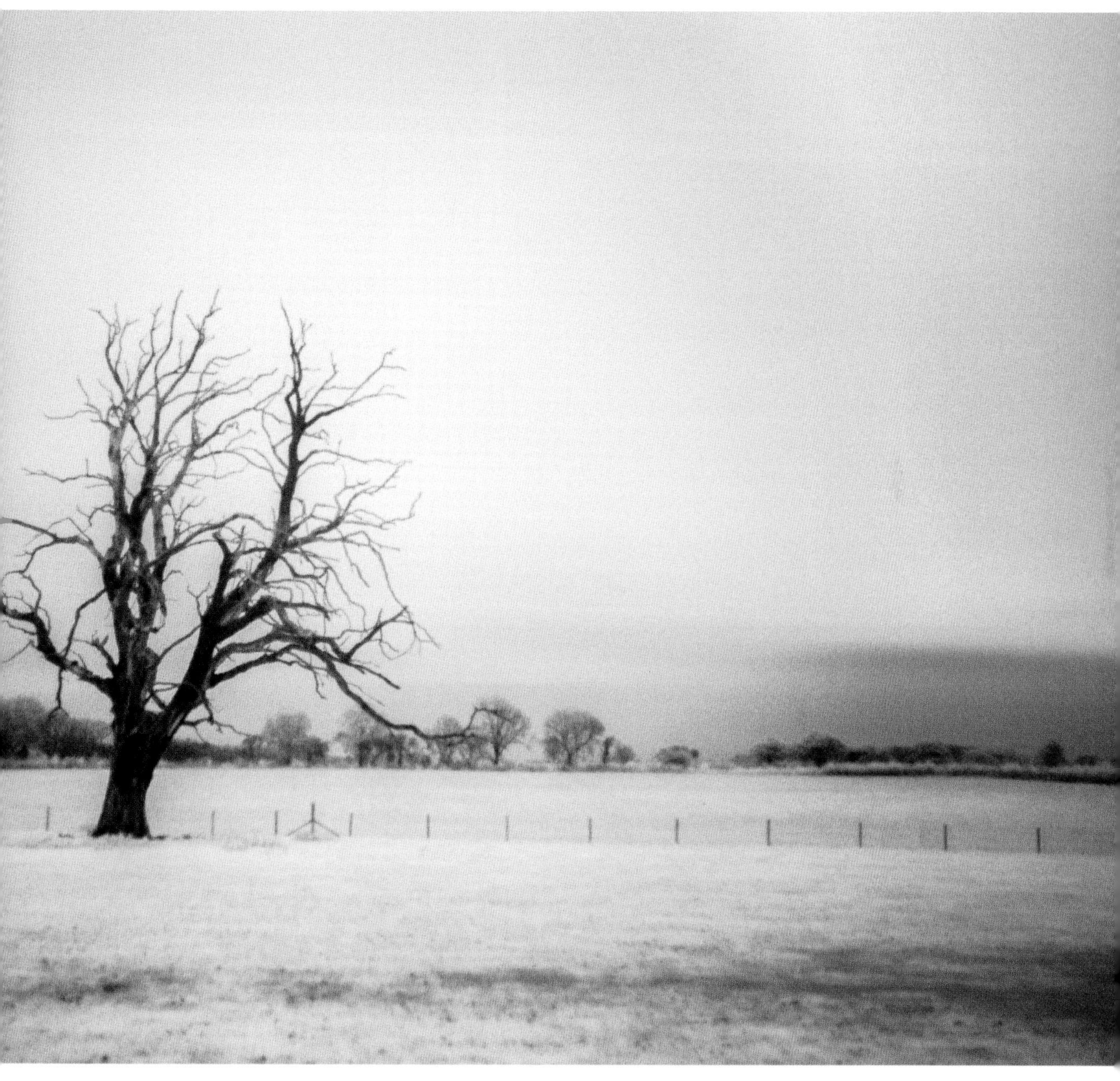

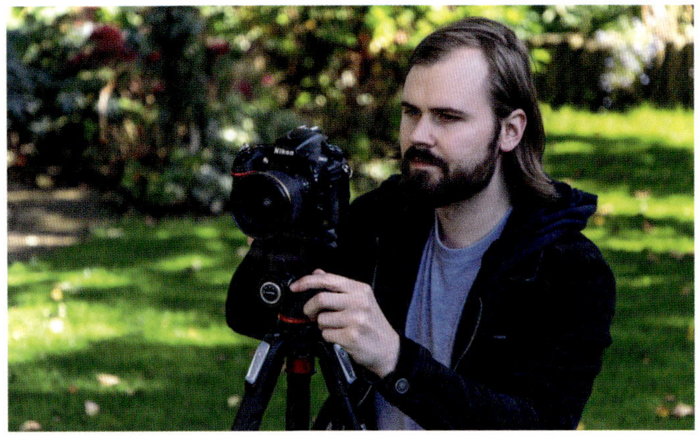

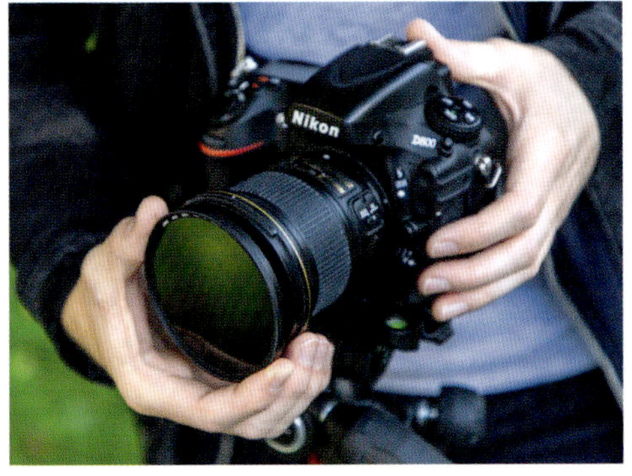


**1 Frame up your shot on a tripod**

Your camera is going to need a very long exposure (probably between 5–10 minutes) to receive enough infrared light for a well-exposed image, so setting it up on a tripod is a must. This is the time to frame up to achieve the composition you want and focus on your focal point – the viewfinder on a DSLR will be totally black when you attach the IR filter.

**2 Attach your IR filter to your camera**

Put your camera into its manual-focus mode to lock it off and carefully screw in the infrared filter, being careful not to knock the zoom or focus rings on the lens. Go into your camera's manual mode, dial in an ISO of 1,600, and open the aperture to its widest value. Make sure you're shooting Raw. Finally, set the shutter speed to bulb mode.

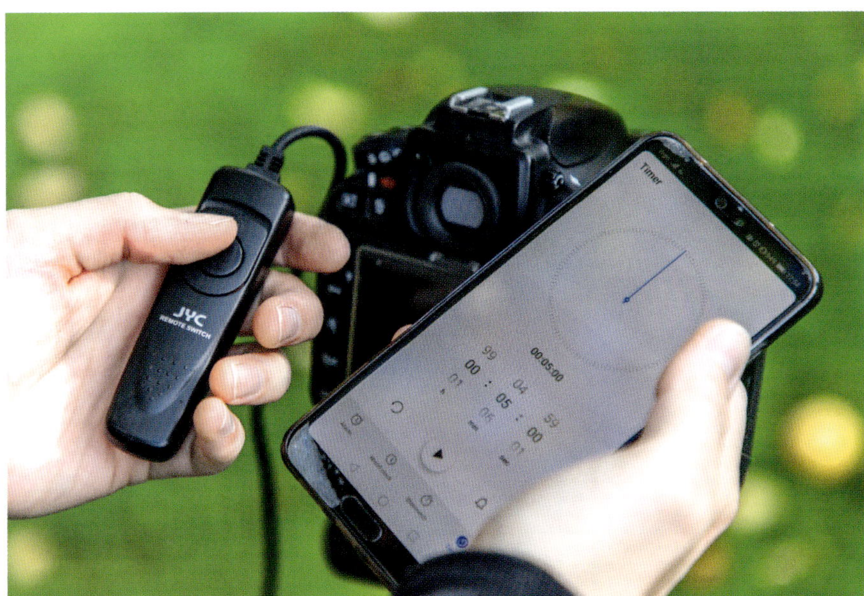


**3 Expose for several minutes**

Plug in your shutter release cable and set a timer on your phone for five minutes. Start the timer, then lock the shutter release button in place until your timer finishes. Check the resulting image – if it's too dark, increase the timer value; if it's too bright, decrease the time or lower the ISO. Take another shot until the exposure looks good.

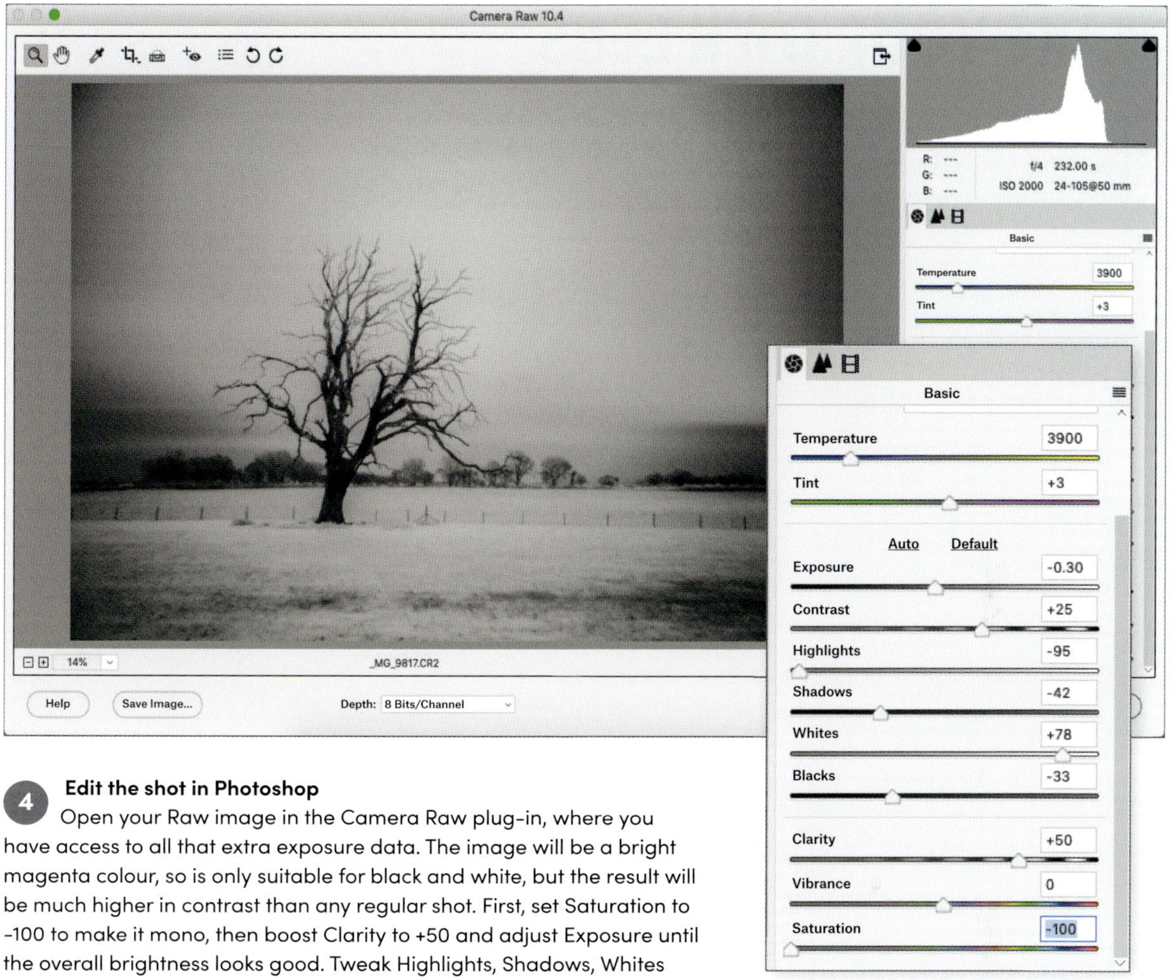

**4** **Edit the shot in Photoshop**

Open your Raw image in the Camera Raw plug-in, where you have access to all that extra exposure data. The image will be a bright magenta colour, so is only suitable for black and white, but the result will be much higher in contrast than any regular shot. First, set Saturation to -100 to make it mono, then boost Clarity to +50 and adjust Exposure until the overall brightness looks good. Tweak Highlights, Shadows, Whites and Blacks to get the contrast you like, then go to the Detail Panel and set Luminance Noise Reduction to 20 to remove image noise.

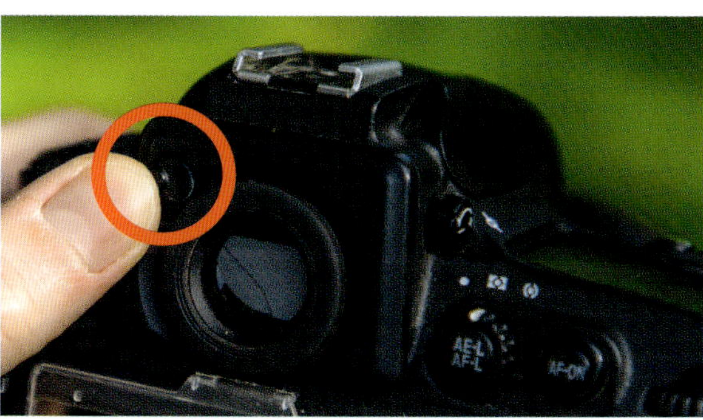


If you're shooting on a DSLR, you'll want to stop light coming in through the viewfinder during your long exposure, as this can create strange flares. Many cameras have a plastic viewfinder blocker on the strap. Others, such as Nikon's D810 and D850 cameras, have one built-in. If you're shooting on a mirrorless camera, you don't need to worry about this problem, as the viewfinder is electronic, not optical.

# MAKE YOUR OWN LENS

**THE IDEA**
**Make a lens from household objects.**

**Time required**: 2 hours

**Kit needed**:
- DSLR or mirrorless camera
- Tripod
- Camera body cap
- Drill
- Pin
- Tape
- Tin foil

**Camera settings**:
Manual exposure, ISO 100

**Skill level**:

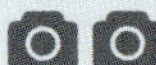 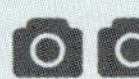 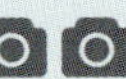

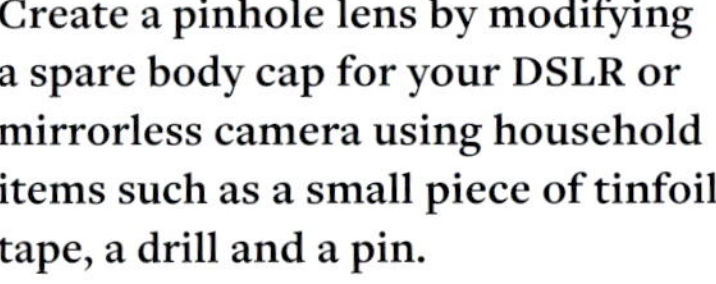

**Create a pinhole lens by modifying a spare body cap for your DSLR or mirrorless camera using household items such as a small piece of tinfoil, tape, a drill and a pin.**

The images you'll be able to take with your custom lens will be reminiscent of those taken using vintage lenses, with a slightly out-of-focus quality to them – they look great in mono, or you could go the other way and super-saturate them with colour. They're great to experiment with for landscapes and portraits, and because it's such a light and portable 'lens', you have no excuse not to take it with you wherever you go.

Making the lens is a fun DIY project that's an excuse to get your power tools out and can be completed in about 20 minutes. All the materials are affordable – providing you already have a drill, the total shouldn't come to more than the price of a cup of coffee. The most expensive component you'll need is a spare body cap for your camera, which can be picked up inexpensively online.

SHOT WITH STANDARD LENS

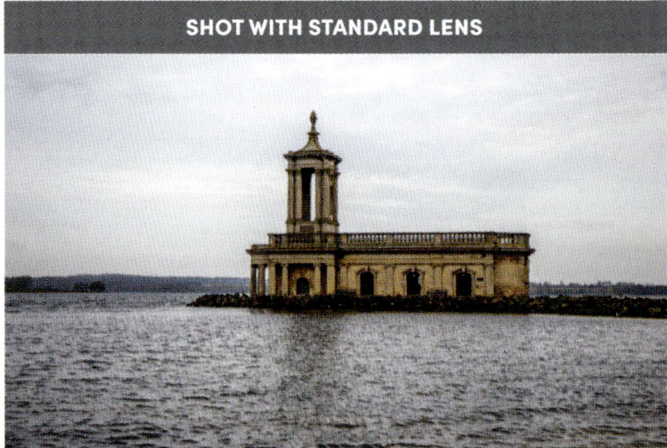

WITH PINHOLE LENS

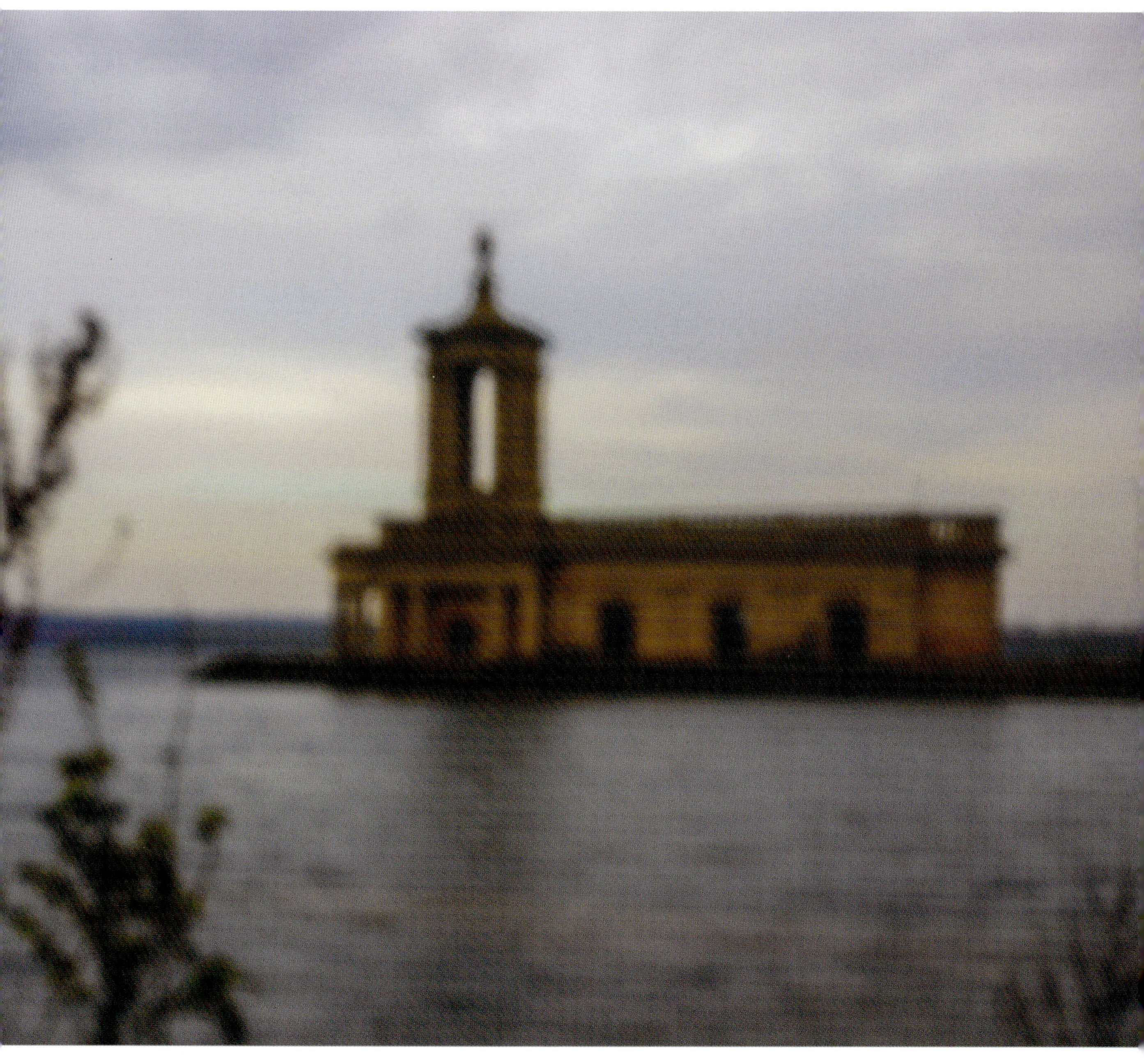

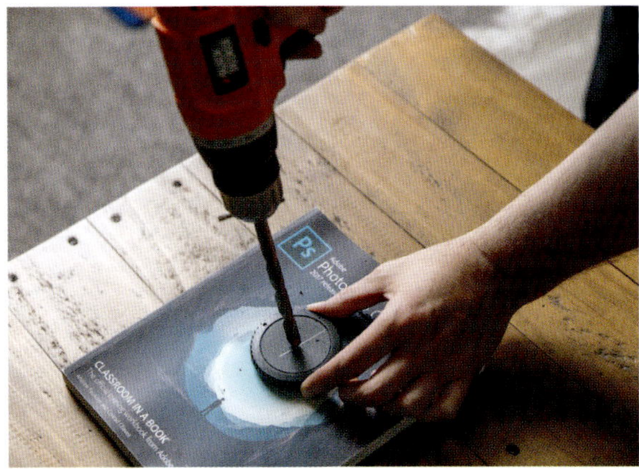


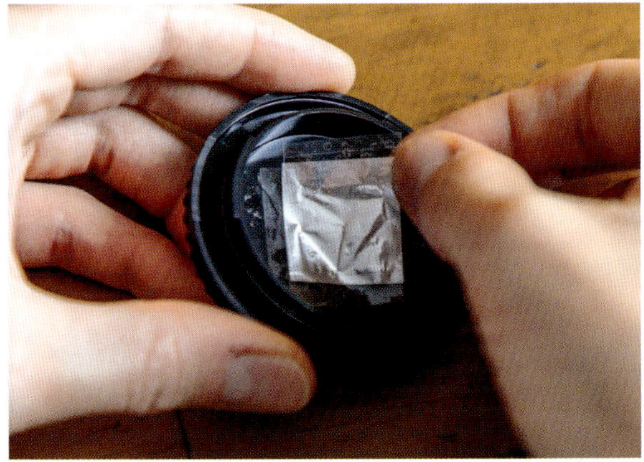

**1 Drill a hole in your body cap**

Drill a hole about 1cm in diameter in the middle of the body cap. Use a ruler to work out the middle and mark it with a pencil. Place your cap on a workbench and clamp it in place, then carefully drill into it to make the first hole. There will be loose bits of plastic that you don't want to get inside your camera, so wipe these away with a cloth. Smooth out any jagged edges around the hole using a craft knife to make it flush, and again wipe away any loose plastic particles.

**2 Tape the foil in place**

Cut out a square of tin foil about 1.5x1.5cm and place it over the hole on the rear side of your body cap. Use a minimal amount of tape to secure it in place, using a sharp pair of scissors to cut thin strips of tape. The foil should be taut, without any folds or kinks in it. When you're finished, the foil should be covering the entire hole in the body cap and be light-tight. (Hold it up against a window to check.)

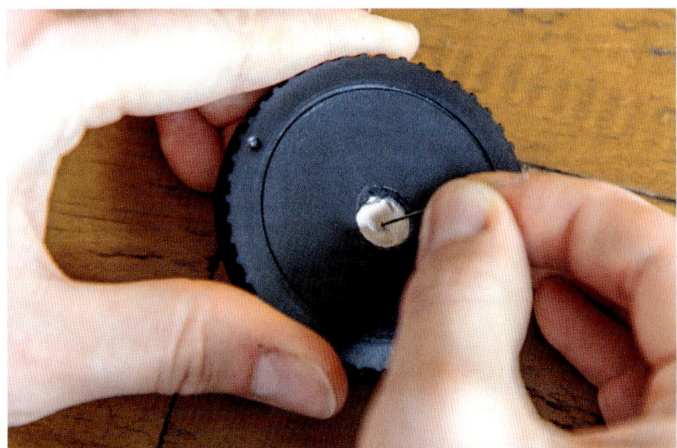

**3 Create your pinhole**

Using a sharp needle or pin, pierce the smallest hole you can right in the middle of the piece of foil. This is the 'pinhole', and is also your aperture, which will let in just a trickle of light. Just like with standard lenses, the smaller the hole, the larger the depth of field is. As there are no optical elements to focus the image, the results will seem somewhat out of focus, but that's all part of the retro vibe that pinhole lenses deliver.

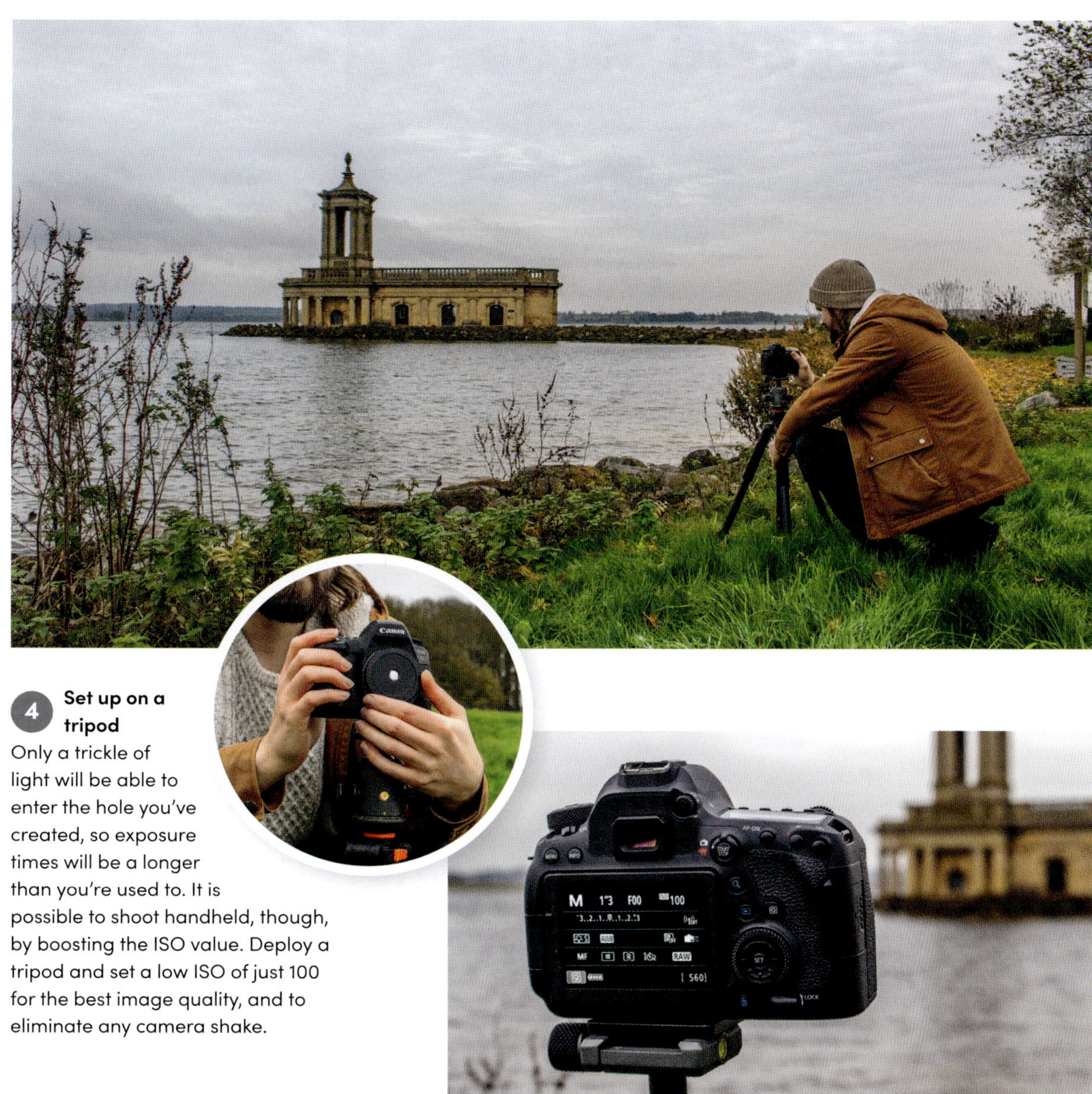


**4 Set up on a tripod**
Only a trickle of light will be able to enter the hole you've created, so exposure times will be a longer than you're used to. It is possible to shoot handheld, though, by boosting the ISO value. Deploy a tripod and set a low ISO of just 100 for the best image quality, and to eliminate any camera shake.

**5 Dial in the settings and shoot**
With your camera in manual mode, the aperture value will read f/00, as a lens won't be detected. Enable Raw file capture and set the ISO to 100. Tweak the shutter speed value until the exposure meter is in the centre. Take a test shot. If the resulting image is too bright, use a faster shutter speed; if it's too dark, increase the shutter speed a little.

# KALEIDOSCOPIC COLOUR

**THE IDEA**
**How to get the best results when using glass prisms for portraits.**

**Time required:** 1 hour

**Kit needed:**
- DSLR or mirrorless camera
- Prime or zoom lens with 50mm focal length
- Glass prism

**Camera settings:**
1/200 sec at f/2, ISO 1600

**Skill level:**

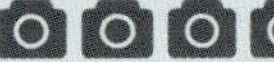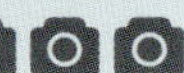

**While we often justify buying a new lens with an ability to open up new creative possibilities, we don't always give accessories the same attention. There is just as much scope to experiment with filters for example, as in this project using Fractals Filters' Classic 3-Pack which may be expensive, but like a new lens, they open up brilliant artistic opportunities and allow you to take unique pictures.**

These prism filters can be held in front of the lens to refract and reflect light. Some create a glitchy pattern while others create a kaleidoscope of colour, making them perfect for portraits – giving your shots an edge that will stand out. Starting with a more affordable option can be a good way to experiment, but investing in more expensive prisms is worthwhile for their superior quality and versatility.

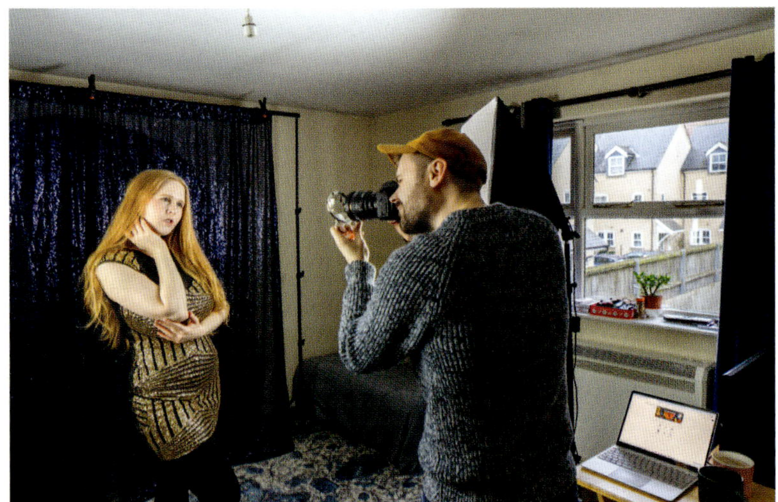

Holding your camera in one hand and a filter in the other can be tricky, so we suggest it's easiest to hold the Fractals Filter by its grip and then use your thumb to rest against the lens barrel to steady yourself, and help you line up the shot perfectly. It's also worth enabling any lens or body-based Image Stabilisation on your camera to help reduce camera shake, too. A tripod can be a better option if you don't need the flexibility of moving and shooting quickly, although it's a good option for shooting video footage with prisms.

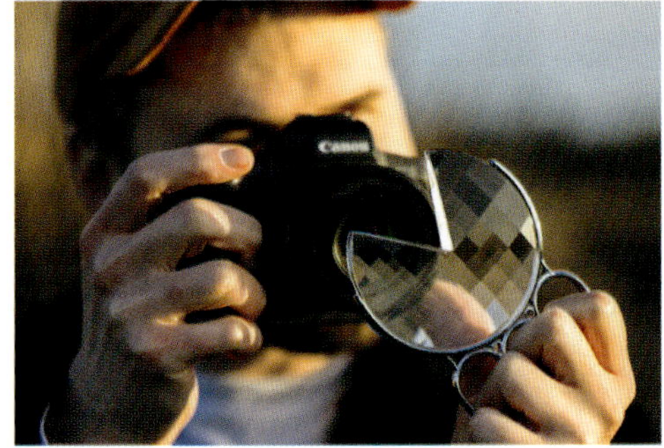

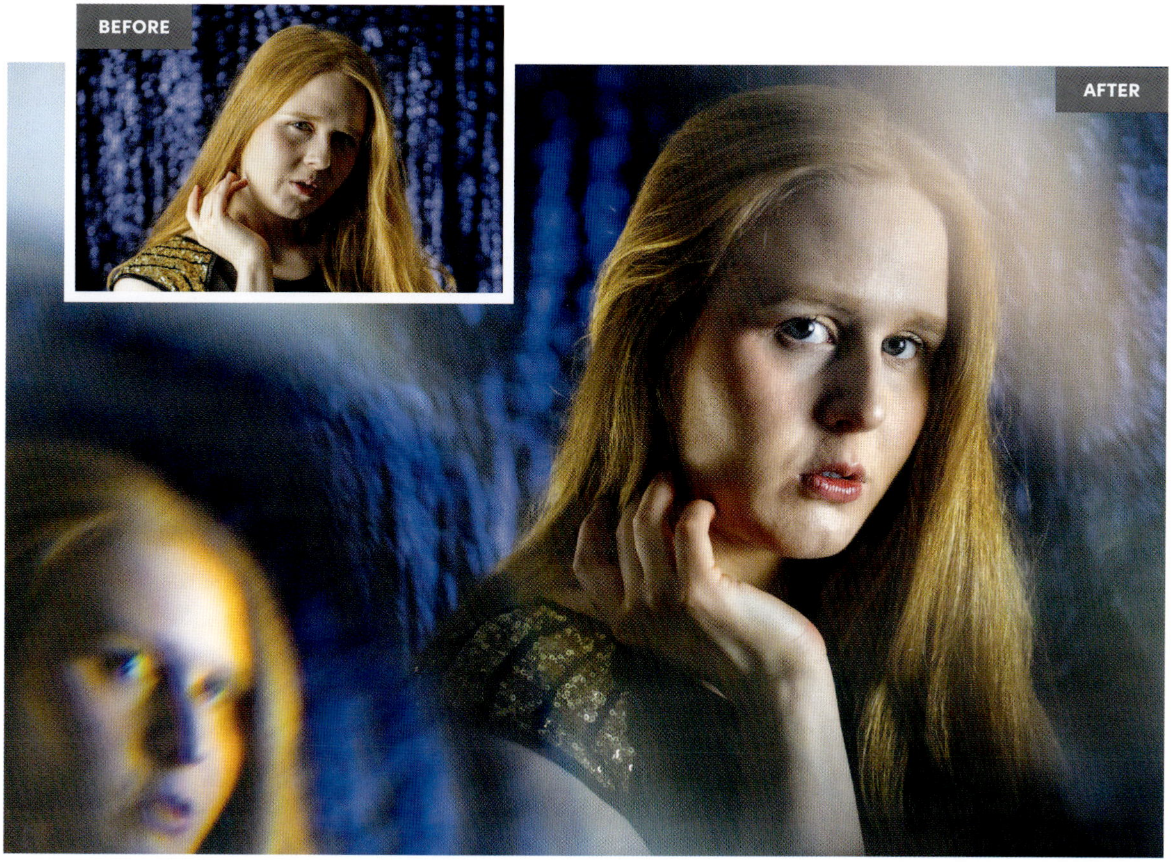

BEFORE

AFTER

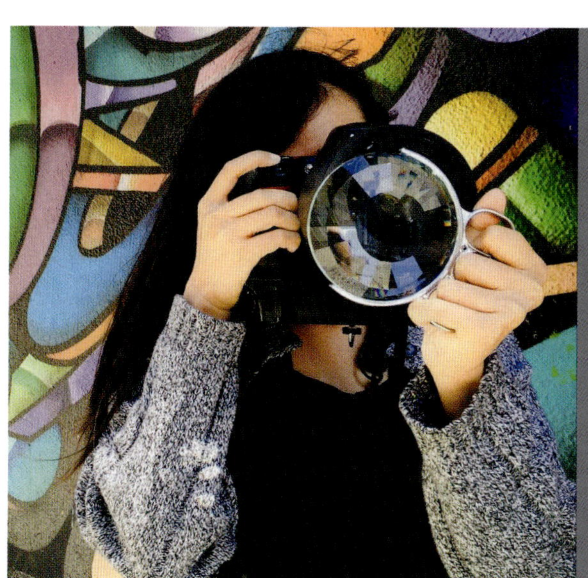

## Expert advice for using prisms

**Any dust, dirt, debris and even greasy fingerprints on your prisms can show up in your photos, and will then need to be removed in software. Carry a microfibre cloth with you and regularly clean your prisms to keep them in good working order. A storage case like the soft bag that comes with the Fractals Classic 3-Pack is designed for stowing away your filters and prisms, keeping them protected when not in use. A shoulder strap and belt loop put the filters within easy reach, too.**

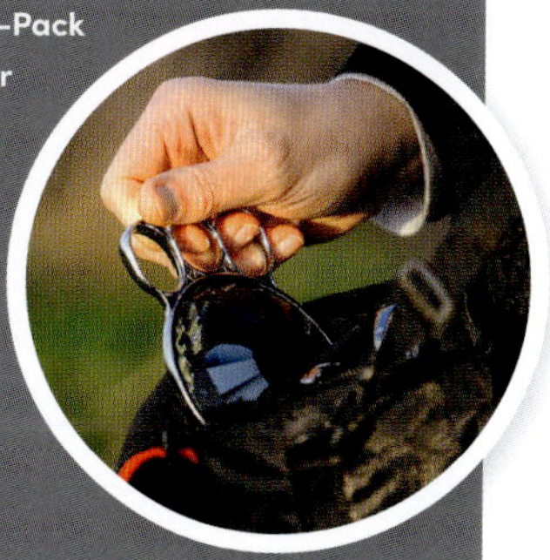

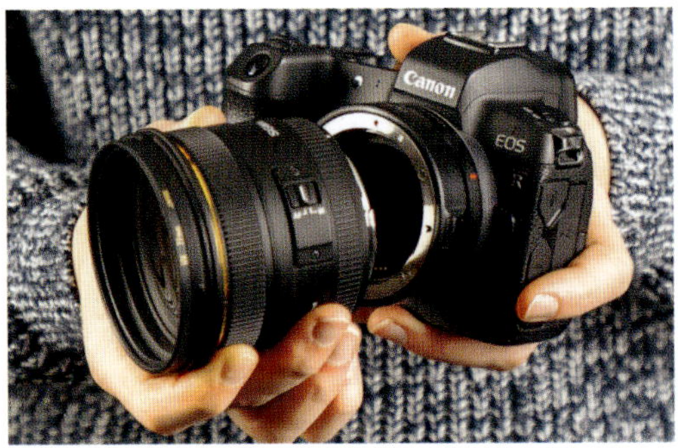


**1 Use a 50mm prime lens**

Start by attaching your lens to your camera. A 50mm prime on a model with a full-frame sensor, or 35mm on a camera with an APS-C sensor, seems to be the sweet spot but you can experiment, of course. Make sure your lens is fitted with a UV filter so that you don't scratch the front element.

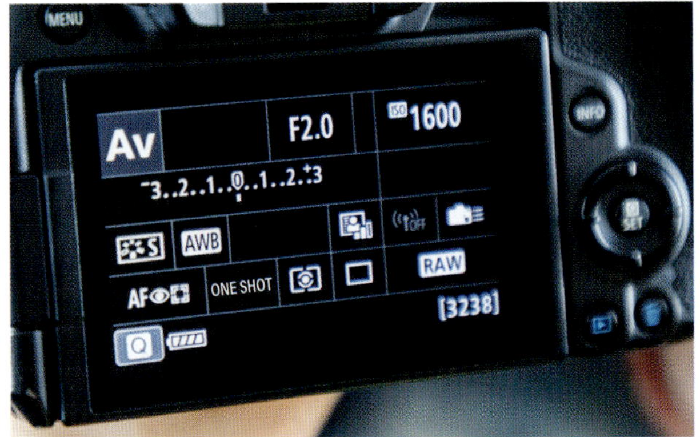


**2 Starting settings**

To begin, go into your camera's Aperture Priority (A) mode and dial in an aperture of f/2 and ISO 1600. You'll want to aim for a shutter speed of at least 1/200 sec to eliminate camera-shake, so you may need to tweak your ISO value depending on daylight levels.

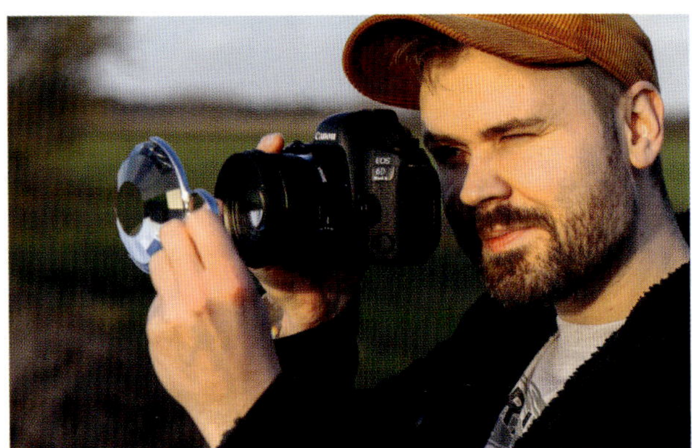

**3 Move the filter around**

First compose your scene and have your model pose as desired, and check the exposure is good. Then compose again but bring your prism into view this time. Try moving it closer or further away from the lens and tilting it towards or away from your model.

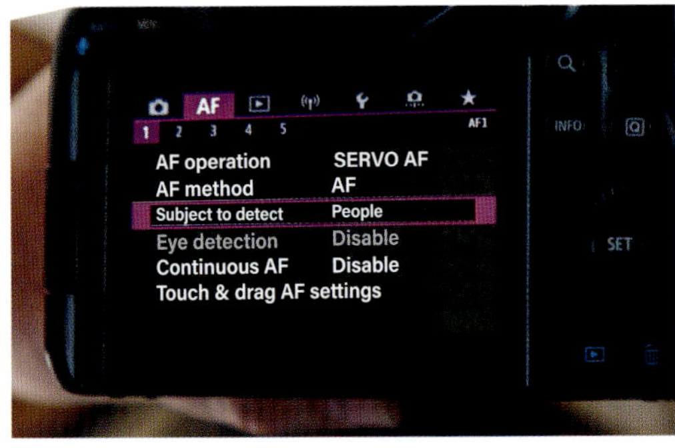


**4 Face detection**

Autofocus can be a challenge when shooting through a prism. On newer mirrorless cameras, Subject Detection makes the process much easier. But for older cameras you'll need to place your active AF point over the model's eyes to make sure they are sharp.

Move the prism away from your lens and use different focal lengths to fine-tune the effect in your composition.

## FRACTALS FILTERS – WHAT'S IN THE BOX?

**Take a closer look at these three classic prism options...**

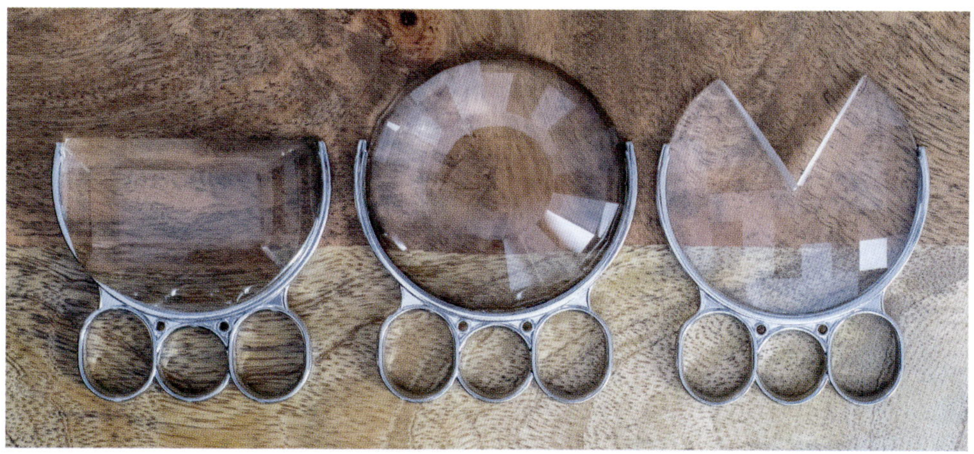

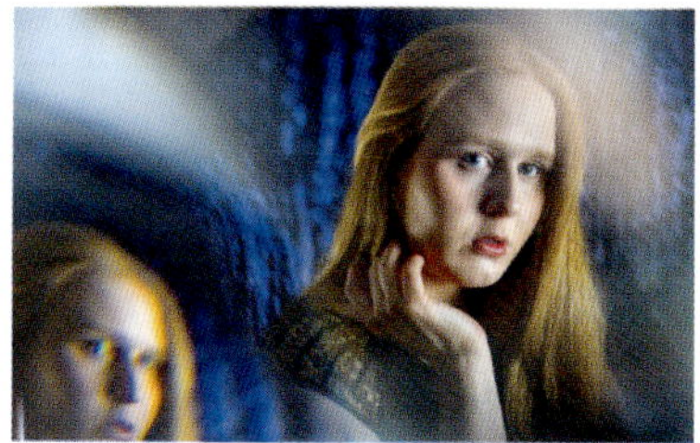

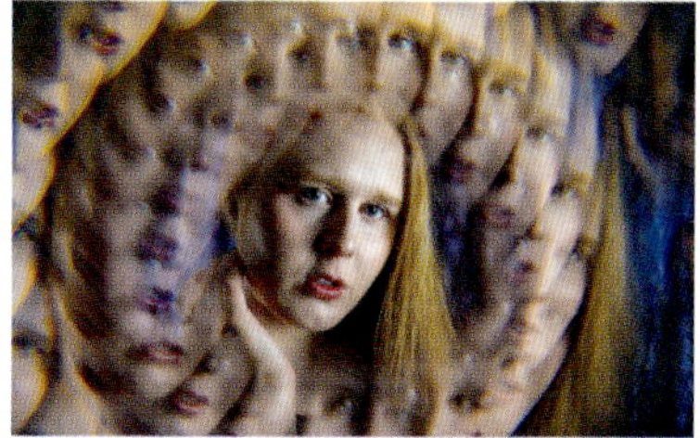

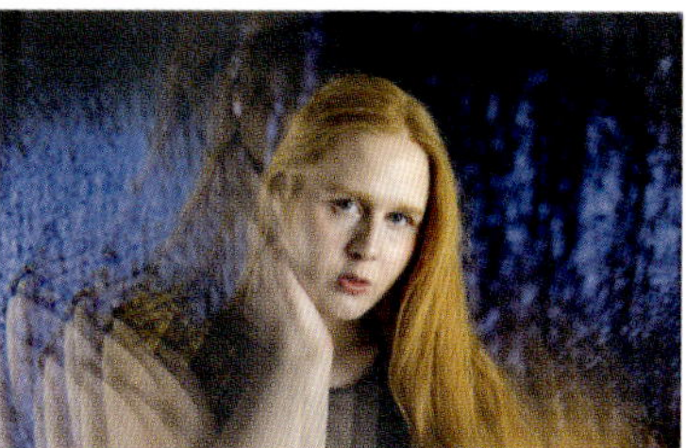

**Pascal**

The Pascal is the heaviest of the three prism filters in the Fractals Filters Classic 3-Pack. Tipping the scales at 255g it's a bit more unwieldy to use than the others. Master it though, and it will allow you to take 'impossible' images, as its chunky glass element has been cut in such a way that allows it to reflect objects from outside your normal field of view. When you're shooting outside, this could be a tree directly behind you! Our model wore a sparkly dress in front of a blue glittery background for extra sparkles that have reflected in the glass.

**Julia**

The Julia filter is perfectly circular with the Fractals Filters' signature knuckle-duster style metal grip so you can hold it comfortably in your left hand, while holding your camera in your right hand. It has an orange segment style pattern cut into it with a clear circular spot in the centre. This central zone gives you an ideal 'sweet spot' in which to position your model's face, with the surrounding frame then being filled with a mesmerising kaleidoscopic view.

**Penrose**

The Penrose filter is the lightest of the trio in the classic 3-Pack with its thin proportions and a section of glass cut out from it. This makes it a joy to use as it can be held and repositioned with ease. The glass has a checkerboard pattern on its front face, breaking the surrounding scenery into a wonderful diffused, glitchy pattern. The cutaway section of glass is ideal for placing your focal point as it leaves this area perfectly sharp. Due to its two pointy 'horns', make sure a UV filter is fitted to your lens to avoid scratches to the front element.

# ACKNOWLEDGEMENTS

This book wouldn't have been possible without the creativity and passion of past and present contributors to *Digital Camera* magazine, whose work appears on these pages: James Artaius, Alistair Campbell, Claire Gillo, Mike Harris, Richard Hill, Rod Lawton, Roddy Llewellyn, Simeon Meinema, Dan Mold, Sebastian Oakley, James Paterson, Dan Pearce and Lauren Scott.

Their photo projects couldn't have made it into print without the work of Digital Camera's Art Editor, Roddy Llewellyn, plus Content Director Chris George, Head of Design Rodney Dive and various designers from Future Publishing's Art Studio. Thanks also to Future's International Licensing Account Director Brendon Bester, International Client and Content Administrator Jane Channon and International Account Manager Phoebe Castledine.

For Ilex Press, I'd like to thank Richard Collins for inviting Future to collaborate on The Ultimate Photography Ideas Book, and Assistant Editor Stephanie Selçuk-Frank and the rest of her team for making it all happen. And thanks to the readers of *Digital Camera* magazine – we hope that we continue to inspire you to get the most from your photography, and that you enjoy reading the magazine as much as we enjoy putting it together every month.

# PIC CREDITS

All content © Digital Camera Magazine/Future Publishing, with the exception of the following.

38 above courtesy app.photoephemeris.com. Photo Ephemeris is a trademark of Crookneck Consulting LLC; 73 below Pexels Javier Martinez/Pexels; 105 below Alexas Fotos/Pexels

126-27 Packaging design © Sainsbury's™. These pages have not been authorised or endorsed by Sainsbury's.



An Hachette UK Company
www.hachette.co.uk

First published in the UK in 2025 by ILEX,
an imprint of Octopus Publishing Group Ltd
Octopus Publishing Group
Carmelite House
50 Victoria Embankment
London, EC4Y 0DZ
www.octopusbooks.co.uk
www.octopusbooksusa.com

The authorised representative in the EEA is
Hachette Ireland,
8 Castlecourt Centre, Castleknock Road,
Castleknock, Dublin 15, D15 YF6A, Ireland

Distributed in the US by Hachette Book Group
1290 Avenue of the Americas, 4th & 5th Floors
New York, NY 10104

Distributed in Canada by Canadian Manda Group
664 Annette St, Toronto, Ontario, Canada M6S2C8



Publisher: Alison Starling
Commissioning Editor: Richard Collins
Managing Editor: Rachel Silverlight
Assistant Editor: Stephanie Selçuk-Frank
Art Director: Ben Gardiner
Design: Chris Robinson
Senior Production Manager: Pete Hunt



ISBN 978-1-78157-963-3

A CIP catalogue record for this book
is available from the British Library

Printed and bound in China

10 9 8 7 6 5 4 3 2 1